D1121630

The Native Peoples
of North America

Recent titles in *Native America: Yesterday and Today*
Bruce E. Johansen, Series Editor

George Washington's War On Native America
Barbara Alice Mann

The Native Peoples of North America

A HISTORY VOLUME II

Bruce E. Johansen

NATIVE AMERICA: YESTERDAY AND TODAY
Bruce E. Johansen, Series Editor

Westport, Connecticut
London

Library of Congress Cataloging-in-Publication Data

Johansen, Bruce E. (Bruce Elliott), 1950–
    The native peoples of North America : a history / Bruce E. Johansen.
        p. cm.—(Native America: Yesterday and Today, ISSN 1552-8022)
    Includes bibliographical references and index.
    ISBN 0-275-98159-2 (set : alk. paper)—ISBN 0-275-98720-5 (vol. 1 : alk.
paper)—ISBN 0-275-98721-3 (vol. 2 : alk. paper)   1. Indians of North
America—Study and teaching.   2. Indians of North America—History.   3. Indians
of North America—Social life and customs.   I. Title.   II. Native America
(Praeger Publishers)

    E76.6.J65 2005
    970.004'97—dc22   2004028732

British Library Cataloguing in Publication Data is available.

Library of Congress Catalog Card Number:
ISBN: 0-275-98159-2 (set)
        0-275-98720-5 (vol. I)
        0-275-98721-3 (vol. II)
ISSN: 1552-8022

First published in 2005

Praeger Publishers, 88 Post Road West, Westport, CT 06881
An imprint of Greenwood Publishing Group, Inc.
www.praeger.com

Printed in the United States of America

The paper used in this book complies with the
Permanent Paper Standard issued by the National
Information Standards Organization (Z39.48-1984).

10 9 8 7 6 5 4 3 2 1

Every reasonable effort has been made to trace the owners of copyrighted
materials in this book, but in some instances this has proven impossible. The
author and publisher will be glad to receive information leading to more
complete acknowledgments in subsequent printings of the book and in the
meantime extend their apologies for any omissions.

Contents

Contents

Introduction

*I*n Benjamin Franklin's time, general opinion among European immigrants in America held that many centuries might pass before their offspring would expand to fill the width of North America. Before the advent of fossil-fueled industry, railroads, the cotton gin, repeating rifles, and massive immigration from Europe, Africa, and Asia, westward movement proceeded slowly—from the Atlantic's shores to the crest of the eastern mountains, for the most part— during roughly 200 years. Within a century after Franklin's death in 1790, however, the U.S. government declared the settlement frontier closed, the buffalo were slaughtered, and the last Native military resistance was quelled. The second volume of this work begins on the West Coast of North America, then follows the last of the "Indian wars" in the Plains. After the massacre at Wounded Knee (1890), Native peoples engaged in an often-covert battle to survive, living in what amounted to open-air concentration camps. The fry bread that is so ubiquitous at today's powwows was born of starvation rations: white flour, lard, a frying pan, and an open fire. From there, the twentieth century tells a story of recovery for North America's Native peoples, including the reclamation of land, language, and cultures.

Chapter 6 begins with a description of Northwest Coast Native peoples, who were unique given their hierarchical social structure and ability to build a high civilization without organized agriculture. By the 1850s, barely fifty years after the Lewis and Clark expedition reached the mouth of the Co-lumbia River, European American immigrants were building the city of Seattle on Puget Sound and lobbying the federal government to make their city the terminus of a transcontinental railroad. Chief Sea'th'l, after whom the city was named, was leading his people across Puget Sound, away from the expanding urban area, following his evocative farewell speech.

At about the same time, Anglo-American immigration slammed into California with notable violence as whole Native peoples were exterminated following initiation of a major gold rush that followed the war with Mexico and the area's acquisition by the United States. By the 1870s, European American migration was closing on North America's interior from the east and the west. Chapter 6 ends with the Long March of Chief Joseph's Nez Perce, more than 1,500 miles over some of North America's roughest and most beautiful country, where on October 7, 1877, Chief Joseph and his people surrendered.

By the last decades of the nineteenth century, the U.S. Army, aided by massive slaughter of the buffalo (the basis of the Plains Native economy) as well as waves of smallpox and other diseases, was isolating the last organized Native resistance in the middle of the continent. Chapter 7 describes Native American peoples who began the century as mounted lords of the plains and ended it as prisoners. Sometimes, as at Sand Creek, they were massacred in these camps. The Navajos were forced from their homelands on a journey they still call the "Long Walk," as the U.S. Army pursued the Apaches, led by a number of notable individuals, including the legendary Geronimo. Resistance, as in the Great Sioux Uprising of 1862, was met with brutal repression—in this case, the largest mass hanging in U.S. history at Mankato, Minnesota.

Another kind of resistance, the defeat of George Armstrong Custer and his troops at the Little Bighorn during the summer of 1876, also was met with a broadside of attacks. Yellow Hair, the Boy General, was hardly a model officer. He was disobeying orders at the time, ignoring the reports of his Native scouts regarding the size of the Indian camp, and driving his forces to exhaustion on a risky publicity stunt, but Custer was nonetheless lionized as an ad hoc hero in another century's war on terror.

Even during the cruelest century for Native Americans, local exceptions to the general tenor of conflict occasionally came to light. The Poncas, for example, were forced off their homeland in northern Nebraska during the late 1870s by a clerical error that deeded their land to the Sioux, their traditional enemies. Exiled in Indian Territory (later called Oklahoma), a band of Poncas led by Chief Standing Bear resolved to walk home against the orders of the U.S. Army. Starving, having eaten their horses and their moccasins, the Poncas arrived in Omaha, then a frontier town, as a newspaperman, Thomas Tibbles, took up their case. The people of Omaha rallied behind the Poncas; the Army was taken to federal court, and the Poncas were declared "persons" under U.S. law, the first time this status had been accorded Native Americans. They were eventually permitted to go home.

More characteristically, however, the nineteenth century brought exile and death to Native leaders, notably Crazy Horse and Sitting Bull, as some well-known European Americans, such as *Oz* books' author L. Frank Baum (then a newspaper editor in South Dakota), called for extermination of remaining Native peoples. Chapter 7 ends with the massacre at Wounded Knee and its aftermath as reported by a Native American woman, Susette LaFlesche, Thomas Tibbles's wife.

As the nineteenth century became the twentieth, Native Americans faced recovery from devastating travails that provoked anthropologists and other non-Indians to call them "the vanishing race." They never vanished, however. Instead, survivors coped with a system that sought to assimilate them as an alternative to outright annihilation. As Richard Henry Pratt, who founded the system of boarding schools, put it: "Kill the Indian, Save the Man." Chapter 8 develops the many forms that assimilation took at century's turn, from boarding schools to allotment of property meant to turn Native Americans into individual farmers. All this was presented to survivors of the nineteenth century holocaust as a favor for their own good, despite the fact that, in some cases, 90 percent of collective land base was taken from them.

Some Native peoples found ways to turn allotment on its head. The Osages, for example, exiled in Indian Territory, found themselves quite by geological accident atop a cache of oil and natural gas at the dawn of the automotive age. In 1906, when allotment came to them, the Osages used its provisions to protect common ownership of their oil and gas, a policy they have since maintained with considerable legal diligence. For most Native peoples, however, allotment was a socioeconomic disaster. The Meriam Report (1928) pointed out just how closely Native poverty could be related to its provisions. During the 1930s, Franklin Roosevelt's Bureau of Indian Affairs, directed by John Collier, reversed the older policies, allowed some additions to Native land base, and implemented limited self-government under the Indian Reorganization Act. By the 1950s, however, established interests were eroding Native American lands again by terminating entire reservations and moving Indian people to urban areas under the "relocation" program.

In the 1960s, a new wave of Native American activism was becoming very direct, personal, and sometimes personally risky for participants. Chapter 9 describes fishing rights protests in the Pacific Northwest that led to a landmark legal ruling by Judge George H. Boldt, opening to Native peoples access to as many as half the salmon returning to local waters. Alcatraz Island, in San Francisco Bay, was occupied during 1969. Native activists seeking to publicize the abrogation of treaties marched across the United States during the late summer and early autumn of 1972, barricading themselves inside the Washington, D.C., headquarters of the Bureau of Indian Affairs. A few months later, activists occupied the village of Wounded Knee on the Pine Ridge Reservation, bringing an avalanche of media attention to the new American Indian Movement. After it ended in May 1973, the Wounded Knee occupation provoked a wave of armed repression at Pine Ridge, during which at least sixty-six people, many of them political activists, were killed by violent means. For a time, the Pine Ridge Reservation had a higher murder rate than Detroit, Michigan, which was reputed at the time to have been the murder capital of the United States. An era of public activism ended during the late

1970s with the pursuit, arrest, trial, and conviction (using questionable evidence) of Leonard Peltier, who later became an international symbol of Native political resistance in the Americas.

Chapter 10 presents a summary of ways in which Native American lifeways have influenced general society in America and, through the spread of its ways of life, the entire world. Aside from the usual important items that we use every day (corn and potatoes, for example), Native history may be traced through items and ideas so often utilized today that most people have forgotten their origins. The place names of half the states, for example, have Native American roots. More than 200 drugs in the U.S. *Pharmacopoeia* were first used by American Indians. Any game that is played with a bouncing ball owes something to Native American sports at some point in its evolution. Before contact with the Americas, Europe had no rubber and thus no rubber balls. The tomatoes in Italian pasta sauces, the "Irish" potato, "Indian" curry, and Jewish potato latkes all at some point in history were borrowed from their first cultivators, American Indians. In addition to material gifts, Sally Roesch Wagner details how much the founding mothers of American feminism, including Elizabeth Cady Stanton and Matilda Joslyn Gage, borrowed from the clan mothers of the Haudanosaunee (Iroquois) Confederacy.

Chapter 11 brings the narrative to the present day with a survey of contemporary reservation economic conditions in South Dakota, a corrective for anyone who thinks that modern-day reservation gambling has made all Native Americans rich. Aside from some of the poorest counties in the United States, Native peoples also occupy some of Canada's most desolate real estate, as characterized here by the village of Pikangikum, where many young people pass the time sniffling gasoline. Alcoholism is still a plague in the cities as well as on rural reservations. Readers will become acquainted in this chapter with the hamlet of Whiteclay, Nebraska, where the major business is selling beer and other alcoholic beverages to Indians of the neighboring Pine Ridge Reservation, where such sales are illegal.

Is gambling the answer? The "new buffalo," as some Native Americans have called it? Some places, such as the Pequots' Foxwoods in Connecticut and some other locales, have been enriched. In other places, such as the New York Oneidas' lands in upstate New York, gambling has provided an enriched upper class the means to hire police to force antigambling traditionalists from their homes. Among the Mohawks at Akwesasne, people have died over the issue. Akwesasne's position on the U.S.–Canadian border also has made smuggling of cigarettes, liquor, other drugs, weapons, and human beings a major industry.

Native America today presents a varied mosaic of life, death, and pervasive struggle. In this book's final chapter, readers will come to know Navajos who mined some of the uranium that powered the nation's nuclear arsenal. Many of them later died painfully, irradiated from the inside out, of lung cancer. Readers also will come to know activists who campaign against the use of

Native symbols as sports mascots, something that often has been handled with deft humor, as in the case of the "Fighting Whities," an intramural basketball team in Colorado, which stirred a national debate by adopting an upper middle class European American image as a mascot. Other activists struggle to remove the word *squaw* (which has been associated with references to Native women's vaginas) from place names. Struggles are ongoing to return Native bones and burial artifacts to the earth and to revive Native languages that are on the verge of disappearing. These are victories—such as naming of Winona LaDuke, an Anishinabe (Chippewa), as a candidate for vice president of the United States on the Green Party ticket with Ralph Nader. From its beginnings to recent years, this is a uniquely American story.

Chapter 6

The Northwest Coast and California

The peoples of the Northwest Coast of North America have proved themselves to be exceptional on several counts. For example, they produced a genuinely high culture (ranking with that of the Pueblos of the Southwest or the temple mound people of the Southeast) without benefit of agriculture, a very rare event in the history of humankind. Instead of pottery and agriculture, the Northwest Coast peoples, extending along the coast from the Alaska Panhandle to coastal Oregon and northern California, created exquisite baskets and wooden bowls that they filled with the bounty of the forests and the sea. The Saskatoon berry, which they harvest, for example, contains three times as much iron as prunes and raisins. The bounty of the ocean and forests was so abundant and so skillfully exploited by the Northwest Coast peoples that most were able during the summer to lay up enough food (much of it dried) to last the winter. The major sources of protein for the Northwest Coast peoples were fish and sea mammals. Among the Makah, the word for "fish" is the same as the word for "food."

The social and economic lifeways of Northwest Coast peoples evolved very differently compared to those of Native peoples across the rest of North America. Although many other American Indian peoples were democratic in their political orientation, the Northwest Coast peoples maintained a very strict caste system. They also maintained an economy that was not communal, like those of many other Native peoples in North America. In a Northwest Coast village, everyone had a class, and everything had an owner.

Economic, political, and ceremonial power were highly prized and unequally distributed among the Northwest Coast peoples. Like few other Native peoples, they paid intense attention to private property. Such wealth was inherited. A chief might own a lodge, salvage rights in nearby forests, and even fishing rights along a portion of coastline for miles offshore. Chiefs also

Wilson Parker, a Makah whaler, carrying sealskin floats and
a harpoon. Photographed by E. S. Curtis. (Courtesy of the
Edward S. Curtis Collection, Library of Congress.)

owned salmon spawning streams and the right to fish in them. A chief also
might own important ceremonial property, such as dances and songs, as well
as the right to present certain rituals. Lesser chiefs owned less-valuable resources. All land that had an economic use was owned by some member of the
nobility. A chief could create power networks under his aegis by allowing
lesser chiefs' families or commoners access to his lands and waters, usually for
a second harvest.

An elderly Makah woman carrying faggots at Neah Bay, Washington.
(Courtesy of the Library of Congress.)

Ownership extended to human beings. Slavery in Northwest Coast cultures was not an imitation of Anglo-American cultures before the U.S. Civil War; it pre-dated European contact. In the richest villages, slaves made up roughly a third of the population; the richest chiefs might own fifty slaves of both sexes. Slaves had no rights and owned nothing except their ability to work. Some male slaves, at least among the Makah, were initiated into the Klukwali (or wolf) Society; during its ceremonies, they participated as equals with nobles and commoners. Members of this secret society also could lodge complaints against each other and discuss grievances regardless of social rank or class, thus bringing some degree of accountability and equality to an otherwise very stratified society.

Slave labor became so important in Tlinget society that upper-class women did little or no work. At puberty, an upper-class Tlinget woman was sent into seclusion for from four months to a year. The longer the period of seclusion, the higher the person's rank and the greater the necessity of having slaves to meet everyday needs. A woman in seclusion was not allowed to engage in any economically productive activity.

Slaves were important commodities in the social economy of the Tlinget. Slaves might be killed or freed to give family and clan "crests" ceremonial value. Slaves were more often freed than killed, however; freed slaves (often captives from other villages) could then assume important positions in Tlinget society, sometimes because of their talents as carvers, dancers, or sorcerers. A skilled slave had some leverage in Tlinget society, and several families might vie for his services.

Native peoples living around Puget Sound were prime targets of their slave-raiding neighbors to the north, with the Makahs (some of whom held slaves themselves) notable as middlemen in the coastal slave trade. Occasionally, the Puget Sound tribes struck back. Chief Sea'th'l (Seattle) gained influence among his people, the Duwamish (who lived on the site of the present-day city of Seattle), in 1810 by leading warriors against tribes in the foothills of the Cascades who had taken some of his people as slaves.

OZETTE: A VILLAGE PRESERVED BY A NATURAL DISASTER

Ozette, on the Pacific coast of present-day Washington State, was one of several hundred Northwest Coast native villages. For archeologists, however, it is a special place. During the fifteenth century, a mudslide sealed the village almost airtight, preserving wooden houses, canoes, and other artifacts that would have decayed if they had been exposed to open air. The Northwest Coast peoples used wood for nearly every article they made, from canoes (which were hollowed out of huge logs) to eating utensils. Most of these implements were carved and painted with exquisite abstract designs depicting cosmology and the natural world. Five hundred years later, in 1966, a team from Washington State University found Ozette (Pascua, 1991, 38–53).

Related families lived together in plank houses flanked by gables, behind house posts carved and painted with family crests. Thus, totem poles are not religious icons, but family heralds, similar in some ways to European coats of arms. The word *totem* (meaning clan) was applied to the poles by European Americans; it stems from central Algonquian and is unrelated to any Northwest Coast language.

The Northwest Coast peoples also traded with their neighbors. The region drained by the Columbia River was a Native crossroads, a network of trade routes, that extended mainly north to south and vice versa along the entire coast; the language of the Chinook was reduced to an elementary form as a trading medium that spread from Alaska to California. Ironically, the Chinook people merged with the Chehalis in the mid-eighteenth century, and quit using their own language, which survived for many years afterward only in the abbreviated form used for trading. One of the words in this trade jargon, *hootchenoo*, became "hooch," slang for alcoholic beverages in American English.

THE POLITICAL AND CEREMONIAL
ECONOMY OF THE POTLATCH

Because the chiefs controlled access to food, shelter, and even spiritual sustenance, the societies of the Northwest Coast peoples were more hierarchical than even the Aztecs or the monarchical societies of Europe during the period of first contacts with Native America. No councils of chiefs existed to exercise restraint on them. Customs did exercise restraint on unbridled power, however. A good chief gathered power by being generous to those "under the arm." The ceremonial potlatch was an expression of this ethic: On one level, it was a display of wealth by the chief or chiefs hosting it; on another level, the intricate gift-giving of the ritual bespoke an inherent desire to distribute the bounteous wealth of Northwest Coast Native American societies. The potlatch thus consolidated the power and authority of its hosts by reminding lesser nobles and commoners that the high chiefs controlled every aspect of village life.

The mild, rainy winters of the Northwest Coast are a time of elaborate socializing and ceremonies. The potlatch often became a festival of wealth squandering between rival chiefs. Everything about the potlatch bespoke ostentation. Guests arrived in ornately carved canoes, flanked by assistants, all dressed in their best clothes. Once at the potlatch, which might have been planned for years, guests were expected to feast until they became ill from overindulgence. Competing chiefs wore headgear topped with special rings that indicated the number of potlatches they had held. In a social and economic context, the potlatch indicated the value the Northwest Coast peoples placed on status. The ostentation of the ritual also bespoke a society of surplus—one so successful at adapting to its environment that its members virtually had resources to burn or otherwise consume with reckless disregard for necessity.

Northwest Coast ceremonies, including the potlatch, were not usually concerned so much with the economic motives of getting and giving as with enhancing social status, honoring ancestors, and sealing personal relationships. According to Duane Champagne, the potlatch "should be understood from within its own cultural and institutional framework, and not be too easily compared with self-interested materialism" (1989, 110). Similarly, the emphasis on rank in Northwest Coast societies was not simply an imitation of Western hierarchical societies. Instead, the Tlinget concept of rank was integrated into that peoples' belief that proper behavior in the present (such as contributing to potlatches, fulfilling one's clan obligations, and submitting to the collective will of the house group) could cause a person to be reborn into a more aristocratic lineage.

The word *potlatch* is anglicized from *patshatl*, meaning "giving." Such giving could take many forms. At a "grease feast," for example, precious oil sometimes was splashed on fires until erupting flames burned members of competing households. Sometimes, the spattering oil set their cedar clothing aflame.

As a potlatch continued, the value of gifts usually rose steadily. After the rival chiefs had given away valuable cedar boxes and other expensive items, one chief might up the ante by sacrificing a slave with a special club called a slave killer. The giving chief might then hurl the scalp of the slain slave at his rival. Slaves also could be freed at potlatches. Another act of potlatch one-upmanship was the giving and destruction of large copper plates that served

Kaw-Claa, Tlinget Native woman in full potlach dancing
costume. (Courtesy of the Library of Congress.)

as currency of very high denomination, in the thousands of dollars if converted into U.S. currency.

Like most other aspects of life among Northwest Coast peoples, the potlatch was carried out with rigid, time-honored formality. Part of the ritual was
rehearsed insults in which one chief often dared the other to give away ever
more precious objects, such as the fabled canoes that were carved out of huge
tree trunks and used to hunt whales. Some of the insults were very personal.
The Kwakiutl may have been adopting a European custom from the Hudson's
Bay Company when they complicated the potlatch by demanding 100 percent

interest on gifts, a postcontact wrinkle in the ritual in which the act of giving now incurred a debt at twice the value of the original gift.

The Northwest Coast peoples hosted a number of other ceremonies and rituals in addition to the potlatch. Some of these rituals were associated with secret societies (exclusive groups of genetically unrelated individuals sometimes called sodalities by anthropologists). Perhaps the most important such ritual among the Kwakiutl-speaking peoples of the British Columbia coast was the cannibal dance, in which an individual, seized by an emotional frenzy, pretended to consume the flesh of another person. Illusions and fakery enjoyed a high degree of prestige among the Northwest Coast peoples, and a small bear might be cooked in such a way that it resembled a human being to be consumed during the cannibal dance. The person doing the cannibal dance might enliven the atmosphere by seizing bits of skin and flesh from members of the audience.

FIRST EUROPEAN CONTACTS

At the time of the American Revolution, English-speaking people on the Atlantic coast had only the slightest knowledge of the Northwest Coast peoples. The first, brief, European contact with them occurred when Vitus Bering, a Dane, sailed from Siberia in search of the strait that now bears his name. A few years after that, Juan de Fuca sailed through the strait between the Olympic Peninsula and Vancouver Island, where he left his name. Bering made only the slightest contact with Native peoples (on Kayak Island) before his ship, the St. Peter, was wrecked on an island between Siberia and Alaska during his return trip. Bering died on that island, but most of his crew survived, eating the flesh of sea otters as they rebuilt the ship. The crew took some of the otters' sleek pelts home with them to Europe. Within a few years, those otter skins ignited a commercial stampede to the Northwest Coast in search of the biggest fur discovery since the beaver.

During 1792, exploring the Pacific Northwest, British navigator George Vancouver found the bones of smallpox victims scattered on the beaches in great numbers. The survivors, noted Peter Puget, a sailor in Vancouver's party, were "most terribly pitted . . . indeed many had lost their eyes" (Mann, 2002, 44). In *Pox Americana* (2001), historian Elizabeth Fenn asserted that the deaths along the Pacific coast were part of a continent-wide pandemic that was almost two decades old, having begun near Boston during 1774, sweeping from Alaska to Mexico.

Employees of the Hudson's Bay Company entered the otter hunt early, as English envoys among the coastal peoples. The company, the premiere vehicle for English trade across the entire north country, was initiated during 1670 to counter the trading acumen of the French *coureurs de bois*, especially in competition for the best of *oiled beaver*, the term for a skin that had been worn with the skin side in, usually by an Indian, for several months to give it a luxurious, subtle texture and shine. In 1796, the Hudson's Bay Company split into two rival factions that engaged in a vicious trade war in which both companies wooed the Indians with 195,000 gallons of liquor in two years. The two factions then merged again until 1821.

In the meantime, whales, caribou, and other sea and land animals that had sustained Native peoples for many thousands of years were hunted nearly to extinction by immigrants in some areas of the Northwest. Freebooting Russian *promyshleniki* killed whatever they could find, from giant (six feet claw to claw) Bering Sea king crabs to beached seals. The freebooters also slaughtered the native Aleuts, whom they described as artistic, mild, polite, and hospitable. The Russians' words seemed to echo those of Columbus nearly three centuries earlier, as he spoke of the Indians' hospitality and then of how easily they might be enslaved. By 1799, when the Russian-American Company (a monopoly granted by the Russian czar) brought the slaughter under control, 90 percent of the Aleuts had been killed. By 1824, the Greek Orthodox Church was recruiting the souls of the few Aleuts who remained. The Aleuts, recalling the violent nature of the Russians they had so regrettably encountered in earlier years, had great respect for any holy man who could save their souls.

Among the Native peoples of the Northwest Coast, the Russians became known as the most ruthless of colonizers. Their demands for tribute in furs were met by armed resistance by the Tlingit, to whom the Russians' British and American colonial competitors happily supplied firearms, even cannons. In 1802, Tlingit war parties, long practiced in internecine warfare up and down the coast, struck at Russian settlements. A large force of Tlingit descended on the Russian colony of New Archangel on Sitka Island, burned most of the structures in the town, and made off with 4,000 sea otter pelts as they killed 20 Russians and 120 vassal Aleuts. The Tlingits held the position for two years, until Russian warships shelled it in 1804. The next year, the Tlingits resumed their insurgency, attacking the Russian settlement of Yakutat, killing twenty-two Russians and many Aleuts. In 1806, roughly 2,000 Native warriors assembled near Sitka in 400 boats. The Russians, warned of the attack, decided to throw a large feast, which defused the planned assault. Nevertheless, the Russian settlements faced regular guerilla raids by smaller native bands for years after that.

A search for a reliable food supply to provision their growing settlements brought the Russians to the California coast shortly after 1800, where they imitated the Spanish missions by establishing farming settlements that used coerced Native labor. Landing at Bodega Bay in 1812, ninety-five Russians and eighty Aleuts founded Fort Ross. The location was appealing because rocky islands offshore allowed the Russians to hunt sea otters for their prized pelts. At the fort, the Russians established vineyards, orchards, and fields of grain. The Russians ordered the fields tended by labor drafted from local Pomo Indians. As the demand for labor rose from fewer than 100 people to more than 250, the Pomos rebelled, burning fields, killing stock, and running from

A Pomo family. (Courtesy of the Library of Congress.)

Russian conscription squads. In the meantime, diseases introduced by the Russians were killing Pomos in larger numbers than slave labor.

Among the Inuit of the Canadian North, trade brought the "summer drunk," during which men, having been paid for their furs, spent the short summer returning their money to the traders in exchange for hard liquor. In the traditional way of life, summer had been a time of hunting and gathering, storing provisions for the long, hard winter. Coming off their summer drunks with empty larders, the Inuit men and their families died en masse during the winter. (In their language, *Inuit* means "real people." The term *Eskimo*, which is Algonquian for "eater of raw meat," has no indigenous meaning.) During 1888, a revenue ship docked at St. Lawrence Island, at the southern aperture of the Bering Strait, to find the entire population of three settlements, 400 people of both sexes and all ages, dead of starvation. Hunters who spent their summers trying to lay up game for winter found that meat animals were getting harder to find every year.

NATIVE AMERICANS AND SLAVERY

The Russians were hardly alone as they enslaved Native Americans. Early Spanish explorers arrived in America planning to take slaves. When De Soto's expedition arrived in Florida, they brought leg irons and metal collars linked with chains for the express purpose of conveying Indian slaves along their line of march. After the Pequot War, in 1675, Massachusetts colonists sold their prisoners into slavery in the West Indies. The Spanish at about the same time were shipping their Native American prisoners of war to Cuba as slaves. The Apaches greatly enhanced their diets by raiding Spanish settlements and missions for cattle, mules, and horses. The Spanish retaliated by capturing Apaches and selling them as slaves. Most of the slaves were compelled to work in Spanish mines. Any Apache was game for enslavement, even those who had come to trade or who had converted to Christianity.

During early English colonial history, several hundred Native Americans were listed as slaves. In 1704, South Carolinians under Colonel James Moore united with Indian allies to invade northern Florida, which was under Spanish control at the time, razing fourteen missions and capturing about 1,000 people, who were taken home as slaves. In 1708, about 1,400 slaves of Native American descent were listed in South Carolina, a quarter of the total slaves in the colony. In 1726, Louisiana, under French control, listed 229 Indian slaves and 1,540 blacks. The Pawnees were captured so often that the word *Panis* became a synonym for "slave" in the language of the French colonies.

Early in the nineteenth century, as Mexico became independent, Navajos, Utes, and Comanches, sometimes working with Mexicans, staged many raids in Hopi country for scalps (to exchange for money) and slaves, to be sold in markets at Santa Fe and Chihuahua. Children were targeted most frequently by the raiders.

The slave trade sometimes became entwined with trade in horses. As noted, Northwest Coast peoples held slaves, so some European Americans were taken and sold as well. Having acquired horses in the early nineteenth century, the Klamaths raided Shasta and Pit River Indian villages in northern California, acquiring slaves who were traded at The Dalles, in present-day Oregon (site of a regional slave market), for more horses and trade goods. With the advent of the fur trade, Russians (and even some Japanese fishermen) sometimes were taken captive for sale and barter at The Dalles.

The trading markets of The Dalles were part of a commercial network maintained by the Chinooks along the lower Columbia River. Native peoples from as far away as Hawaii sometimes changed hands in The Dalles slave markets, where canoes and blankets, as well as horses, also were exchanged. Some of the treaties signed by Isaac Stevens in Washington Territory contained legal prohibitions of slave-taking by Native Americans, an indication that the practice was economically significant at the time. After the Civil War, agents of the U.S. government actively tried to suppress the Native American slave trade, causing prices to rise. During 1830, the going rate for a young, healthy, male slave in The Dalles' market was about ten blankets. Within a few decades, the Haida were paying up to 200 blankets per slave.

On balance, however, many more Native Americans were enslaved by Europeans than vice-versa. Los Angeles maintained a thriving slave market in the shell of an old mission, to which Indians were delivered after they had been arrested for drunkenness. The *aguardiente* sold to the Indians was very powerful alcohol; it was sometimes mixed with corrosive acids. This addictive poison was sometimes called *forty rod*, the estimated distance that an Indian might stagger before dying after drinking it. Indians were said to go insane from it following wild drunks. Thousands of Indians may have died in this way. The death toll from alcohol and murder was never tallied. Anyone with a need for cheap labor could bail Indians out for a day at $2 or $3 a head, renting them from the drunk tank as slave labor.

Into the 1860s, Native Americans who had been picked up for drinking by the Los Angeles police were "sold" to local farmers and ranchers as day labor. In 1850 and 1860, the newly established state of California enacted laws that allowed for Indian "apprenticeship," a state-approved grant of a form of near-slavery by which a property owner could obtain the labor of as many Native young people as he wished, on stipulation that he feed and clothe them and treat them "humanely." The measure was promoted as a means of teaching the Indians "civilized" habits. A debate rose over the terms of the laws, which in effect made several thousand Indian young people indentured servants at the same time that California had been admitted to the United States as a "free" state. In the 1850s, the going sales price for an adult Indian was about $50. The indenture law was repealed in 1863 (as part of the nationwide Civil War debate over slavery), but illegal kidnappings and sales of Indians continued through at least the 1870s, although in smaller numbers. Travel literature sometimes drew the attention of potential immigrants to the advantages of free Indian labor that was not available in other states.

The Aztecs also held slaves, but their society invoked some social sanctions against mistreatment of domestic servants. Slaves were said to be under the protection of their own god, Tezcatlipoca, who, it was believed, could ruin the lives of rich people who mistreated them. It was said that Tezcatlipoca could cause mistreated slaves to be freed and their cruel masters to lose their wealth. Aztec society not only was stratified, but also offered people some degree of social mobility, both upward and downward. Not infrequently, an affluent individual might fall into slavery for debt. Gamblers sometimes put their personal liberty up for sale when they had lost all else (Soustelle, 1961, 159). When the Spanish conquered Tenochtitlán, they incorporated some of the Aztecs' slavery system into their own economy. According to the Spanish chronicler Bernadino de Sahagún, "In the first years there was such haste to make slaves that they poured into Mexico City from all directions, and throughout the Indies they were taken like sheep in flocks to be branded" (de Zorita, 1963, 207).

The Spanish god did not reproach them for mistreating slaves, so Native Americans often were worked to death in the mines or as personal porters who were compelled to carry Spanish household goods and merchandise on their backs, as many as a thousand porters at a time, for hundreds of miles. According to official edict, Indian labor was "voluntary." According to Sahagún, "In actual fact, the Indians never go voluntarily." Women and children were pressed into the porters' brigades along with men, "loaded down with [Spaniards'] household furnishings, beds, chairs, tables, and all the other appointments for their household and kitchen service. Thus weighted down . . . they returned to their homes half dead, or died along the way" (de Zorita, 1963, 208). Indians in New Spain, according to Sahagún, "have also been laid low by the labor of making sheep, cattle, and pig farms, fencing those farms, of putting up farm buildings, and by their labor on roads, bridges, watercourses, stone walls, and sugar mills," as well as mines (ibid., 209). On top of all this labor, Indian villages were compelled to pay tribute to the Spanish, at central collection sites. Sahagún believed that the labor the Spanish imposed on the Indians destroyed them: "So the Indian returns home worn out from his toil, minus his pay and his mantle, not to speak of the food that he had brought with him," he wrote, continuing: "He returns home famished, unhappy, distraught, and shattered in health. For these reasons, pestilence always rages among the Indians" (ibid., 215).

EXTERMINATION OF THE CALIFORNIA NATIVES

The Spanish mission system was a form of slavery in all but name. Women in some of the missions around San Francisco Bay aborted their children rather than allow them to grow up under the subjugation of the missions. Captive Apaches, Navajos, Comanches, Utes, Pawnees, and Wichitas served as muleteers, household servants, day laborers, shepherds, silversmiths, blacksmiths, masons, and weavers. California Indians, who lived in hundreds of independent groups, were generally unable to mount organized resistance to the Spanish mission system, but they went into service of the Catholic Church without enthusiasm. So testified numerous friars, who nonetheless impressed Indian labor to cultivate bountiful crops and create a rich variety of salable crafts.

The Spanish empire and its mission system in California came to a very sudden end between 1811 and 1825, after 300 years of virtual slavery for thousands of Native American peoples. During the decade and a half after 1811, most of Spain's colonies in the New World achieved their independence. Mexico became an independent kingdom in 1821 and a republic in 1824. California, at first a province of Mexico, secularized its wealthiest missions in 1834. In theory, the land that had comprised the missions was to be returned to the Indians who had worked on them, making them self-sustaining peoples. Instead, most of the land became part of private ranches, and most of the Indians were driven away. By the time the mission lands and other property had been distributed to California's new Hispanic upper class, the United States conquered the area between 1846 and 1848.

Like most of Mexico's northern half, California became a territory of the westward-expanding United States. In 1848, gold was discovered; within a year, California was flooded by gold-rushing "Forty-niners." In 1848, before California became a state, its non-Indian population was about 15,000. By 1850, the population had increased to 93,000 according to the federal census. At least 100,000 Indians had lived in the area before the gold rush; the best estimate in 1856 was 40,000. The Native American population of the area fell to fewer than 30,000 in 1864 and 19,000 in 1906 as the immigrant population continued to swell.

With the discovery of gold in present-day Nevada, the Paiutes, who had lived in the Great Basin at least 10,000 years, were forced to face a tidal wave of European American settlement. The gold-seekers surged into Virginia City and other quickly erected commercial centers so fast that some of the Paiutes, who had no warring tradition and no capacity for armed resistance, tried to get away as quickly as they could. Some Paiutes buried their children up to the necks in the desert sand and piled clumps of brush over their heads. The Paiutes had hoped to retrieve the children later, but most of them were never able to return to a land suddenly awash with a flood of miners and land speculators.

Stands of pinon trees, with nuts that had been a staple in the Paiutes' diet, were cut in huge swaths for firewood, and cattle, sheep, and horses denuded the dryland prairie. Cholera quickly killed 2,000 Paiutes. A few of the survivors, skirting starvation, joined with Shoshonis and Utes in occasional petty theft from white settlements. During the 1860s, the Paiutes were subjugated by military force and vigilantes. Within a generation, the only means of survival open to a Basin Indian was menial work as a housekeeper or field hand. By 1874, 10,000 years of a people's life in the Great Basin were nearly wiped clean from humankind's memory.

For several decades, the new immigrants in California and Nevada took part in what may have been the largest unprovoked slaughter of Native peoples during the bloody nineteenth century. In one massacre, thirty Indians were butchered in retaliation for the wounding by a Native man of a single steer. The Indians were not able to organize a mass resistance, but every hint of trouble was met by hastily organized "volunteer" Indian fighters, who later billed the federal government for their services on the theory that they were doing the work of the U.S. Army. During the 1850s, the federal government reimbursed California almost $1 million (several million dollars today) for freelance Indian hunting. The victims of the volunteers, who had none of the scruples displayed by some regular Army officers, were mainly (but hardly exclusively) Native American men.

The earliest gold rush was led by single men. Although they did not kill Native women as frequently as men, women suffered rape and assault. Venereal diseases from prostitution ravaged the native women of California. Even the immigrants' newspapers protested frequent gang rapes of native women by miners. Between 3,000 and 4,000 Indian children were stolen to be sold as servants or slaves between 1852 and 1867, not including women forced into having sex or adults taken into slavery (often to redeem debts) for field labor.

A few Natives fought back. One was a Modoc called Captain Jack by the immigrants (his native name was Kintpuash), leader of a renegade band that rebelled against intolerable reservation conditions by escaping to the northern California lava beds of their homeland. With about sixty compatriots, Captain Jack kept as many as a thousand soldiers at bay for seven months in the rugged country. After they kidnapped several children, Captain Jack and his allies were regarded as terrorists by farmers in the Yureka area of northern California.

Troops arrived in 1872 to force Captain Jack and his men back to their as-signed reservation. Before the Army hanged him and three of his close friends, Captain Jack led a campaign through the lava beds of northern California that took the lives of more than 100 soldiers. At a peace conference, Captain Jack shot General E. R. S. Canby, the leader of the non-Indian treaty commissioners, to death. After the killing of Canby, the Army shelled the lava beds with field guns to drive Captain Jack and his band out. Captain Jack wore Canby's uniform until the day he was hanged.

MARTIAL LAW IN WASHINGTON TERRITORY

Beginning in 1843, continuing until the middle 1850s, Washington Territory Governor Isaac Stevens "negotiated" at least 50 heavy-handed treaties with the Natives of the Pacific Northwest. Most of his effort was concentrated east of the Cascades, in the areas that today comprise eastern Washington, eastern Oregon, and Idaho. The Native peoples felt insulted by most of the treaties, by which they were cajoled and threatened into signing away 157 million acres.

The 1855 Walla Walla Treaty galled them the most. The Yakimas, claim-ing that Stevens had bought off their leaders, recruited allies from several other tribes and waged an armed guerilla war with the U.S. Army that spread over the mountains to the Pacific coast. The Army brought the rebellion under control after three years of occasionally bloody fighting. During the rebellion, Dr. Marcus Whitman (whom, it was said, had come to the Walla Walla area to civilize the Indians with a Bible in one hand and a whip in the other) was murdered, along with his wife and twelve other immigrant European Amer-icans. A freelance posse formed immediately and hung five captured Cayuse in retribution.

Although settlement of the coastal Northwest began at the same time as California, accelerating about 1850, most of the people who traversed the continent along the Oregon Trail were not looking for gold or other quick riches. Most sought farms (some planned utopian communes), and they found alliances with the Native peoples of the area to be in their interests. Some even aided Indians who were dissatisfied with the terms of a series of treaties negotiated by Governor Stevens. When his white opponents sought the protection of local courts, Stevens called up a militia of a thousand men, declared martial law, closed the courts, and arrested the chief justice of the territory— a rare example of government by fiat in the face of settlers' resistance to ill treatment of Indians. By that time, European American immigrants were flooding the area around Puget Sound as the Duwamish (led by chief Sea'th'l) abandoned their homelands peacefully as the urban area approached.

After the chief's first trial ended with a hung jury, the judge in the second trial refused to instruct jurors that killing an enemy soldier in war was not considered murder. Chief Leschi was convicted and sentenced to death. On appeal, the territorial Supreme Court refused to consider new evidence showing that Chief Leschi had been miles away when Colonel Moses was killed.

A brief but bloody native uprising followed, ending with the hanging of Chief Leschi, the leader of the Native people opposing the treaties, in 1858. Chief Leschi was hanged for killing Colonel A. Benton Moses of the territorial militia during the region's Indian war of 1855. The historical court was led by the chief justice of the State Supreme Court, Gerry L. Alexander. It ruled that if Chief Leschi did in fact kill Colonel Moses, a murder charge was not justified because they were lawful combatants in a time of war. "I'm just happy; this is really about the future," said Cynthia Iyall, a descendant of Chief Leschi's sister and chairwoman of the Committee to Exonerate Chief Leschi. "This is for all the kids: they need to know who that man was and what truthfully happened to him" ("Indian Chief," 2004). During December 2004, Chief Leschi was exonerated by a historical court, nearly a century and a half after he was hanged. The unanimous verdict by a seven-judge panel was not legally binding, but it drew cheers from several hundred people who gathered at the Washington State history museum to hear the decision.

The historical trial's verdict thus came to agree with the U.S. Army, which refused to execute Chief Leschi at the time because military leaders believed the rules of war should have prevented him from being charged with murder. Instead, civilian Pierce County authorities oversaw his execution on February 19, 1858. Leschi's hangman, Charles Grainger, later said, "I felt then I was hanging an innocent man, and I believe it yet" ("Indian Chief," 2004). Chief Leschi's name is remembered in the region. His name appears on schools, monuments, a park, and a Seattle neighborhood.

Chief Sea'th'l (Seattle) and Angeline with views of Mt. Rainier and Seattle.
(Courtesy of the Library of Congress.)

Sea'th'l's Haunting "Farewell Speech"

Sea'th'l (Duwamish/Suquamish, ca. 1788–1866) probably was born on Blake Island in Puget Sound. He was a principal chief of the Duwamish, whose original homeland is today an industrial area immediately south of downtown Seattle. Sea'th'l was described in 1833 by William Fraser Tolmie, a Hudson's Bay Company surgeon, as "a brawney Suquamish with a Roman countenance and black curley [sic] hair, the handsomest Indian I have ever seen" (Johansen and Grinde, 1997, 341). David Denny, one of the first white settlers of Seattle, said that Sea'th'l's voice could be heard a half-mile away when he spoke, and that he led his people by force of his considerable intellect.

Son of the Duwamish chief Schweabe, Sea'th'l was about seven years of age when George Vancouver sailed the *Discovery* into Puget Sound and met briefly with the Duwamish and their allies, the Suquamish. Sea'th'l later aided his father and other Duwamish in the construction of the Old Man House, a community longhouse 1,000 feet long that housed 40 families. The Duwamish and the Suquamish formed an alliance that ringed central Puget Sound. Sea'th'l took a wife, La-da-ila, and he became chief of the Duwamish-Suquamish alliance at the age of 22. La-da-ila had died by 1833, when the Hudson's Bay Company established a trading post at Nisqually, in southern Puget Sound. In 1841, the first "Bostons," as the Duwamish called whites (they had arrived from Boston), sailed into Central Puget Sound in Sea'th'l's territory. Ten years later, the schooner *Exact* delivered the first settlers in what later became the city of Seattle.

From the beginning, Sea'th'l resolved to cooperate with the settlers, but when they proposed naming their city after him, he protested that his spirit would be disturbed if his name was mentioned after he died. The settlers retained the name anyway, in an anglicized form. Sea'th'l, who had been a Catholic since the 1830s when he was converted by missionaries, adopted the biblical name Noah at his baptism and began regular morning and evening prayers among his people.

Sea'th'l and his band moved westward across Puget Sound after signing the Treaty of Point Elliot with Washington Territorial Governor Isaac Stevens during 1854. As his people prepared to move, Sea'th'l delivered a haunting farewell speech that has come to be recognized as one of history's great pieces of Native American oratory. The speech was given in Salish and translated by Dr. Henry Smith, who published it in 1887, which was 33 years after the original oration. Given the amount of time between the speech and its publication, the fact that Sea'th'l was not speaking English (Smith heard a translation), and numerous modern embellishments of the original printed text, modern versions sometimes are unreliable.

Environmental conservation was not a subject of general debate and controversy in the mid-nineteenth century, as Euro-American settlement sped across the land mass of the United States. Yet, from time to time, the records of the settlers contain warnings by Native leaders whose peoples they were displacing describing how European-bred attitudes toward nature were ruining the land, air, and water. Perhaps the most famous warning of this type came from Chief Sea'th'l's farewell speech.

> Our dead never forget the beautiful world that gave them being. They still love its verdant valleys, its murmuring rivers, its magnificent mountains, sequestered vales and verdant-lined lakes and bays.... Every part of this soil is sacred in the estimation of my people. Every hillside, every valley, every plain and grove has been hallowed by some sad or happy event in days long vanished. Even the rocks, which seem to be dumb and dead as they swelter in the sun along the silent shore, thrill with memories of stirring events connected with the lives of my people. (Vanderwerth, 1971, 120–121)

In the development of environmental philosophy, Chief Sea'th'l's words are often cited in the late twentieth century as evidence that many Native Americans practiced a stewardship ethic toward the earth long before such attitudes became popular in non-Indian society. The debate ranges from acceptance of several versions of Sea'th'l's speech to a belief that the original translator, Dr. Henry Smith, as well as many people who followed him, put the ecological concepts into the chief's mouth.

Regardless of the exact wording of Sea'th'l's speech, it did contain environmental themes. Sea'th'l was not telling the immigrants what they wanted to hear because they displayed no such ideological bent. The farewell speech, as recorded, also touched on fundamental differences between cultures:

> The white man's god cannot love his red children[,] or he would protect them....
> We are two distinct races with separate origins and separate destinies....To us,
> the ashes of our ancestors are sacred and their resting place is hallowed ground.
> You wander far from the graves of your ancestors, seemingly without regret. Your
> religion was written on tables of stone by the iron fingers of your God so that you
> cannot forget it. The Red Man could never comprehend nor remember it. Our
> religion is the tradition of our ancestors—the dreams of our old men, given to
> them in the solemn hours of the night by the Great Spirit, and the visions of our
> sachems; and it is written in the hearts of our people. Your dead cease to love you
> and the land of their nativity as soon as they pass the portals of the tomb and
> wander away among the stars. They are soon forgotten and never return. Our dead
> never forget the world that gave them being. (Furtwangler, 1997, 14–15)

> It matters little where we pass the remnants of our days. They will not be many. A
> few more moons, a few more winters—and not one of the descendants of the
> mighty hosts that once moved over this broad land ... will remain to mourn over
> the graves of a people once more powerful and hopeful than yours. But why
> should we repine? Why should I murmur at the fate of my people? Tribes are
> made up of individuals and are no better than they. Men come and go like waves
> of the sea. A tear, a *tahmanawis* [a mourning ceremony], a dirge, and they are
> gone from our longing eyes forever. Even the white men, whose God walked and
> talked with him, is not exempt from the common destiny. We *may* be brothers
> after all. We shall see. (emphasis in original; Smith, 1887, n.p.)

In the mid-1850s, when the Yakima War spilled over the Cascades into Seattle under Chief Leschi, Sea'th'l and his people looked on from their retreat on the western shores of Puget Sound. He died there in 1866.

Whites Arrested for Aiding "Renegade" Indians

During the hostilities with Chief Leschi and his allies, Governor Stevens's militia also arrested several settlers suspected of aiding "renegade" Indians. Lion A. Smith, Charles Wren, Henry Smith, John McLeod, Henry Murray, and another man asserted that they were taken from their land claims in Pierce County "without process of law, and without any complaint or affidavit being lodged against them" ("A Brief Notice," 1856, 385). The men were escorted against their will to Fort Steilacoom (near Tacoma), where they were held, at Stevens's request, on charges of treason.

Following complaints by attorneys for the men, Stevens issued a martial law declaration suspending civil liberties in Pierce County, accusing the arrested settlers of giving "aid and comfort to the enemy" ("A Brief Notice," 1856, 386). A few days later, Stevens ordered the men back to Olympia, out of Pierce County, because a judge there had issued a writ of habeas corpus on their behalf. Later, the case was taken up in the court of Honorable Edward Lander, chief justice of the territory. When Judge Lander convened court to hear the case, a column of militiamen filed into his courtroom and arrested him, leading the judge and the clerk of the court from the bench. The arrests occurred on May 6; by May 9, the judge was released. A few days later, Stevens extended martial law to Thurston County, including Olympia, the territorial capital.

A legal ballet ensued in which Governor Stevens refused to honor the writ of habeas corpus. Members of the militia stood outside the house in which Chief Justice Lander was holding court. "The marshal, being ordered to keep the room clear of armed men, was compelled to lock the door. . . . The counsel engaged inside could distinctly hear the men [outside] cocking their rifles," said a contemporary statement. An officer of the militia called on Judge Lander to surrender once again. He refused. Finally, the armed men barged into the courtroom, seized the judge and clerk, and transported them to the office of Governor Stevens. An observer said the judge was "kidnapped" ("A Brief Notice," 1856, 389). The judge was told that he would be freed if he stopped issuing orders contrary to the decree of martial law. The judge flatly refused. Stevens had violated his oath of office by refusing to respect a writ of habeas corpus, an act that the U.S. Constitution says may be suspended only by Congress.

CHIEF JOSEPH LEADS THE NEZ PERCE LONG MARCH

The Nez Perce became steadfast U.S. allies as immigrants moved into the Pacific Northwest in the face of opposition from Great Britain. They even rescued a body of U.S. troops in 1858. Nevertheless, during the same year, the United States signed a treaty with Nez Perce "treaty commissioners" who did not represent the nation. The treaty ceded the Nez Perce's Wallowa Valley to the United States, opening it for settlement. Chief Joseph (father of Young Joseph, whose long march with his people subsequently became legendary) protested that the treaty was illegal, a violation of another signed only three years earlier.

Joseph the Elder died in 1871, passing the leadership of his Nez Perce band to Hinmaton Yalatik, Thunder Rolling Over the Mountains (1841–1904), whom English speakers at first called Young Joseph and later Chief Joseph. Like his father, Young Joseph refused to surrender to reservation life.

Chief Joseph, Younger. (Courtesy of Smithsonian National
Anthropological Archives.)

The Nez Perce in Joseph's band stayed in the valley, tending their large herds
of prized horses, as European American immigrants moved in around them,
sparking several violent incidents.

As Young Joseph assumed leadership of his Nez Perce band, government
emissaries continued to press the Nez Perce to move to a reservation where they
would be allocated far too little land to run the blue Appaloosas that the Nez
Perce used for hunting and war. Under pressure from the United States, during
1871 Joseph and his band signed the last treaty negotiated by any Native nation

with the United States. Under the terms of the treaty, the Nez Perce agreed to move to Lapwai, Idaho. As the logistics of the move were being worked out, settlers stole hundreds of the Nez Perce's horses. A renegade band of young Nez Perce led by young Wahlitis, whose father had been murdered by whites two years earlier, retaliated by killing eighteen settlers. The Army was brought in to arrest the "hostiles." Instead of surrendering, the entire band of about 500 men, women, and children decamped and marched into the mountains.

During the next several months, the vastly outnumbered Nez Perce led U.S. Army troops on a 1,500-mile trek through some of the most rugged country on the continent, north into Canada, then south again. Joseph, with at most 200 warriors, fought more than a dozen engagements with four U.S. Army columns, evading capture every time. On one occasion, in a night raid, the Nez Perce made off with the pursuing Army's pack animals. At other times, the Nez Perce so skillfully evaded Army pincer movements that the two closing columns ran into each other without capturing a single hostile. The Army did inflict casualties on the Nez Perce at other times. Eighty-nine were killed in one battle, fifty of them women and children. Despite the deaths, the Nez Perce continued.

Chief Joseph instructed his warriors not to take scalps. The Nez Perce earned praise for their military acumen from General William Tecumseh Sherman, who said the Indians went to great lengths to avoid killing innocent settlers. General Nelson A. Miles, whose troops brought the Nez Perce's long march to an end, seconded Sherman's opinion: "In this skillful campaign, they have spared hundreds of lives and thousands of dollars worth of property that they might have destroyed" (Johansen and Grinde, 1997, 189).

Through the Bitterroot Mountains and the present-day Yellowstone National Park, to the headwaters of the Missouri, then to the Bear Paw Mountains, Joseph's band fought a rear-guard action with unquestioned brilliance. At one point, the Indians were harbored briefly in Canada by Sitting Bull's Lakota, who also had been exiled from their homelands. Exhausted, the Nez Perce surrendered October 5, 1877, at Eagle Creek, roughly 30 miles south of the Canadian border. Many of the Nez Perce were starving. Several also were maimed and blind. Joseph handed his rifle to General Miles, and said he was

> tired of fighting. . . . My people ask me for food, and I have none to give. It is cold, and we have no blankets, no wood. My people are starving to death. Where is my little daughter? I do not know. Perhaps, even now, she is freezing to death. Hear me, my chiefs. I have fought, but from where the sun now stands, Joseph will fight no more forever. (Johansen and Grinde, 1997, 189)

Chief Joseph then drew his blanket over his face and walked into the Army camp, a prisoner. Of roughly 650 Nez Perce who had begun the long march, only about 400 remained at its end.

At roughly the same time, a band of 297 Cheyennes, unhappy with life on an assigned reservation near Fort Reno, Oklahoma, walked a thousand miles back to their homelands along the eastern slopes of the Rockies, to the northwest. After an extremely arduous journey, about a hundred of them were captured and imprisoned at Fort Robinson, Nebraska. The Cheyennes refused to march south again in the middle of winter, and officers at the fort decided to deny the native people food until they changed their minds. Instead of changing, the captive Cheyenne burst out of the barracks, killing several soldiers. They were eventually recaptured, along with the rest of the band, and dispersed to several reservations against their wills. Meanwhile, a large number of the men, women, and children died of exposure and starvation. The march of the Cheyennes was described in Mari Sandoz's historical novel *Cheyenne Autumn*, which in turn provided the material for John Ford's 1964 movie of the same name. It was the only motion picture that Ford, the famous director of westerns, made from a Native point of view.

In 1879, Chief Joseph appealed to Congress (speaking in person to a full chamber) to let his people return home. "It has always been the pride of the Nez Perce that they were the friends of the white men," he began, recounting how the Indians helped support the first few immigrants. "There was room enough for all to live in peace, and they [Joseph's ancestors] were learning many things from the white men that appeared to be good.... Soon [we] found that the white men were growing rich very fast, and were greedy to possess everything the Indian had." He recalled how his father had refused to sign a treaty with Washington territorial governor Isaac Stevens: "I will not sign your paper.... You go where you please, so do I; you are not a child; I am no child; I can think for myself.... Take away your paper. I will not sign it." (Nabokov, 1991, 130–131). Joseph said that the Nez Perce had given too much, and that they had only gone to war when the immigrants forced them off their cherished homeland.

The War Department refused Chief Joseph's request to let his people resettle in their homeland. Instead, they were imprisoned at Fort Leavenworth, Kansas, where many who had survived the Long March died of malaria. In 1885, the 268 surviving Nez Perce were marched to Indian Territory (later Oklahoma), where more died.

Later in 1885, roughly seven score survivors were finally allowed to return to the Northwest, some to Lapwai, Idaho, and others to the Colville reservation in eastern Washington. The Nez Perce were provided no supplies as they arrived at the onset of winter. They experienced profound suffering. Lieutenant Wood, who had witnessed Chief Joseph's surrender speech and later wrote a narrative of the Nez Perce's long march, said: "I think that, in his long career, Joseph cannot accuse the Government of the United States of one single act of justice" (Johansen and Grinde, 1997, 190). Joseph died at Colville in 1904, his heart still yearning to go home to the land where he had buried his father.

A VISE CLOSES ON THE PLAINS

By the last third of the nineteenth century, the settlement frontier was closing in on the plains and steppes of North America, the continent that Benjamin Franklin once had speculated would not be occupied by settlers for a thousand years. The development of transportation technology (notably the railroad) had complemented the lure of land and gold, among other resources, to push Native peoples into isolated pockets of resistance. For most Native peoples in North America, this was a time of profound cultural change, often accompanied by acute suffering, especially from European diseases. A long decline of Native populations followed a brief flash of prosperity that had come with the advent of widespread trade with Euro-Americans. The settlement frontier soon would close in 1890 in Wounded Knee, a small hamlet on the windswept plains of South Dakota.

FURTHER READING

Anderson, Eva Greenslit. *The Life Story of Chief Seattle*. Caldwell, ID: Caxton Publishers, 1950.

Baily, L. R. *Indian Slave Trade in the Southwest*. Los Angeles: Westernlore Press, 1973.

Beal, Merrill D. *I Will Fight No More Forever*. Seattle: University of Washington Press, 1963.

"A Brief Notice of the Recent Outrages Committed by Isaac Stevens...May 17, 1856." Cited in W. H. Wallace, "Martial Law in the Washington Territory," *The Annals of America*, 1856, 384–389.

Calloway, Colin. *New Worlds for All: Indians, Europeans, and the Remaking of Early America*. Baltimore: Johns Hopkins University Press, 1997.

Chalmers, Harvey. *The Last Stand of the Nez Perce*. New York: Twayne, 1962.

Champagne, Duane. *American Indian Societies: Strategies and Conditions of Political and Cultural Survival*. Cambridge, MA: Cultural Survival, 1989.

Davis, Russell, and Brant Ashabranner. *Chief Joseph: War Chief of the Nez Perce*. New York: McGraw-Hill, 1962.

DeVoto, Bernard. *Across the Wide Missouri*. Cambridge, MA: Harvard University Press, 1947.

De Zorita, Alonso. *Life and Labor in Ancient Mexico*. Translated by Benjamin Keen. New Brunswick, NJ: Rutgers University Press, 1963.

Drucker, Philip. *Indians of the Northwest Coast*. New York: McGraw-Hill, 1955.

Fee, Chester. *Chief Joseph: The Biography of a Great Indian*. New York: Wilson Erickson, 1936.

Fenn, Elizabeth. *Pox Americana: The Great Smallpox Epidemic of 1775–82*. New York: Hill & Wang, 2001.

Furtwangler, Albert. *Answering Chief Seattle*. Seattle: University of Washington Press, 1997.

Gibson, Arrell Morgan. *The American Indian: Prehistory to Present*. Lexington, MA: Heath, 1980.

Gunther, Erna. *Indian Life on the Northwest Coast of North America.* Chicago: University of Chicago Press, 1972.

Howard, Helen A., and Dan L. McGrath. *War Chief Joseph.* Caldwell, ID: Caxton, 1952.

Howard, Oliver O. *Nez Perce Joseph.* Boston: Lea & Shepherd, 1881.

Indian Chief Hanged in 1858 Is Cleared. *New York Times,* December 12, 2004. Available at http://query.nytimes.com/mem/tnt.html?oref=login&tntget=2004/12/12/national/12chief.html&tntemail1.

Johansen, Bruce E., and Donald A. Grinde, Jr. *The Encyclopedia of Native American Biography.* New York: Henry Holt, 1997.

Joseph, Chief [In-mut-too-yah-lat-lat]. An Indian's View of Indian Affairs. *North American Review* 128(April 1879):415–433.

Josephy, Alvin, Jr. *The Patriot Chiefs.* New York: Viking, 1961.

Josephy, Alvin M. *The Nez Perce Indians and the Opening of the Northwest.* New Haven, CT: Yale University Press, 1965.

Lavender, David. *Let Me Be Free.* San Francisco: HarperCollins, 1992.

Mann, Charles C. 1491: America before Columbus was More Sophisticated and More Populous than We Have Ever Thought—and a More Livable Place Than Europe. *The Atlantic Monthly,* March 2002, 41–53.

Maxwell, James A. *America's Fascinating Indian Heritage.* Pleasantville, NY: Reader's Digest, 1978.

McNickle, D'Arcy. *They Came Here First: The Epic of the American Indian.* New York: Harper and Row Perennial Library, 1975.

Moore, John H. How Giveaways and Pow-wows Redistribute the Means of Subsistence. In John H. Moore, ed., *The Political Economy of North American Indians.* Norman: University of Oklahoma Press, 1993: 240–269.

Nabokov, Peter, ed. *Native American Testimony.* New York: Viking, 1991.

Oberg, Kalervo. *The Social Economy of the Tlinget Indians.* Seattle: University of Washington Press, 1973.

Olexer, Barbara. *The Enslavement of the American Indian.* Monroe, NY: Library Research Associates, 1982.

Pascua, Maria Parker. Ozette: A Makah Village in 1491. *National Geographic,* October 1991, 38–53.

Ruby, Robert H., and John A Brown. *Indian Slavery in the Pacific Northwest.* Spokane: Arthur H. Clark, 1993.

Sahagún, Bernardino de. *General History of the Things of New Spain: Florentine Codex.* Book 12, *Conquest of Mexico.* Translated by A. J. O. Anderson and C. E. Dibble. Salt Lake City: University of Utah Press, and Santa Fe, NM: School of American Research, 1950.

Smith, Henry A. Early Reminiscences. Number Ten. Scraps from a Diary. Chief Seattle—a Gentleman by Instinct—His Native Eloquence, etc., etc. *Seattle Star,* October 29, 1887, n.p.

Snell, William Robert. Indian Slavery in Colonial South Carolina, 1671–1795. Ph.D. dissertation, University of Alabama, 1972.

Soustelle, Jacques. *Daily Life of the Aztecs on the Eve of the Spanish Conquest.* Translated by Patrick O'Brian. Palo Alto, CA: Stanford University Press, 1961.

Tebbel, John, and Keith Jennison. *The American Indian Wars.* New York: Bonzanza Books, 1960.

Vanderwerth, W. C., ed. *Indian Oratory: Famous Speeches by Noted Indian Chieftains.* Norman: University of Oklahoma Press, 1971.

Waters, Frank. *Brave Are My People: Indian Heroes Not Forgotten.* Santa Fe: Clear Light, 1992.

Weeks, Philip. *Farewell, My Nation: The American Indian and the United States, 1820–1890.* Arlington Heights, IL: Harlan Davidson, 1990.

Wood, H. Clay. *The Status of Young Joseph and His Band of Nez Perce Indians.* Portland, OR: Assistant Adjutant General's Office, Department of the Columbia, 1876.

CHAPTER 7

The Frontier Closes on the Southwest and Great Plains

By the 1850s, the demographic fingers of European American immigration extended into the North American continent from both coasts. The last great series of "Indian wars" began on the plains and prairies and in the American Southwest. At the time, an estimated 200,000 of 300,000 Native people were living in the center of the continent. Some (such as the Mandan) had lived in the area for centuries; others, including the Lakota (Sioux) were recent immigrants, crowded westward by surges of European American movement from the east. Still others, notably the Five Civilized Tribes, formerly of the South, had been removed from their homelands to the southern plains on the trails of tears.

European American immigration accelerated with the laying of rails across the continent. Although the earliest European American immigrants had traversed the open country in ox-drawn covered wagons, averaging 20 miles a day (the speed of a brisk walk), by 1870 the railroads conveyed them across the continent at nearly the speed of modern automobiles on interstate highways. Many of the Plains Indian wars began as disputes over whether, and where, railroads ought to run.

ECONOMIC IMPACT OF THE HORSE

Before arrival of the horse from the Spanish colonies to the south, beginning about 1600, the economic life of Plains peoples was simple, even stark. Peoples' belongings were restricted to the bulk that they could move on an A-shaped travois pulled by a dog or a human being. Not surprisingly, horses were first greeted as a larger, stronger kind of dog. Native peoples who acquired horses usually affixed travois to them before learning to ride. A number of Native peoples gave horses names based on their earlier nouns for dogs: the Assiniboin called them *sho-a-thin-ga* and *thongatch-shonga*, both meaning "great dog." The Gros Venture called horses *it-shou-ma-shunga*, meaning "red dog." The Blackfeet called them *ponokamita*, for elk dog. The Cree called horses *mistatim*, meaning "big dog." The Comanche, whose horsemanship became legendary, gave horses names that translated as medicine dogs, good dogs, or mystery dogs. The Lakota, who used horses to extend the range of their buffalo hunts, called their wonderful newly domesticated beasts *honk-a-wakan*, meaning "mystery dog" or "amazing dog" (Roe, 1955, 61). The Lakota had such a high regard for the horse that they sometimes also called it sacred dog (Johnson, 1984, 67).

Ethnohistorian Dean Snow described the diffusion of the horse through the Plains:

> The Shoshones adopted Spanish horses quickly, taking them north and east, introducing them to the Indian societies of the Great Plains. Algonquians such as the Blackfeet, Gros Ventres, and Arapahos, as well as some Crees and Ojibways, abandoned forest hunting and gathering to become mounted nomadic hunters on the Great Plains.... Later, the horticultural Cheyennes (Algonquians) entered the Plains as well, quickly becoming the quintessential American Indian nation in the eyes of many. (1996, 193)

Horses diffused northward after Spanish settlement began in New Mexico after 1600 C.E., but as early as the 1500s some horses escaped Spanish herds and bred wild in New Mexico and Texas. These "Indian ponies" averaged less than 1000 pounds in weight, smaller than modern-day riding horses; these agile, fast horses were interbred with larger animals acquired from Spanish (and later Anglo-American) herds.

The Pawnees, who were strategically located on the plains of latter-day Nebraska, later built a trade in horses that nearly spanned the continent. Patrick Henry bought a "Santa Fe" horse through a chain of merchants who included the Pawnees during the 1750s. The Pawnees especially became known as horse traders on the Plains. These horses probably were traded to the Pawnees by native horse merchants who tapped supplies in Mexico (Wissler, 1914, 2, 10).

Horses may have been introduced to some Native American peoples as long ago as the Coronado expedition of the early 1540s, but the Native American horse culture probably sprang from the herds the Spanish built at Santa Fe following the Oñate expedition a half-century later. During the seventeenth and early eighteenth centuries, horses spread rapidly among Native American peoples from the Apaches in present-day New Mexico (on one occasion, Apaches stole nearly every horse at the Santa Fe garrison).

The horse turned a subsistence lifestyle on the harsh high plains of North America into a festival of ornamentation, and a brief period of prosperity for many Native peoples before disease and settlement frontiers reached them, killing a large majority of Native peoples there. Maximilian described the Sioux in 1833: "Many of the Sioux are rich, and have twenty or more horses, which they obtained originally from the Spanish" (Roe, 1955, 90). Many Native nations on the Plains and in the adjacent Rocky Mountains became rich in horses. The various divisions of the Lakota, Nakota, and Dakota; the Crow; and the Nez Perce are only a few examples of many.

Horses became such an essential part of many North American Indian cultures that the Apaches, for example, incorporated them into their oral history as gifts of the gods. The horse completely changed the lifestyles of some Plains Indian nations, who adapted their use to the hunting of buffalo and other animals. The image of the warrior Sioux on horseback firing his rifle at buffalo or calvarymen, which became fixed in many twentieth century non-Indian minds as the sine qua non of "Indianness" actually was a product of European trade and technology. The horses came from the Spanish to the south, and the guns and trade beads on buckskin arrived with the French and English. Guns aided hunting and raised the level of violence in wars that once had been mainly ceremonial. Trade also brought to the Native peoples of the Plains the "traditional" flowing-feather headdresses that now adorn so many generic Indians from coast to coast. In addition, the same metamorphosis transformed the Cheyenne, who also moved westward in advance of the Euro-American frontier, to the high plains of Wyoming and Montana and southward.

The horse extended Native peoples' ranges, as well as control over their environments. A Native group on foot was limited to a few miles a day; with horses, a camp could be moved 30 miles or more in the same period. A small party of warriors on horseback could cover a hundred miles of rough country in a day or two. By 1659, Spanish reports indicated that the Apaches were stealing horses from them despite their best efforts to keep the valuable animals out of Indian hands. At roughly the same time, the Apaches and Pueblos traded for horses; by shortly before 1700 C.E., the Utes and Comanches had acquired mounts. After that, Native peoples' use of horses diffused across the continent. By 1750, the horse frontier had reached a line stretching roughly from present-day eastern Texas, northward through eastern Kansas and Nebraska, then northwest through Wyoming, Montana, Idaho, and Washington.

Native Americans explored different ways of training horses. Unlike the English and Spanish, the Cheyennes, for example, did not usually "break" their horses. Instead, they "gentled" them. Boys who tended horses stroked them, talked to them, and played with them. An owner of a horse might sing to it or smoke a pipe and blow smoke in its face. At age 18 months, the horse would begin more intense training, but was still sung to, smoked over, and stroked with eagle-wing fans. Gradually, the horse was habituated to carrying a human being, saddle, and bridle. Horses were trained specifically for war or hunting.

The horse shaped economic behavior in many ways. One was the productivity of raiding, which acquired considerable status. By the early nineteenth century, raiding on horseback was the Apaches' major economic activity; the greatest fame a Crow could earn came when he was able to snatch a tethered horse from under the nose of an enemy. "What must certainly be considered a really remarkable feature in the Plains Indian horse culture is the almost phenomenal rapidity with which they mastered their early fears and developed into one of the two or three foremost equestrian peoples on earth," commented historian Frank Gilbert Roe (1955, 56).

The horse also changed some peoples' housing styles from fixed lodges to mobile tipis and allowed the size of the average tipi to increase because a horse could haul a tipi as large as 18 to 20 feet in diameter, much larger than a dog or a human being could carry. Some tipis weighed as much as 500 pounds and required three horses. The horse reduced economies of scale in hunting, especially of buffalo, making hunting parties smaller. The increased mobility brought by horses energized trade, as well as intertribal conflict, because ease of transport brought more contact between diverse peoples, friendly and not (Anderson, 1995, 59–61).

When they provided the major form of land transportation in North America, horses were invested with considerable financial value. Cortés personally kept track of the Spaniards' stable as the Aztecs were conquered: "When anything happened to a horse, he does not fail to notice it," a Spanish observer said of Cortés (Roe, 1955, 35). Once Spanish colonization of New Mexico began about 1600 C.E., the immigrants were conscious of their monopoly on the horse as they sought to outlaw use of the animals by Native peoples.

THE ROLE OF DISEASE ON THE PLAINS

The U.S. Army killed fewer Native people during the conquest of the American West in the nineteenth century than freelance Indian fighters (who often were reimbursed by the federal government) or imported diseases. Between 1789 and 1898, the Army was responsible for killing about 4,000 Native people, probably less than 1 percent of those who died because of imported influences.

Disease was by far the biggest killer of Native people along the frontier. Euro-American settlement brought a host of ailments for which the Native people had no immunity and no cure. Some of these diseases were not usually fatal to whites, even in the nineteenth century: whooping cough, measles, scarlet fever. These "minor" maladies killed Indians by the thousands. The diseases that killed some European Americans, such as cholera and smallpox, nearly extinguished large numbers of Indians. Often, the disease frontier preceded sustained Euro-American immigration. European diseases often arrived in Native communities with the English honeybees, which traveled more quickly than the immigrants themselves.

All along the expanding frontier, initial contact with European Americans initially caused drastic population declines among Native groups, mainly because of diseases. After this initial decline and before the Indian peoples were subjugated in a series of wars that accompanied the settlement frontier, many Native tribes and nations recouped population because of trade and general prosperity brought by the fur trade. Jeanne Kay has made a case that during the late eighteenth and early nineteenth centuries, the Fox, Sauk, Menominee, and Winnebago experienced "significant population increases"— some on the order of five to eight times the number of people who survived the initial epidemics (Kay, 1984, 265).

Native settlement patterns sometimes defined whether groups lived or died in large numbers. The Lakota may have enjoyed a brief flash of prosperity during the early contact period not only because of trading patterns and their ability to adopt to European imports such as the horse, but also because they were favored by vectors of disease; their villages were relatively small and widely scattered, offering some insulation from the waves of smallpox and other diseases. The same diseases ravaged other Plains peoples who practiced agriculture and lived in larger, more permanent towns. This seemed to be true across the continent. In the Northwest, two-thirds of the Makah, who lived in villages along the coast, were killed by smallpox, measles, and other diseases shortly after intensive settlement of the area began in the 1850s (Pascua, 1991, 40).

Richard White wrote of how "winter counts," pictorial histories of bands or tribes, often drawn on hides, provided records of epidemics.

The Brule winter counts record smallpox in 1779–1780, 1780–1781 and 1801–1802 (the epidemics were dated slightly differently in other winter counts), but their loses were slight when compared to those of the Arikaras, Hidatsas, and Mandans. In 1795, Truteau reported that the Arikaras had been reduced "from 32 populous villages" to two and from 4,000 warriors to 500—a loss of population which, in turn, caused severe social and economic disruption. The smallpox reached the Mandan and Hidatsa villages in 1781, inflicting loses proportionate to those of the Arikaras. (1978, 325)

The Pawnees and Omahas also were ravaged by disease during the early nineteenth century. In 1806, Zebulon Pike counted roughly 4,000 Pawnees (1,973 men and 2,170 women); in 1859, agent William Dennison listed 820 men and 1,505 women. Both figures were low (the counters missed many people), but the proportions probably were roughly correct. The Pawnees' population had been cut nearly in half during one horrible winter, in 1831, when smallpox ravaged their villages. People under the age of 30, lacking immunity from earlier epidemics, died in very large numbers. The population of the Pawnees, a sedentary, corn-growing people, fell from about 25,000 before the epidemic to 12,500 afterward. "Not one under 33 years of age escaped this monstrous disease, it having been the length of time since it visited them before," wrote John Dougherty, who was present at several of the villages during the epidemic (Johnson, 1984, 13). The loss of so many young people crippled the Pawnee for almost a century. Smallpox ravaged the area again in 1837–1838, and cholera surged through Pawnee country in 1849. The population of the Pawnees continued to decline and did not begin to rise again until after 1920.

The disproportionate loss of men was caused by war with the Sioux. In 1843, Sioux warriors destroyed a Pawnee village and inflicted sixty-seven deaths. The Pawnees were forced to retreat to the Platte River, where hostile whites awaited them. By 1850, the Omahas, Otos, and Poncas had given up attempts to hunt on the western plains because of the area's domination by growing bands of Sioux. By 1873, the Sioux harassment of the Pawnees became so intense that the latter asked federal Indian agents to remove them to the Indian Territory (White, 1978, 13).

Roughly 1,500 of 1,600 Mandans were killed by a series of smallpox epidemics after Lewis and Clark encountered them but before immigration started in the western Dakotas, their homeland. Half the Blackfeet died before the settlement frontier reached their country. More than half the Kiowas and Comanches, also high plains peoples, died of cholera. From the coasts of Oregon, Washington, and California, inland to the Pawnee territory along the Platte River—more than 1,500 miles—a half-dozen diseases raged during the middle of the nineteenth century. Henry Schoolcraft, who served as an Indian agent among the Mandans at this time, said at one point that their surviving population shrank to thirteen people. Wolves roamed abandoned Pawnee villages from lodge to lodge, ripping flesh off human carcasses.

THE ECONOMIC ROLE OF THE BUFFALO

The buffalo was the basis of the Plains Native economy. When European American settlement began to encroach on the area early in the nineteenth century, an estimated 30 million buffalo lived in a large area from present-day Texas in the south to northern Alberta. Buffalo ranged from present-day New York State to Alabama and Mississippi, to Idaho and eastern Oregon. Within three-quarters of a century, competition from European Americans, including deliberate slaughter, reduced the buffalo population to about 100,000 animals. By 1995, a concerted effort to replenish buffalo herds had raised the population to about 200,000.

The Native peoples there had learned to make dozens of products essential to their lives from this one animal. They ate meat and marrow, tongue, intestines, and other innards. They drank buffalo blood and preserved its fat and marrow, among other parts, in jerky, the original trail food. From the tanned hide of the buffalo, Plains people fashioned tipi covers, moccasin tops, shirts, dresses, leggings, breechcloths, robes, bedding, belts, caps, mittens, bags, pouches, dolls, and items for trade. From raw buffalo hides, Plains peoples made containers, sheaths, soles for moccasins, shields, rattles, drums, saddles, bridles and other horse tack, lariats, masks, bindings, snowshoes, and bodily ornaments. The horns were raw material for cups, spoons, ladles, powder flasks, toys, parts of head-dresses, and rattles, as well as knives, arrowheads, shovels, hoes, runners for sleds, war clubs, and tool handles. The hair of the animal provided parts of headdresses, stuffing and padding, and ornaments. Hooves were used to manufacture glue. The bladder supplied pouches, buckets, cups, water basins, and cooking vessels; the chips provided fuel (Johnson, 1984, 60–61).

Native acquisition of the horse had an immense impact both on the hunting of buffalo and on the economic behavior and social structure of Native societies. A large number of Native societies transformed themselves into roving buffalo-hunting bands. Elite societies of young men skilled at buffalo hunting emerged, forming the basis of the Plains warrior societies, who pursued the animals. A male buffalo can weigh a ton and can charge at 30 miles an hour.

Most Native peoples worked nature into their rituals and customs because their lives depended on the bounty of the land around them. Where a single animal formed the basis of a Native economy (such as the salmon of the Pacific Northwest or the buffalo on the plains), strict cultural sanctions came into play against killing of such animals in numbers that would exceed their natural replacement rate. On the plains, the military societies of the Cheyenne, Lakota, and other peoples enforced rules against hunting buffalo out of season and against taking more animals than a people could use. Many Plains societies had special police who maintained discipline before and during communal buffalo hunts. An individual who began the hunt early could be severely punished.

Before they acquired horses, Native bands sometimes hunted Buffalo by herding them over "jumps," cliffs that were nearly invisible to the stampeding animals until they were pushed over the edge by animals behind them. Following such a stampede, the hunters and their wives worked quickly to preserve the meat, often by drying it in the sun to make jerky. In the heat of summer, when buffaloes were usually hunted, undressed meat could spoil within a day.

THE SLAUGHTER OF THE BUFFALO

Before 1870, large buffalo herds still roamed the southern plains, and many thousands of Native people still lived as they preferred, with the buffalo at the base of their economies. The slaughter of the vast buffalo herds that roamed the plains and prairies until the 1840s reached a million animals a year during the 1870s. Along their newly opened tracks, the railroads ran special excursions from which self-styled sportsmen shot buffalo from the comfort of their seats. General Phil Sheridan remarked that buffalo hunters had done more in two years to defeat the Indians than the entire regular Army had been able to do in the previous thirty years. "I would not seriously regret the total disappearance of the buffalo from our western prairies, in its effect upon the Indians, regarding it rather as a means of hastening their dependence upon the products of the soil" (Morris, 1992, 343). At one point, Sheridan suggested rewarding buffalo poachers by giving them medals with an engraving of a dead buffalo on one side and a discouraged-looking Indian on the other.

The buffalo herds of the central plains had been finished off during the 1860s with a technological boost from a new line of high-powered hunting rifle. Hunters of the dwindling herds were followed by skinners, who (depending on market conditions) might strip the hides or just remove the slain buffaloes' tongues. No one ever counted the number of buffalo that fell. The death toll was probably at least 20 million.

By the 1870s, European Americans were killing more buffalo than the Native Americans. Of 1.2 million buffalo skins shipped east on the railroads in 1872 and 1873, about 350,000 (28 percent) were supplied by Indians. By that time, the plains were swarming with unemployed railroad workers, would-be farmers whose homesteads would not sustain their families, and hopeful miners caught between gold rushes. By the time buffalo populations were reduced to levels that would no longer sustain the trade during the 1880s, there were an estimated 5,000 non-Indian hunters chasing them.

By the early 1880s, the U.S. Army's version of total war against the Plains Indians had reached its goal: The buffalo were nearly extinct. Ten years earlier, some of the Plains Indians still had an ample supply of food; by the early 1880s, they were reduced, as General Sheridan had intended, to the condition of paupers, without food, shelter, clothing, or any of those necessities of life that came from the buffalo.

CHANGES IN THE NATURE OF PLAINS WARFARE

A major aim of Plains warfare during prosperous times was acquisition of goods, often an enemy's best horses. In its essence, Plains Native warfare before full-scale white contact was an elaborate ritual that called for splendid dressing and skilled fighting that only rarely did a great deal of human damage. The main aim (other than making off with horses) was "counting coup" (*coup* is French for "a blow")—touching, but not injuring, an enemy in battle. Scalps were not regarded as trophies by most Lakota (the Tetons were an exception). Plains war was more than a game or a ritual, however. Skirmishes did take place. Warriors were killed and seriously injured, although not on the scale of European set-piece warfare.

The scale and violence of intertribal warfare increased with the advent of horses, guns, and bids for alliance by Euro-Americans. The systematic destruction of the buffalo herds by non-Native hunters sharpened competition for remaining animals between some Native groups. This competition resulted in additional warfare, raising the death toll for societies that also were suffering epidemics of disease. All of these factors, along with the crowding caused by immigration sped by the advent of the railroad (after the middle 1860s), provoked further Native societal deterioration.

In 1849, the United States established two forts on the Platte River. Two years later, the largest gathering of Plains Native peoples in memory took place at Fort Laramie. Between 8,000 and 12,000 people—Lakota, Cheyenne, Assiniboins, Crows, Shoshonis, and others—negotiated a treaty with representatives of the United States that allowed unhindered crossing for wagon trains heading to California and the Oregon Territory. The United States promised to keep troops on the plains to protect Native peoples against aggression by European American immigrants.

The Plains wars began two years later with provocations that sound absurd, considering the intensity of retribution later exacted against Native peoples. In one case, an Indian killed an immigrant's stray cow. This incident occurred ten miles from Fort Laramie during 1854. The cow-napping was reported by a white transient at Ft. Laramie; the transient asserted that neighboring Indians owed him $25 for the cow. A spokesman from the Minneconjou Sioux camp offered $10. An argument developed, and a $15 disagreement prompted the arrival of a hotheaded junior officer with thirty-two men and a battery of large field guns. The officer ordered a Native elder shot on the spot. The Sioux then retaliated by killing the officer and all the soldiers. The following summer, 1,300 troops marched against the recalcitrant Plains tribes from Fort Leavenworth, Kansas, killing 86 Natives. After that, battles became steadily more frequent and brutal, a set of circumstances made worse by the immigration of several thousand non-Native people after gold was discovered near Denver during 1858.

THE FRONTIER CLOSES IN THE SOUTHWEST

The Apaches and Navajos migrated from the area today called the Yukon (home of the Athapascan peoples) several centuries before the Spanish invaded their new home in present-day Arizona, Utah, and New Mexico. The word *Apache* is Zuni for "enemy." The Navajos, originally a band of Apaches, settled in an abandoned pueblo the Spanish called Navaho. The Spanish called them Apaches de Navaho. After that, the Navajos moved to the homeland that is familiar as Navajo country today, increasing in numbers. By the late nineteenth century, the Navajos were one of the largest Native groups in the region. Pursuing a quiet ranching life from their widely dispersed hogans (traditional Navajo residences), living "the Right Way," as they say, the Navajos also have become one of the most populous of Native peoples in the present-day United States.

The Navajos adopted sheep herding, weaving, and silversmithing from the Spanish and became expert at all of them. From the Pueblos they adopted kivas, sand paintings, and several religious rituals. By the time the U.S. frontier reached them, the Navajos had been totally made over into a new people by both Spanish and regional Native influences. They had little organized political or tribal life, at least at first, because they were so widely dispersed in solitary hogans or very small settlements. With the Hopis, the Navajos stood their ground on land that very few non-Indians coveted until coal and uranium were discovered there during the early twentieth century.

The Hopis never left their traditional mountain homes, preserving their way of life as well as their name (from Hopitou, "the peaceful ones") as tides of Spanish and Anglo-American settlement ebbed and flowed around them. Likewise, until recent times, many Navajos had never even heard the name the Spanish gave them. Because the Navajos' language contains no sound for the letter "v," many native-speaking Navajos cannot pronounce it. The Navajos' own name is Dine, which means, "the people." Indicative of their origins, the name is very similar to Dene, the term by which some Native groups in the Canadian Northwest refer to themselves today.

Although the Navajos and Hopi sought as best they could to distance themselves from the invading colonists (Spanish and English), the Apaches, rarely by choice, found themselves embroiled in nettlesome relationships with both groups of colonizers. The Apaches had long experience with Europeans, the first being the Spanish, who made a habit of drawing up ambitious plans (which never succeeded) to exterminate them. After Mexican independence, the northern states offered bounties for Apache scalps. As late as 1866, U.S. officials in Arizona were paying as much as $230 per Apache scalp, an amount worth several thousand dollars today. In 1837, scalp bounty fever ran through Anglo-American trappers in the area. A number of trappers invited a group of Mimbres Apaches to a social gathering at the Santa Rita copper mines, then quickly slaughtered all of them and cashed in their scalps. Until that time, the Mimbres had not been troublesome to Anglo-Americans in the area; afterward, surviving members of the victimized families haunted the mines like vengeful ghosts.

Such murders galled the Apaches, but what inflamed them even more was abduction of their women and children, who were sold into slavery or prostitution. This practice began under the Spanish but continued under the Anglo-Americans despite antislavery legislation. By 1821, all forms of involuntary servitude had been officially outlawed in newly independent Mexico; in the United States, the Civil War was fought over this issue, among others. Nevertheless, in 1866, after that war ended, between 2,000 and 10,000 Apaches were enslaved to whites. Other Apaches also were being held as slaves in the Mexican states of Sonora and Chihuahua.

THE NAVAJOS' LONG WALK

Kit Carson, who was dispatched from Fort Defiance, Arizona, to subdue the Navajos, disdained killing women and children or taking slaves, but he showed no remorse when it came to burning Navajo villages, razing their fields, and scattering their flocks. Men who elected to remain free of U.S. government control were killed by Carson's forces. Women and children (as well as men who surrendered) were promised new lands and food. Carson wore down the Navajos over months of pursuit.

A final confrontation took place as Carson and his men backed a substantial majority of the surviving Navajos into their sacred Canyon de Chelly, a gorge between towering cliffs and mesas. The Navajos were rounded up and bound with ropes. The first group of imprisoned Navajos departed on March 6, 1864, on a 300-mile forced march from Fort Defiance to Fort Sumner in Bosque Redondo, 185 miles southeast of Santa Fe. About 2,400 people departed; only the very young, the very old, and the infirm were allowed to ride. The weather was very cold, even for early March, and many of the Navajos (no one recorded the total number) died along the way. The series of forced marches continued until December 1864.

About 80 percent of an estimated 10,000 Navajos were forced onto a march that they called the Long Walk. At Fort Sumner, government agents tried to remake the Navajos in the white man's image as literate, Christian yeoman farmers, but most Navajos refused to cooperate. They were sharing 40 square miles of arid land with another tribe, and the alkaline waters of the Pecos River sickened them. There was no way to gather wild plants or to hunt, and government agents never issued them any housing materials or shelter. Many of the Navajos had to burrow into the ground to escape the elements. In 1868, the government gave up its intensive indoctrination and allowed the Navajos to return to their homelands.

Before they became reestablished, the Navajos survived several years as hunters and gatherers. Even after the government issued stock to them, the people found themselves facing frequent drought. As circumstances allowed, they took up old agricultural ways, tending small flocks of sheep, goats, and other animals issued them by the government.

WAR AGAINST THE APACHES

The Apaches' reputation as homeless raiders was a product of attacks against them as the frontier warfare invaded their homelands. Before they were driven from them, Apaches often lived in humble rancherias and practiced agriculture in areas where moisture and soil conditions permitted. Starting in 1864, a number of Army expeditions killed several hundred Apaches. General Edward Ord, while commanding the Army's Department of California, encouraged his troops to capture and root out the Apache by every means, to hunt them, he said, as they would wild animals.

Cochise (also known as Hardwood, Chiricahua Apache, ca. 1823–1874), a major leader in the Apache Wars of the 1870s, was the son of an Apache chief who became the leader of his father's band after his death. Everyone who dealt with Cochise held him in high regard. He was a powerfully built man who carried himself with dignity. In peaceful situations, Cochise was mild mannered, but during war he was capable of ferocity, great courage, and cruelty. Ultimately, he understood that a lasting peace was the only way to ensure the survival of his people in the Southwest.

During the 1860s, Cochise waged a formidable campaign to retain the traditional homelands of the Apaches. In 1861, Cochise was summoned to see Lieutenant George N. Bascom at Apache Pass because a rancher had accused Cochise of stealing cattle and kidnapping Mickey Free, a white settler's child. Cochise arrived under a flag of truce along with members of his family, including a son, Naiche, to meet with Bascom. Bascom accused Cochise of the earlier raid. Although Cochise denied any wrongdoing, Bascom attempted to arrest him. A fight ensued, and Cochise was badly wounded. He then slashed his way through the tent with a knife and managed to escape. One Apache was killed, and Bascom took the others hostage. During the next few days, Cochise took a number of whites as prisoners, offering them in exchange for the Apache captives. When Cochise's negotiations with Bascom broke down, both sides killed their hostages.

The Bascom fiasco started the Apache Wars. Soon, the Mimbreno Apaches under Cochise's father-in-law, the leader Apache Mangas Coloradas, joined the Chiricahuas and the White Mountain (Coyotero) Apaches in war against the invading Anglo-Americans. Mangas Coloradas had been well known since the early 1850s, when American miners captured him and cut his back to ribbons with a whip. During the Apache Wars, Cochise and Mangas Coloradas led raiding parties that wreaked havoc along the Arizona frontier during the early years of the Civil War, when many of the U.S. Army's troops had been recalled to battles in the east. They drove most settlers out of the area for a time. The only sizable U.S. settlement in the territory during the Apache uprising was Tucson, where the population dwindled to about 200 people.

As the Civil War wound down, garrisons were replenished in the area. Volunteer Indian fighters organized and billed the War Department for their services. Some of the volunteers had arrived from California and were men who had recently taken part in the wholesale slaughter of many peaceful, unorganized Native bands. Any tactic sufficed for the War Department as long as it killed Indians. Many times, vigilantes invited Indians to fake "treaty conferences," at which they were gunned down. Red Sleeves was killed at such an event in 1863. After killing Mangas Coloradas, soldiers cut off his head and boiled it, deliberately offending an Apache belief that a person goes to the afterlife in his or her bodily condition at death.

During the early Civil War years, Apache depredations sought to drive both Mexicans and Anglo-Americans from Arizona. During July 1862, there were 3,000 California volunteers under Colonel James H. Carleton sent to remedy the situation. Meanwhile, Mangas Coloradas and Cochise set a trap for the newly arrived troops. At Apache Pass, with about 500 men behind fortifications, the Apaches held off the California forces until Carleton utilized howitzers against them. The Apaches then retreated to Mexico with a wounded Mangas Coloradas; Cochise sought out a Mexican surgeon, who healed his father-in-law's wounds. For more than a decade, Cochise and about 200 warriors raided Anglo-American settlements along the Butterfield Trail and adjacent areas from his "stronghold" in the Dragoon Mountains of southern Arizona. He resisted all efforts to exterminate him and his men.

In 1871, Colonel George Crook took command of the Army's Department of Arizona. Realizing the futility of warfare aimed at annihilating the Apaches, Crook developed a group of highly effective Indian scouts who pursued Cochise and his supporters in the rugged terrain of southern Arizona. At one point, General Crook arranged Cochise's surrender, but when Cochise heard plans that his band would be sent to a reservation near Fort Tularosa, New Mexico (and not set free), he renounced the agreement. As a result, General Oliver O. Howard was dispatched by President U. S. Grant to meet with Cochise. After eleven days of deliberations during the fall of 1872, Howard granted Cochise's request for a reservation along Apache Pass. Shortly after this meeting, Cochise's 200 men surrendered, and Cochise promised to keep order along the pass. He remained peaceful until his death in 1874.

Also during 1871, American, Mexican, and Papago Indian residents of Tucson slaughtered eighty-five Natives who had put themselves under protection of the Army at Camp Grant. The Army tried to stop the massacre but arrived too late. The camp was razed, the dead bodies of twenty-one women and children were scattered across the ground, and some of their brains were beaten out with stones. Two of the women were raped during the massacre, and nearly all of the dead were mutilated. One ten-month-old infant was shot twice, and one of his legs was nearly hacked off.

The first phase of the war against the Apaches took ten years and cost about 1,000 Anglo-American lives, as well as those of uncounted Native people. The dying did not end in 1871, although some of the excessively brutal episodes did after a nationwide outcry over the massacre at Camp Grant and associated depredations. As whites flowed back into the area, opening old mines, farms, and commercial centers, vigilantes chased Apache bands into the rugged mountains, preying on what was left of their rancherias. The Apaches retaliated by making life very difficult for prospectors and settlers. Knowledge that Apaches might be in the area chilled the blood of just about every non-Indian in the territory as rumors spread that Apaches tormented their captives by such methods as tying them, feet up, over crackling fires as flames slowly roasted their brains. True or not, the rumors only enhanced the Anglo-American immigrants' beliefs that their own murderous retaliation was justified. General George Crook negotiated peace with many of the bands and rounded up those who would not agree to cease raiding. He also enlisted a number of Apache scouts.

Taza, Cochise's oldest son, who became chief after his death, attempted to continue the peace agreement. When Taza died, however, Naiche (another of Cochise's sons) joined forces with Geronimo. After Cochise's death in 1874, the number of Chiricahua raids in Mexico increased despite efforts by agent Thomas J. Jeffords. Apache war parties crossed into Mexico, then returned to use the reservation at Apache Pass on the Butterfield Trail as a safe haven. After an altercation involving the killing of two stagecoach attendants, the reservation was dissolved by the U.S. government. Subsequently, John P. Clum, Indian agent to the Chiricahuas, moved residents of Apache Pass north to the San Carlos Reservation in Arizona, where they joined 4,000 other Apaches from other bands.

GERONIMO'S WAR: THE APACHES' FINAL REBELLION

During the late 1870s, the Indian Bureau made a practice of moving Apache bands from one reservation to another without asking their consent. Resentment regarding this practice provoked the last great Apache uprising, led by the legendary Geronimo.

The man the Spanish would call Geronimo (Goyathlay, Chiricahua Apache, ca. 1830–1909) was born along the upper Gila River, very likely on the Arizona side of the New Mexico-Arizona border. Taklishim, his father, was a Chiricahua, as was his mother Juana, although she had been a captive among the Mexicans during childhood. After he was born among the Bedonkohe Apaches about 1830, the man who would lead the Apaches' final rebellion was named Goyathlay, "One Who Yawns."

In his youth, Geronimo served under Cochise and Mangas Coloradas. Although Geronimo was not a hereditary chief, his repute among the Apaches increased because of his bravery and prowess in battle. In 1858, Mexicans killed his wife, mother, and three children, provoking Geronimo to mount campaigns against the Mexicans for revenge. Given the ferocity of the avenging raids that followed, it is said that the Spanish invoked St. Jerome (Geronimo in Spanish, the Catholic saint of lost causes) whenever they crossed paths with him.

In the 1860s, Geronimo married into the Chiricahua Apaches and began a new life as medicine man, warrior, leader, and avenger of his family. During ensuing years, the Army and mercenaries waged a bitter war of attrition against Apaches who remained off assigned reservations, including Geronimo and his band. Part of the problem was the departure of the conciliatory General George Crook and his replacement by General Nelson A. Miles. Miles sent Crook's Apache scouts to talk Geronimo into surrendering with promises of humane treatment.

Geronimo and his band then escaped, fleeing into Mexico, taking refuge in the Sierra Madre. Geronimo's band merged with Juh's Nednhi band, carrying out raids on the American side of the river. Following these raids, in April 1877, Geronimo was captured and transported to the San Carlos Reservation. Victorio, a Mimbreno, was relocated along with his Warm Springs band at that time as well. Victorio fled San Carlos in the fall of 1877, resisting U.S. control until his death in 1880. During the late 1870s, Geronimo remained at San Carlos, although he went raiding in Mexico once with Juh, withdrawing quickly to San Carlos because of retaliation by Mexican troops.

Geronimo. (Courtesy of the Nebraska State Historical Society.)

The U.S. Army decided on August 30, 1881, to arrest Nakaidoklini, a White Mountain Apache prophet. He was seized for espousing a new vision that postulated the resurrection of dead warriors to overwhelm the whites. The U.S. Army killed Nakaidoklini at a battle near Cibecue Creek. Subsequently, some of Nakaidoklini's group attacked Fort Apache unsuccessfully as military reinforcements were summoned against the rebellious Apaches to forestall further chaos. In September 1881, after the battle at Cibecue Creek, Geronimo, Juh, Naiche, hereditary chief Chato, and seventy-four followers left

San Carlos for Mexico. Returning in April 1882 to raid the reservation, Geronimo and others slew the chief of police and forced Loco and his band of Mimbrenos to follow them into Mexico, uniting them with Nana's more war-like Mimbrenos.

At the end of 1882, General George Crook was ordered to the Southwest to subdue the Apaches. Believing in the virtues of mobility, Crook quickly developed a number of mounted units with Apache scouts who could track fellow Apaches effectively. Crook, in May 1883, led units into the Sierra Madre of Mexico, with Mexican government permission, led by Captain Emmet Crawford and Lieutenant Charles Gatewood. Because of desert conditions, they used mules instead of horses. On May 25, 1883, the U.S. military struck Chato's camp. As a result, some Apache leaders agreed to return to the reservation. It was a year before all bands complied. Although Juh had died earlier in an accident, Nana, Naiche, Loco, and Chato slowly returned to San Carlos with their bands. Geronimo returned to the reservation as one of the Apaches' most revered war chiefs in March 1884.

A year later, Geronimo, Nana, Naiche, and about 150 others abandoned reservation life and headed for Mexico again. Crook's men trailed them until the fleeing Apaches agreed to talk at Canyon de los Embudos on March 25, 1886. Crook insisted that the Apaches submit to unconditional surrender and imprisonment in the east for two years. Geronimo initially agreed to the Army's terms. While being escorted to Fort Bowie, however, Naiche, Geronimo, and twenty-four followers escaped. To capture the escaped Apaches, the U.S. Army placed 5,000 soldiers in the field with Apache scouts. While leading a unit into Mexico, Captain Henry Ware Lawton skirmished with the Apaches on July 15, 1886. However, Geronimo was able to escape the grip of the Army. After avoiding the Army for another month, Geronimo agreed to surrender, but only to Miles personally. At Skeleton Canyon, sixty-five miles south of Apache Pass, Geronimo and the remaining members of his group surrendered for the last time.

Following their surrender, Geronimo and his band were shuttled off to Florida in chains, via railroad, where the warriors were housed in one prison camp, and their families (along with some "peaceful" Apaches) in another. Later, the families were reunited at another camp in Alabama. Tuberculosis, the damp climate, "swamp fevers," and other diseases killed at least a quarter of the Apaches in the camps. The scouts had agreed to talk Geronimo into surrendering on a promise that, once captured, Apache warriors would not be separated from their families. The breaking of this latest promise only deepened Geromino's bitterness toward the invading Euro-Americans.

The Aravaipas-Pinal band returned to Arizona, but Geronimo's and Naiche's Chiricahuas were not allowed to return to their homelands. Eventually, Geronimo and his followers accepted the Comanches' and Kiowas' offer to share their reservation in the Indian Territory. In 1894, the remaining incarcerated Apaches were relocated to Fort Sill in western Oklahoma. At Fort

Sill, Geronimo played baseball and became a member of the Dutch Reformed Church. He also collaborated with S. M. Barrett on the publication of his memoirs, *Geronimo's Story of His Life*, published in 1906. Geronimo also tried farming and sold souvenirs, including photos of himself, at expositions and fairs. He took occasional engagements with Buffalo Bill's (originally Pawnee Bill's) Wild West Show. Geronimo rode in President Teddy Roosevelt's inaugural parade at his request in 1905. Geronimo died of pneumonia on February 17, 1909, at Fort Sill, never having been allowed to return to his beloved homeland.

OFFICIALLY SANCTIONED INDIAN EXTERMINATION IN TEXAS

Mexico, seeking to contain increasing Anglo-American settlement of the area that was later called Texas during the 1820s, forbade further colonization and strengthened central authority over the province. The Mexicans outlawed slavery, causing the Anglos to rebel in 1835 and to declare their own republic in 1836. The Texans applied for entry to the United States, but admission was put off several years by pressures from northern states, representatives of which argued that addition of the Lone Star Republic would provide the South with a powerful new ally.

Sam Houston, the first president of the independent republic of Texas, moved swiftly to make peace with the numerous bands of Native peoples who occupied the area—Comanches, Lipan Apaches, Kiowas, Wichitas, Wacos, and Caddos, among others. In 1838, however, Mirabeau Lamar defeated Houston for the presidency on a campaign platform that included a legalized war of extermination against Texas Natives. After four years of bloody warfare against Native peoples, Texans again elected Houston on a peace platform. The hero of the Texas revolution tried to arrange an Indian territory in the western part of the state, even sending Texas Rangers to keep settlers out of it for a time. During the next decade, however, increasing numbers of immigrants squatted on Indian lands anyway, and the Rangers proved as ineffective at stopping the migration as the British Army had been at enforcing the Proclamation of 1763, which had been meant to halt European settlement at the crest of the Appalachians.

In 1845, Texas became a state that retained title to all open land within its borders. There was no federal land in Texas and, many Texans maintained, no federal jurisdiction over relations with the Indians. Federal agents negotiated a number of treaties with Natives in Texas, only to watch the state and the rapidly increasing number of Anglo-American immigrants ignore them. The Indian wars in Texas resumed and reached such a pitch by 1859 that the federal government, unable to control the aggressiveness of Anglo-American immigration, legally sanctioned the removal of all Indians in Texas, most of them to Indian Territory (later Oklahoma) to the north.

Those Native peoples who could be persuaded by the federal agents moved to the Indian Territory; those who would not leave Texan territory largely migrated to its less-densely populated western steppes. Both groups developed a generally bitter enmity with the Anglo-American settlers concentrated in eastern Texas, establishing de facto (at least for a time) the line of demarcation that Sam Houston had sought. By the 1870s, however, the last of the great buffalo herds was shrinking, and discontent was rising among the Kiowas and Comanches, many of whom pledged to ride with young firebrand war chiefs on numerous raids into settled areas. The names Satanta, Big Tree, Satank, Eagle Heart, and others were seared into the memories of homesteaders from the southern rim of Indian Territory to the arid high plains of the Texas Panhandle. The Kiowas and Comanches also drew Southern Cheyenne war parties into these raids.

During the summer of 1871, General Sherman ordered the arrest of Satanta and Big Tree, asserting that they had bragged openly to informants about robbing and killing white people. Both were taken to the Texas state penitentiary. Humanitarian groups protested the imprisonment as unjust, and while the Kiowas' lesser-known chiefs continued raids in the absence of their two most influential leaders, the government decided to release Big Tree and Satanta. All the time, Indian anger was rising on the reservations of Indian Territory because of immigrant horse thieves (probably roaming from Kansas), a lack of promised government rations, and the unwillingness of the reservation's poor land to yield to the plows with which the government so earnestly hoped to turn the Natives into Jeffersonian yeomen.

Slowly, the raids diminished as the ravages of alcohol eroded the Indians' ability to fight back. During the remainder of the 1870s, a series of military campaigns subjugated the surviving Kiowas, Comanches, Cheyenne, and others. It was a slow, arduous war of attrition. Some of the Natives died in Texas prisons, including Satanta, who had been sentenced to life. Satanta was so discouraged by the prospect of a lifetime in confinement that he jumped to his death from a prison window on March 11, 1878.

THE ARMY CLOSES ITS VISE ON THE GREAT PLAINS

During the years between 1860 and 1890, when the massacre at Wounded Knee heralded the closure of the frontier, the last great wave of Indian wars was spurred by more than prospects of land and gold. This wave of conquest also occurred under the aegis of an ideology based on Darwinistic principles in biology that stressed the "survival of the fittest." This doctrine, called social Darwinism, had been called into service to justify manifest destiny, the belief that the laws of nature (as well as the laws of the Christian God) had sanctioned the westward explosion of settlement. Darwin's work itself was hardly bereft of politics. His *Origin of Species* (1859) was first published with a now-forgotten subtitle: *The Preservation of Favored Races in the Struggle for Life*. In the *Voyage of the Beagle* (1839), Darwin wrote: "at some future period, not very distant when measured by centuries, the civilised races of man will almost certainly exterminate, and replace, the savage races throughout the world" (1962, 433–434). It was in this frame of mind that many of the pioneers (the word is archaic French for foot soldier) met the Great Sioux Nation and dozens of other Plains peoples.

The Native people who were so transformed as the frontiers closed around them have been called the Sioux (an archaic French word meaning snake or enemy). Their own name was Lakota, Dakota, and Nakota (allies). They sometimes called themselves *Ochheti shakowin* (the seven council fires, a confederacy). The Lakota moved to the plains from the Great Lakes area as the frontier expanded westward.

THE GREAT SIOUX UPRISING OF 1862

By the mid-nineteenth century, the Bureau of Indian Affairs, which had been transferred from the War Department to the Interior Department in 1849, was readying its version of the welfare state for subjugated Plains Native peoples. One by one, Native peoples were defeated, forced into camps, and promised supplies that often did not arrive. Despite occasional exposés in the press, "Indian rings" made graft a fine art in the bureaucracy, siphoning goods and money meant to purchase supplies for reservation-bound peoples. The Indians, now cut off from their traditional hunting economy, had no other means of survival. Some reservation-bound Indians ate their horses, many of which also were starving. When they had finished with the emaciated horses, the Indians ate the bark of trees and their moccasins. After that, they starved, sometimes hundreds at a time.

The Minnesota Sioux (Santee) signed a treaty in 1851 and moved onto reservations. By the early 1860s, with the outbreak of the Civil War, the U.S. government fell so far behind on providing promised food supplies and payment of annuities that many Santees were starving. By August 1862, the situation was so desperate that Santees from the Upper Agency (the northern part of the reservation) broke into a government warehouse and took enough pork and flour to feed their families. Santees under the jurisdiction of the Lower Agency, who also were starving, requested emergency rations. Indian agent Thomas Galbraith flatly refused to supply the food, telling the Santees to "eat grass or their own dung" (Weeks, 1990, 92). The desperation of hunger, combined with Galbraith's insult, provoked a revolt that came to be known as the Great Sioux Uprising of 1862. This uprising ended with the largest mass hanging in U.S. history.

Little Crow, then about sixty years old, led the uprising, which began during the early hours of August 18, 1862, with strikes on outlying farms. The Indians quickly killed several hundred immigrants. Individuals with whom the Indians had specific grievances (such as the Indian trader Andrew Myrick) were found slain, with grass stuffed in their mouths, recalling Galbraith's remark. After three days of intensive raiding, reinforcements joined troops in the area, driving the Santee back slowly, under orders from President Lincoln to quell the uprising at any cost. "Necessity knows no law," Lincoln reportedly told Army commanders in the area (Weeks, 1990, 94). Colonel Henry Hopkins Sibley of the Third Minnesota Volunteer Regiment issued orders to "destroy everything they own and drive them out into the Plains.... They are to be treated as maniacs or wild beasts" (ibid., 94).

The Santees killed more than 700 settlers and 100 soldiers before the Army drove them westward into the plains. A large number of Santees who had not taken a direct role in the uprising stayed in Minnesota. They expected to be treated as neutrals, but the immigrants' thirst for revenge fell on them. After the uprising was quelled, a military court condemned 303 of 392 imprisoned Santees to death by hanging. President Lincoln demanded a review of the sentences and cut the number to be executed to 38. Lincoln asserted that each of the accused had taken part in the massacre, raped women, or both. The 38 Santees died on a single scaffold at Fort Mankato on December 26, 1862, the largest mass hanging in U.S. history. William J. Dudley, who lost two children to the Santees' scalping knives during the massacre, cut the rope that hung the Santees.

The bodies of the executed men were removed from their mass grave after nightfall by medical doctors, who used them as laboratory specimens. Army units trailed the Santees who had escaped Minnesota to the Badlands of South Dakota. On August 4, 1864, Sibley's forces killed more than 500 Santee warriors in a single day. A dwindling number of survivors moved westward and took shelter with the Cheyennes. They forged parts of an alliance that General George A. Custer would face at the Little Big Horn a dozen years later.

Little Crow escaped Sibley's raids. He later was shot by a farmer (some say the farmer's son made the shot) as he foraged for berries in a nearby field. The farmer did not know until later that he had shot the man who started the Great Sioux Uprising. The Minnesota legislature voted the farmer a $500 honorarium. On May 4 and 5, 1863, two steam boats were boarded by 1,300 neutral Santees, most of them women and children, going into exile from their homelands. Settlers on shore threw rocks at them.

THE SAND CREEK MASSACRE (1864)

During the spring of 1864, Reverend J. M. Chivington, an officer with the Colorado volunteers (militia), reported that Cheyennes had stolen a number of cattle. The report may have been faked as an excuse to retaliate, which he did, attacking Cheyenne camps and indiscriminately killing women and children as well as warriors. The governor of Colorado persuaded the Cheyennes to settle peacefully at Sand Creek. Shortly thereafter, again acting on his own volition, Chivington raised between 600 and 1,000 men, mostly volunteers seething to

Mankato hanging, 1862. (Courtesy of the Nebraska State
Historical Society.)

drive the Indians out, and mounted a surprise attack on the village. Chivington
shouted: "Kill and scalp all the big and little; nits make for lice" (Virtual Truth
Commission, 1998).

The Southern Cheyennes had lived peacefully during their early years of
contact with immigrants in and around the new city of Denver. A village of
Arapahoes camped in the heart of Denver around 1860. In 1861, Arapaho and
Southern Cheyenne "treaty chiefs" were pressured into signing an agreement
with the federal government without consulting their nations as a whole.
Resentment rose among the Indians as more settlers and gold seekers moved
in, further encroaching on their hunting lands.

As Black Kettle (Moketavato, ca. 1800–1868), the ranking chief in the village, hoisted a white flag and the stars and stripes, Chivington's men tore the
Indians apart with sadistic enthusiasm. Black Kettle's wife was shot nine times
but somehow survived. Black Kettle himself survived the Sand Creek massacre, only to be killed by George Armstrong Custer's Seventh Calvary four
years later in the Washita massacre.

Another leader of the encampment at Sand Creek, White Antelope, stood in
front of his lodge and sang his death song: Nothing, he sang, lives long, except
the earth and the mountains. The elderly White Antelope was shot as he sang,

along with at least 300 other Native men, women, and children. Chivington's detachment never accurately counted the casualties. The volunteers severed several Indians' limbs and heads, took them to Denver, and charged admission at a theater for a glimpse of the bloody body parts.

David Hurst Thomas described the aftermath of the Sand Creek massacre (1864): "One trooper cut off White Antelope's testicles, bragging that he needed a new tobacco pouch. . . . Returning to Denver, the Sand Creek heroes paraded through the streets, to the cheers of throngs. Theatergoers applauded an intermission display of Cheyenne scalps and women's pubic hair, strung triumphantly across the stage" (2000, 53). Shortly after the massacre, according to Thomas's account, several of the victims were packed into crates "[a]fter the corpses were beheaded, [and] the skulls and bones were defleshed" for shipment to the newly established Army Medical Museum in Washington, D.C. (ibid., 53). Some of these remains later became part of the Smithsonian Institution's collections. Army doctors often cut first and asked questions later, if at all. On another occasion, "Upon the death of a young Yankton Sioux woman—a 'squaw having remarkable beauty'—a post surgeon in the Dakotas dug up her grave, severed her head, and dispatched it to Washington [D.C.] as 'a fine specimen'" (ibid., 57).

The behavior of Chivington and the Colorado volunteers was so reprehensible to Kit Carson that he called Chivington's men cowardly dogs. The surviving Cheyennes retaliated with fire and fury, killing uncounted immigrants during the next three years. Four years after Chivington's attack, a federal commission concluded that he and his men had acted with a degree of barbarism that even the most brutal of Indians could not match.

Following the Sand Creek massacre, Black Kettle labored without success to restore the peace. Survivors of the massacre camped near the Washita River in Oklahoma. During the winter of 1868, they were attacked again by troops with orders to raze the village, hang all the men, and take women and children captive. The leader of this attack was George Armstrong Custer, the brash "boy general" whose enthusiasm for a big victory later would cost him his scalp at the Little Big Horn. Custer, the U.S. Army's youngest general, a rank that he held on a brevet (temporary) basis, won a number of battlefield promotions during the Civil War. Custer's attack on the Southern Cheyennes' camp at Washita during 1868 was his first experience in the Indian wars. Between 40 and 110 Indians were killed, including Black Kettle. During the attack, Arapahoes, Comanches, and Kiowas came to the rescue of the Cheyennes, forcing Custer and his troops to withdraw prematurely.

RED CLOUD FORCES THE U.S. ARMY TO RETREAT DURING THE LATE 1860s

When Red Cloud (Makhpiya-luta, Oglala Lakota, ca. 1820–1909, whose name refers to an unusual formation of crimson clouds that hovered over the

Red Horse's depiction of the Custer battle, 1876. (Courtesy of
Smithsonian National Anthropological Archives.)

western horizon) was born about 1820 near the forks of the Platte River in
present-day Nebraska, only a few European Americans lived in that area. By
the time he died, in 1909, Red Cloud's people had been pushed onto a tiny
fraction of their former lands, imprisoned in concentration camp conditions,
famished, and impoverished. Born into the heyday of the Plains horse culture,
Red Cloud died in the era of the "vanishing race."

As a young man, Red Cloud learned to fight and hunt, as did most other
Oglala Lakota boys. Very quickly, he proved himself adept at both. Red Cloud
was especially known as a fierce warrior who was always ready to personally
take an enemy's scalp. Red Cloud also had five children and possibly as many
as six wives. Red Cloud became a major leader of the Oglala Lakota during the
late phases of the Plains Indian wars. At one point, during the 1860s, Red
Cloud and his allies forced the United States to concede considerable territory
in and around the Black Hills, borders of which were outlined in the Fort
Laramie Treaty of 1868.

In 1865, the Lakota refused to sign a treaty permitting passage across their
lands from Ft. Laramie, along the Powder River, to the gold fields of Montana.
They dominated the northern plains as the energies of the U.S. Army were
being directed toward fighting the Civil War. When U.S. Army troops built
forts without Lakota permission, war parties cut off food supplies to Fort
Phil Kearney in northern Wyoming and laid siege to the outpost for two

years. During this offensive, in December 1866, Captain William J. Fetterman bragged that he could ride with eighty men across the whole of Sioux country. He set out with eighty-one men and high ambitions only to be led into a deadly ambush by Crazy Horse, a son-in-law of Red Cloud, and a dozen warriors.

In 1868, with the wagon road still closed, the government signed a treaty at Fort Laramie that caused its forts to be dismantled. The Powder River country and the Black Hills were reserved for the Lakotas forever, or so the treaty said. Red Cloud advised trading with the immigrants, but otherwise avoiding them. Red Cloud's valor as a warrior was legendary. He counted more than eighty coups and once returned from battle against a contingent of Crows with an arrow through his body.

Once Red Cloud was asked by a trader at Wolf Point why he continued to pursue diminishing herds of buffalo rather than settle on a reservation despite cold and near starvation:

> Because I am a red man. If the Great Spirit had desired me to be a white man, he would have made me so in the first place. He put in your heart certain wishes and plans, in my heart he put other and different desires. Each man is good in his sight. It is not necessary for eagles to be crows. Now we are poor but we are free. No white man controls our footsteps. If we must die, we die defending our rights. (Johansen and Grinde, 1997, 313)

During the 1870s and 1880s, Red Cloud fought the Army and the reservation system, but at the same time he provided aid to Yale professor Othniel C. March, who was searching the area for dinosaur bones. In exchange, March said he would take Lakota allegations of mistreatment "to the highest levels" of government (Milner, 1990, 387). March and his crew excavated two tons of bones during the midst of the war for the Black Hills. March investigated Red Cloud's complaints of rotten food and unmet promises. The Yale professor also documented massive profiteering by Indian rings in the Grant administration, sparking a congressional investigation and several newspaper exposés. At one point, March confronted Grant personally. March and Red Cloud became friends for the rest of their lives, into the twentieth century. Red Cloud said that he appreciated the fact that March, unlike many whites who dealt with Indians, did not forget his promises after he got what he wanted.

Red Cloud's biographer George E. Hyde characterized him in old age as "wrinkled, stooped, and almost blind" (1967, 336). Red Cloud was sometimes given to ironic bitterness over what had become of him and his people: "I, who used to control 5,000 warriors, must tell Washington when I am hungry. I must beg for that which I own" (ibid., 336). Red Cloud spent his final years in retirement, having little to do with his people's affairs. He died December 10, 1909.

GEORGE ARMSTRONG CUSTER'S LAST INDIAN WAR

Best known as the loser of the Battle of the Little Big Horn (1876), George Armstrong Custer (1839–1876) had earned the enmity of Native Americans for his participation in earlier campaigns against them, as well as for leading an Army expedition into the Lakota's sacred *Paha Sapa* (Black Hills) in 1874.

Six years after his men killed the Southern Cheyenne Black Kettle, Custer headed an Army column that marched into the Lakota Sioux's sacred *Paha Sapa*, despite legal reservation of the area to the Sioux in the 1868 Fort Laramie Treaty. The expedition was less a military invasion than a geological assay; Custer brought with him a sixteen-piece brass band, as well as civilians to catalogue the area's flora and fauna, most notably its rich deposits of gold.

As he returned to Fort Abraham Lincoln in September 1874, Custer telegraphed news to Chicago and Denver that the whole area was thickly veined with gold, as he put it for maximum emphasis, from the grass roots downward. The news soon sparked a stampede of fortune seekers into the *Paha Sapa*. The power of the stampede was slackened only slightly by Lakota warriors who murdered a small number of miners. The miners ignored several federal edicts directing them away from land that belonged to the Lakota by treaty. Commanding officers faced a problem that often had perplexed the U.S. Army during the years of westward expansion: How strenuously did soldiers dare to enforce unpopular laws against citizens of their own country? Most soldiers escorted miners out of the Black Hills, leaving them free to return via different routes.

The invasion of the Black Hills changed the demographic balance in the entire surrounding area. In 1870, fewer than 5,000 whites had lived in the Dakota Territory. By 1880, the non-Indian population had grown to 134,000, with 17,000 of these individuals digging gold in the Black Hills.

Crazy Horse (Tashunka Witco, Oglala Lakota, ca. 1842–1877), who had led the decoy mission that had ambushed the bragging Fetterman, was among the best-known Lakota war leaders during the time that the Black Hills gold rush began. Crazy Horse had a reputation that spanned the Plains for sometimes-shrewd and often-reckless bravery. Crazy Horse, a daring military strategist, was a major leader of the Lakota during the last half of the nineteenth century, during the final phases of the Plains Indian wars. Alone among the Native leaders of the Plains wars, he never signed a treaty with the United States. Crazy Horse repudiated the idea of living on a reservation until his violent death at age 35. He never wore European-style clothing, and his photograph was never taken. To the Oglala Lakota and to many other Native people generally, his memory has become the essence of resistance to European colonization. Alvin Josephy Jr. wrote that "To the Sioux, he is the greatest of all their leaders" (1961, 259). Crazy Horse was of average height, with a complexion that was lighter than most other Lakota. He was known to wander away from his village after a battle with the detachment of a poet.

Crazy Horse is an old name among the Oglalas, having been handed down generation to generation. For several centuries, Crazy Horse's ancestors kept historical records for the Oglalas on buckskin, a method of historical record keeping related to the "winter counts" of other Sioux tribes. Crazy Horse married a Cheyenne and thus cemented the alliance that functioned during the final phases of the Plains Indian wars.

Crazy Horse was born about 1842 on what would later become the site of Rapid City, South Dakota. His father was a Lakota holy man, and his mother was Brule Sioux. As a youth, Crazy Horse was called the Light-haired One or Curly. He received the name Crazy Horse from his father after a battle with the Arapahos in 1858, at about sixteen years of age. From an early age, Crazy Horse was a master of the psychological aspects of Plains warfare. He often rode into war naked, except for a breechclout around his loins, "his body painted with white hail spots, and a red lightning streak down one cheek. . . . His battle cry was 'It's a good day to die!'" (Waters, 1992, 152). Crazy Horse was never seriously injured in battle, and he made a point of never scalping anyone he killed. After attaining "shirt wearer" rank in 1865, he attended leadership meetings, but rarely spoke. Introverted and eccentric, Crazy Horse was shot in the face and relieved of the shirt of rank in 1870 following an attempt to steal another man's wife.

During mid-1870s, the U.S. Army had ordered all Plains Indians onto assigned reservations. Several Sioux and Cheyenne bands roamed in their accustomed patterns between summer and winter camps despite the Army orders. In December 1875, the government's Indian Bureau, alarmed that the Sioux were not staying on their reservation, sent out orders that all "roving bands" must return to stations assigned them within two months. The winter was severe, and so many of the Sioux, including Crazy Horse's and Sitting Bull's bands, ignored the order so that they could replenish their depleted stores of buffalo meat and other game. When the government's orders were not obeyed, the Army sent General Crook to attack the Natives' winter camps.

General George Crook set out with ten cavalry units and two infantry companies, one of the largest forces the Army ever sent into the field against Indians. Having spotted Crazy Horse's camp, Crook dispatched Colonel J. J. Reynolds and 450 men to round them up. Reynolds's detachment took the Sioux almost completely by surprise—the warriors had just enough warning to scatter into the nearby woods as Reynolds ordered the burning of their village and the capture of their ponies. Crazy Horse then emerged from the woods, leading a frenzied charge that not only drove Reynolds out of the razed village with heavy losses, but also reclaimed the ponies. Crazy Horse did not stop there. His force chased Reynolds's retreating force back to Crook's camp, where warriors stole the cattle that fed them. Without meat animals, caught in a bleak, cold Plains winter, Crook was forced to retreat to Fort Fetterman.

By 1876, several allied peoples, Lakota, Cheyenne, and others, were camped at the Little Big Horn when they were presented with an unexpected opportunity to avenge Custer's invasion of the Black Hills. Their camp, perhaps as many as 5,000 people, including about 2,000 warriors, followed the Little Bighorn River for about three miles. The Seventh Calvary, under Custer, had expected only about a thousand because he had ignored reports of his Crow scouts. Even after Custer discovered that the camp was twice the size that he had expected, Custer decided to attack the Indians on their home ground. That decision resulted in the deaths of Custer and his entire force of about 225 men, who were exhausted from having marched most of the previous night.

The Seventh Calvary rode into a battle that the Lakota chief Kill Eagle likened to a hurricane or bees swarming out of a hive. Riding horses exhausted after a 350-mile night ride, completely surrounded, and cut off from reinforcements stationed only nine miles away, Custer's force was cut to ribbons during one furious, bloody hour on a battleground that nearly disappeared under a huge cloud of dust. The Lakota religious leader Black Elk (Hchaka Sapa, Oglala Lakota, 1863–1950) was heartened by the outcome: "I was not sorry at all. I was a happy boy. Those *wasi'chus* [takers of the fat, or greedy ones, e.g., white men in Lakota] had come to kill our mothers and fathers and us, and it was our country" (Weeks, 1990, 185). The battle provoked momentary joy among the Lakota and Cheyennes, who for decades had watched their hunting ranges curtailed by what Black Elk called "the gnawing flood of the *wasi'chu*" (Gibson, 1980, 426).

Black Elk came of age during the late nineteenth century, as European settlement reached his homeland. His views of Native life at that time reached large audiences in the twentieth century through the books of John Neihardt; the best known of these books is *Black Elk Speaks* (Black Elk, [1932] 1972). Black Elk was eleven years old during the summer of 1874 when, by his account (published in *Black Elk Speaks*), an expedition under the command of Custer invaded the *Paha Sapa*. In the words of Black Elk, the Lakota and Cheyennes painted their faces black—went to war—to regain the Black Hills. In *Black Elk Speaks*, Black Elk told Neihardt that he had been a young warrior at the battle of the Little Big Horn, and that he had witnessed the battle. Young Black Elk tried to take the first scalp at that battle. The soldier under Black Elk's hatchet proved to have an unusually tough scalp, so Black Elk shot him instead.

News of Custer's defeat spoiled the U.S. centennial celebrations of July 1876. After the battle, the aging Lewis Henry Morgan, who had founded American anthropology four decades earlier with his landmark work on the Iroquois, *The League of the Haundenosaunee* ([1851] 1962), wrote in *The Nation* that the Lakota and Cheyenne who had defeated Custer's troops were only defending their birthright (Hoover, 1976, 157, 277). Morgan's point of view was not popular among non-Indians, however. Retaliation against the Lakota, Cheyenne, and others followed, by progressively larger Army units, drawn into the last "untamed" section of the continental United States.

Black Elk, *left*, about 19 years of age, on tour in Europe.
(Courtesy of the Smithsonian National Anthropological Archives.)

After the battle of the Little Big Horn, Indians who remained free of reservations were hounded relentlessly by reinforced U.S. Army troops. The Sioux who had defeated Custer were pushed onto the Great Sioux Reservation, band by band. Crazy Horse and his contingent of 800 Oglalas, 145 lodges with 1,700 ponies, were among the last to surrender. On May 5, 1877, the Oglalas formed a parade two miles long as they marched into Red Cloud Agency, where they surrendered their horses and guns. Red Cloud met the Oglalas en route and guided them to Fort Robinson, near the agency.

Shortly after the surrender, Crazy Horse's wife Black Shawl became sick with tuberculosis. He asked permission to take her to Spotted Tail's people at the Brule Agency, forty miles away, but was denied. Crazy Horse then departed Fort Robinson anyway. Several dozen soldiers chased Crazy Horse to the Brule Agency but failed to catch him. Instead, the Brule Indian agent and Spotted Tail himself convinced Crazy Horse to return to Ft. Robinson.

Crazy Horse began to return; fifteen miles from the Brule Agency, he was surrounded by forty of Spotted Tail's government-employed scouts. Crazy Horse was taken prisoner and escorted back to Ft. Robinson. Rumor had it that Crazy Horse would be killed or taken in chains to Fort Augustine, Florida, to be imprisoned for life. At Fort Robinson on September 5, 1877, Crazy Horse was led toward a stockade. He rebelled at the sight of the prison and tried to escape. Little Big Man and several other Indians grabbed Crazy Horse as Private William Gentles ran his bayonet through his body. Crazy Horse was about thirty-five years of age at the time.

On his deathbed, Crazy Horse recalled why he had fought:

> I was not hostile to the white man.... We had buffalo for food, and their hides for clothing and our tipis. We preferred hunting to a life of idleness on the reservations, where we were driven against our will. At times, we did not get enough to eat, and we were not allowed to leave the reservation to hunt. We preferred our own way of living. We were no expense to the government then. All we wanted was peace, to be left alone.... They tried to confine me, I tried to escape, and a soldier ran his bayonet through me. I have spoken. (Johansen and Grinde, 1997, 88–89)

After Crazy Horse's assassination, about 240 Lakota lodges occupied by people who had supported him migrated to Canada, where they joined Sitting Bull's people. With the "Crazy Horse band," Sitting Bull's camp grew to about 800 lodges.

SITTING BULL'S EXILE IN CANADA

Tatanka Yotanka (ca. 1830–1890), or Sitting Buffalo (or, as he was more widely known, Sitting Bull), was the Lakota's best-known political leader

Sitting Bull. (Courtesy of the Nebraska State Historical Society.)

during the late nineteenth century. He was a Hunkpapa Teton Sioux, a seer of visions and an esteemed statesman as well as a warrior.

Sitting Bull, whose Lakota name portrays a large bull buffalo at rest, was one of the principal war chiefs who negotiated the Fort Laramie Treaty of 1868, which forced the United States to abandon several forts and to respect the Lakota's claim to their sacred *Paha Sapa*, "the heart of everything that is."

Sitting Bull was known among the Lakota as an outstanding warrior as a young man; in later years, he was best known as a spiritual leader—a visionary and a dreamer. Before the Battle of the Little Big Horn, Sitting Bull experienced a vision that portended a native victory. After the battle, the Army forced Sitting Bull and his people into exile in Canada.

Captain Edmund Fechet, who observed Sitting Bull's influence after he surrendered to reservation life during the 1880s, later wrote: "Since the days of Pontiac, Tecumseh, and Red Jacket, no Indian has had the power of drawing to himself so large a following . . . and molding it and wielding it against the authority of the United States" (Johansen and Grinde, 1997, 352).

Born at a site the Hunkpapas called Many Caches along the Grand River in Dakota Country, Sitting Bull's first childhood name was Slow. He apparently resented the stigma and worked to prove himself from a very early age. At ten, he killed a buffalo. At age fourteen, he counted coup on an enemy and received his adult name. Sitting Bull, as a teenager, also showed promise as a medicine man by undertaking an early vision quest. Shortly after that, he was initiated into the Strong Heart warrior society. Sitting Bull assumed leadership in the society during 1856, after he killed a Crow in combat and sustained a bullet wound that forced him to limp for the rest of his life. From early in his life, Sitting Bull was conscious of his leadership role in battle as well as the buffalo hunt. White Bull, a Hunkpapa Sioux leader, remarked: "Wherever he was, and whatever he did, his name was great everywhere" (Johansen and Grinde, 1997, 353). Sitting Bull's enemies held his name in such awe that Hunkpapa warriors could intimidate enemies by shouting "*Tatanka-Iyotanka tahoksila*," meaning "We are Sitting Bull's Boys." Sitting Bull grew to be both a great warrior and *wichasha wakan*—a man of mystery, a "medicine man."

Sitting Bull was reluctant to engage the U.S. Army in war until the Hunkpapas' land was invaded. After that happened, he allied with other Sioux bands, as well as Cheyennes, to try to stem the flood. Sitting Bull and his allies closely watched the invasion of the Black Hills by Custer in 1874 and played a key role in rallying the Lakota and Cheyennes to defeat Custer in 1876 at the Little Big Horn. Sitting Bull's dreams foreshadowed the defeat of Custer. In June 1876, a large Sun Dance was held on the west bank of the Rosebud River. Sitting Bull performed the dance 36 hours straight, after which he had a vision that U.S. Army soldiers without ears were falling into a Sioux village upside down. The lack of ears signified ignorance of the truth, and the upside-down positioning indicated that they would die. Sitting Bull said of the battle: "Let no man say that this was a massacre. They came to kill us and got killed themselves" (Johansen and Grinde, 1997, 353).

Later in the 1870s, Sitting Bull and about 200 other Lakota escaped the Great Sioux Reservation and took refuge in Canada. In Canada, Sitting Bull was afforded the deference due a visiting head of state. He received visitors from around the world. In 1881, Sitting Bull and his band returned to the

United States and surrendered. By this time, his once-vast following had dwindled to 44 men and 143 women and children. Sitting Bull was taken to the Standing Rock Agency, where he ridiculed efforts to sell Indian land: "Take a scale and sell it by the pound!" he is said to have shouted in derision (Johansen and Grinde, 1997, 354). On the Great Sioux Reservation, millions of acres were being sold to non-Indians, and epidemics were spreading. Sitting Bull staunchly opposed any form of allotment, and although he adopted farming and sent his children to reservation schools, Sitting Bull maintained until his death that "I would rather die an Indian than live as a white man" (ibid., 354).

THE TRAVAIL OF STANDING BEAR'S PONCAS: 1877–1879

The Ponca Standing Bear (ca. 1830-1902) gained national notoriety in the late 1870s, during a time of forced removal for the Ponca and other native peoples on the Great Plains. Standing Bear and his companions soon became engaged in the first court case to result in a declaration that American Indians should be treated as human beings under the law of habeas corpus. Thus, under U.S. law, the Army could not relocate Standing Bear's party by force without cause.

Before they were forcibly removed from their homeland along the Niobrara River, along the northern border of present-day Nebraska, the Poncas had gone to great lengths to maintain friendly relationships with the United States. In 1858, they ceded part of their homeland along the Niobrara in exchange for a homeland in the same area that was said, at the time, to be theirs in perpetuity. Ten years later, the United States, in a classic example of sloppy bureaucracy, signed the Poncas' land over to the Sioux, their traditional enemies, in the Laramie Treaty of 1868.

During 1877, federal troops removed 723 Poncas from three villages along the Niobrara River to Indian Territory. The tribe was moved at bayonet point after eight of their leaders had inspected and refused to accept the arid land that the government wanted the Poncas to occupy in Oklahoma. During their march to Indian Territory, several of the Poncas died of starvation and disease.

A year after their removal, a third of the Poncas had died. One of the dead was a son of Standing Bear. Following that death, Standing Bear, determined to bury the bones of his son in the lands of his ancestors, escaped northward, toward the Niobrara, with thirty other Poncas. Standing Bear recalled: "It was winter. We started for home on foot. We barely lived [un]til morning, it was so cold. We had nothing but our blankets. We took the ears of corn that had dried in the fields; we ate it raw. The soles of our moccasins wore out. We went barefoot in the snow" (Massey and the Omaha Indian Center, 1979, n.p.). After two months of walking, including a ten-day stop among the Otoes, the group led by Standing Bear took shelter on land owned by the Omahas.

Standing Bear, Ponca chief. (Courtesy of the Nebraska State
Historical Society.)

They had run out of food, eaten their horses, and finally consumed their
moccasins. Their bare, bloody feet left tracks in the snow.

During March 1879, troops under General George Crook arrested Standing
Bear and his party and conveyed them to Fort Omaha, just north of the
growing frontier city of the same name. Once he had arrived at the fort, which
was serving as his headquarters, Crook called Omaha newspaperman Thomas
Tibbles, whose dispatches were wired to larger newspapers on the East Coast,
causing a storm of protest letters to Congress on the Poncas' behalf.

Crook already had announced his disgust at how Standing Bear's party
was being treated: "An Irishman, German, Chinaman, Turk, or Tarter will be

protected in life and property" under the laws of the United States, General Crook had said, "But the Indian can command respect for his rights only so long as he inspires terror for his rifle" (Mathes, 1989, 46).

Tibbles, who was thirty-nine years of age at the time, described himself as the "ebullient, volatile assistant editor of the Omaha *Daily Herald*" when he first met Standing Bear (Tibbles, [1880] 1972, xii). Before taking a job at the Omaha *Herald*, Tibbles had been an outspoken abolitionist, a scout in the Civil War, and a circuit-riding preacher.

The day that General Crook brought the Poncas to town, Tibbles put the Sunday newspaper to bed at 4:30 A.M., slept for two and a half hours, then rose at 7 A.M. and walked five miles north from the newspaper's downtown offices to Fort Omaha. After he interviewed members of Standing Bear's group, Tibbles then made his way south again, running part of the way, stopping at every church he could find, asking pastors if he could address their congregations about the travail of the Poncas. At a Congregational church, the pastor, Reverend Mr. Sherill, allowed Tibbles to speak between the opening hymns. After hearing Tibbles's account, two churches passed resolutions to the Interior Department and Secretary Carl Schurz on the Poncas' behalf. By the next day, Tibbles was preparing wire dispatches for newspapers in Chicago, New York, and other cities as he searched for attorneys who would represent Standing Bear and his people in Omaha federal district court.

Omaha citizens obtained a writ of habeas corpus and brought the Army into the federal court of Judge Elmer Dundy, who ruled during 1879 that an Indian is a person within the meaning of the law, and no law gave the Army authority to forcibly remove them from their lands. After initially refusing to let Standing Bear speak during the trial on April 30, 1879, Judge Dundy relented. Standing Bear spoke in Ponca through an interpreter. Another translation was provided later by Tibbles. Standing Bear spoke with the passion of a man who had lost a brother, a sister, two daughters, and two sons during the Poncas' diaspora.

Standing Bear raised one of his hands and said: "This hand is not the same color as yours, but if I pierce it, I shall feel pain. If you pierce your hand you will also feel pain. The blood that will flow from mine will be the same color as yours. I am a man. The same God made both of us" (Bob Reilly, Reilly, and Reilly, 2003, 29–30). Standing Bear said that the Poncas were like a family trying to escape a river in flood, stumbling up a cliff, finding only one way out. Finally, he said, they spot a passage. "But a man bars that passage. He is a thousand times more powerful than I. Behind him I see soldiers as numerous as the leaves of the trees. They will obey that man's orders.... If he says I cannot pass, I cannot" (ibid., 30). Standing Bear turned to Dundy, and concluded: "You are that man" (ibid., 30). The judge wept, as did several other people in the courtroom. Dundy handed down his historic ruling a week later.

Further, Dundy ruled that the right of expatriation is "a natural and inherent right of all people, indispensable to the enjoyment of the rights of life, liberty, and the pursuit of happiness. An Indian," wrote Judge Dundy, "is a person within the meaning of the law, and there is no law giving the Army authority to forcibly remove Indians from their lands" (Johansen and Grinde, 1997, 367).

Shortly after Omaha federal Judge Dundy denied the Army's power to relocate Standing Bear and his party forcibly, his brother Big Snake tested the ruling by moving roughly 100 miles in Indian territory, from the Poncas' assigned reservation to one occupied by the Cheyennes. He was arrested by troops and returned. On October 31, 1879, Ponca Indian Agent William H. Whiteman called Big Snake a troublemaker and ordered a detail to imprison him. When Big Snake refused to surrender, contending he had committed no crime, he was shot to death. Later, the U.S. Senate called for an investigation of the shooting and other aspects of the Poncas' tragedy. Big Snake was unaware of the fact that Judge Dundy had limited his ruling to the Poncas who appeared before his court. In so doing, he did not deny the Army's power to relocate other Natives by force of arms.

In 1990, the Ponca tribe of Nebraska was restored to tribal status by an act of Congress, signed by President George H. W. Bush, following termination of its status in 1965. Across the United States, several dozen Native nations were following the same path. In 1992, the Poncas moved into new tribal offices at Niobrara, Nebraska.

THE ROAD TO WOUNDED KNEE

By 1890, the surviving Lakota people had been corralled into reservations on the plains. The Ghost Dance religion arrived at their lowest ebb. Originated by the prophet Wovoka, a Paiute, the Ghost Dance spread among the destitute Native peoples of the West, from Oregon to Nebraska, into the Dakotas, where Sitting Bull endorsed its vision of Native restoration. Wovoka's English name was Jack Wilson. Born a Paiute, he had spent his childhood, after age 14, with a white Christian family. Wovoka's father regularly read the Bible at meals. As Handsome Lake did before him, Wovoka combined Native and Christian symbols into a religion that evoked a messiah not in a person but in the promised delivery of Native people from misery that came with oppression by Euro-Americans. Wovoka's instructions to ghost dancers contained references to Christ as well as prophecies of native restoration: "Do not tell the white people about this. Jesus is now upon the earth. He appears like a cloud. The dead are all alive again. I do not know when they will be here; maybe this fall or in the spring. When the time comes there will be no more sickness and everyone will be young again" (Powers, 1973, 225).

The Lakota took to the Ghost Dance with a frenzy that Wovoka had not anticipated. Lakota medicine men also said that special "ghost shirts" would shield the Sioux from soldiers' bullets. Driven by hunger, desperation, and a determined desire to escape from their new, brutal reality, many Sioux ghost dancers worked themselves into a frenzy during which they said they had seen the return of the buffalo and spoken with dead relatives.

By late 1890, an estimated 3,500 people were gathered against their will in the hills near Wounded Knee Creek, which bisects the Pine Ridge Indian reservation. Many of them demanded the right to practice the Ghost Dance religion, which held that God would create a new world for them in which the buffalo would return, and white men would vanish. The rules of the reservation laid down by the Indian Bureau forbade practice of the religion.

Non-Indian immigrants demanded protection from what they regarded as an attempt to rally Native peoples against them. Several thousand U.S. Army troops converged on the area in anticipation of renewed conflict. "What treaty that the whites have kept has the red man broken?" Sitting Bull asked before his assassination, as his people were guarded by nervous soldiers. "Not one. What treaty that the whites ever made with us red men have they kept? Not one. When I was a boy, the Sioux owned the world. The sun rose and set in their lands. They sent 10,000 horsemen to battle. Where are the warriors today? Who slew them? Where are our lands? Who owns them?" (Johansen and Grinde, 1997, 355).

William Cody (1846–1917), the creator of Buffalo Bill's Wild West Show, figured into the last days of Sitting Bull's life as he tried to defuse tensions between Pine Ridge Indian agents and the aging chief. Cody had been born near Davenport, Iowa, but moved at the age of eight to Kansas, where his father became embroiled in antislavery politics. When he was eleven years of age, Cody's father died from an attack motivated by his politics. The younger Cody then moved to Colorado, where he tried panning for gold and spent some time as a rider on the Pony Express. During the early 1860s, Cody began serving as a scout for the U.S. Army. The name Buffalo Bill was given him by Union Pacific railway workers to whom he supplied buffalo meat under contract about 1866.

By 1868, Cody again was working as an Army scout; he may have killed the Cheyenne leader Tall Bull. In the meantime, Edward Zane Carroll Judson was beginning to glorify Buffalo Bill's real and imagined exploits in the earliest of 1,700 dime novels. By 1872, Cody had taken advantage of the publicity to become an entertainer, engaged in Wild West shows staged by a number of Army scouts who toured the eastern urban areas of the United States. Between show tours, Cody himself returned to work as an Army scout. On July 17, 1876, Cody reportedly killed and scalped the Cheyenne chief Yellow Hair. By the early 1880s, the Indian wars were winding down, and Cody became a full-time showman with his own Wild West Show that included Native Americans as a major attraction. Cody was known as a benevolent employer as he became friends with some of the same Native leaders he had once pursued as a scout. One of his closest friends was Sitting Bull. A publicity poster for the Wild West Show showed Sitting Bull and Cody clasping hands over the caption, "Foes in '76, Friends in '85."

Sitting Bull and Buffalo Bill Cody. (Courtesy of the Nebraska State Historical Society.)

As tensions mounted in South Dakota late in 1890, Cody was returning from a tour of Europe with forty-five Sioux, many of whom had been prominent leaders during the final years of the Plains Indian wars. In November 1890, trains pulled out of Omaha carrying troops bound for Pine Ridge Agency, newspaper reporters, and the Sioux from Buffalo Bill's troupe. The train carrying the forty-five Sioux arrived at Rushville, Nebraska, the train depot nearest the Pine Ridge Agency, on November 20. Cody had been asked for help in defusing tensions at Pine Ridge by General Nelson Miles, an adversary of Standing Rock Indian agent James McLaughlin. On his arrival at the agency, Cody was detained by associates of McLaughlin, who urged him to get drunk at the Fort Yates officers' mess. McLaughlin had Cody's authority rescinded as he pursued his own plans to arrest Sitting Bull.

Tension continued to intensify between McLaughlin, who was pressuring the Sioux to sign new treaties ceding more of their territory, and Sitting Bull, who had campaigned all his life against signing away Native homelands.

Sitting Bull was killed December 15, 1890, a few days before the massacre at Wounded Knee, as forty-three tribal police tried to arrest him. Accounts of Sitting Bull's assassination vary, but it appears that Bullhead, a police officer employed by the Indian agency, served a warrant on Sitting Bull as he protested that no reason existed for his arrest. Bullhead then shot him in the thigh, as his partner, Sargent Red Tomahawk, shot Sitting Bull in the head. A riot ensued, during which six policemen and eight of Sitting Bull's followers, including his son Crow Foot, also were killed.

L. Frank Baum, who later would author the *Oz* books, edited the Aberdeen, South Dakota, *Saturday Pioneer* from 1888 to 1891. During this time, he penned two vitriolic editorials that fanned racial hatred in the area. On December 20, 1890, days after the assassination of Sitting Bull and slightly more than a week before the Wounded Knee massacre, he wrote:

> The proud spirit of the original owners of these vast prairies...lingered last in the bosom of Sitting Bull. With his fall, the nobility of the Redskin is extinguished, and what few are left are a pack of whining curs who lick the hand that smites them. The Whites, by law of conquest, by justice of civilization, are masters of the American continent, and the best safety of the frontier settlements will be secured by the total annihilation of the few remaining Indians. Why not annihilation? Their glory has fled, their spirit broken, their manhood effaced; better that they should die than live [as] the miserable wretches that they are. (Stannard, 1992, 126)

A week after the massacre, the demand for annihilation was repeated in Baum's newspaper, with one difference. He misspelled "extermination" as "extirmination."

Baum was not alone. The Omaha *Bee* invoked the stereotype of Indian-as-devil to justify the assassination of Sitting Bull on December 10, 1890. Calling Sitting Bull "always hostile to the white man [and] ever the foe of civilization," the *Bee* said that Sitting Bull's demise should "give a sense of relief" to whites in South Dakota. "No sentiment should be wasted upon the death of Sitting Bull," wrote the *Bee,* echoing the opinion of L. Frank Baum in Aberdeen, South Dakota. "Whatever the circumstances...he deserved his fate as a rebellious and implacable enemy.... It cannot fail to have a salutary effect on his bloodthirsty followers" (Hugh Reilly, 1997, 201–202).

The Omaha *World-Herald,* influenced by Tibbles, reacted very differently from the *Bee* or Baum. It wrote of Sitting Bull's assassination: "The killing was only part of the unwarranted severity and oppression that the United States is now inflicting on the Indians.... There seems to be no end to the blunders, crimes, and atrocities into which the government is led in the treatment of the Indians. It is time for a change" (Hugh Reilly, 1997, 202–203).

According to Hugh Reilly's analysis of newspaper coverage of the Indian wars, unverified rumors regarding events at Wounded Knee were presented as reports from reliable sources, idle gossip became purported fact, and "a large number of the nation's newspapers indulged in a field day of exaggeration, distortion, and just plain faking" (1997, 183). In many ways, Wounded Knee was a journalistic training ground for sensational, mass-market newspaper provocation of the Spanish-American War eight years later.

While many newspapers stoked European American fears of Indian unrest in the months before the massacre at Wounded Knee, the Omaha *World-Herald,* influenced by Tibbles and Susette LaFlesche, struck a moderate tone. In an editorial November 8, 1890, the newspaper said the Ghost Dancers should be left alone. "The United States [government] takes this matter very stupidly—it always takes everything connected with the Indians stupidly," the newspaper said.

> All this is but a part of the general impression which the government and the people in it have always cherished, that the Indian has no right to any ideas of his own, or indeed to any nationality of his own. The Indian is not an idolater. He is distinctly religious. His ideas concerning the unknown are far from contemptible, yet they have never been respected." (Hugh Reilly, 1997, 183)

Among the reporters on the trains that departed from Omaha on November 18, 1890, bound for Pine Ridge country were Charles H. Cressey of the *Bee* and Carl Smith of the *World-Herald,* who covered the situation until he was replaced in late November by LaFlesche and Tibbles. LaFlesche thus became, according to Hugh Reilly (1997), one of the first female war correspondents to be officially employed by any American newspaper, and certainly America's first female, as a Native American war correspondent. While LaFlesche and Tibbles interviewed Native Americans, Cressey spun imaginative tales as he read conspiracies of intrigue and impending violence into expressions on the faces of Indians returning home after performing in Buffalo Bill Cody's Wild West Show. Cressey, for example, filed a report featuring an invented plot by Indians to attack a troop train at Valentine, Nebraska, just south of Pine Ridge. The attack never occurred.

The *Bee's* Cressey compared the Indians he saw at Pine Ridge to "cigar sign models" who replied to questions with "a grunt and a foolish look." Cressey

Susette LaFlesche. (Courtesy of Smithsonian
National Anthropological Archives.)

seemed to relish the stylistic turn of his stereotypes when, on December 8,
he further described the cigar sign models as "half-animated, long-haired,
blanket-swathed musk bags that make up nine-tenths of the inhabitants [who]
swim their tepees in tears and then go blind" (Hugh Reilly, 1997, 199).

The *World-Herald*, by contrast, reported that the fears of local ranchers and
farmers had no factual foundation, as the *Bee's* headlines, according to Reilly's
account, screamed "Fears of an Ambush" and "A Squaw's Warning." Cressey
reported that Sioux were dancing with rifles strapped to their backs, threat-
ening to "cut off soldiers' ears and otherwise maim them" (Hugh Reilly, 1997,
189–190). By Reilly's account, Cressey on November 21 quoted an unnamed
"prominent officer" as saying that "Nothing but a miracle could save us from
Custer's fate, and I hope to God that reinforcements will arrive before the
red devils make their break" (ibid., 190). Two days later, the *World-Herald*

published an editorial headlined "No Need for War" (ibid., 191), which compared the Ghost Dance to religious excitement experienced by the European Druids and the early Methodists. "And yet," said the *World-Herald*, "no arms were brought to bear on them. No retributions were prepared in the shape of a Hotchkiss gun or otherwise." On November 30, the newspaper quoted General Nelson A. Miles's opinion that the Ghost Dance troubles were more of a "correspondents' scare than an Indian scare" (ibid., 193).

In its editions of December 17, less than two weeks before the massacre, the *Bee* invented an entire battle under the headline, "Bloody Battle with Reds." The account said that the Indians had been routed by soldiers with "heavy losses" as the Army lost fifty men and two officers. In the midst of the story, the account was said to be "not authenticated" (Hugh Reilly, 1997, 205). After that statement, the *Bee* then continued to weave its fable in great detail. At the same time, Tibbles reported ten days before the massacre that events were coming to a head. He also worried (as reported later in his book *Buckskin and Blanket Days*, 1957) about complaints from his editors that his dispatches were not exciting enough.

The *World-Herald* often published LaFlesche's accounts under the headline "What Bright Eyes Thinks." Unlike most other correspondents, LaFlesche stressed the common humanity of the Ghost Dancers: "The causes that brought about the 'Messiah scare' may seem to be very simple if one stops to think, first of all, that the Sioux are human beings with the same feelings, desires, resentments, and aspirations as all other human beings" (Hugh Reilly, 1997, 198).

DEATH AT WOUNDED KNEE

During the days before the clash at Wounded Knee, roughly 120 men and 230 women and children led by Big Foot were intercepted and surrounded by General Whitside of the Seventh Cavalry, Custer's former unit, as they emerged from open country to surrender. Big Foot, weakened from pneumonia, could barely speak as Whitside's men herded the Indians into a circle and demanded their guns. Big Foot's band was surrounded by 500 cavalry and four Hotchkiss guns. When few firearms were forthcoming (most of which were broken), Whitside ordered a search of the camp. Tension mounted as Yellow Bird, a healer, began a Ghost Dance, throwing handfuls of dirt into the air, calling on warriors to be brave of heart and telling them that if they danced, their Ghost Shirts would protect them.

Hugh Reilly described the incident on December 29 that set off what the Army still maintains was a "battle."

The soldiers began to search the men for weapons [as] one young man leapt to his feet angrily, holding aloft his gun and saying he had paid good money for it and would not give it up. Some Indian witnesses said he was named Black Coyote, and others said it was a man named *Hosi Yanka*, which means "deaf."

Survivors of the Wounded Knee massacre, 1890. (Courtesy of
the Library of Congress.)

Two soldiers came behind the young man and tried to seize his weapon. In the
scuffle, it went off. (1997, 209)

At that point, by Hugh Reilly's account, "Several young warriors threw off
their blankets and fired a brief volley into the soldiers' ranks" (1997, 209).
The Seventh Cavalry answered these few shots with massive retaliation that
included not only bullets, but also devastating fire from Hotchkiss guns, a
turn-of-the-century combination of a small cannon with an early model of
machine gun. The withering fire quickly tore the Indian camp to shreds.

Many of the Indians sought refuge in a nearby ravine, which turned out
to be a trap as, according to Hugh Reilly, "the Hotchkiss guns on the ridge . . .
raked the camp," taking deadly aim at people hiding in the ravine (1997,
209). At least 170 Indians died (some of whom were tracked down and shot
miles from the scene of the original altercation). Most of them were women
and children. The Army lost twenty-nine killed and thirty-nine wounded.
Because much of the fire was delivered from a roughly circular position
around the Indian camp, an unknown number of the soldiers were killed or
wounded by their compatriots' own friendly fire.

Tibbles was on his way to the telegraph office at Pine Ridge to file a dispatch when he heard shooting and returned to the scene. Cressey saw at least some of the battle himself. His first dispatch was headlined: "Red Devils Bite the Dust" (Hugh Reilly, 1997, 210). Cressey's accounts during the ensuing two days called the incident "ghastly work of treacherous Reds" whom, wrote Cressey, fired at least 100 shots at the Seventh Cavalry before the soldiers, afraid of hitting their own men, replied. Cressey wrote that the men of the Seventh Cavalry had "once more shown themselves to be heroes in deeds of daring." Editorially, the *Bee* said that there should be no more "truckling in dealing with the murderous Sioux" (ibid., 211).

As the Indians took fire at point-blank range, some of them flew into desperate rages, fighting back with their hands or whatever they could find. Survivors were chased and gunned down by troops after the actual battle. After the shooting stopped, a blizzard swept the area, burying most of the Indian dead in drifts. The dead were later dragged out of the snow, heaped onto wagons, and buried in a common grave.

The *World-Herald* treated the conflict as a massacre rather than a battle, using headlines such as "All Murdered in a Mass." The newspaper's accounts emphasized the difference in the amount of firepower available to each side and the large number of women and children in the Native camp. Editorially, the *World-Herald* called what had happened at Wounded Knee "a crime against civilization." The paper asked: "What sentiment dignifies and raises it from the low estate of murder to that of war. . . . On a field on which there can be no honor" (Hugh Reilly, 1997, 211–212).

The *Bee's* reports emphasized the dying agonies "of . . . wounded and dying soldiers—gallant, utterly fearless, Seventh Cavalry boys, whose bravery in the discharge of their duties none . . . can ever fully appreciate" (Hugh Reilly, 1997, 213). The *Bee* created an illusion that the battle at Wounded Knee was only the precipitating spark of a far wider Indian war in which thousands would die.

While Cressey and the *Bee's* editorialists railed against "murderous Redskins," LaFlesche, under the headline "Horrors of War," described the sufferings of Indian women and children who had been seriously wounded in the shooting. This account, as compiled by Hugh Reilly, makes for wrenching reading. Susette LaFlesche was nearly alone in reporting the suffering of the Native people at Wounded Knee:

> There was a woman sitting on the floor with a wounded baby on her lap and four or five children around her, all her grandchildren. Their father and mother were killed. There was a young woman shot through both thighs and her wrist broken. Mr. Tibbles had to get a pair of pliers to get her rings off. There was a little boy with his throat apparently shot to pieces. . . . When we fed this little boy, we found that he could swallow. We gave him some gruel and he grabbed with both his little hands a dipper of water. When I saw him yesterday afternoon he looked worse than the day before, and when they fed him now, the food and water came out the side of his neck. (Hugh Reilly, 1997, 215)

Burial of the dead at Wounded Knee. (Courtesy of the Nebraska
State Historical Society.)

The anger of Bright Eyes was palpable. The Sioux believe that they have
been made to suffer because the whites want their land, she wrote. "If the
white people want their land and must have it, they can go about getting it
some other way than by forcing it from them by starving them or provoking
them to war and sacrificing the lives of innocent women and children" (Hugh
Reilly, 1997, 215).

Black Elk was one of the Lakota holy men who had performed the Ghost
Dance during the days before the massacre. In *Black Elk Speaks*, he recalled
how the Lakota's indignation had risen in 1874, when General Custer opened
the Black Hills, seeking "the yellow metal that drives white men crazy" (1972,
79). He remembered answering Crazy Horse's call to war at the Little Bighorn
and the brutal subjugation that followed. Black Elk visited Wounded Knee
a day or two after the blizzard and later told John G. Neihardt that his grief
was tempered by his belief that the Lakota who had died were now in a
better place.

Black Elk described the scene of the massacre as follows:

We followed down the dry gulch, and what we saw was terrible. Dead and
wounded women and children and little babies were scattered all along where

they had been trying to run away. The soldiers had followed along the gulch, as they ran, and murdered them in there. Sometimes they were in heaps because they had huddled together, and some were scattered all along. Sometimes bunches of them had been killed and torn to pieces where the wagon [Hotchkiss] guns hit them. I saw a little baby trying to suck its mother, but she was bloody and dead. (Collier, 1947, 104–105)

Eighteen U.S. Army troops received the Congressional Medal of Honor for actions at Wounded Knee Creek:

1st Sgt. William G. Austin	Pvt. George Hobday
Musician John E. Clancy	Sgt. George Loyd
Pvt. Mosheim Feaster	Sgt. Albert W. McMillan
1st Lt. Ernest A. Garland	Pvt. Thomas Sullivan
1st Lt. John C. Gresham	1st Sgt. Jacob Trautman
Pvt. Matthew B. Hamilton	1st Sgt. Frederick E. Toy
Pvt. Joshua B. Hartzog	Sgt. James Ward
2nd Lt. Harry L. Hathorne	Cpl. Paul H. Weinert
Pvt. Marvin C. Hillock	Pvt. Hermann Ziegner (Byrd, 2003, 1)

In addition, five other soldiers were awarded the Medal of Honor for participating in skirmishes along White Clay Creek as part of a search-and-destroy mission:

Sgt. Bernhard Jetter	1st Sgt. Theodore Ragner
Pvt. Adam Neder	Cpl. William O. Wilson (Byrd, 2003, 1)
Farrier Richard J. Nolan	

By awarding so many Medals of Honor, the Army supported its official version of events at Wounded Knee as a battle rather than a massacre. The Army also excused the murder of one of its officers, Lt. Edward W. Casey, by Plenty Horses, an Oglala Lakota, to maintain its version of events. When Plenty Horses was brought to trial in a civilian court, the Army refused to support the prosecution, maintaining that the murder, which had taken place in daylight under otherwise peaceful conditions, was an "act of war."

After five years at Carlisle Indian School, Plenty Horses returned to the Pine Ridge Indian reservation angry and alienated, just in time to witness the 1890 massacre at Wounded Knee. A few days after the massacre, on January 7, 1891, he shot Casey in the back, hoping to be hung for his bravery, to die as a man and a warrior in the Oglala Lakota tradition. Plenty Horses' wife, Roan Horse, also was killed in the ensuing melee.

After his arrest, Plenty Horses said that he killed Casey because

> I am an Indian. Five years I attended Carlisle and was educated in the ways of the white man. When I returned to my people, I was an outcast among them. I was no longer an Indian. I was not a white man. I was lonely. I shot the lieutenant so I might make a place for myself among my people. I am now one of them. I shall be hung, and the Indians will bury me as a warrior. They will be proud of me. I am satisfied. (Johansen and Grinde, 1997, 293)

Plenty Horses was imprisoned at Fort Meade and tried in Sioux Falls, South Dakota. Instead of convicting Plenty Horses and sentencing him to hang, a judge threw the case out because a state of war had existed on the Pine Ridge Reservation—the same state of war that the Army was using as a reason not to prosecute the soldiers who had taken part in the massacre. Plenty Horses was sent home to Rosebud, still very confused and alienated. He died at Pine Ridge during the 1930s.

Wovoka, who had initiated the Ghost Dance, was deeply saddened by the massacre at Wounded Knee. The massacre convinced Wovoka that the religion ought to be abandoned. Sadly, Wovoka told his followers that the path he had advised them to follow was now choked with sand and covered with grass. "My children," he preached, "I call upon you to travel a new trail, the only trail now open—the White Man's Road" (Tebbel and Jennison, 1960, 298).

After the Wounded Knee massacre, Black Elk watched his people, once the mounted lords of the plains, become hungry, impoverished prisoners, pent up on thirteen government reservations. Black Elk surveyed the scene with sadness: "The nation's hoop is broken and scattered. There is no center anymore, and the sacred tree is dead" (Johansen and Grinde, 1997, 36).

FURTHER READING

Ambrose, Stephen E. *Crazy Horse and Custer*. New York: New American Library, 1986.

Anderson, Terry L. *Sovereign Nations or Reservations: An Economic History of American Indians*. San Francisco: Pacific Research Institute for Public Policy, 1995.

Armstrong, Virginia Irving. *I Have Spoken: American History through the Voices of the Indians*. Chicago: Swallow Press, 1971.

Barrett, S. M. *Geronimo's Story of His Life*. New York: Duffield & Company, 1906.

Black Elk. *Black Elk Speaks, as told to John G. Neihardt*. New York: William Morrow, [1932] 1972.

Black Elk. *The Sacred Pipe: Black Elk's Account of the Seven Rites of the Oglala Sioux*. Edited by Joseph Epes Brown. New York: Penguin Books, 1973.

Branch, Douglas E. *The Hunting of the Buffalo*. Lincoln: University of Nebraska Press, 1973.

Brown, Dee. *Bury My Heart at Wounded Knee*. New York: Holt, Rinehart, Winston, 1970.

Byrd, Sydney. Wounded Knee: We Must Never Forget. *Lakota Journal*, January 3–10, 2003, 1. Available at http://www.lakotajournal.com/front.htm.

Calloway, Colin. *New Worlds for All: Indians, Europeans, and the Remaking of Early America*. Baltimore: Johns Hopkins University Press, 1997.

Clark, Robert A. *The Killing of Crazy Horse*. Lincoln: University of Nebraska Press, 1976.

Collier, John. *Indians of the Americas*. New York: New American Library, 1947.

Crosby, Alfred W. *The Columbian Voyages, the Columbian Exchange, and Their Historians*. Washington, DC: American Historical Association, 1987.

Custer, Elizabeth. *Boots and Saddles*. New York: Harper & Brothers, 1885.

Custer, George Armstrong. *My Life on the Plains*. Lincoln: University of Nebraska Press, 1966.

Darwin, Charles. *The Origin of Species by Means of Natural Selection, Or the Preservation of Favoured Races in the Struggle for Life*. London: John Murray, 1859.

Darwin, Charles. *The Voyage of the Beagle*. Garden City, NY: Doubleday, [1839] 1962.

Denhardt, Robert M. *The Horse of the Americas*. Norman: University of Oklahoma Press, 1975.

Drinnon, Richard. *Facing West: Indian Hating and Empire Building*. New York: Schoken Books, 1990.

Driver, Harold E. *Indians of North America*. Chicago: University of Chicago Press, 1969.

Dugan, Bill. *Sitting Bull*. San Francisco: HarperCollins, 1994.

Edmunds, R. David, ed. *American Indian Leaders: Studies in Diversity*. Lincoln: University of Nebraska Press, 1980.

Giago, Tim. Book Lacks Lakota View. *Indian Country Today*, August 4, 1993, n.p.

Gibson, Arrell Morgan. *The American Indian: Prehistory to Present*. Lexington, MA: Heath, 1980.

Graham, W. A. *The Custer Myth*. Lincoln: University of Nebraska Press, 1953.

Hamilton, Charles. *Cry of the Thunderbird*. Norman: University of Oklahoma Press, 1972.

Hodgson, Bryan. Buffalo: Back Home on the Range. *National Geographic* 186:5(November 1994):64–89.

Hoig, Stan. *The Sand Creek Massacre*. Norman: University of Oklahoma Press, 1961.

Holder, Preston. *The Hoe and the Horse on the Plains*. Lincoln: University of Nebraska Press, 1970.

Homaday, William T. *The Extermination of the American Bison*. Washington, DC: Annual Report of the U.S. National Museum, 1869.

Hoover, Dwight W. *Red and Black*. Chicago: Rand-McNally, 1976.

Hyde, George E. *A Sioux Chronicle*. Norman: University of Oklahoma Press, 1956.

Hyde, George E. *Red Cloud's Folk: A History of the Oglala Sioux Indians*. University of Oklahoma Press, 1967.

Jensen, Richard E., R. Eli Paul, and John E. Carter. *Eyewitness at Wounded Knee*. Lincoln: University of Nebraska Press, 1991.

Johansen, Bruce E., and Donald A. Grinde, Jr. *The Encyclopedia of Native American Biography*. New York: Henry Holt, 1997.

Johnson, Lowell. The Buffalo. In *The First Voices*, ed. Lowell Johnson. Lincoln, NE: Nebraska Game and Parks Commission, 1984: 60–61.

Josephy, Alvin, Jr. *The Patriot Chiefs*. New York: Viking, 1961.

Kay, Jeanne. The Fur Trade and Native American Population Growth. *Ethnohistory* 31:4(1984):265–287.

Massey, Rosemary, and the Omaha Indian Center. *Footprints in Blood: Standing Bear's Struggle for Freedom and Human Dignity.* Omaha, NE: American Indian Center of Omaha, 1979.

Mathes, Valerie Sherer. Helen Hunt Jackson and the Ponca Controversy. *Montana: The Magazine of Western History* 39:1(Winter 1989):42–53.

McLaughlin, James. *My Friend, the Indian.* Boston: Houghton Mifflin, 1910.

McNickle, D'Arcy. *They Came Here First: The Epic of the American Indian.* New York: Harper and Row Perennial Library, 1975: 177–178.

Milner, Richard. Red Cloud. In *The Encyclopedia of Evolution,* ed. Richard Milner. New York: Henry Holt, 1990: 387–388.

Monoghan, Jay. *Custer.* Lincoln: University of Nebraska Press, 1959.

Moore, John H. *The Cheyennes.* London: Blackwell, 1997.

Morgan, Lewis Henry. *League of the Iroquois.* Secaucus, NJ: Corinth Books, [1851] 1962.

Morris, Roy, Jr. *Sheridan: The Life and Wars of General Phil Sheridan.* New York: Crown, 1992.

Nabokov, Peter, ed. *Native American Testimony.* New York: Penguin Books, 1991.

Neihardt, Hilda. *Black Elk and Flaming Rainbow: Personal Memories of the Lakota Holy Man.* Lincoln: University of Nebraska Press, 1995.

Olson, James C. *Red Cloud and the Sioux Problem.* University of Nebraska Press, 1965.

Pascua, Maria Parker. Ozette: A Makah Village in 1491. *National Geographic,* October 1991, 38–53.

Powers, William K. *Indians of the Northern Plains.* New York: Capricorn Books, 1973.

Reilly, Bob, Hugh Reilly, and Pegeen Reilly. *Historic Omaha: An Illustrated History of Omaha and Douglas County.* San Antonio, TX: Historical Publishing Network, 2003.

Reilly, Hugh. Treatment of Native Americans by the Frontier Press: An Omaha, Nebraska Study, 1868–1891. Masters thesis, University of Nebraska at Omaha, 1997.

Rice, Julian. *Black Elk's Story.* Albuquerque: New Mexico University Press, 1991.

Roberts, David. Geronimo. *National Geographic,* October 1992, 46–71.

Roe, Frank Gilbert. *The Indian and the Horse.* Norman: University of Oklahoma Press, 1955.

Rosenberg, Bruce A. *Custer and the Epic of Defeat.* University Park: Pennsylvania State University Press, 1974.

Sandoz, Mari. *Crazy Horse: Strange Man of the Oglalas.* New York Knopf, 1942.

Schmitt, Martin F., and Dee Brown. *Fighting Indians of the West.* New York: Ballantine Books, 1948.

Snow, Dean. The First Americans and the Differentiation of Hunter-Gatherer Cultures. In Bruce G. Trigger and Wilcomb E. Washburn, eds., *The Cambridge History of the Native Peoples of the Americas.* Cambridge, England: Cambridge University Press, 1996, 125–199.

Stannard, David. *American Holocaust: Columbus and the Conquest of the New World.* New York: Oxford University Press, 1992.

Tebbel, John, and Keith Jennison. *The American Indian Wars.* New York: Bonanza Books, 1960.

Thomas, David Hurst. *Skull Wars: Kennewick Man, Archaeology, and the Battle for Native American Identity*. New York: Basic Books/Peter N. Nevraumont, 2000.

Tibbles, Thomas Henry. *Buckskin and Blanket Days; Memoirs of a Friend of the Indians Written in 1905*. Garden City, NY: Doubleday, 1957.

Tibbles, Thomas Henry. *The Ponca Chiefs: An Account of the Trial of Standing Bear*. Edited by Kay Graber. Lincoln: University of Nebraska Press, [1880] 1972.

Utley, Robert. *The Lance and the Shield: The Life and Times of Sitting Bull*. New York: Henry Holt, 1993.

Vestal, Stanley. *Sitting Bull: Champion of the Sioux*. Norman: University of Oklahoma Press, [1932] 1957.

Virtual Truth Commission. Telling the Truth for a Better America; Reports by Name: Col. John M. Chivington. June 22, 1998. Available at http://www.geocities.com/~virtualtruth/chiving.htm.

Walker, James R. *Lakota Society*. Edited by Raymond J. DeMallie. Lincoln: University of Nebraska Press, 1982.

Waters, Frank. *Brave Are My People*. Santa Fe: Clear Light, 1992.

Weeks, Philip. *Farewell, My Nation: The American Indian and the United States, 1820–1890*. Arlington Heights, IL: Harlan Davidson, 1990.

White, Richard. The Winning of the West: The Expansion of the Western Sioux in the Eighteenth and Nineteenth Centuries. *Journal of American History* 65:2(1978): 319–343.

Wissler, Clark. The Influence of the Horse in the Development of Plains Culture. *American Anthropologist* 16(1914):1–25.

CHAPTER 8

The Rise of the "Vanishing Race"

NATIVE AMERICAN ADAPTATIONS
TO ASSIMILATION

During the first half of the twentieth century, U.S. Indian policy vacillated between the two poles: aggressive assimilation and preservation of tribal identity to some degree. One can watch this cyclical evolution in the decisions of the courts, the acts of Congress, and the positions of various presidents, as well as in the responses of Native peoples themselves. The duality of conquest and curiosity about the cultures being crushed (and some evolving sense of respect for Native peoples' own desires) may be traced to the beginnings of colonization, to the 1630s, when Roger Williams rejected the idea that the Puritans had a divine right to the land they occupied. The somewhat tortured definition by the Marshall court (in *Worcester v. Georgia*, 31 U.S. [6 Pet.] 515 [1832]) that Native people comprised "dependent domestic nations" also illustrates this duality. Beginning in 1790, the federal government also passed a number of "nonintercourse acts" meant to restrain state and private taking of Native lands. Some of these laws have been used in recent years to support land claims, especially in the northeastern United States.

During the late nineteenth century, this duality was expressed in allotment legislation and the beginnings of the boarding schools, both undertaken expressly in what some European Americans took to be the Indians' best interests, as alternatives to extermination. By the first half of the twentieth century, European American responses to surviving Native presence varied from the progressivism of John Collier, under Franklin Roosevelt, to the renewed assimilationism of termination during the Eisenhower era.

Assimilation and alienation of land base usually was favored under business-oriented Republicans. Dissolution of the Indian estate and cultures was expressed legislatively in allotment and termination, the last great legal attempt at midcentury to eliminate the "vanishing race." The other pole of policy usually was implemented by Democratic presidents, such as Franklin Delano

Roosevelt, who brought John Collier into his administration to construct the Indian New Deal during the 1930s. This policy generally recognized Native peoples' right to exist in distinct groups on their own land but under governmental control. As a whole, however, the terms of debate on Native questions had changed little since the days when President Andrew Jackson squared off with Chief Justice John Marshall. Termination and programs urging Indians to move from reservations to urban areas were expressions of the same assumptions that produced removal policies during the 1830s and 1840s. The Indian New Deal (legislated as the Indian Reorganization Act in 1934) was an elaboration of Chief Justice Marshall's opinion that the Indians occupied "dependent domestic nations."

The twentieth century began with most Native Americans at their lowest point, considering population as well as social and economic organization and well-being, following three centuries of intensive subjugation by European American immigrants in North America. In less than one century, the United States had spread westward across most of North America's land mass. The removal of the Cherokees from their homelands near the Atlantic coast (1838) and the massacre at Wounded Knee (1890) occurred during the life spans of many individuals. The dominant national mindset at the turn of the century vis-à-vis Native Americans was still baldly imperialistic. President Theodore Roosevelt raised few white eyebrows when he said that the extermination of Indians and expropriation of their lands was "as ultimately beneficial as it was inevitable." Roosevelt believed that such a state of affairs was "sure to come when a masterful people, still in its raw barbarian prime, finds itself face to face with the weaker and wholly alien race which holds a coveted prize in its feeble grip." Roosevelt once quipped that "I don't go so far as to think that the only good Indians are dead Indians, but I believe that nine out of ten are, and I shouldn't like to inquire too closely about the case of the tenth" (Stannard, 1992, 245).

Among the self-professed non-Indian guardians of the Native body and soul, the alternatives seemed, late in the nineteenth century, to be assimilation or extinction. Remaking the Indian in a European American image was widely regarded as the more humane alternative. That Native Americans might be able to choose their own future seemed a precluded option outside Indian country itself. The government, under the influence of reformers, along with the customary cabal of special economic interests set about to solve the U.S. "Indian problem" by dissolving Native cultures and land bases into the great Anglo-American melting pot.

Beginning about 1960, Native Americans themselves took the debate outside the former ideological confines by advocating a much greater degree of self-determination. The phrase became a rallying cry throughout the 1960s and was officially embraced by President Nixon in the early 1970s, just as a new wave of Native self-assertion crested most visibly in the seizure of Alcatraz Island in 1969, followed by the occupation of the Washington, D.C., Bureau of Indian Affairs (BIA) offices in 1972 after a continent-spanning march called the Trail of Broken Treaties. The 71-day confrontation at Wounded Knee in 1973 was followed by a protracted, bloody battle at Pine Ridge in South Dakota between assimilationists (backed by the BIA and Federal Bureau of Investigation) and Native traditionalists allied with the urban, militant American Indian Movement.

By the end of the twentieth century, Native American peoples and nations were making measured, determined strides to reclaim their cultures, histories, and some measure of their treaty-guaranteed land bases. By the 1990 census, the number of people in the United States who identified themselves as Native American had grown to almost 2 million from about 250,000 at the turn of the century. The most interesting irony at the end of the twentieth century may have been the wave of popular interest in all things Native, in stark contrast to the assumptions of assimilation or annihilation that had opened it. A sizable number of people actually were faking being Native American. America's European immigrants were again discovering that their "errands in the wilderness" had shaped them as well as the continent's original inhabitants. One might imagine how the "reformers" of the late nineteenth century would regard the legions of plastic medicine men plying their wares a century later. These themes are developed in chapter 9.

ASSIMILATION

During much of its first century under the Constitution, the United States dealt with Indian nations as semisovereign political entities by treaty. The legal interpretation of this relationship was set down by Chief Justice John Marshall in his Marshall Trilogy. In 1871, however, Congress stopped treaty-making and embarked on a number of other measures aimed at assimilation.

Many Indians did not desire the future that was being constructed for them by powers beyond their control. General Philip Sheridan, one of the principal U.S. Army commanders during the Indian wars of the western plains, remarked in 1878, as the wars were ending: "We took away their [the Sioux's] country and their means of support, broke up their mode of living, their habits of life, introduced disease and decay among them, and it was for this and against this that they made war. Could anyone expect less?" (Morris, 1992, 376).

As early as 1819, the U.S. Congress passed an act to establish a "civilization fund" for Native Americans, notably the construction of schools. The act urged that the schools be used to introduce among the Indians "habits and arts of civilization," including "agriculture . . . and for teaching their children in reading, writing, and arithmetic." The act asserted that its provisions would be "for the purpose of providing against the further decline and final extinction of the Indian tribes" (Johansen, 1998, 22). Congress allotted $10,000 a year for the fund's first year.

In 1872, the commissioner of Indian affairs was quoted as saying that the reservation must become "a legalized reformatory" where Native Americans would adopt non-Indian ways "peaceably if they will, forcibly if they must." Some supporters of assimilation put the case for it in more ethnocentric terms, such as the Office of the Commissioner of Indian Affairs, in 1901: "Indian dances and so-called Indian feasts should be prohibited. In many cases these dances and feasts are simply subterfuges to cover degrading acts and disguise immoral purposes. You [Indian agents] are directed to use your best efforts in the suppression of these evils" (Johansen, 1998, 23).

The Rules for the Court of Indian Offenses on the Pine Ridge Reservation in 1908 included a ban on the Sun Dance, all other similar dances, as well as other religious ceremonies. An Indian convicted of dancing could, on the first offense, be deprived of rations (that is, semistarved) for as many as ten days. A second offense called for deprivation of rations for fifteen to thirty days or up to thirty days in the agency prison.

In 1875, Congress moved to make Indians on reservations subject to federally supervised policing. Family, religious, and economic affairs of Indians were strictly regulated by the BIA by 1882, and Congress established mechanisms to enforce an individualized property-holding ethic among Indians in the General Allotment Act of 1887.

From the points of view of many Native Americans, assimilation was the essence of political oppression on a very personal level. The Winnebago spiritual leader Reuben Snake (1991) recalled:

> The steam-rolling effort of the "civilized society" upon the Indian people has wreaked a havoc that extends far beyond that of loss of material possessions. The American Indian and Alaskan Native are caught in a world wherein they are trying to find out who they are, and where they are. . . . The land that was once their "mother," giving them food and clothing, was taken. Their spiritual strengths were decried as pagan and familial ties broken. Their own form of education, i.e. that of legends, how to live, how to respect themselves and others, were torn asunder by the White society's reading, writing, and arithmetic. No culture could, or can be, expected to be thrust into a world different from its own and adapt without problems of culture shock.

As assimilation was being legislated, the Supreme Court denied citizenship to Indians who wished to take the policy to its logical conclusion. In 1884, in *Elk v. Wilkins* (112 U.S. 94 [1884]), Indians were denied the right to vote despite the wording of the recently passed Fourteenth Amendment, which had extended the franchise to blacks.

THE GENESIS OF ALLOTMENT LEGISLATION

During the 1880s, plans were developed by the federal government to effectively nullify the several hundred treaties that had set aside land, much of

Henry Laurens Dawes. (Courtesy of the Library of Congress.)

which non-Indians deemed worthless at the time. Perhaps ironically in retrospect, the one legislative act most responsible for dismembering what remained of the Native land base evolved out of liberal concern for Indians' condition that developed after the Civil War.

As the Plains Indians were subjected to conditions like those of a concentration camp, a wave of compassion was stirred by publication of Helen Hunt Jackson's *Century of Dishonor* in 1881. Jackson (1830–1885) also wrote a novel, *Ramona*, which put the depredations she had described factually in *Century of Dishonor* into a novelistic format. The book went through about 300 printings and later inspired several movies. Jackson said at the time that she wanted Ramona to raise indignation regarding mistreatment of Indians to the degree that Harriet Beecher Stowe's *Uncle Tom's Cabin* had done regarding black slavery.

Despite her intentions as a reformer, Jackson's work often was used to support legislation, such as the Dawes (Allotment) Act, passed by Congress in 1887, that distributed many Native Americans' common landholdings among individuals in 80- or 160-acre parcels. Such allotments often were sold to non-Indians, eroding the Native American land base, cultures, and languages. "Surplus" lands, those remaining after assignment of individual plots, usually were sold to non-Natives. In some cases, these tracts comprised as much as 90 percent of some reservation land bases.

In the late 1800s, very few non-Indian reformers asserted a Native right to land, language, and culture. Instead, they sought, as General William Pratt, founder of the boarding school system, often said, to "kill the Indian and save the man" as an alternative to outright extermination. Jackson's work played into the plans of reformers who supported allotment. The Allotment Act evolved into yet another land grab by the Indian rings even though its expressed purpose was to turn surviving Indians into yeoman farmers in the Jeffersonian image.

The Dawes Severalty Act (1887) was sponsored primarily by Senator Henry Dawes of Massachusetts. Dawes was no expert in Indian Affairs but considered himself as such after a fact-finding mission that included a short tour of the Cherokee Nation of Oklahoma, which had been rebuilt largely along the lines of the prosperous republic that had been built in the Southeast before the Trail of Tears. In 1883, Dawes marveled at the prosperity that the Cherokees had hewn out of the land but then condemned Native peoples because they held their lands in common:

> There is not a pauper in that nation, and the nation does not owe a dollar. It built its own capitol . . . its schools and hospitals. Yet the defect of the system is apparent. They have got as far as they can go, because they hold their land in common. . . . There is no selfishness, which is at the bottom of civilization. (Hendrix, 1983, 32)

With allotment, selfishness definitely got the upper hand. Treaty-guaranteed land that was left over after allotment—often as much as 90 percent of native peoples' commonly held estate—was then sold to non-Indian immigrants.

The Dawes Act was designed to remedy this "defect," to "civilize" the Indians by breaking up their communal lands into individual farmsteads. Often, however, the family tracts (which were as small as ten acres each) were too small to sustain the people assigned to them, and farming was a highly uncertain business because of the variability of temperatures and precipitation across much of the northern and western high plains. More than 100 reservations were allotted, centering in the plains, where large tracts of several states had earlier been assigned to Native peoples by treaty. Most of these treaties had been signed within memory of a middle-aged person when allotment began to break up the Native peoples' communal estate.

The Allotment Act was passed by Congress at a time of growing non-Indian pressure to open remaining Native American lands for settlement. At the time, several Lakota, Natoka, and Dakota peoples still owned most of western South Dakota; the Flatheads and Blackfeet held title to much of western Montana, and a coalition of local Native nations, such as the Kiowa, and "removed" Indians, such as the Cheyennes and Apaches, occupied western Oklahoma. The Crow held a large area in southern Montana.

Allotment was only one way that land speculators used the government to seize ownership of Native American land. In 1857, for example, 127,000 acres in southeastern Nebraska were set aside for Indians of mixed blood who had no other reservation base. At a time when most other reservation land was held in common, the land of the Nemaha Half-Breed Reservation was individually allotted. Most of the land was quickly transferred to a number of land sharks, the majority from the eastern seaboard. This number included James W. Denver (after whom the city was named), who also was serving at the time as commissioner of Indian affairs, a fox in the henhouse.

According to research by Bill Moran, a middle school teacher in Auburn, Nebraska, Denver did not transfer the land directly to himself but through his father-in-law, Matthew Rombach. "Together, they acquired thousands of acres," said Moran. He traced the pattern of land purchases by checking records at local county courthouses. "Rombach's name [was] all over the place," said Moran (Associated Press, 1991, 16). Rombach and others were drawn to the land because they thought a railroad would be built through the area, raising the land's value. The speculation proved groundless because the Union Pacific eventually laid its tracks through Council Bluffs and Omaha. Denver served as a member of Congress from California, where he was privy to railroad planning; he later was appointed territorial governor of Kansas.

Although the introduction of private property was advanced ideologically as an aid in civilizing Native peoples, in reality allotment was a government-sponsored real estate agency that transferred land from Indians to European Americans. In 1880, before allotment became the law of the land, approximately 150 million acres were under Native title. Within two generations, two-thirds of that land, an area roughly the size of North and South Dakota combined, had been transferred to European Americans. The loss of this land sealed many Native people into poverty and dependence on promised government supplies and annuities.

The Allotment Act contributed importantly to the reduction of Native American population in the United States to about 250,000 between 1880 and about 1920. At the beginning of the twentieth century, even the friends of the Indian called them the vanishing Americans. This characterization was considered by some to be an act of compassion. Harold E. Driver, in *Indians of North America*, provides the following Native population figures for the continental United States (not including Alaska or Hawaii): about 250,000 in 1890; 271,000 in 1900; 336,000 in 1920 (1969, 527). D'Arcy McNickle, in *They*

Came Here First, asserted that the figure of 255,000 reported by the federal government in 1880 was the lowest population point for Native Americans in the United States (McNickle, 1975, 227–228).

As a mechanism for the transfer of land from one group of people to another, allotment worked hand in glove with the practice of homesteading, the granting of land to immigrating European Americans. The amount of land granted immigrants by homesteading peaked in 1884, three years before the passage of the Allotment Act.

Because allotment was based on the model of the Anglo-American nuclear family, many Native Americans who were subjected to its provisions were required to do more than change their property-holding customs. Indian extended families were devastated by the allotment system, in which close relatives who had lived together often were given distant parcels of land. Long-established ties between grandmothers and their children were severed, and a long-standing family structure destroyed. Native men who were married to more than one wife were told to divest all but one. Vine Deloria, Jr., recalled the tearful response of the Kiowa chief Quanah Parker, who, when told that he must give up his extra wives, "told the [Indian] agent that, if he must give them up, he could not choose which one to surrender and that the agent must do it for him" (Deloria and Lytle, 1983, 197).

The Allotment Act also authorized the Secretary of the Interior to sell timber from allotted land and strengthened existing powers authorizing the government to lease land for the supposed benefit of the allottees. Income from such activities was deposited in a BIA account, called Individual Indian Monies (IIM) to be paid to allottees only if the bureau deemed them "worthy." A scandal subsequently ensued in Oklahoma when full-blooded members of the Five Civilized Tribes in Oklahoma Territory died of starvation despite the fact that they had IIM accounts worth hundreds of thousands of dollars. The BIA had been diverting their income to pay for construction of schools and churches. During the late twentieth century, a number of IIM account holders asked for their money, only to be told that the BIA's records were so haphazard that the funds could not be located. A very large class action lawsuit followed.

According to legal scholar Charles F. Wilkinson: "Allotment and the other assimilationist programs that complemented it devastated Indian land base, weakened Indian culture, sapped the vitality of tribal legislative and judicial processes, and opened most Indian reservations for settlement by non-Indians" (1987, 19). The U.S. political leaders understood this to be the upshot of allotment at the time. President Theodore Roosevelt, for example, said: "The General Allotment Act is a mighty pulverizing engine to break up the tribal mass. It acts directly upon the family and the individual" (Johansen, 1997, 21). Over the generations, many individual allotments were subdivided into miniscule plots by inheritances, rendering many of them nearly useless for agriculture.

The breakdown of Native American estate, political traditions, and family relations was the stated aim of allotment legislation. BIA publications acknowledge that the trust of U.S. Indian policy in the 1870s and 1880s was to "further minimize the functions of tribal leaders and tribal institutions and to continually strengthen the position of the government representative and his subordinates, and to improve the effectiveness of their programs to break down traditional patterns within the Indian communities" (Johansen, 1997, 20–21).

A few non-Indians protested allotment and other forms of assimilation. Ethnologist Lewis Henry Morgan, known as the founder of American anthropology, predicted that a result of allotment for the Indian "would unquestionably be, that in a very short time he would divest himself of every foot of land and fall into poverty" (Johansen, 1998, 18). Morgan was echoing the minority opinion of the House Committee of Indian Affairs on the Allotment Act:

> The real purpose of this bill is to get at the Indian lands and open them up to [non-Indian] settlement. The provisions for the apparent benefit of the Indians are but the pretext to get his lands and occupy them.... If this were done in the name of greed, it would be bad enough; but to do it in the name of humanity, and under the cloak of an ardent desire to promote the Indian's welfare by making him like ourselves whether he will or not, is infinitely worse. (Johansen, 1997, 21)

The same minority report scoffed at the Allotment Act's professed humanitarianism. Representative Henry M. Teller of Colorado said that allotment was "a bill to despoil the Indians of their land and to make them vagabonds on the face of the earth." He said that the Indians would someday "curse the hand that was raised professedly in their defense" (Weeks, 1990, 220–221).

Although allotment impoverished many Indians as Morgan foresaw, the BIA prospered. In 1881, Native Americans owned 155.6 million acres of land; by 1890, their holdings had dropped to 104.3 million acres. By the turn of the century, the Native estate was 77.9 million acres. Between 1887 and 1934, as Native American estate was reduced to less than half what it had been before allotment had begun, the Indian Bureau increased its staff by 6,000 people and its budget 400 percent.

If the goal of allotment was to turn Native people into yeoman farmers in the Jeffersonian image, the experiment was an unmitigated failure. Many peoples who had practiced agriculture themselves preferred their own farming methods, especially in the West, where lands that often were wracked by drought were simply unsuited for agricultural methods developed in Europe and refined in humid eastern North America. In addition, for Native Americans, farming the staples of life (especially corn) often was closely associated with religious practices; among the Hopis and Pueblos, for example, the breaking of the ground with a plow was considered a sacrilege comparable to slashing the breast of Mother Earth. For peoples who had never farmed, the situation was often worse:

Chitto Harjo, or Crazy Snake. (Courtesy of the Library of Congress.)

Conversion of tribal land into individual allotments did not lead to family self-sufficiency. For the Cheyennes and Arapahoes, only 16 years had passed between their confinement on reservations in 1875 and allotment of their lands in 1891. Except for the most assimilated mixed-bloods, they had not made the transition from independent nomadism to settled commercial farming, nor had many of the men come to accept agricultural labor as anything more than complete humiliation. (Olson and Wilson, 1984, 88)

Native unwillingness to accept allotment occasionally erupted into violence. At the turn of the century, Chitto Harjo, a full-blooded Creek, established the

Snake Society, which formed a native-controlled tribal government. Harjo and his followers asserted that the United States could not annul legally signed treaties without the consent of native signers, despite legislation by Congress enacted in 1871, which had done that unilaterally. In 1901, the reorganized Creeks rejected allotment. Harjo's band assaulted some Creeks who had accepted individual parcels of land. The Snake Uprising was crushed quickly by federal troops as resistance to allotment began to spread to the Cherokees and Choctaws, who, like the Creeks, were descended from people who had been forced to march the trails of tears from the Southeast in the 1830s. For years after their turn-of-the-century uprising was crushed, many of the Snakes refused to live on their allotments. Instead, they camped on church, school, tribal, or government property. Their example was followed by some other members of the Five Civilized Tribes, some of whom even refused to cash royalty checks for oil found under the lands that had been assigned individually.

HOW THE OSAGES KEPT THEIR OIL

The Allotment Act occasionally was used in some novel ways to protect Native collective estate, quite opposite its original intention to "pulverize tribal mass." For example, the Osages, finding themselves exiled to Oklahoma atop a massive cache of oil, managed to write their version of the Allotment Act in 1906 to protect their collective ownership of natural resources, an arrangement that has been maintained since.

Thus, a law meant to convert Native Americans from collective property owners to individual Anglo-Saxon-style landholders was used at a key juncture to uphold collective Osage control of oil and other mineral rights. At every turn since 1906, the Osage tribal government has protected its rights to manage oil production for the common good of the nation, even as private interests have tried to assail it. Through several decades, the Osages have used legal resources to lobby Congress to use its plenary power to maintain its right to manage the nation's natural resources. Leases and royalties from oil and gas generated about $50 to $75 million annually during the 1990s.

The Osage reservation occupies nearly all of the roughly 1.5 million acres of Osage County in north central Oklahoma, adjacent to the Kansas border, a land that varies from woods to open plains and grasslands. Osage County, which is roughly the size of Delaware, is the largest county in Oklahoma and the only one created explicitly to accommodate an Indian reservation. The county was created because the Osages feared that Oklahoma statehood might crimp their ability to control their own affairs.

The Osage originally migrated from the banks of the Ohio River to present-day Missouri before contact with Europeans, which occurred in 1673 on the banks of the Osage River. The Osages were shuffled through several treaty councils, moved from their ancestral homelands, and deposited, during 1871, in Indian Territory, where nature had a surprise waiting for them. The lands assigned them contained some of the richest oil deposits in the United States. By 1906, smallpox and intermarriage had reduced the Osage population to about 2,200 people, about half of mixed blood. (In the mid-1990s, the tribal roll contained about 12,000 people.)

Oil was discovered under the Osages' land during 1896. Tribal records indicate that on March 16, 1896, the Osage Tribe executed an oil and gas lease to Edwin H. Foster for ten years, allowing him to explore anywhere on the 1.5 million acres of the reservation. The lease expired March 16, 1906, after which it was extended another ten years to March 1916, during which time Foster executed subleases to several other corporations.

During the Roaring Twenties, oil and gas royalties hit their height. Many white men married Osage women to tap into their headrights (individual shares of oil and gas royalties). Terry P. Wilson, in *The Underground Reservation: Osage Oil*, wrote that "It was commonly believed that in rural Osage County there were more Pierce Arrows [expensive automobiles] than in any other county in the United States" (1985, xi). During this time, Pawhuska, the major town on the reservation, had a population of roughly 8,000. The town supported the services of eighty attorneys and did so in style, according to Wilson (ibid., 140) Osage County also became the scene of several spectacular (and often unsolved) murders. Earnings per headright reached a height of $13,200 per year in 1925, then plummeted to $585 in 1932 with the onset of the Great Depression.

A letter from the Secretary of the Interior (July 16, 1917) contained regulations for the leasing of Osage lands for oil and gas mining. On April 28, 1922, House Resolution 10401 (66th Congress, First Session) contained an amendment adding a provision "preserving Osage tribal ownership of all oil, gas, coal, or other minerals." On February 26, 1921, House Report 1377 extended Osage Tribal mineral estate to April 7, 1946, at the same time allowing Oklahoma to collect a production tax "in lieu of all other State and county taxes." The same legislation also declared Osages to be U.S. citizens and allowed collection of an additional 1 percent gross production tax for roads and bridges in Osage County.

The Osages' collective exercise of leasing rights has been challenged by private interests. In 1931, 25 years after the 1906 Allotment Act, the Texas Company and the Indian Territory Illuminating Oil Company, holders of mineral leases from the Osage Tribal Council, made a case that they owned the land (and any oil, gas, etc. below its surface), having purchased it from individual Osage allottees. In *Adams et al. v. Osage Tribe of Indians et al.* (No. 642 District Court N. D. Oklahoma 50 F. 2d 918, 1931 U.S. Dist), a federal district judge found that "The contention of the complainants is untenable. A careful consideration of the various acts of Congress involved discloses that the complainants have never by reason of their purchase become vested with the title in and to the oil and gas and other minerals found under the lands involved in this action."

The court upheld the Osage Nation's right to control mineral rights. By act of Congress on March 3, 1921 (41 Stat. 1249), the Osage government's right to control mineral rights was extended to April 8, 1946; by act of Congress on March 2, 1929 (45 Stat. 1478), the "trust period over such mineral rights" was extended again, to 1959. In 1957, tribal control vis-à-vis the 1906 Allotment Act provision was extended from 1959 to 1984. The same right subsequently has been extended into our time.

The Osages' collective control of oil and gas leasing has been extended by Congress over the unsuccessful protests of the Osage County Homeowners' Association, a group of non-Indians who sought to control reservation oil and gas production for themselves. The right of Congress to extend the terms of the 1906 Allotment Act was justified as use of its plenary power in relationships with Indian nations, stemming from *Worcester v. Georgia* and several other federal cases.

The 1906 clause came up again in *United States v. Stanolind Crude Oil Purchasing Company; United States v. Gulf Oil Corporation; United States v. Sinclair Prairie Oil Company* (Numbers 1975–1977; 113 F. 2d 194 [10th Cir. 1940]). This case evolved from a dispute over royalty rates owed the Osages by companies producing oil from its leases, specifically the industry custom of deducting 3 percent from the volume of oil pumped to account for impurities, sediment, and shrinkage. The court found that the companies were entitled to the 3 percent deduction. This case, however, shows how aggressively the United States sometimes exercised its responsibility to act as the Osages' legal advocate in oil-related cases.

THE CURIOUS CONCEPT OF "WARDSHIP"

Assimilation was the basic rationale for a state of wardship, which has framed U.S. Indian policy from its beginnings. *Wardship* has come to refer to a legal doctrine, said to be based on opinions by U.S. Supreme Court Chief Justice John Marshall during the 1820s and 1830s, that Native Americans live in "dependent domestic nations" and are therefore wards of the federal government. The BIA was initially established to hold Indians' land and resources "in trust." Wardship status rationalized the establishment of Indian reservations and schools to assimilate Native Americans into mainstream U.S. culture.

The concept of wardship also lay behind the storage of thousands of Native skeletal remains and burial artifacts in many federal and state research institutions. The idea of Native sovereignty in modern times has been developed in large part in opposition to wardship doctrines. Indians reacted to a social control system that was so tight that in many cases (for example, if a will affected the status of allotted land) individual actions of Native American people were subject to approval by the Secretary of the Interior.

The assertion of states' rights over Native territory in the southeastern United States provided the legal grist for a 1832 Supreme Court decision written by Chief Justice John Marshall. In *Worcester v. Georgia*, Justice Marshall wrote that inhabitants of Native nations had assumed a relationship of "pupilege" in their relations with the United States. Using this doctrine, which has no constitutional basis, the executive branch of the U.S. government, principally through the BIA, created a superstructure of policies and programs that have had a vast impact on individual Native Americans and their governments. Through the use of the plenary power of Congress, such policies as allotment divested much of the Indian estate.

A concept of wardship also has been used since the mid-nineteenth century to construct for Native Americans a cradle-to-grave social control system that was described this way during the mid-twentieth century by legal scholar Felix Cohen:

> Under the reign of these magic words [wardship and trust] nothing Indian was safe. the Indian's hair was cut, his dances forbidden, his oil lands, timber lands, and grazing lands were disposed of by Indian agents and Indian commissioners for whom the magic word "wardship" always made up for lack of statutory authority. (Johansen, 1997, 19)

Although Chief Justice Marshall's opinions have been used as a legal rationale for government policies that have treated American Indians as wards, "There is nothing," according to Robert T. Coulter, executive director of the Indian Law Resource Center, "in the rulings of the Marshall Court [which] even remotely suggested that the United States could unilaterally impose a guardian-ward relationship on Indians, that it held trust title to Indian lands, or that, as trustee, it could dispose of lands without Indian consent" (Coulter and Tullberg, 1984, 199).

Wardship as historically practiced by the BIA differs markedly from the legal status of non-Indian wards. Under most conditions, wardship is usually taken to be a temporary condition with established standards for cession. Civil guardianship and custody law must allow people who have been deprived of their civil rights means of regaining them in accordance with the Due Process Clause. As developed by the BIA, however, Indian wardship has no standard for cession and no ending date. An Indian is defined as a ward regardless of his or her accomplishments or other actions, as the object of a policy that may have misinterpreted Marshall's intent.

REMAKING THE MIND: INDIAN EDUCATION

Assimilation was the goal of a paternalistic educational system established for Indian young people late in the 1870s by General Richard Henry Pratt (1840–1924), a reformer who coined the assimilationist slogan "Kill the Indian, save the man." The phrase was designed initially as an advertising

Classroom at Indian Industrial School, Carlisle, Pennsylvania.
(Courtesy of the Library of Congress.)

slogan in Congress to request appropriations for Indian education for a nationwide complex of schools around 1900.

Pratt's Indian schools were run with Army-style boot camp discipline, the idea being to make the Indian children anew in the image of small farmers and urban workers with the rudiments of Anglo-American cultural heritage. The Carlisle Indian Industrial School, Pratt's first, was run on an Army model. Students were strictly regimented and forced to divest themselves of all vestiges of Indian identity. They wore uniforms, and their hair was cut. Missionaries also were brought in to teach them Christianity. Runaways were punished severely. Discipline was sometimes personal and petty. Albert White Hat, an instructor of Lakota at Sinte Gleska University on the Rosebud Reservation in South Dakota, recalled instances at St. Francis Indian School in which he and his classmates had their mouths washed out with soap for speaking their Native languages.

Pratt described his philosophy in a book, *Battlefield and Classroom: Four Decades with the American Indian, 1867–1904* ([1964] 1987). His educational experiment began in the 1870s with seventy-two Native men, most of them Cheyenne, who were imprisoned in an old Spanish fort at St. Augustine,

Florida. In 1878, this class "graduated," and Pratt approached Congress for an appropriation to begin an Indian industrial school on an abandoned army post at Carlisle, Pennsylvania. To recruit students for his new school, Pratt visited the Sioux of the high plains. One hundred and sixty-nine students traveled eastward in 1879 to form Carlisle's first class. Included was Luther Standing Bear, who later became a well-known author. Standing Bear recalled his days at Carlisle in *My Indian Boyhood* ([1931] 1988).

The schools were established at a time when industrial enterprises were expanding rapidly in the United States; at the same time, the European American settlement frontier was crossing the western half of the present continental United States. The curriculum of the schools was intensely vocational. "This is to be an industrial school to teach young Indians how to make a living among civilized people by practicing agricultural and mechanical pursuits and the usual industries of civilized life," Pratt wrote in his book, *Battlefield and Classroom* ([1964] 1987, 235). Pratt approached Congress for money to buy a long list of items to further Indians' induction into what he regarded as civilized industrial society: carpenter's tools, blacksmith's forges and anvils, sewing machines, paint brushes, tools for making shoes and harnessing horses, printing presses and type.

Pratt ran the boarding schools on a model that was appropriate for training a factory workforce during the late nineteenth century. Thus, the communal lifeways of many American Indians were to be replaced by an emphasis on individual labor regarded as a commodity in the capitalistic marketplace. Pratt continuously stressed the value of boarding school education and the white man's world of work as two stops on the same avenue of assimilation for Native Americans.

By the 1880s, as the Anglo-American settlement frontier closed in the middle of the continent, government policy toward Indian education was marked by debate. One faction wanted to remove Native children from their homes under governmental or religious sponsorship and remake the Indians into English-speaking, God-fearing participants in an agricultural and industrial economy, person by person, within one generation. The other faction advocated establishment of reservation-based schools and a slower path to assimilation.

Even as many boarding school students were stunted by oppression and hundreds died in influenza and tuberculosis epidemics, other students overcame all obstacles to shine in Anglo-American culture. Jim Thorpe, a graduate of Carlisle Indian School, was named the greatest American athlete in America during the first half of the twentieth century by the Associated Press. Luther Standing Bear, a Lakota author, is another prominent example. Thus, mixed with memories of pain, isolation, and despair, the boarding schools produced occasional testaments to their value as havens from an aggressive European American world that could be very hostile to the few hundred thousand Native American peoples who survived the Indian wars.

Luther Standing Bear. (Courtesy of the Nebraska State Historical Society.)

Jim Thorpe with his family. (Courtesy of the Library of Congress.)

Born near Prague, Oklahoma, during 1888 of Irish, French, and Fox/ Potawatomi descent, Jim Thorpe (Wathohuck, the Bright Path) was an out- standing college and professional football player and a gold medal Olympic athlete. Some sports historians have called him one of the greatest all-around athletes of any era. Thorpe's mother was a granddaughter of the Sauk leader Black Hawk.

Thorpe was an all-American college football player in 1911 and 1912, as Coach Glenn S. (Pop) Warner turned the Carlisle Indian School into a na- tional football power. Thorpe also won letters in ten sports besides football while at Carlisle: baseball, track, boxing, wrestling, lacrosse, gymnastics, swimming, hockey, handball, and basketball. He also was a prize-winning marksman and excelled at golf. Thorpe represented the United States at the 1912 Olympics in Stockholm, where he won both the decathlon and the pentathlon, the first time the same person had ever won both events in the same Olympic games. King Gustav of Sweden called him the greatest athlete in the world. His gold medals were taken from Thorpe later when it was discovered that he had played professional baseball for a short time in 1911, violating Olympic rules.

Thorpe played professional baseball between 1913 and 1919 for the New York Giants and Boston Braves. During the 1920s, he began another professional sports career in football with the Chicago Cardinals and other teams. Thorpe also recruited an all-Native American team (the Oorang Indians) for the fledgling National Football League. The team played two seasons. In 1921, the team won two games and lost six; in 1922, before the team was disbanded, the Oorang Indians won one game and lost ten.

During the 1930s, Thorpe's sports career declined. He made celebrity appearances, played bit parts in a few movies, and returned to Oklahoma for a time to delve into tribal politics. During World War II, Thorpe joined the Merchant Marine, and after that, in 1950 and 1951, he took part in the filming of the movie *Jim Thorpe—All-American*. Thorpe died in Lomita, California, in 1953. The next year, two villages in Pennsylvania, Mauch Chunk and East Mauch Chunk, merged and named themselves for him.

In 1982, the Jim Thorpe Foundation was established to work for restoration of his Olympic medals. Replicas of the medals were presented to Thorpe's family in 1983. A year later, Dennis Banks and other members of the American Indian Movement helped organize the Longest Run, during which Indian runners saluted Thorpe with a relay across North America. The run began at Onondaga, New York, and ended at the site of the 1984 Summer Olympics in Los Angeles, where the return of his medals was celebrated.

Unlike Jim Thorpe, another Native American athlete, Big Hawk Chief (Kootahwecoosoolelehoolashar, Pawnee, born ca. 1850) is virtually unknown today. He probably ran a mile in less than four minutes nearly three-quarters of a century before anyone else. Big Hawk Chief joined the U.S. Army scout corps under Captain Luther North in 1876; he fought the Sioux and their allies in the final years of the Plains Indian wars. As he was waiting for orders to muster out of the Army, Big Hawk Chief twice ran a mile in under four minutes at Fort Sidney, Nebraska.

Captain North set up a mile-long course and put two stopwatches on Big Hawk Chief, who was reputed to be the fastest of a number of outstanding Pawnee runners. Big Hawk Chief was reported to have run the first half of the course in two minutes and the second half in one minute fifty-eight seconds at a time when the fastest recorded mile run by any other human being was 4:49. Captain North remeasured the course, and Big Hawk Chief duplicated the effort in the same time to the astonishment of nearly everyone at the fort. The next sub-four-minute mile would be run by Roger Bannister, an Englishman, in 1954, three-quarters of a century later.

Thorpe was probably the most notable single alumnus of Pratt's boarding school system. Unlike Thorpe, most students were being prepared for anonymous lives in an industrializing country. Boarding schools were usually purposefully located far from children's homes to break down ties to their families and cultures. During their scholastic careers, many native children were "outed" to European American families for as many as three years. Students who were outed often performed domestic labor (for women) and farm or urban wage labor (for men). Young men were trained in agriculture, carpentry, blacksmithing, harness and shoe-making, printing, tailoring, and baking. Young women were trained in cooking, sewing, and laundry.

The outing policy was based on an assumption that Native American children were less intelligent than European Americans. During the 1940s, the BIA and University of Chicago researchers set out to test this assumption. They compared Indian children's intelligence with that of non-Indians in a rural Midwestern area. They used performance tests in which comprehension of English was not the main factor in defining intelligence, testing Hopi, Navajo, Sioux, Papago, and Zuni children. A group of Hopis averaged a score of 111 to 117 on a battery of tests. A comparison group of European American children scored 101 to 103 on the same tests. Pine Ridge children averaged 101 to 114 on the tests, and the other Indian groups scored in similar ranges (Havighurst and Hilkevitch, 1944).

Native peoples also displayed an intense attachment to their traditions that the government did not expect. Sometimes, the curriculum of the boarding schools so profoundly rejected Native values and self-worth that they were self-defeating, propelling students to suicide or alcoholism (also eventually a form of suicide). Some rebelled outright at the contradictions they were being taught compared to the lives they knew and the traditions they were taught at home. The boarding school system had a curious effect on some of its best students. It turned some of them into the Indian militants of the 1960s. Even such a transformation is not totally unique to the twentieth century, however. Wovoka, who initiated the Ghost Dance, was raised in a Christian settler family during the early years of the boarding schools.

The boarding school system was based on an assumption that making students accept the degradation of their traditions as an objective fact would cause them to accept acculturation. The Carlisle School published one essay that its teachers regarded as "excellent":

Question: To what race do you belong?
Answer: The human race.
Question: How many classes belong to this race?

Answer: There are five classes belonging to the human race.
Question: Which was the first?
Answer: The white people are the strongest.
Question: Which are the next?
Answer: The Mongolian or yellows.
Question: The next?
Answer: The Ethiopians or blacks.
Question: Next?
Answer: The American or reds.
Question: Tell me something of the white people.
Answer: The Caucasian is way ahead of all the other races. He thought more than any other race, he thought that somebody must [have] made the earth, and if the white people did not find that out, nobody would ever know it—it is God who made the world. (Weeks, 1990, 224–225)

The world into which many Native Americans were born during the early twentieth century brings to mind George Orwell's novel *1984*. The influence of the BIA pervaded every aspect of its wards' lives, from cradle to grave, in the image of Big Brother. The minions of government usually thought they were doing the Indians a favor, shaping them into melting pot Americans. They were imposing a way of life that many Native people did not want and often did their best, under difficult circumstances, to avoid.

If the BIA forbade traditional ceremonies such as the Sun Dance and the rituals of the kiva, Native people took them underground. The same was true of shamanistic practices, which survived stringent attacks in which they were called "paganism." The off-reservation boarding schools were designed to immerse Native students in anglicized culture and to strip them of their own, beginning with language. English was taught and enforced as the *lingua franca*. The speaking of Native languages often was punished, sometimes violently. Even under such pressure, many Native languages, the vessels of many hundreds of cultures, survived.

By the time that treaty-making ended in 1871, the smothering bureaucratic arms of the BIA were reaching into the lives of most surviving Native Americans. According to the "reformers" of the post–Civil War era, this nullification of tribal sovereignty—by which Native peoples often had to go to court to fight to regain what had been guaranteed them, often in eternal terms, by treaties signed only a few years earlier—served the same purpose as Indian boarding school education.

As allotment reduced the Native land base, enrollment in BIA-sponsored schools increased. Between 1895 and 1905, the number of off-reservation boarding schools designed on the Carlisle model rose from 19 to 25, and their enrollment doubled to 9,736. The number of boarding schools on reservations increased from 75 to 93, with enrollment rising from 8,068 to 11,402 (Olson and Wilson, 1984, 90–100).

RE-LIVING THE BOARDING SCHOOL
EXPERIENCE IN CANADA

The paternalistic assumptions of Pratt's schools also informed Canadian educational policies. The Canadian minister of Indian affairs, Frank Oliver, forecast in 1908 that the residential school system would "elevate the Indian from his condition of savagery" and "make him a self-supporting member of the state, and eventually a citizen in good standing" (Johansen, 2000, 12). Canadian officials sent delegations south of the border to study boarding schools in the United States before establishing their own system. By the early twenty-first century, hundreds of Canadian Native Americans were suing churches and the federal government there because of maltreatment at these schools.

Even after decades, the memories of Native Americans who were forced to attend Canadian boarding schools have a searing quality. "It was like jail," Warner Scout, who was 54 years of age in 1999, told the *Calgary Herald*. "The scar will be there for the rest of our lives" (Lowey, 1999, A-1). Scout, who is one of 2,000 Canadian natives seeking legal redress for boarding school abuse, recalled regular beatings and taunts that he was "an ugly savage."

More than 100,000 Native American students attended residential schools across Canada until the 1980s. Most of these schools were funded by the Canadian federal government and operated by employees of the Catholic, Anglican, Presbyterian, and United churches. During the past few years, hundreds of men and women have filed lawsuits outlining the physical and sexual abuse they said they were forced to endure in these schools as children. Eventually, settlements could reach billions of Canadian dollars, possibly devastating the financial resources of the churches that had maintained the schools.

Scout was taken from his adopted family to attend the St. Paul residential school, operated by the Anglican Church of Canada on the Blood Reserve near Lethbridge, in southern Alberta. There, he said, "Teaching . . . was beaten into us" (Lowey, 1999, A-1). Scout watched as one Indian student was forced to eat his own vomit after he threw up into a bowl of porridge. Students who wet their beds had urine rubbed in their faces, and those who spoke the Blackfoot language had their heads shaven.

Jackie Blackface, who was 52 in 1999, recalled being beaten with a tractor's fan belt at an Anglican school on the Siksika First Nation Reserve east of Calgary. Federal Canadian law at the time gave the Indian agent on each Native reserve authority to invade homes and order children aged seven or older into residential schools. Parents who did not cooperate were threatened with time in jail.

Why has a drive to apologize and compensate for the abuses of boarding schools developed in Canada while the issue has been virtually untouched in the United States? The seeds were sown almost a decade ago with the summer of fire and iron at Oka, Quebec, on and near the Kanesatake Mohawk Reserve. That confrontation over a long-ignored land claim reverberated across Canada during and after 1990, causing intense soul-searching by many non-Native Canadians. This wave of questioning expressed itself in the appointment of the Royal Commission on Aboriginal Peoples, which in 1996 published a massive, multivolume study of the many ways in which Native Americans had been abused of their lands and rights during Canadian history.

Part of the report (volume 1, chapter 10) by the Royal Commission documented the abuses of the boarding schools, providing a basis for establishment of a $350 million "healing fund" by Canada's federal government as well as a tidal wave of lawsuits. The healing fund is reserved for community projects, not for individual compensation. Individual compensation must be sought through the Canadian court system or by negotiation with agencies of the federal government.

The graphic sexual nature of boarding school abuses shocked many Canadians. Their sense of disgust was not alleviated by the fact that many of the abuses took place at the hands of priests, nuns, and other clerics. The scope of the abuse also has shocked Canadians. The Royal Commission found that abuse was systemic, not occasional or accidental. Thousands of Native young people are said to have died in the schools, and thousands more were scarred for life by physical and sexual abuse.

Aboriginal people often realized the purpose of the schools at the beginning, according to the report of the Royal Commission:

> The Aboriginal leader George Manuel, a residential school graduate, was rather more blunt. The schools, he wrote, were the laboratory and production line of the colonial system...the colonial system that was designed to make room for European expansion into a vast empty wilderness needed an Indian population that it could describe as lazy and shiftless...the colonial system required such an Indian for casual labor. (Royal Commission, 1996)

The Royal Commission on Aboriginal Peoples found that the residential schools' concerted campaign to obliterate those habits and associations, Aboriginal languages, traditions, and beliefs and its vision of radical resocialization were compounded by mismanagement and underfunding, the provision of inferior educational services, and the woeful mistreatment, neglect, and abuse of many children—facts that were known to the department and the churches throughout the history of the school system.

The boarding school system was designed to transform Native children into Europeans from the ground up. In the words of the Royal Commission's report, their purpose was as follows:

> [To] release [the children] from the shackles that tied them to their parents, communities and cultures. The civilizers in the churches and the department understood this and, moreover, that it would not be accomplished simply by bringing the children into the school. Rather it required a concerted attack on the

ontology, on the basic cultural patterning of the children and on their world view. They had to be taught to see and understand the world as a European place within which only European values and beliefs had meaning; thus the wisdom of their cultures would seem to them only savage superstition. (Royal Commission, 1996)

The main enforcement mechanism in this transformation from "permissive" aboriginal life to white Canadian discipline was punishment, much of it violent. In 1943, the principal of St. George's School (located on the Fraser River, just north of Lyttons, BC) disclosed that a set of shackles had been used routinely "to chain runaways to the bed." Furthermore:

At the heart of the vision of residential education—of the school as home and sanctuary of motherly care—there was a stark contradiction, an inherent element of savagery in the mechanics of civilizing the children. The very language in which the vision was couched revealed what would have to be the essentially violent nature of the school system in its assault on child and culture. The basic premise of resocialization, of the great transformation from "savage" to "civilized", was violent. (Royal Commission, 1996)

In 1936, G. Barry, district inspector of schools in British Columbia, described the Alberni School on Vancouver Island, "where every member of staff carried a strap" and where "children have never learned to work without punishment" (Royal Commission, 1996). In 1896, according to the Royal Commission's report, Agent D. L. Clink refused to return a child to the Red Deer School because he feared "he would be abused." Without reprimand from the principal, a teacher had beaten children severely on several occasions, one of whom had to be hospitalized. "Such brutality," Clink concluded, "should not be tolerated for a moment" and "would not be tolerated in a white school for a single day in any part of Canada" (ibid.).

The Royal Commission also included a report by a senior official in western Canada, David Laird, on Norway House in 1907 detailing "frequent whippings" over an eight-year period of a young boy, Charlie Clines, for bedwetting. The severity of his punishment was not, Laird asserted, "in accordance with Christian methods." Clines hated the new Anglo world that was being thrust on him so much that he ran away from the school and slept in weather so severe that several toes froze and he lost them.

In 1902, Johnny Sticks found his son, Duncan, dead of exposure after he fled from the Williams Lake, British Columbia, industrial school. Nearly four decades later, in 1937 at the Lejac School, four boys ran away and were found frozen to death on the lake within sight of their community. They were wearing only summer clothes. In both cases, investigations uncovered a history of neglect and violence in evidence given by staff, children, and some graduates. Some students complained that they were given rotten, worm-ridden meat and punished if they did not eat it.

During 1921, a visiting nurse at Crowstand School discovered nine children "chained to the benches" in the dining room, one of them "marked badly by a strap" (Royal Commission, 1996). Children were frequently beaten severely with whips, rods, and fists; chained and shackled; bound hand and foot; and locked in closets, basements, and bathrooms.

The Royal Commission reported that, in 1919, a runaway student from the Anglican Old Sun's school was captured, then shackled to a bed, with his hands tied, and was "most brutally and unmercifully beaten with a horse quirt until his back was bleeding." The accused, P. H. Gentlemen, admitted to having used a whip and shackles. Canon S. Gould, the general secretary of the Missionary Society, mounted a curious defense: that such a beating was the norm "more or less, in every boarding school in the country." Gentlemen remained at the school.

Writing in 1991 of her experience in both Anglican and Catholic schools, Mary Carpenter (Johansen, 2000, 19) told an-all-too-familiar story: After a lifetime of beatings, going hungry, standing in a corridor on one leg, walking in the snow with no shoes for speaking Inuvialuktun, and having a heavy, stinging paste rubbed on her face (to stop her from expressing the Eskimo custom of raising eyebrows for "yes" and wrinkling noses for "no"), she lost the ability to speak her native language.

The Aboriginal Commission found the following:

> By the mid-1980s, it was widely and publicly recognized that the residential school experience . . . like smallpox and tuberculosis in earlier decades, had devastated and continued to devastate communities. The schools were, with the agents and instruments of economic and political marginalization, part of the contagion of colonization. In their direct attack on language, beliefs and spiri- tuality, the schools had been a particularly virulent strain of that epidemic of empire, sapping the children's bodies and beings. In later life, many adult sur- vivors, and the families and communities to which they returned, all manifested a tragic range of symptoms emblematic of "the silent tortures that continue in our communities." (Royal Commission, 1996)

Although school supervisors acknowledged and sometimes even took pride in stern discipline, including corporal punishment, they said very little about the deepest secret of the system: sexual abuse of the children. The official files ignore the issue almost completely. Any references were encoded in the lan- guage of repression that marked the Canadian discourse on sexual matters. One report at Red Deer School commented that "the moral aspect of affairs is deplorable." Others wrote of "questions of immorality" of "the breaking of the Seventh Commandment" (Royal Commission, 1996).

In 1990, the Toronto *Globe and Mail* (Johansen, 2000, 19) reported that Rix Rogers, special advisor to the minister of national health and welfare on child sexual abuse, had commented at a meeting of the Canadian Psychological Association that the abuse revealed to date was "just the tip of the iceberg" and that closer scrutiny of treatment of children at residential schools would show that all children at some schools were sexually abused. A 1989 study sponsored by the Native Women's Association of the Northwest Territories found that eight of ten girls under the age of eight had been victims of sexual abuse, and 50 percent of boys the same age had been sexually molested as well.

On January 7, 1998, Minister of Indian Affairs Jane Stewart read a Statement of Reconciliation into the record of Canada's federal Parliament at Ottawa that acknowledged the damage done to the Native population, including the hanging of Louis Riel after he led a rebellion of Indian and mixed-race people in western Canada in 1885. The government apology stopped short of pardoning Riel, a step that aboriginal leaders have demanded for decades. Stewart did, however, apologize for the government's assimilation policies, including the abuses of boarding schools.

"Attitudes of racial and cultural superiority led to a suppression of aboriginal culture and values," Stewart said. She continued:

> As a country, we are burdened by past actions that resulted in weakening the identity of aboriginal peoples, suppressing their languages and cultures, and outlawing spiritual practices. We must recognize the impact of these actions on the once self-sustaining nations that were disaggregated, disrupted, limited or even destroyed by the dispossession of traditional territory, by the relocation of aboriginal people, and by some provisions of the Indian Act. The time has come to state formally that the days of paternalism and disrespect are behind us and we are committed to changing the nature of the relationship between aboriginal and non-aboriginal people in Canada. (Bourrie, 1998)

Phil Fontaine, leader the Assembly of First Nations, a coalition of nationwide aboriginal groups, said that the apology paves the way for lasting peace between Native peoples and the Canadian government. "This celebrates the beginning of a new era," Fontaine told Interpress Service. "It is a major step forward in our quest to be recognized as a distinct order of government in Canada" (Bourrie, 1998).

Some aboriginal leaders were not happy with the reconciliation statement. Representatives of Inuit, Native women's groups, and Metis said they did not believe the apology was strong enough. They were critical because the statement did not refer in more detail to the wrongs done to their communities. The same groups also maintained that the money involved in recompense was too little, too late. Inuit and Metis leaders, who are not included in the Assembly of First Nations, also complained that Stewart's later statements did not mention specific programs for them.

Stewart's statement sparked a retort in the Canadian *Financial Post* from columnist David Frum, who wrote, in part:

> Let the groveling begin.... The descendants of the Europeans have had the good taste never to demand a thank-you from the descendants of the

aboriginals. . . . But at the very least they are entitled to refuse to bow and scrape and abase themselves for the sin of having tamed and civilized this inhospitable land. (Hipwell, 1998, 18)

Frum's column, published January 13, 1998, drew several indignant letters to the editor, one of which was from Bill Hipwell, a lecturer in political geography at Ottawa's Carlton University. Instead of apologizing, Hipwell suggested, Euro-Canadians should thank Native peoples for several things, among them democratic ideas: "The civilizations of the Mi'kmaq and the Haudenosaunee (Iroquois) Confederacy [which] taught Europeans such basic principles as human rights. . . . Jefferson borrowed liberally from the Haudenosaunee political system" (1998, 18).

Other non-Indian Canadians complained that the surge of lawsuits for residential school abuse would clog the court system, bankrupt some religious denominations, and strain the Canadian federal budget, requiring new taxes. By the end of the year 2002, according to the Canadian government, more than 19,000 Native persons had entered some form of claim, a number equal to roughly 15 to 20 percent of the boarding schools' living alumni.. This legal backlog included four class action suits. Indian plaintiffs won all five boarding school abuse trials held during the late 1990s, two in Saskatchewan and three in British Columbia.

By early 1999, the Canadian federal government had paid out roughly $20 million worth of individual compensation, including awards to several victims of staff at the Gordon Reserve in Saskatchewan (which was run by the government without church affiliation). Late in 1998, the federal government and the Catholic Church also reached an out-of-court settlement with eleven men who were abused by Oblate priests while attending St. Joseph's residential school near Williams Lake, British Columbia, during the 1960s.

During late October 1998, the United Church of Canada, the country's largest Protestant body (including 3 million Presbyterians, Congregationalists, and Methodists) issued an apology for physical and sexual abuse meted out to Native students at boarding schools it had operated. The apology was made shortly after disclosure of evidence indicating that church officials knew of the abuse as early as 1960 and did nothing to stop it. Peter Grant, an attorney for former students at a British Columbia boarding school, had presented evidence indicating that the vice principal at the Port Alberni residential school was convicted of indecently assaulting male students between 1948 and 1968. Arthur Plint, who supervised the school's dormitories, pleaded guilty in 1995 to "dozens of sexual assaults," according to the Associated Press. He was sentenced to eleven years in prison. British Columbia Court Justice William Brenner ruled that both the federal government and the church were "vicariously responsible" for Plint's assaults on Native young people.

"I apologize for the pain and suffering that our church's involvement in the Indian residential school system has caused," the Rev. Bill Phipps, the church's chief executive (or moderator) told a news conference on October 27 (Associated Press, 1998). "We are aware of some of the damage that some of this cruel and ill-conceived system of assimilation has perpetuated on Canada's first nations," Phipps said. "We are truly and humbly sorry" (McIlroy, 1998, 5).

One of Grant's clients, Willy Blackwater, said that the church should be prepared to compensate abuse victims with money as well as words. Harry Daniels, president of the Congress of Aboriginal peoples, said "These things are nice to hear, but talk is cheap" (Associated Press, 1998). The Anglican and Roman Catholic churches of Canada expressed repentance for their role in boarding school abuses, but as of 2002 had not apologized, in part because they fear legal liability. The United Church seems to have decided that it will settle with litigants out of court.

The Royal Commission concluded the following:

> The terrible facts of the residential school system must be made a part of a new sense of what Canada has been and will continue to be for as long as that record is not officially recognized and repudiated. Only by such an act of recognition and repudiation can a start be made on a very different future. Canada and Canadians must realize that they need to consider changing their society so that they can discover ways of living in harmony with the original people of the land. (Royal Commission, 1996)

The Royal Commission called for a full investigation into Canada's residential school system "to bring to light and begin to heal the grievous harms suffered by countless Aboriginal children, families and communities as a result of the residential school system." Although not the forum the Royal Commission may have intended, such a public inquiry has begun to unfold, case by specific case, in many Canadian courtrooms. The economic stakes of boarding school compensation in Canada were reflected by the fact that, by late 2002, the Canadian federal government had reserved $1.7 billion to settle up to 18,000 native residential school lawsuits brought for physical and sexual abuse. The government was planning to require plaintiffs to waive rights to future litigation, including claims based on loss of language and culture.

The Anglican diocese of Caribou, British Columbia, during 2001 announced plans to close (to place its assets in trust) following a costly legal fight over compensation for victims of abuse at residential schools in which some of its ministers had a role. This is the first Canadian church to give up its corporate identity because of these claims. The churches in the small archdiocese will continue to operate, however. The diocese, which includes about 4,700 parishioners in British Columbia's interior, has legal bills totaling more than $350,000 from residential litigation according to the Canadian Broadcasting Corporation. After more than a decade of battling in court, it has paid out settlements to a small number of victims. All of the diocese's liquid assets have now been spent, according to officials.

ELK V. WILKINS *AS COUNTERPOINT TO ASSIMILATION*

During the same decade that the U.S. Congress sought to assimilate American Indians by requiring them to follow Anglo-American property-holding conventions and educational systems, the U.S. Supreme Court refused voting rights to a Native American who requested them. The Court held in *Elk v. Wilkins* that an American Indian is not a U.S. citizen under the Fourteenth Amendment to the U.S. Constitution. This position held even if the Indian is living apart from his nation or band.

At issue was the constitutional status of American Indians for purposes of citizenship and voting. The Fourteenth Amendment granted citizenship to "all persons born or naturalized in the United States, and subject to the jurisdiction of the United States." Did American Indians fall under this definition? A federal district court ruled that it did not apply to Indians who had not been "born subject to its jurisdiction—that is, in its power and obedience" (*McKay v. Campbell* 16 Fed. Cas. 161 [1871] [No. 8840]).

John Elk had been born outside U.S. jurisdiction but moved to Omaha as an adult and lived what the court described as a "civilized" life. He sought to become a citizen and to exercise the right to vote in Omaha elections during 1880. The Supreme Court ruled that the Fifteenth Amendment (which grants the right to vote to all persons regardless of race) did not apply in Elk's case because he was not born in an area under U.S. jurisdiction. Therefore, Elk was not a citizen within the meaning of the Fourteenth Amendment. The fact that Elk had abandoned his Indian relatives and style of life did not matter to the court. Elk's citizenship and voting rights were denied because the court held that an affirmative act was required of the United States before an Indian could become a citizen. The Supreme Court's opinion cited a dozen treaties, four court rulings, four laws, and eight opinions of the U.S. attorney general requiring "proof of fitness for civilization" as a precondition of granting Indians citizenship and voting rights.

Six years after John Elk's request for citizenship was denied, Congress passed the Indian Territory Naturalization Act (26 Stat. 81, 99–100), which allowed any Indian living in Indian Territory to apply for citizenship through the federal courts. The aim of this act was to break down communal loyalties among Native Americans in Indian Territory as it moved toward statehood as Oklahoma.

Thus, following the logic of *Elk v. Wilkins*, while federal courts were busy maintaining the plenary power of Congress over Indians, classifying Native Americans as wards of the federal government, and denying an international dimension to their political existence, individual Native Americans seeking to exercise constitutional rights were being told that they were, in effect, no more than the children of foreign subjects.

At a time when federal policy accentuated the dominance of European heritage, some Native Americans became well known for crossing cultural lines. Two examples were Arthur Parker, a Seneca who became notable in the world of museums, and the Kansa and Osage Charles Curtis, who served as a congressman and U.S. vice president in the administration of Herbert Hoover.

Arthur C. Parker: A Seneca Museum Curator

Some Native Americans adapted to the dominant society by becoming professionally proficient in lines of work, such as museum curating, that acted as gateways to the society's experience with indigenous peoples and cultures. One example was Arthur C. Parker (Gawasowaneh), a Seneca, who brought the word *museologist* into the English language. Joy Porter's *To Be Indian* (2001) was the first full-scale biography of Parker, long-time curator at the Rochester Municipal Museum, later known as the Rochester Museum and Science Center. Porter is a senior lecturer in American history at Anglia Polytechnic University in Cambridge, England.

Porter brings Parker to life:

> Although not tall, at perhaps five feet six inches, he cut a dignified figure in his smart clothes with his dark hair and hazel eyes winking out from under his trademark fedora. Some thought he looked quintessentially "Indian"; others thought of him as "white." However they encountered him, people seemed to have warmed to Parker because of his skill at putting them at ease. A lover of puns and word games, he was friendly, with a charming sense of humor. (2001, xvii)

Parker was best known as a museum director, but he also was a prolific writer, with roughly 500 pieces that ranged from books to journal and magazine articles (published and not), radio scripts, plays, and others. Porter's (2001) portrait of Parker is richly detailed, delineating a man walking the cusp of Indian and non-Indian worlds (he was one-fourth Seneca), a person always acutely aware of the interplay between the two. He was both a thirty-third degree Freemason as well as an adopted member of the Seneca Bear Clan.

Porter described a man who was intensely aware of prevailing ideological winds, with special attention throughout much of his life to a eugenic point of view that went severely out of intellectual fashion after Hitler's Nazis took its tenets to especially cruel extremes between 1933 and 1945. Before the Meriam Report (Meriam, 1928) and the Indian Reorganization Act (1934), Parker voiced doubts that Native Americans could maintain their cultural identity in the midst of popular demands for a breakdown of reservation land bases (through the Allotment Acts and other measures) and suffocating policies of assimilation.

As Parker sometimes favored restrictions on immigration to reduce the proportion of the "less fit," Porter wrote that he was "simply following a fashion" (2001, 30). After all, Porter wrote, Woodrow Wilson and George Eastman (of the Eastman-Kodak fortune) made similar statements. Later in the book, however, Porter raised doubts as to whether even the sterilization of 2 million defectives by the Nazis provoked Parker to "begin a fundamental reassessment of his deeply held assumptions about 'race' and human development" (ibid., 215). Until his retirement in 1946, after World War II had ended, Parker continued to "mull them over in print" (ibid., 215). At one point, Porter quoted Parker as having argued for "the preservation of racial type—that of the Aryan white man." He held forth against "indiscriminate blood-blending and inharmonious race contacts." At roughly the same time, circa 1920, Parker, according to Porter, "accepted a new imperative— white cultural and racial perpetuation" (ibid., 137).

Within a decade, however, the intellectual wind had begun to shift, and Parker started to shift with it. Native self-determination and preservation of identity became fashionable by the 1930s. Parker ended his professional life best known for popular innovation in museums, which he called "the university of the common man." On his death in 1955, Parker was recalled very warmly by Ray Fadden, who wrote to Martha Parker that "the Chief," as he often was called, "was a great person, desiring nothing for himself, and ever ready to do good for everyone, no matter who" (Porter, 2001, 241). Obscuring his earlier doubts about Native American cultural survival and his eugenic ruminations, Parker's affectionate personality won out in the end—a tribute to his essential humanity.

Charles Curtis: A Native American U.S. Vice President

At the same time that assimilation became the dominant ideology in Indian affairs, a Native American served as U.S. vice president. As a Republican politician, Charles Curtis (1860–1936), Kansa and Osage, also served as a member of the U.S. House of Representatives and as a U.S. senator. Curtis became a leading spokesperson for some assimilationist measures, including the General Allotment Act.

Born on Indian land that later was incorporated into North Topeka, Kansas, Curtis was the son of Oren A. Curtis (an abolitionist and Civil War Union cavalry officer) and Helen Pappan (Kaw/Osage). His mother died when he was three, and he was raised under the care of his maternal grandmother on the Kaw Reservation and in Topeka. Following an attack on Kaw Indians at Council Grove by Cheyenne militants, Curtis (who was one-eighth Indian) left the Indian mission school on the Kaw Reservation in 1868 and returned to Topeka, where he attended Topeka High School. For several years as a young man, he was a jockey and worked odd jobs until he met A. H. Case, a Topeka lawyer. Studying the law and working as a law clerk, Curtis was admitted to the Kansas bar in 1881.

Entering politics, Curtis was elected county prosecuting attorney in 1884 and 1886. From 1892 to 1906, he served eight terms in the U.S. House of Representatives. He authored the Curtis Act of 1898, which dissolved tribal governments and permitted the institution of civil government within the

Indian Territory, later Oklahoma. The Curtis Act, which attempted to force assimilation on American Indian peoples, brought the allotment policy to the Five Civilized Tribes of Oklahoma, who previously had been exempted from the initial Allotment Act. In essence, the Curtis Act paved the way for Oklahoma statehood in 1907 by destroying tribal land titles and governments.

Curtis served in the U.S. Senate from 1907 to 1913 (he was the first U.S. senator of American Indian ancestry) and 1915 to 1929. During his tenure in the Senate, Curtis was Republican party whip (1915–1924) and then majority leader (1924–1929). As chair of the Senate Committee on Indian Affairs in 1924, Curtis sponsored the Indian Citizenship Act. After an unsuccessful campaign for the presidential nomination, he ran as vice president with Herbert Hoover in 1928. He served as vice president from 1929 to 1933. Curtis was a deft politician who used his Indian background for personal advantage, even though his political adversaries called him "the Injun." Although a fiscal conservative, he supported veterans' benefits, farm relief, women's suffrage, and national prohibition.

The Hoover-Curtis ticket's bid for a second term was defeated in 1932 by Franklin Delano Roosevelt. On his retirement from politics in 1933, Curtis had served longer in the nation's Capitol than any active politician at that time. After leaving public office, Curtis headed the short-lived National Republican League and practiced law in Washington, D.C. He was also president of a gold mining company in New Mexico. In 1936, Curtis died of heart disease.

DESKAHEH OPPOSES ASSIMILATION

Assimilative policies were vigorously opposed by some important Native leaders. One example was Deskaheh (Levi General, Cayuga, 1873–1925), who was Tadadaho (speaker) of the Iroquois Grand Council at Grand River, Ontario, in the early 1920s, when Canadian authorities closed the traditional longhouse, which had been asserting independence from Canadian jurisdiction. Canadian authorities proposed to set up a governmental structure that would answer to its Indian affairs bureaucracy. With Canadian police about to arrest him, Deskaheh traveled to the headquarters of the League of Nations in Geneva, Switzerland, with an appeal for support from the international community.

Several months of effort did not win Deskaheh a hearing before the international body, in large part because of diplomatic manipulation by Great Britain and Canada, governments that were embarrassed by Deskaheh's mission. Lacking a forum at the League of Nations, Deskaheh and his supporters organized a privately organized meeting in Switzerland that drew several thousand people, who roared approval of Iroquois sovereignty.

In his last speech, March 10, 1925, Deskaheh had lost none of this distaste for forced acculturation. "Over in Ottawa, they call that policy 'Indian Advancement,'" he said. "Over in Washington, they call it 'Assimilation.' We who would be the helpless victims say it is tyranny.... If this must go on to

Deskaheh (Levi General). (Courtesy of John Kahionhes Fadden.)

the bitter end, we would rather that you come with your guns and poison gas and get rid of us that way. Do it openly and above board" (Johansen and Grinde, 1997, 111).

As he lay dying, relatives of Deskaheh who lived in the United States were refused entry into Canada to be at his bedside. Deskaheh died two-and-a-half months after his last defiant speech.

THE NATIVE AMERICAN CHURCH'S RESPONSE TO OPPRESSION

One of the most effective responses to the severe repression of Native peoples and cultures at the turn of the century was religious. After the Ghost

Dance played a role in the massacre at Wounded Knee, most practice of Native American religions went underground. There was no more showing of ghost shirts to be shot at by the cavalry. The Native American Church is historically important not only because it took native culture underground (and therefore revived forms of community that were being lost to assimilation), but also because it was an early example of a successful pan-Indian movement. Like the religion begun by the Iroquois Handsome Lake a century earlier, the Native American Church sought native members only and sometimes carried the air of a secret society, especially in the eyes on non-Indians. Both religions rejected aspects of European culture that had proved particularly harmful to American Native people, especially alcohol. Both religions mixed Native belief and custom with some aspects of Christianity. Both continue to attract adherents today.

The secrecy of the Native American Church (at least to European American eyes) caused some non-Indian observers to cry "paganism." The practice that brought down the wrath of non-Indians on the church's members was their use of peyote. Chewing peyote produces mild hallucinations; in the early years of the Native American Church, members took peyote to aid meditation. The so-called peyote cult arose in Mexico and spread among the Apaches and Comanches during the 1870s. After the decline of the Ghost Dance religion in the 1890s, peyotism swept over the plains and prairies in the central part of North America. The Native American Church itself was founded in 1918. By 1955, people associated with roughly eighty Native tribes and nations practiced some form of peyotism (Olson and Wilson, 1984, 90). Peyote was used as a religious sacrament and to blunt the pain and alienation of reservation life at its worst.

Some of the opposition to peyotism came from nonpracticing Native Americans. In 1940, the Navajo Tribal Council, dominated by Christians, outlawed the use of peyote. The Taos Pueblos, White Mountain Apaches, and several Sioux communities passed laws forbidding its use. Many of these were enacted at the behest of traditionalists, who saw the Native American Church as a threat to existing tribal religions. The territorial legislature of Oklahoma outlawed peyote's use outside Indian Territory in 1898. By 1923, fourteen states had banned use of peyote. Customs agents began seizing peyote crossing the border from Mexico. In 1940, Congress outlawed the shipment of peyote through the mail. The BIA tried, but failed, to enact laws to ban the use of peyote nationwide. Not enough non-Indians used peyote to fuel a good drug scare. By the 1990s, with legal protection of Native American religious practice in place, the use of peyote in religious ritual was legalized.

THE INDIAN CITIZENSHIP ACT (1924)

At the same time that Deskaheh was attempting to present the Iroquois case before the League of Nations, citizenship in the United States was extended to all Native Americans in the Citizenship Act of 1924. This was only four decades after the Supreme Court, in *Elk v. Wilkins* (1884), had denied the petition of an individual Indian for the same rights. Ironically, citizenship had been offered to some tribes as early as 1850, sometimes on condition that their lands be allotted to private ownership.

The granting of U.S. citizenship dovetailed with the abolition of Native national autonomy. Although citizenship for all Native Americans was not legislated until 1924, many Native people had been made citizens (often without their consent) decades earlier. By 1924, two-thirds of American Indians had been extended citizenship piecemeal. Citizenship was extended to individual Native persons when their land was allotted. In 1888, a year after passing the Allotment Act, Congress made Native people who married U.S. citizens eligible for citizenship. In 1890, as Oklahoma moved toward statehood, reservation residents in Indian Territory were offered citizenship if they applied to federal courts. In 1919, an act of Congress extended citizenship to Native American veterans of World War I. In 1901, Congress extended citizenship rights to all Native people living in what was then called Indian Territory.

Many Native people refused citizenship (or did their best to avoid it), especially after it was tied to the loss of communal land through allotment. Citizenship was to begin after the allotted land had been held in trust for 25 years. Some Native peoples have rejected citizenship, notably members of the Haudenosaunee (Iroquois) Confederacy and other Native people in New York State. During World War II, the Iroquois made a point of their sovereignty by declaring war on the Axis powers independent of the United States. Even today, many Iroquois abstain from voting in state and national elections, and a number have refused to pay income taxes. Some of the six Iroquois nations (Mohawk, Oneida, Onondaga, Tuscarora, Cayuga, and Seneca) issue their own vehicle license plates, as do several other Native American nations. The Iroquois Confederacy at Onondaga goes one step further: It sends diplomats to other countries with their own passports.

THE MERIAM REPORT (1928): A REPUDIATION OF ALLOTMENT

Shortly after 1920, a wave of sympathy emerged in response to the cruelties imposed on Native Americans during the nadir of the reservation era. This wave of political opinion produced the Meriam Report (Meriam, 1928), which documented the horrid condition of human health and welfare under the BIA's "wardship."

The Meriam Report also brought the argument on allotment full circle: from alleged harbinger of a new American Indian future, to the dismal, culturally destructive real estate agency it had become. The report laid the intellectual and political basis for the revolution that John Collier wrought in Indian Affairs during the early 1930s. The Meriam Report came to be widely regarded as the most important indictment of the BIA since Helen Hunt Jackson's *A Century of Dishonor* (1881). Although *A Century of Dishonor* was used to advance the merits of allotment, the Meriam Report became a political tool to repudiate it.

By 1923, an organized committee of influential Indians and non-Indians, the Committee of One Hundred, was lobbying for more respectful and humane treatment of Native Americans. Collier was an early member, with William Jennings Bryan, Clark Wissler, General John J. Pershing, Bernard Baruch, William Allen White, and the Seneca Arthur C. Parker. Parker was elected presiding officer at a convention in Washington, D.C., during December 1923. Under his aegis, in 1924 the group published its findings under the title *The Indian Problem* (Otis, 1924). This document formed the basis for the better-known Meriam Report four years later.

The Meriam Report was an exhaustive, 870-page narrative and statistical portrait of Native American life at a time sometimes called the era of the vanishing race. It covered health, education, economic conditions, legal aspects, and missionary activities, among others. The Meriam Report found generally that the government was failing miserably at its professed goal of protecting Indians, their land, and resources. Of the Allotment Act (1887), the report said the following:

> When the government adopted the policy of individual ownership of the land on the reservations, the expectation was that the Indians would become farmers.... It almost seems as if the government assumed that some magic in individual ownership of property would in itself prove an educational civilizing factor, but unfortunately this policy has for the most part operated in the opposite direction. (Meriam, 1928, 7)

The Meriam Report provided graphic evidence of just how badly the federal government's Indian wards were being treated. Infant mortality on Indian reservations, for example, was nearly three times that of European-descended Americans generally. Large numbers of Indians were dying from tuberculosis, trachoma, measles, and other diseases that had been largely eradicated in mainstream society. In this sea of disease, health services on reservations were ill-equipped and lacking sufficient trained staff. Diets heavy on cheap, government-issued carbohydrates were producing malnutrition in people who often were otherwise overweight. The government provided 11 cents a day to feed students at its boarding schools and skimped on equipment and salaries for teachers. Schools often were unsanitary. Per capita income for native reservation residents was less than $200 a year at a time when national average earnings were $1,350. All of this contributed to an average life span among Indians of 44 years.

According to the Meriam Report, the essential Indian problem was poverty caused by the fact that the U.S. government had done little to replace traditional Native economies with self-sustaining structures that could provide Indians a livelihood. The report found that forced assimilation did little to improve Indians' economic conditions; many of its recommendations, such as an end to allotment, were essentially rearguard actions meant to ameliorate problems caused by forced assimilation during the previous century.

Belief that government should address its mistakes regarding Indian affairs became a popular political theme after the release of the Meriam Report. Even before John Collier (who had been accused of communist tendencies during the "red scare" of the early 1920s) became Indian commissioner, a liberal tendency was evident under the otherwise conservative presidency of Herbert Hoover. Hoover brought Ray Lyman from the presidency of Stanford University to become secretary of interior. Hoover also chose Charles J. Rhoades, a devout Quaker, as commissioner of Indian Affairs. Rhoades enjoyed little success in his efforts to reform the federal bureaucracy to implement the Meriam Report. More fundamental reforms would have to wait until the presidency of Franklin D. Roosevelt and his appointment of John Collier as commissioner of Indian Affairs.

JOHN COLLIER'S BUREAU OF INDIAN AFFAIRS

John Collier filled the post of Indian commissioner for nearly the entire length of Franklin Roosevelt's presidency, twelve years, more time than any other person. His policies initiated a Native resurgence to some degree. Some land was added to the Native estate, reversing a U.S. trend of a century and a half. Although he was reviled frequently for favoring Native communalism over assimilation, Collier also encountered considerable criticism from Native people for ignoring their traditional systems of governance. He recognized that Native cultures and land bases should be maintained but thought that they ought to exist subject to the government's rules. The result of this synthesis was the Indian Reorganization Act (IRA), passed by Congress and signed into law by President Roosevelt during 1934. Mixing liberalism with bureaucratic prerogative, the IRA offered Native people a measure of self-government but demanded that those governments be created and conducted by its rules.

The IRA was the most fundamental and far-reaching piece of legislation relating to Native Americans passed by Congress during the first half of the twentieth century. The IRA eliminated the allotment system and established Native American governments for some reservations under systems that were partially self-governing. The IRA also established hiring preferences for Native Americans within the BIA. Although it was criticized by some Native American groups, some of the IRA's changes also were widely acclaimed at the time of its origins. For example, Native peoples were allowed by this act to resume their ceremonies openly, after a half-century of repression.

Before passage of the IRA, Native tribes and nations had been operated more or less as colonial enclaves by the United States. They were legally held to be subject to Congress and the president, delegated through the BIA. According to legal scholars Russel Barsh and James Henderson, "No local laws or assemblies were recognized, and a special police force was established to maintain federal supremacy. Traditional leadership was deposed, prosecuted, and sometimes killed when in conflict with federal Indian policy" (1980, 209). Under the IRA, colonialism was relaxed somewhat. Leaders were no longer appointed but were elected under constitutions that themselves were subject to U.S. government veto. In many cases, even individual ordinances passed by councils were subject to Interior Department review.

The IRA was introduced by Representative Edgar Howard of Nebraska and Senator Burton K. Wheeler of Montana and became known popularly as the Wheeler-Howard Act. The initial drafts of the fifty-page bill were the work mainly of John Collier, whom Roosevelt had appointed commissioner of Indian affairs. Before its provisions were modified during debates in the House and Senate, the IRA declared a federal policy that American Indians be encouraged to establish and control their own governments. Another part of Collier's draft required Indian schools to develop materials relevant to Native American histories and cultures. The third version of the original bill stopped allotment of Indian land and restored title to surplus lands still held by the government, as well as created reservations for Native American groups left without land by the usurpation of the previous century. Collier's bill also called for a Court of Indian Affairs. After compromise in the legislative process, many of Collier's ideas were discarded. Even so, the IRA established a new framework for Indian affairs, a hybrid of Collier's ideas and the older paternalistic system.

Native nations and tribes were given two years after the passage of the IRA to accept or reject its provisions. Within that period, 258 elections were held, with 181 Native groups accepting the terms of the IRA and 77 voting negatively. Some of those who rejected the IRA objected to its requirements that the federal government approve policies on land use, selection of legal counsel, and other matters (including constitutions). Although the act rhetorically upheld Native self-determination, it imposed a federal veto power over most major (and many minor) decisions that each Native government had proposed.

Frank Fools Crow, a Sioux, described the effects of the Indian New Deal in this way: "Being beaten in war was bad enough. Yet being defeated and placed in bondage by programs we could not understand ... is worse, especially when it is done to one of the most powerful, independent, and proudest of the Indian nations of North America" (Mails, 1990, 146–147). Fools Crow believed that, for the Sioux people, the "years from 1930–1940 rank as the worst ten years I know of." Fools Crow stated that the traditional family structure was crumbling because of the following:

> Individual independence and ... irresponsibility was being encouraged among the young people. Bootleggers were after the Indian's money, and were hauling

cheap wine and whiskey onto the reservation by the truckload.... Even the young women were drinking now, and this assured a future tragedy of the worst possible proportions. (ibid., 146–147)

California was a major center of opposition to Collier's Indian New Deal. One of the principal leaders of this opposition was Rupert Costo, a young Cahuilla who had attended college and had the respect of his people. Costo believed that the Indian New Deal was a "great drive to assimilate the American Indian." Costo felt that the IRA was a program to colonize Indians because, in his view, genocide, treaty-making and treaty-breaking, substandard education, disruption of Indian culture and religion, and the Dawes Allotment Act had failed. Costo knew that partial assimilation already had taken place in native societies through the use of "certain technologies and techniques," but he knew that total assimilation which meant "fading into the general society with a complete loss of" culture and identity was another thing altogether. Costo called the IRA the Indian Raw Deal (Mails, 1990, 146).

By 1940, the IRA had come under enough criticism to prompt congressional hearings to consider its repeal. As of that date, according to Indian law scholar Lawrence C. Kelly, 252 Indian nations and bands had voted on the IRA as required by the act, including 99 small bands in California with a total population of less than 25,000. Seventy-eight groups had rejected it. Nationwide, 38,000 Indians voted in favor of IRA governments; 24,000 voted against. Another 35,000 eligible voters did not take part, most as a silent protest against the IRA.

THE INDIAN CLAIMS COMMISSION

The Meriam Report emphasized that no long-term solution of the Indian problem could occur without establishment of a commission to adjudicate compensation for outstanding land claims. Several legislative attempts to create such a body were made without success during the late 1920s and 1930s. After World War II, however, the United States was facing pressure regarding treatment of minorities at home after having criticized the human rights records of the Axis powers during the war. As a result, the Indian Claims Commission (ICC) was established by Congress in 1946.

By that time, much of the impetus of the Indian New Deal had ended, but the creation of the ICC in that year represented the final reform measure of the era. Before the enactment of the ICC, Native American nations were required to obtain the consent of Congress through special legislation to sue the federal government for violations of treaties and agreements. The Indian Claims Commission Act created a three-person commission to hear and determine claims existing prior to the bill's passage. The Congress felt that the ICC was to be part of a process that would enable to Native American groups to become autonomous.

A special tribunal was required to settle Indian claims because claims based on violation of Indian treaties had been barred from the jurisdiction of the general U.S. Court of Claims in 1863. Absent special congressional action, Indians in effect had no forum under U.S. law in which to present their claims until the Indian Claims Commission Act was passed in 1946. Under the act, suits were allowed by tribes, bands, or other "identifiable" groups of Native peoples. Appeals were permitted to the general Court of Claims and, via *certiorari*, to the U.S. Supreme Court. The Indian Claims Commission Act consolidated federal legal actions related to Indian claims for illegal taking of land, which heretofore had been dealt with through 142 different statutes. Congress created the ICC in an effort to extinguish all outstanding claims.

The ICC expired in 1978, at which time the 102 cases remaining on its docket were transferred to the U.S. Court of Claims. Between 1945 and 1975, the commission awarded $534 million to Indian claimants, $53 million of which was paid in attorney's fees. In all, the commission docketed 605 individual claims cases, nearly half of which resulted in monetary awards. The commission had originally been created for five years, but the volume of cases and the complexity of the commission's proceedings caused its bureaucratic life to be extended four times. Even so, when jurisdiction was transferred by Congress to the general Court of Claims, only 40 percent of the petitions filed had been adjudicated. The claims that were settled were paid conservatively, with land usually being valued at its cost when it was taken, usually in the late nineteenth century, without the benefit of several decades of increasing prices and land values. Many of the settlements amounted to less than $1 per acre.

THE 1950S: RELOCATION AND TERMINATION

By the 1950s, the economic rationale of allotment had become obsolete. The myth of the yeoman farmer had dissolved into the reality of large-scale, global agribusiness. Most Americans lived and worked in cities. Advocates of termination and relocation saw themselves generally as modernists and realists, promoting the eradication of Native land, identity, and lifeways for the Natives' own good to ease their transition into a modern industrial economy—the benign, all-knowing hand forever shaping the soft underside of conquest.

Between 1954 and 1966, Congress passed legislation terminating federal recognition and services to 109 Native American nations and bands. Some of them disappeared as organized communities. Their members moved to other places, particularly cities, where the BIA, through its "relocation" program, was busily shuttling Native Americans from reservations to cities. Some of the children of relocation would return to haunt the BIA as members of the self-determination generation of the 1960s and 1970s—a crisp contradiction of the belief that the hand of BIA paternalism would stir the last of Indian identity into the vast American urban melting pot.

Political momentum toward termination was accelerating as Dwight Eisenhower assumed the presidency in 1952. Eisenhower appointed Glenn L. Emmons, a supporter of Watkins's termination legislation, as commissioner of Indian affairs. Between 1953 and 1962, Congress passed legislation terminating federal recognition and services to 60 native nations and tribes.

Congress sometimes held up land claims payments until the Native tribe or nation in question also agreed to termination proceedings, thereby obliterating both past and present land bases. In 1963, for example, the Claims Commission awarded the Kalispels $3 million, an award that was held by Congress (under legislation passed at the behest of Idaho Senator Frank Church) until they agreed to termination. Sometimes, the pitch was different, but no less subtle. The Klamaths, holding title to a million acres of prime timber in Oregon, were enticed into terminating after BIA agents promised them per capita payments of $50,000. Only afterward did the Klamaths learn painfully that "going private" can be expensive. They found themselves paying rent, utilities, health care costs, and taxes they had never faced.

The Menominees of Wisconsin shared ownership of property valued at $34 million when their termination bill was enacted in 1953. By 1961, the federal government was out of Menominee Country, and each member of the former tribe had become the owner of 100 shares of stock and a negotiable bond valued at $3,000, issued in the name of Menominee Enterprises Incorporated (MEI), a private company that held the former tribe's land and businesses. Governmentally, the Menominee Nation had become Menominee County, the smallest (in terms of population) and poorest (in terms of cash income) in Wisconsin.

As a county, Menominee had to raise taxes to pay for its share of services, including welfare, health services, utilities, and the like. The only taxable property owner in the county was MEI, which was forced to raise the funds to pay its tax bill by restructuring so that stockholders had to buy their homes and the property on which they had been built. Most of the Menominees had little savings except for their $3,000 bonds, which were then sold to MEI to make the required residential purchases. Many Menominees faced private sector health costs, property taxes, and other expenses with no more money than they had possessed before termination. Unemployment rose to levels that most of the United States had known only during the Depression of the 1930s. By 1965, health indicators in Menominee County sounded like a reprint of the Meriam Report almost four decades earlier. Tuberculosis afflicted nearly 35 percent of the population, and infant mortality was three times the national average. Termination, like allotment, had been an abject failure at anything other than alienating Indian land.

One of the major opponents of relocation (and other assimilationist policies) was Felix Cohen (1907–1953), the author of *The Handbook of Indian Law* (1942), a basic reference book of the field for decades. He also was a student of Native American societies and a social critic, as well as a defender of Native

American estate as associate solicitor in the Interior Department. Cohen was a professor of law at the City University of New York and Yale.

Many of termination's opponents were Native American traditionalists, who believed that distinct cultures and land bases should be maintained. During the renaissance of native activism in the 1960s, they were joined in this effort by the young, urbanized children of an earlier generation that had made its own long marches, one by one or family by family, from their homelands to the cities at the behest of the BIA. Between 1953 and 1972, more than 100,000 Native Americans moved to urban areas; by 1980, about half of the Native Americans in the United States lived in cities. Young Native Americans raised in urban areas in the 1960s began to reverse relocation's effects. By the 1970s, many young urban Indians, often veterans of the Vietnam War who had served terms in state and federal prisons, were returning to the reservations.

FURTHER READING

Adams et al. v. Osage Tribe of Indians et al. No. 642 District Court N. D. Oklahoma 50 F. 2d 918, 1931 U.S. Dist.

Archuleta, Margaret L., Brenda J. Child, and K. Tsianina Lomawaima, eds. *Away from Home: American Indian Boarding School Experiences, 1879–2000.* Phoenix: Heard Museum, 2000.

Associated Press. *Omaha World-Herald,* December 9, 1991, 16.

Associated Press Canada. Canada's United Church Apologizes for Abuse at Indian Schools. October 28, 1998.

Barsh, Russel, and James Henderson. *The Road: Indian Tribes and Political Liberty.* Berkeley: University of California Press, 1980.

Bourrie, Mark. Canada Apologizes For Abuse of Native Peoples. Interpress Service, January 8, 1998. Available at http://www.oneworld.org/ips2/jan98/canada2.html.

British Columbia Anglican Diocese Set To Close over Lawsuit. Canadian Broadcasting Corporation News On-line, December 30, 2001. Available at http://cbc.ca/cgi-bin/view?/news/2001/12/30/anglican_011230.

Cohen, Felix. *The Handbook of Indian Law.* Washington, DC: U.S. Government Printing Office, 1942.

Cohen, Felix. *The Legal Conscience: The Selected Papers of Felix S. Cohen.* Edited by Lucy Kramer Cohen. New Haven, CT: Yale University Press, 1960.

Coulter, Robert T., and Steven M. Tullberg. Indian Land Rights, In Sandra L. Cadwallader and Vine Deloria, Jr., eds., *The Aggressions of Civilization.* Philadelphia: Temple University Press, 1984: 185–214.

Deloria, Vine, Jr., and Clifford Lytle. *American Indians, American Justice.* Austin: University of Texas Press, 1983.

Deskaheh (Levi General) and Six Nations Council. *The Redman's Appeal for Justice.* Brantford, Ontario, Canada: Wilson Moore, 1924.

Driver, Harold E. *Indians of North America.* 2nd ed. Chicago: University of Chicago Press, 1969.

Elk v. Wilkins. 112 U.S. 94 (1884).

Fadden, Ray, and John Kahionhes Fadden. *Deskaheh: Iroquois Statesman and Patriot.* Six Nations Indian Museum Series. Akwesasne, NY: Akwesasne Notes, n.d.

Havighurst, Robert J., and Thea R. Hilkevitch. The Intelligence of Indian Children as Measured by a Performance Scale. *Journal of Abnormal and Social Psychology* 39(1944):419–433.

Hendrix, Janey B. Redbird Smith and the Nighthawk Keetoowahs. *Journal of Cherokee Studies* 8:1(1983):17–33.

Hipwell, Bill. Apology Should Have Been a Thank You. *The Financial Post* [Ottawa, Ontario], February 3, 1998, 18.

Jackson, Helen Hunt. *A Century of Dishonor: A Sketch of the United States Government's Dealings with Some of the Indian Tribes.* New York: Harper and Brothers, 1881.

Jackson, Helen Hunt. *Ramona.* Boston: Roberts Brothers, 1884.

Johansen, Bruce E. The BIA as Banker: Trust Is Hard when Billions Disappear. *Native Americas* 14:1(Spring 1997):14–23.

Johansen, Bruce E. *The Encyclopedia of Native American Legal Tradition.* Westport, CT: Greenwood Press, 1998.

Johansen, Bruce E. "Education—The Nightmare and the Dream: A Shared National Tragedy, a Shared National Disgrace." *Native Americas* 17:4(Winter 2000):10–19.

Johansen, Bruce E., and Donald A. Grinde, Jr. *The Encyclopedia of Native American Biography.* New York: Henry Holt, 1997.

Josephy, Alvin M., Jr. Modern America and the Indian. In Frederick E. Hoxie, ed., *Indians in American History: An Introduction.* Arlington Heights, IL: Harlan Davidson, 1988: 251–272.

Kelly, Lawrence C. The Indian Reorganization Act: The Dream and the Reality. *Pacific Historical Quarterly* 64(August 1975):291–312.

Kelly, Lawrence C. *The Assault on Assimilation: John Collier and the Origins of the Indian Reorganization Act.* Tucson: University of Arizona Press, 1983.

Levitan, Sar A. *Big Brother's Indian Programs—with Reservations.* New York: McGraw-Hill, 1971.

Lowey, Mark. Alberta Natives Sue Over Residential Schools. *Calgary Herald*, January 3, 1999, A-1.

Mails, Thomas E. *Fools Crow.* Lincoln: University of Nebraska Press, 1990.

McKay v. Campbell. 16 Fed. Cas. 161 (1871) (No. 8840).

McIlroy, Anne. Canadians Apologize for Abuse. *Manchester Guardian Weekly*, November 8, 1998, 5.

McLaughlin, Michael R. The Dawes Act, or Indian General Allotment Act of 1887: The Continuing Burden of Allotment. *American Indian Culture and Research Journal* 20:2(1996):59–105.

McNickle, D'Arcy. *They Came Here First: The Epic of the American Indian.* New York: Harper Perennial Library, 1975.

Meriam, Lewis. *The Problem of Indian Administration.* Baltimore: John Hopkins University Press, 1928.

Morgan, Lewis Henry. *League of the Iroquois.* Seacaucus, NJ: Citadel Press, [1851] 1962.

Morgan, Lewis Henry. *Houses and House-Life of the American Aborigines.* Edited by Paul Bohannon. Chicago: University of Chicago Press, 1965.

Morris, Roy, Jr. *Sheridan: The Life and Wars of General Phil Sheridan*. New York: Crown, 1992.

National Resources Board, Land Planning Committee. *Indian Land Tenure, Economic Status, and Population Trends*. Washington, DC: Government Printing Office, 1935.

O'Brien, Sharon. *American Indian Tribal Governments*. Norman: University of Oklahoma Press, 1989.

Olson, James S., and Raymond Wilson. *Native Americans in the Twentieth Century*. Urbana: University of Illinois Press, 1984.

Orwell, George. *1984*. London: Secker & Warburg, 1949.

Otis, Joseph E. *The Indian Problem: Resolution of the Committee of One Hundred Appointed by the Secretary of the Interior and a Review of the Indian Problem*. Washington, DC: U.S. Government Printing Office, 1924.

Parman, Donald L. *The Navajos and the New Deal*. New Haven, CT: Yale University Press, 1976.

Philip, Kenneth R. *John Collier's Crusade for Indian Reform, 1920–1954*. Tucson: University of Arizona Press, 1977.

Porter, Joy. *To Be Indian: The Life of Iroquois-Seneca Arthur Caswell Parker*. Norman: University of Oklahoma Press, 2001.

Pratt, William Henry. *Battlefield and Classroom: Four Decades with the American Indian, 1867–1904*. Edited by Robert M. Utley. Lincoln: University of Nebraska Press, [1964] 1987.

Prucha, Francis P. *Documents of United States Indian Policy*. Lincoln: University of Nebraska Press, 1975.

Resek, Carl. *Lewis Henry Morgan: American Scholar*. Chicago: University of Chicago Press, 1960.

Rostkowski, Joelle. The Redman's Appeal for Justice: Deskaheh and the League of Nations. In Christian F. Feest, ed., *Indians and Europe*. Aachen, Germany: Edition Herodot, 1987.

Royal Commission on Aboriginal Peoples. Vol. 1, chapter 10, 1996. Available at http://www.prsp.bc.ca/vol1ch10_files/Vol1%20Ch10.rtf. Accessed February 25, 2003.

Russell, Don. *The Lives and Legends of Buffalo Bill*. Norman: University of Oklahoma Press, 1960.

Sell, Henry B., and Victor Weybright. *Buffalo Bill and the Wild West*. New York: Oxford University Press, 1955.

Snake, Reuben. Personal interview with Bruce E. Johansen, in Seattle, WA, October 12, 1991.

Standing Bear, Luther. *My Indian Boyhood*. Lincoln: University of Nebraska Press, [1931] 1988.

Stannard, David. *American Holocaust: Columbus and the Conquest of the New World*. New York: Oxford University Press, 1992.

Thorpe, James, and Thomas F. Collinson. *Jim Thorpe's History of the Olympics*. Los Angeles, 1932.

Todd, Douglas. Natives' Abuse Suits Creating a Dilemma. *Vancouver Sun*, December 15, 1998, A-1.

Turtle Island Native Network. British Columbia Residential School Project. No date. Available at http://www.turtleisland.org/healing/infopack1a.htm.

United States v. Stanolind Crude Oil Purchasing Company; United States v. Gulf Oil Corporation; United States v. Sinclair Prairie Oil Company. 113 F. 2d 194 (10th Cir. 1940).

Waldman, Carl. *Who Was Who in Native American History*. New York: Facts on File, 1990.

Washburn, Wilcomb. *The Assault on Indian Tribalism: The General Allotment Law (Dawes Act) of 1887*. Philadelphia: J. B. Lippincott, 1975.

Weeks, Philip. *Farewell My Nation: The American Indian and the United States, 1820–1890*. Arlington Heights, IL: Harlan Davidson, 1990.

Wilkinson, Charles F. *American Indians, Time, and the Law: Native Societies in a Modern Constitutional Democracy*. New Haven, CT: Yale University Press, 1987.

Wilson, Terry P. *The Underground Reservation: Osage Oil*. Lincoln: University of Nebraska Press, 1985.

Worcester v. Georgia. 31 U.S. (6 Pet.) 515 (1832).

.

CHAPTER 9

A People's Revival—1961 to 1990

NATIVE SELF-DETERMINATION

In 1961, Native American voices of protest were raised at the American Indian Chicago Conference, which brought together more than 500 Native people from more than sixty groups. This conference was the opening salvo for a decade-plus wave of Native activism that would change the legal, social, and economic face of Native America. It was organized at the behest of President John F. Kennedy by Sol Tax, professor of anthropology at the University of Chicago, as a forum to enable Native peoples to express their views regarding their own futures. This gathering helped to ignite a social and political movement among many Native Americans that had an influence on later, better-known events. Also during 1961, a group of young, college-educated American Indians formed the National Indian Youth Council (NIYC). This organization had deep roots in impoverished, traditional Indian communities.

By 1964, the first modern civil disobedience by Native Americans was taking place on Puget Sound salmon streams as Indian "fish-ins" dramatized Native assertion of treaty rights to harvest fish that state authorities had long ignored. At roughly the same time, Native American militant organizations also were springing up in other cities as well. In 1968, the American Indian Movement (AIM) was formed in Minneapolis to resist selective law enforcement policies (and brutality toward American Indians) on the part of the Minneapolis police. Initially, an "Indian patrol" was established to follow police in Native American neighborhoods. Arrest rates of Native Americans declined to the general average in the city within nine months after the AIM patrols were introduced.

American Indian activism and nationalism was transformed by the occupation of the former Federal Penitentiary at Alcatraz Island by about 300 Native Americans and supporters on November 9, 1969. They were requesting title to the island under a federal law that gave Indians first refusal on federal "surplus" property. Activists executed a march across the United States during 1972 to protest broken treaties; this was followed, during the last week of the 1972 election, by an occupation of the Bureau of Indian Affairs (BIA) headquarters in Washington, D.C., followed by the occupation of Wounded Knee (1973).

Following the Wounded Knee occupation, more than sixty AIM members and supporters were killed on and near the Pine Ridge Reservation in South Dakota. Two Federal Bureau of Investigation (FBI) agents also lost their lives in the tense aftermath of Wounded Knee at Pine Ridge, deaths for which Leonard Peltier was convicted on what his defenders to this day contend was falsified evidence.

Copious media attention provided a national platform for discussion of American Indian issues relating to self-determination during this wave of activism. On December 16, 1969, the occupants of Alcatraz said the following:

> We are issuing this call in an attempt to unify our Indian brothers behind a common cause.... We are not getting anywhere fast by working alone as individual tribes. If we can get together as brothers and come to a common agreement, we feel that we can be much more effective, doing things for ourselves, instead of having someone else doing it, telling us what is good for us. So we must start somewhere. We feel that we are going to succeed, we must hold on to the old ways. This is the first and most important reason we went to Alcatraz Island. (Johansen, 1998, 13)

The occupants departed Alcatraz during 1971 without achieving their expressed goals of gaining title to the island and building an American Indian culture center there. The occupation did focus attention, as no one had done before, on the issues of American Indian identity, self-determination, and tribal lands.

Militant activities became more frequent in the early 1970s. During the spring of 1972, AIM leaders openly castigated the Chippewa tribal councils for allowing non-Indians to exploit reservation resources (especially fishing rights). For a few days at the Cass Lake Convention Center (Minnesota), AIM leaders blocked traffic and demanded that the tribal leadership reassert treaty fishing rights (the non-Indians, afraid of AIM's tactics, reluctantly accepted tribal control of resources as a result of this confrontation). At the same time, AIM led 1,000 American Indian people into Gordon, Nebraska, to protest the murder of Raymond Yellow Thunder by five European Americans. Protests over the death of Richard Oakes (a leader of the Alcatraz occupation) at the hands of a prison guard in California also flared up in 1972.

During the summer of 1972, Hank Adams (a leader of fish-ins in Washington) and Dennis Banks, a founder of AIM, met in Denver to plan a Trail of Broken Treaties caravan. Dennis Banks (Chippewa), who was born on the Leech Lake Reservation in northern Minnesota during 1932, became familiar to television news viewers along with Russell Means as the two most easily recognizable leaders of AIM.

Participants in the Trail of Broken Treaties aimed to marshal thousands of protesters across the United States to march on Washington, D.C., to dramatize issues related to American Indian self-determination. In Minneapolis, the group issued its Twenty Points, a document that sought to revive tribal sovereignty completely. Summarized, the Twenty Points advocated the following:

1. Repeal of the 1871 federal statute that ended treaty-making;
2. Restoration of treaty making status to native nations;
3. Establishment of a commission to review past treaty violations;
4. Resubmission of unratified treaties to the Senate;
5. That all Native Americans be governed by treaty relations;
6. Elimination all state jurisdiction over American Indian affairs. (Deloria, 1974a, 48–52)

Armed with their demands, the Trail of Broken Treaties caravan moved on to Washington, D.C. On their arrival on November 3, 1972, within days of a national election, the protesters learned that there was not enough lodging, so they elected to stay in the BIA building for several hours until security guards sought to forcibly remove them. At that point, events turned violent. The protesters seized the building for six days as they asserted their demands that Native sovereignty be restored and immunity be granted to all protesters. Files were seized, and damage was done to the BIA building (AIM leaders asserted that federal agents had infiltrated the movement and had done most of the damage). On November 8, 1972, federal officials offered immunity and transportation home to the protesters. The offer was accepted, and the crisis was resolved for the moment.

AMERICAN INDIAN MOVEMENT AT PINE RIDGE: THE OCCUPATION OF WOUNDED KNEE

Local issues at Pine Ridge laid the basis for the national attention given AIM as it occupied the small village of Wounded Knee early in 1973. Many traditional people on the Pine Ridge Reservation had rallied around AIM. Some people detested the brutality of the tribal police; others wanted help in settling fractionalized heirship problems that inhibited ranching and agriculture on the reservation.

The tiny hamlet of Wounded Knee, South Dakota, on the Pine Ridge Indian Reservation, the site at which more than 200 Sioux and others were massacred in 1890, became a symbolic site again as members of AIM were quickly surrounded by armored troops.

The seventy-one-day occupation of Wounded Knee began February 28, 1973. In early March, George McGovern and James Abourezk, U.S. senators from South Dakota, met with AIM leaders and the federal authorities to calm tempers. On March 11, 1973, AIM members declared their independence as the Oglala Sioux Nation, defining its boundaries according to the Treaty of Fort Laramie (1868). At one point, federal officials considered an armed attack on the camp at Wounded Knee, but the plan was ultimately discarded. Dennis Banks and Russell Means, AIM's best-known leaders, stated that they would hold out until the Senate Foreign Relations Committee had reviewed all broken treaties and the corruption of the BIA had been exposed to the world. After much gunfire and negotiation, AIM's occupation of Wounded Knee ended on May 7, 1973.

The occupation of Wounded Knee by Native American activists had a profound impact on non-Indians because news of the conflict was spread worldwide through the media. The occupation had a major effect on American culture: A book by Dee Brown, titled *Bury My Heart at Wounded Knee*, became an international best-seller. At the 1973 Academy Awards, held as Wounded Knee was being occupied, Marlon Brando, via his spokesperson Sacheen Littlefeather, refused to accept an Oscar to protest the treatment of American Indians.

Pine Ridge tribal police supported tribal chairman Richard Wilson (Oglala Lakota, 1936–1990). From the early 1970s until his defeat for the chairman's office by Al Trimble in 1976, Wilson outfitted a tribal police force that was often called the goon squad. This police force, which took goon to mean guardians of the Oglala Nation, was financed with money from the federal government. The local context of the occupation included an effort to confront Wilson's policies publicly, which often favored non-Indian ranchers, farmers, and corporations.

The struggle between AIM and Wilson also was taking place within the realm of tribal politics. When Wilson sought reelection in 1974, Russell Means, an Oglala who had helped found AIM, challenged him. In the primary, Wilson trailed Means, 667 votes to 511. Wilson won the final election over Means by fewer than 200 votes in balloting that the U.S. Commission on Civil Rights later found was permeated with fraud. The Civil Rights Commission recommended a new election, which was not held; Wilson answered his detractors by stepping up the terror, examples of which were described in a chronology kept by the Wounded Knee Legal Defense-Offense Committee. One of the goons' favorite weapons was the automobile. Officially, such deaths could be reported as traffic accidents.

Wilson had a formidable array of supporters on the reservation, and many criticized AIM for being urban based and insensitive to reservation residents' needs. Mona Wilson, one of Wilson's daughters, who was 17 years of age when Wounded Knee was occupied, recalled seeing him crying in his mother's arms at the time. Recalling the events two decades later, Wilson's wife, Yvonne, and two daughters recalled him as a kind and compassionate father who had the interests of his people at heart. They said that Wilson supported AIM when it protested the 1972 murder of Raymond Yellow Thunder in the reservation border town of Gordon, Nebraska. Only later, as events culminated in the siege of Wounded Knee, did Wilson and AIM leaders become deadly enemies.

Wilson was the first Oglala Lakota tribal chairman to serve two consecutive terms. He worked as a self-employed plumber, owner of a gas station, and on other short-term projects after his defeat by Trimble for the tribal chairmanship in 1976. Wilson's family recalled that he also had a traditional side. He was a pipe carrier, as well as a practicing Episcopalian. Wilson was known for feeding anyone who came to his door, and he had a major role in beginning a Lakota community college on the reservation, as well as a number of other tribal enterprises. Wilson died of a heart attack in 1990 as he was preparing to run for a third term as tribal chairman.

Following the occupation of Wounded Knee, Banks and Means were charged with three counts of assault on federal officers, one charge each of conspiracy, and one each of larceny. Banks and Means, facing five charges each, could have been sentenced to as many as eighty-five years in prison. For several months in 1974, a year after the occupation of Wounded Knee, the defense and prosecution presented their cases in a St. Paul, Minnesota, federal court. On September 16, Judge Fred J. Nichol dismissed all the charges. The judge said that the FBI's agents had lied repeatedly during the trial while under oath and had often furnished defense attorneys with altered documents. Judge Nichol said that R. D. Hurd, the federal prosecutor, had deliberately deceived the court. "The FBI," said Judge Nichol, "has stooped to a new low." To the chagrin of the judge and jurors, the Justice Department responded by presenting Hurd with an award for "superior performance" during the trial (Johansen and Maestas, 1979, 91).

THE FEDERAL BUREAU OF INVESTIGATION'S PURSUIT OF LEONARD PELTIER

An activist in the American Indian Movement during the 1973 confrontation at Wounded Knee, Leonard Peltier (Anishinabe, born 1944) was caught in a shootout with FBI agents and state police at the Jumping Bull Compound on the Pine Ridge Indian Reservation during June 1975. He was later convicted of killing two FBI agents, Jack Williams and Ronald Coler. The trial, which was held in Fargo, North Dakota, Federal District Court in 1977, has since become the focus of an international protest movement aimed at obtaining a retrial.

Before Peltier's trial opened in March 1977, the prosecution's case began to fall apart. Discovery proceedings produced an affidavit, signed by government witness Myrtle Poor Bear, dated February 19, 1976 (before two others known to the defense, dated February 23 and March 31), which said that the woman had not been on the scene of the June 25, 1975, gun battle in which the two FBI agents had been shot to death. This information, contained in an affidavit that had not been sent to Canada by the U.S. government during Peltier's extradition hearing, contradicted the other two statements attributed to Poor Bear.

Leonard Peltier. (Courtesy of the University of Washington *Daily.*)

More importantly, Poor Bear herself recanted. On April 13, out of earshot of the jury, Poor Bear told the court (having been called by the defense) that she had never seen Peltier before meeting him at the trial. Furthermore, Poor Bear said that she had not been allowed to read the three affidavits that bore her name and implicated Peltier in the murders, and that FBI agents David Price and Bill Wood had threatened physical harm to herself and her children if she did not sign them.

Judge Paul Benson refused to let the jury hear Poor Bear's testimony, ruling it "irrelevant" to the case. The next day, the judge changed his mind and ruled the testimony relevant but still would not let the jury hear it. He ruled this time that Poor Bear's testimony was prejudicial to the government's case and, if believed, could confuse the jury.

Prosecution testimony, which occupied the first five weeks of the trial, ranged far afield from what happened on the day of the shootings. The prosecution was allowed to bring up extraneous charges against Peltier on which he had not been tried, and testimony that ran counter to the federal rules of evidence. The defense's planned two weeks of testimony was reduced to two-and-a-half days by Judge Benson, who limited defense testimony to events directly connected with the shootings themselves.

The only evidence that directly linked Peltier to the killings of Coler and Williams (other than that fabricated in Poor Bear's name) came from Frederick Coward, an FBI agent, who said he had recognized Peltier from half a mile away through a seven-power rifle sight. The defense team replicated the sighting and found that the feat was impossible through such a sight at such a distance, even for a person with excellent vision. In court, defense attorneys offered to duplicate their experience for the jury so that its members could judge for themselves the veracity of the FBI agent's statement. Judge Benson refused the request. "Finally," said Bruce Ellison, a member of the defense team, "we brought in someone from a gun shop, who said that an idiot could tell you that it is impossible to recognize someone, even someone you know, from a half-mile away through a seven-power sight" (Johansen and Maestas, 1979, 114).

Three Native juveniles also testified that they had seen Peltier at the scene. Each of them also testified, under cross-examination, that their testimony had been coerced by the FBI. One of them, Mike Anderson, testified that he had been threatened with beating. Another, Wish Draper, said that he had been tied and handcuffed to a chair for three hours to elicit his statement. The third, Norman Brown, swore that he was told that if he did not cooperate he "would never walk the Earth again" (Johansen and Maestas, 1979, 115).

The prosecution, its eyewitness testimony in dispute, linked Peltier to the use of an AR-15, a semiautomatic rifle, which was not introduced as evidence because it had been blown apart during a Kansas freeway explosion on September 10, 1975. The prosecution also asserted that Peltier's thumbprint had been found on a bag containing a gun belonging to one of the dead agents. The bag and the gun were found on November 14, 1975, after the two men police described as Peltier and Dennis Banks had escaped their dragnet near Ontario, Oregon.

Following his conviction, Peltier became the object of a growing popular movement demanding a new trial. Peltier's request for a new trial was rejected by a U.S. Circuit Court (in St. Louis) during 1978; his appeal also was declined by the U.S. Supreme Court in 1978 and 1986. In the meantime, Peltier's support spread to the Soviet Union and Europe. In the Soviet Union, by 1986 an estimated 17 million people had signed petitions in his support. Peter Matthiessen's *In the Spirit of Crazy Horse* was readied for publication in the early 1980s and made a case for Peltier's innocence. The publisher, Viking, withdrew the book after former South Dakota Governor William Janklow threatened to sue for libel over passages in the book that linked him to the rape of a young Native American woman. Bootlegged copies of the book began to circulate, and it was published in 1991 after Janklow's case was dismissed by the South Dakota Supreme Court. *In the Spirit of Crazy Horse* presents, in an epilogue appended after the book had been suppressed for eight years, a case that Peltier was not the murderer of the two FBI agents. In an interview, a Native man known only as X confesses to the murders. In the meantime, the FBI had withheld from the public 6,000 pages of documents on the case for reasons the agency associated with national security.

Dennis Banks had eluded capture during the FBI dragnet that followed the shooting deaths of two agents at Pine Ridge for which Peltier was convicted. Banks went underground before receiving amnesty from Jerry Brown, governor of California. Banks earned an associate of arts degree at the University of California (Davis campus) and during the late 1970s helped found and direct Deganawidah-Quetzecoatl University, a Native-controlled college. After Jerry Brown's term as California governor ended, Banks in 1984 was sheltered by the Onondagas on their reservation near Syracuse, New York.

In 1984, Banks surrendered to face charges stemming from the 1970s in South Dakota. He later served 18 months in prison, after which he worked as a drug and alcohol counselor on the Pine Ridge Reservation. During the late 1980s, Banks's energies were concentrated on measures to protect Native American graves and human remains. He organized a campaign in Kentucky, where he lived as a single parent; the campaign resulted in statewide legal protections after robbers desecrated Native graves in Uniontown. Banks also organized several more ceremonial runs in the United States and Japan. His autobiography, *Sacred Soul*, was published in Japan during 1988.

Banks remained active in Native American politics throughout the 1990s, although he was not as often in the national spotlight. He had acting roles in several films, including *War Party*, *The Last of the Mohicans*, and *Thunderheart*. During the first half of 1994, Banks helped organize a five-month Walk for Justice across the United States on behalf of Peltier. About 400 people took part in the march, and 28 walked the entire 3,000 miles. The Walk for Justice ended in Washington, D.C., July 15 at a rally calling on President Bill Clinton to pardon Peltier. Clinton refused repeated pardon appeals throughout his presidency.

During the 1980s and 1990s, Peltier's appeals for a new trial were denied several times by U.S. federal courts. He was serving two life terms at Marion Federal Penitentiary, Illinois, and at Leavenworth Federal Penitentiary in Kansas, developing his talents as an artist, creating posters, paintings, and designs for a line of greeting cards that were sold nationwide. Peltier's case also became the focus of the feature film *Thunderheart* and a documentary, *Incident at Oglala*.

Peltier's case came to the attention of Amnesty International and the government of Canada, from which Peltier was extradited to face trial on the basis of the Poor Bear affidavits. Peltier's appeals were directed by several well-known legal personalities, including former U.S. Attorney General Ramsey Clark and attorney William Kunstler. His third appeal for a new trial was turned down by the Eighth Circuit Court of Appeals (St. Paul, MN) in 1993, exhausting his remedies within the U.S. court system.

THE DEATH OF ANNA MAE AQUASH (MICMAC), 1945–1976

Anna Mae Aquash (MicMac, 1945–1976) was one of the most note-worthy of more than sixty people who were killed for political reasons on the Pine Ridge Reservation during the three years following the Wounded Knee occupation. Aquash, from Nova Scotia, Canada, became involved in AIM during its peak of activity shortly after 1970; she was a close friend of Peltier, Banks, Means, and others who were arrested and charged in connection with the Wounded Knee occupation in 1973 and other events. Following the shooting deaths of FBI agents Ronald Coler and Jack Williams at the Jumping Bull Compound on the Pine Ridge Indian Reservation in June 1975, Aquash was pursued and arrested by the FBI as a possible material witness to the crime.

On February 24, 1976, Roger Amiott, a rancher, found Aquash's body near Wanblee, in the northeastern section of the Pine Ridge Indian Reservation. Dr. W. O. Brown, a pathologist who performed autopsies under contract with the BIA, arrived the following day. After examining the body, Brown an-nounced that the woman, who still had not been officially identified, had died of exposure to the brutal South Dakota winter.

The FBI decided that the only way to identify the woman was to sever her hands and send them to the FBI's crime laboratories in the Washington, D.C., area. Agents on the scene reasoned that the body was too badly decomposed to take fingerprints at Pine Ridge. Ken Sayres, BIA police chief at Pine Ridge, would say later that no one had been called to the morgue to attempt iden-tification of the body before the hands were severed.

A week after the body was found, Aquash—now missing her hands as well as her identity—was buried at Holy Rosary Catholic Cemetery, Pine Ridge. On March 3, the FBI announced Aquash's identity.

Aquash's family was notified of the death March 5. They did not believe that she had died of natural causes. At 32 years of age, Aquash had been in good health and was trained to survive in cold weather. She did not drink alcohol or smoke tobacco. Her friends remembered that she had smuggled food past federal government roadblocks into Wounded Knee during another brutal South Dakota winter, almost three years to the day before her body had been found. A new autopsy was demanded.

In the midst of the controversy, Aquash's body was exhumed. Her family retained an independent pathologist, Dr. Gary Peterson, of St. Paul, Minne-sota. Dr. Peterson reopened the skull and found a .32-caliber bullet, which he said had been fired from a gun placed at the base of Aquash's neck. The bullet was not difficult to find: "It should have been discovered the first time,"

Peterson said (Johansen and Maestas, 1979, 106). Asked about the bullet he had not found, Dr. W. O. Brown, the BIA coroner, replied, according to an account in the Washington *Star* May 24, 1976, "A little bullet isn't hard to overlook" (ibid., 106).

Following identification of Aquash's decomposed body, the Canadian government and the U.S. Commission on Civil Rights demanded an investigation. The U.S. Justice Department announced that it would look into the case, but the "investigation" languished in bureaucratic limbo. Aquash's friends refused to let her spirit pass away. On March 14, Aquash's body was wrapped in a traditional star quilt as several women from Oglala Village mourned her passing for two days and two nights.

Twenty-seven years after Aquash's murder, federal agents on April 2, 2003, arrested a man and charged him with the death. Arlo Looking Cloud, 49, was arrested in Denver and pleaded innocent to a charge of first-degree murder. Looking Cloud worked as a security guard for AIM, checking people at the gates of events and patrolling the grounds, said Paul DeMain, editor of the bimonthly newspaper *News from Indian Country*. AIM was beset by internal disputes (and was infiltrated by FBI informers) at the time, DeMain said (Walker, 2003). On February 6, 2004, Looking Cloud was convicted of the murder.

BATTLES OVER FISHING RIGHTS IN WASHINGTON STATE

One of the most notable Native rights issues beginning during the 1960s was the right to fish in Pacific Northwest waters in accordance with treaties signed during the 1850s—a right that had been routinely denied by state authorities to that time.

To the Northwest Indian nations, the salmon was as central to economic life as the buffalo on the plains; 80 to 90 percent of the traditional Puyallup diet, for example, was fish. The salmon was more than food; it was the center of a way of life. A cultural festival accompanied the first salmon caught in the yearly run. The fish was barbecued over an open fire and bits of its flesh parceled out to all. The bones were saved intact, to be carried by a torch-bearing, singing, dancing, and chanting procession back to the river, where they were placed into the water, the head pointed upstream, symbolic of the spawning fish, so the run would return in later years.

Washington became a territory of the United States on March 2, 1853, with no consent from the Indians who occupied most of the land. Isaac Stevens was appointed governor and superintendent of Indian affairs for the territory. As governor, Stevens wished to build the economic base of the territory; this required the attraction of a proposed transcontinental railroad, which in turn required peace with the Indians. Stevens worked with remarkable speed; in 1854 and 1855 alone, he negotiated five treaties with 6,000 Indian people

Indians fishing for salmon at Celilo Falls, Oregon.
(Courtesy of the Library of Congress.)

west of the Cascades. By signing the treaties, the Indians ceded to the United States 2,240,000 acres of land, an immense sacrifice for the right to fish.

In 1914, about 16 million fish were caught annually; by the 1920s, annual catches had declined to an average of 6 million. In the late 1930s, following construction of several large hydroelectric dams on the Columbia River and its tributaries, the annual catch had fallen as low as 3 million, about one-sixth of what Native peoples alone had been harvesting a century earlier. By the 1970s, with more aggressive conservation measures in place, including construction of fish ladders at most major dams, the annual catch rose to 4 to 6 million, just short of a third of the precontact harvest.

Native American peoples who had signed the Medicine Creek Treaty and others were having a more difficult time harvesting enough fish to survive. By the early 1960s, state fisheries police were conducting wholesale arrests of Indians, confiscating their boats and nets. Denied justice in the state courts, the tribes pursued their claim at the federal level. During the 1960s and early 1970s, they also militantly protected their rights in the face of raids by state fisheries authorities. A nucleus of fishing rights activists from Franks Landing, living only a few miles from the site at which the Medicine Creek Treaty had

Spearing salmon. (Courtesy of the Library of Congress.)

been signed, continued to fish on the basis of the treaty, which gave them the right to fish as long as the rivers run.

The fish-ins continued for years, attracting multiethnic support from many places including, most notably, El Centro de la Raza of Seattle. Celebrities, including Marlon Brando, made a point of stopping by to pull a few nets. On February 12, 1974, U.S. District Court Judge George Boldt ruled that Indians were entitled to an opportunity to catch as many as half the fish returning to off-reservation sites that had been the "usual and accustomed places" when the treaties were signed. Boldt had put three years into the case; he used 200 pages to interpret one sentence of the treaty in an opinion that some legal scholars say is the most carefully researched and thoroughly analyzed ever handed down in an Indian fishing rights case. The nucleus of Boldt's decision had to do with nineteenth century dictionaries' definitions of "in common with." Boldt said the words meant to be shared equally. During the next three years, the Ninth Circuit Court of Appeals upheld Boldt's ruling, and the U.S. Supreme Court twice let it stand by refusing to hear an appeal by the state of Washington.

State officials and the fishermen whose interests they represented were furious at Boldt. Rumors circulated about the sanity of the 75-year-old judge. It was said that he had taken bribes of free fish and had an Indian mistress, neither of which was true. Judge Boldt was hung in effigy by angry non-Indian fishermen, who on other occasions formed "convoys" with their boats and rammed Coast Guard vessels that had been dispatched to enforce the court's orders. At least one with the Coast Guard was shot.

Among state officials during the middle and late 1970s, a backlash to Indian rights formed, which would become the nucleus for a nationwide non-Indian campaign to abrogate the treaties. Washington State Attorney General (later U.S. Senator) Slade Gorton called Indians supercitizens with special rights and proposed that constitutional equilibrium be reestablished not by open state violation of the treaties (Boldt had outlawed that) but by purchasing the Indians' fishing rights and abrogating the treaties on which they were based. The tribes, which had been listening to offers of money for Indian resources for a century, flatly refused Gorton's offer. To them, the selling of fishing rights would have been tantamount to termination.

FISHING RIGHTS IN EASTERN WASHINGTON

The 1974 Boldt decision restored recognition of treaty rights regarding salmon fishing west of the Cascades. East of the Cascades, during the 1980s, the fishing rights battle continued in a form that reminded many people of the Frank's Landing fish-ins of the 1960s. Many Native people along the Columbia River and its tributaries also fished for a livelihood long before European Americans migrated to their land, but they had no treaties protecting their right to do so. For years, David Sohappy (Wanapam, 1925–1991), his wife Myra, and their sons erected a riverbank shelter and fished in the traditional manner.

The Sohappys' name came from the Wanapam word *souiehappie*, meaning shoving something under a ledge. David Sohappy's ancestors had traded salmon with members of the Lewis and Clark expedition. The Wanapams never signed a treaty, wishing only to be left in peace to live as they had for hundreds, if not thousands, of years. By the early 1940s, Sohappy's family was pushed off its ancestral homeland at Priest Rapids and White Bluffs, which became part of the Hanford Nuclear Reservation. Hanford was located in the middle of a desert that Lewis and Clark characterized as the most barren piece of land that they saw between St. Louis and the Pacific Ocean. Still, David Sohappy fished, even as his father, Jim Sohappy, warned him that if he continued to live in the old ways, "The white man is going to put you in jail someday" (Johansen and Grinde, 1997, 363).

During the 1950s, development devastated the Celilo Falls, once one of the richest Indian fishing grounds in North America. Most of the people who had fished there gave up their traditional livelihood and moved to the nearby Yakima reservation or into urban areas. David Sohappy and his wife, Myra, moved to a sliver of federal land called Cook's Landing, just above the first of several dams along the Columbia and its tributaries. They built a small longhouse with a dirt floor. Sohappy built fishing traps from driftwood. As the fish-ins of the 1960s attracted nationwide publicity, Sohappy fished in silence until state game and fishing officials raided his camp, beat family members, and in 1968, put Sohappy in jail on charges of illegal fishing. He then brought legal action, and the case *Sohappy v. Smith* (302 F. Supp. 899 [D. Oregon, 1969]), produced a landmark federal ruling that was supposed to prevent the states of Washington and Oregon from interfering with Indian fishing except for conservation purposes.

The state ignored the ruling and continued to harass Sohappy and his family. Under cover of darkness, state agents sunk their boats and slashed their nets. In 1981 and 1982, the states of Washington and Oregon successfully (but quietly) lobbied into law a federal provision that made the interstate sale of fish taken in violation of state law a felony—an act aimed squarely at Sohappy. Eight months before the law was signed by President Reagan, the state enlisted federal undercover agents in a fish-buying sting that the press called Salmonscam to entrap Sohappy. He was later convicted in Los Angeles (the trial had been moved from the local jurisdiction because of racial prejudice against Indians) of taking 317 fish and sentenced to five years in prison. During the trial, testimony about the Sohappy's religion and the practice of conservation was not allowed.

Sohappy became a symbol of Native American rights across the United States. Myra Sohappy sought support from the United Nations Commission on Human Rights to have her husband tried by a jury of his peers in the Yakama Nation's Tribal Court. The new trial was arranged with the help of Senator Daniel Inouye, chair of the Senate Select Committee on Indian Affairs. The Yakama court found that the federal prosecution had interfered with Sohappy's practice of his Seven Drum religion.

Released after 20 months in prison, Sohappy had aged rapidly. Confinement and the prison diet had sapped his strength. Sohappy suffered several strokes during the months in prison, when he was even denied the use of an eagle prayer feather for comfort (it was rejected as contraband by prison officials). Back at Cook's Landing, Sohappy found that vindictive federal officials had tacked an eviction notice to his small house. Sohappy took the eviction notice to court and beat the government for what turned out to be his last time. He died in a nursing home in Hood River, Oregon, on May 6, 1991.

A few days later Sohappy was buried, his Wanapam relatives gathered in an old graveyard. They sang old songs as they lowered his body into the earth, having wrapped the body in a Pendleton blanket. He was placed so that the early morning sun would warm his head, facing west toward Mount Adams. Tom Keefe, Jr., an attorney who had been instrumental in securing Sohappy's release from prison, stood by the grave and remembered:

And while the sun chased a crescent moon across the Yakima Valley, I thanked David Sohappy for the time we had spent together, and I wondered how the salmon he had fought to protect would fare in his absence. Now he is gone, and the natural runs of Chinook that fed his family since time immemorial are headed for the Endangered Species Act list. "Be glad for my dad," David Sohappy, Jr. told the mourners. "He is free now, he doesn't need any tears." (Keefe, 1991, 6)

FURTHER READING

American Friends Service Committee. *Uncommon Controversy: Fishing Rights of the Muckleshoot, Puyallup, and Nisqually Indians.* Seattle: University of Washington Press, 1970.

Ball, Milnar. Constitution, Court, Indian Tribes. *American Bar Foundation Research Journal* 1(1987):1–140.

Barsh, Russel L. *The Washington Fishing Rights Controversy: An Economic Critique.* Seattle: University of Washington School of Business Administration, 1977.

Bates, Tom. The Government's Secret War on the Indian. *Oregon Times*, February–March 1976, 14.

Bluecloud, Peter. *Alcatraz Is Not an Island.* Berkeley, CA: Wingbow Press, 1972.

Brack, Fred. Fishing Rights: Who Is Entitled to Northwest Salmon? *Seattle Post-Intelligencer Northwest Magazine*, January 16, 1977, 8–10.

Brand, Johanna. *The Life and Death of Anna Mae Aquash.* Toronto: Lorimer, 1978.

Brown, Bruce. *Mountain in the Clouds: The Search for the Wild Salmon.* New York: Simon and Schuster, 1982.

Brown, Dee. *Bury My Heart at Wounded Knee: An Indian History of the American West.* New York: Holt, Rinehart and Winston, 1970.

Canby, William C., Jr. *American Indian Law.* St. Paul, MN: West, 1981.

Churchill, Ward. *Struggles for the Land.* Monroe, ME: Common Courage Press, 1993.

Churchill, Ward, and Jim Vander Wall. *Agents of Repression: The FBI's Secret War Against the Black Panther Party and the American Indian Movement.* Boston: South End Press, 1990a.

Churchill, Ward, and Jim Vander Wall. *The Cointelpro Papers.* Boston: South End Press, 1990b.

Deloria, Vine, Jr. *Behind the Trail of Broken Treaties.* New York: Delacorte, 1974a.

Deloria, Vine, Jr. *The Indian Affair.* New York: Friendship Press, 1974b.

Deloria, Vine, Jr. *The Nations Within.* New York: Pantheon, 1984.

Deloria, Vine, Jr. *American Indian Policy in the Twentieth Century.* Norman: University of Oklahoma Press, 1985.

Deloria, Vine, Jr. *Custer Died for Your Sins: An Indian Manifesto.* Norman: University of Oklahoma Press, 1988.

Deloria, Vine, Jr. *Behind the Trail of Broken Treaties.* Austin: University of Texas Press, 1990.

Deloria, Vine, Jr., and Clifford Lytle. *American Indians: American Justice.* Austin: University of Texas Press, 1984.

Gates, Paul W., ed. *The Rape of Indian Lands.* New York: Arno Press, 1979.

Hertzberg, Hazel W. *The Search for an American Indian Identity: Modern Pan-Indian Movements.* Syracuse: Syracuse University Press, 1971.

Jaimes, M. Annette, ed. *The State of Native America: Genocide, Colonization and Resistance.* Boston: South End Press, 1992.

Johansen, Bruce E. Peltier and the Posse. *The Nation,* October 1, 1977, 304–307.

Johansen, Bruce E. The Reservation Offensive. *The Nation,* February 25, 1978, 204–207.

Johansen, Bruce E., ed. *The Encyclopedia of Native American Legal Tradition.* Westport, CT: Greenwood Press, 1998.

Johansen, Bruce E., and Donald A. Grinde, Jr. *The Encyclopedia of Native American Biography.* New York: Henry Holt, 1997.

Johansen, Bruce E., and Roberto F. Maestas. *Wasi'chu: The Continuing Indian Wars.* New York: Monthly Review Press, 1979.

Josephy, Alvin, Jr. *Red Power.* New York: McGraw-Hill, 1971.

Keefe, Tom, Jr. A Tribute to David Sohappy. *Native Nations,* June/July 1991, 4–6.

Kickingbird, Kirke. *Indian Sovereignty.* Washington, DC: Institute for the Development of Indian Law, 1983.

Kilborn, Peter. Pine Ridge, A Different Kind of Poverty. *Omaha World-Herald,* September 30, 1992, 9.

LaMay, Konnie. 20 Years of Anguish. *Indian Country Today,* February 25, 1993, n.p.

Matthiessen, Peter. *In the Spirit of Crazy Horse.* New York: Viking, 1991.

Miller, Bruce J. The Press, the Boldt Decision, and Indian-White Relations. *American Indian Culture and Research Journal* 17:2(1993):75–98.

O'Brien, Sharon. *American Indian Tribal Governments.* Norman: University of Oklahoma Press, 1989.

Sohappy v. Smith. 302 F. Supp. 899 (D. Oregon, 1969).

U.S. Commission on Civil Rights. Report of Investigation: Oglala Sioux Tribe, General Election, 1974. Washington, DC: Civil Rights Commission, October 1974. Mimeographed.

United States v. Washington 384 F. Supp. 312 (1974).

Walker, Carson. Man Is Arrested in Activist's Death. April 2, 2003. Available at IndigenousNewsNetwork@topica.com.

Weir, David, and Lowell Bergman. The Killing of Anna Mae Aquash. *Rolling Stone*, April 7, 1977, 51–55.

Weisman, Joel. About That "Ambush" at Wounded Knee. *Columbia Journalism Review*, September/October 1975, 28–31.

CHAPTER 10

Majority Culture Borrowings from Native American Peoples and Cultures

For many years, European American immigrants to the continent they came to call North America studied history as if they had shaped its first peoples—it was *their* westward movement, *their* religion, *their* civilization, *their* conquest. Often left unexamined until recent years are the many ways in which the more recent immigrants absorbed Native foods, sports, social and political ideas.

As they acquired new foods and tools from Native Americans, early European American colonists also adopted Native American place names. Twenty-six of the states in the United States of America today bear names first spoken (at least in part) before Europeans immigrated here in large numbers. Thousands of words have entered English and other European languages from American Indian sources; they are too numerous even to survey in this brief overview. Assertions also have been made that Indian contributions helped shape Euro-American folk songs, locations for railroads and highways, ways of dying cloth, and even bathing habits (Frachtenberg, 1915, 64–69; Edwards, 1934, 255–272).

The U.S. Army did more than subjugate the Plains Indians. As troops chased the Lakota, they also learned from them. Many Plains people used sign language. Their smoke signals could be seen for many miles in open country. The Sioux later devised a system of signaling by mirrors. The U.S. Army adopted some of these signaling systems (in some cases, symbol-bearing blankets became flags), and they became the basis of the techniques used in the modern U.S. Army Signal Corps.

Even after more than five centuries in America, Europeans are still discovering the lands and inhabitants of a place their ancestors called the New World. Felix Cohen, author of the *Handbook of Federal Indian Law*, a basic reference in that field, compared Native American influence on immigrants from Europe to the ways in which the Greeks shaped Roman culture:

> When the Roman legions conquered Greece, Roman historians wrote with as little imagination as did the European historians who have written of the white man's conquest of America. What the Roman historians did not see was that captive Greece would take captive conquering Rome [with] Greek science [and] Greek philosophy. (1952, 180)

Cohen wrote that American historians had too often paid attention to military victories and changing land boundaries while failing to see that "in agriculture, in government, in sport, in education, and in our views of nature and our fellow men, it is the first Americans who have taken captive their battlefield conquerors" (1952, 180). American historians "have seen America only as an imitation of Europe," Cohen asserted. In his view, "the real epic of America is the yet unfinished story of the Americanization of the white man" (ibid., 180).

Many borrowings are indirect and so deeply ingrained in present-day culture that we have forgotten for the most part where they came from. The word *tuxedo*, for example, is anglicized from the Delaware (Lenni Lenape) word for wolf, *p'tuksit*. Neither wolves nor most American Indians wore tuxedos when this borrowing took place during the 1880s, of course. The tuxedo was first worn in a New York village by the name of Tuxedo, however. In our time a "Tux" is taken to be very conventional dress, but in the 1880s, young men wore it as an alternative to the older fashion of jackets with tails.

By 2002, however, the study of ways in which Native American ways of life shaped the rest of the world had become deep enough to sustain a 384-page reference book, Emory Dean Keoke and Kay Marie Porterfield's *Encyclopedia of American Indian Contributions to the World: 15,000 Years of Inventions and Innovations*. This book contains some surprises even for the avid student of cross-cultural communication. As its title suggests, the *Encyclopedia of American Indian Contributions to the World* is the first attempt to compile a comprehensive array of such material and intellectual influences under one cover. It is a wide-ranging effort, and one that may surprise even the most diligent student of ways in which Native American cultures have shaped others worldwide.

This encyclopedia merits reading cover to cover. It is a groundbreaking compilation of Native American contributions to sciences, technology, foods, lifeways, government, and other aspects of history and modern life. It is also, at the same time, a reminder of cultural amalgamation, that everything ultimately finds itself mixed with everything else. This was as true 500 years ago as today, with accelerated communication and transportation. Consider "Indian" (that is, Indian subcontinental) curry. The spices that comprise it actually began as a chili in what is now Brazil. They were transported to India by Portuguese seamen, then mixed with Asian spices to produce the mixture we know today (Keoke and Porterfield, 2002, 9, 78). One wonders what the Italians ate before tomato sauce, what the Irish consumed before potatoes, and what Jewish celebrants of Hanukkah used in lieu of potatoes for their latkes.

The idea of playing a game with a bouncing ball is indigenous to the Americas, particularly to Mesoamerica, where the Aztecs and Mayas played a game that had attributes of basketball, American football, and soccer. Europeans had no rubber before Columbus and thus no rubber balls. The Olmec, who lived in the Yucatan Peninsula, invented a way to treat raw latex to make usable items from rubber as early as 1700 C.E. They used it to make balls, soles for sandals, hollow bulbs for syringes, and waterproofed ponchos. This process was similar to vulcanization, which was patented by Charles Goodyear in 1844. Baseball shares attributes of English cricket and a Choctaw ballgame.

Numerous Native American contributions have become so familiar for so long that many of us have forgotten their origins. When we "sleep on it," for example, we forget that we are invoking an Iroquois custom, in which chiefs in council are implored to let at least one night intervene before making important decisions. The passage of time was said to allow the various members of a Haudenosaunee council to attain unanimity—"one mind"—necessary for consensual solution of a problem. The Grand Council also prohibited carrying debate after sunset to avoid hasty decision making caused by stress. Similarly, to "bury the hatchet" refers to the Iroquois practice of sequestering weapons under the Great Tree of Peace.

Pre-Colombian American Indian astronomers (notably the Maya) used a sophisticated system that could calculate celestial events such as solar eclipses. The Maya also created calendar systems, complete with corrections that were based on detailed observations of the sun and moon. Mayan astronomers' observations were so accurate that by the fifth century B.C. they had calculated a year's length to within a few minutes of today's calendars.

Keoke and Porterfield asserted that indigenous Americans employed technology that was in some respects more advanced than European techniques. They wrote, for example, that American Indian metallurgists invented electroplating of metals hundreds of years before its discovery in Europe. The Moche, who lived on the coast of northern Peru, utilized electroplating between 200 B.C.E. and 600 C.E. Europeans did not discover the process of electroplating until Sir Humphrey Davy's experiments during the late 1700s (2002, 98).

Keoke and Porterfield also weighed into the debate regarding who invented scalping. Their verdict: Native Americans did not do it. Keoke and Porterfield relied on precontact records indicating that Europeans took scalps, often buying them, centuries before the practice was utilized in North America. The practice was a well-established tradition for Europeans as early as 440 years before the common era, when the Greek historian Herodotus noted the practice. Much later, the English paid bounties for Irish scalps because they were easier to transport and store than entire heads. Keoke and Porterfield displayed records indicating that the English Earl of Wessex scalped enemies during the 11th century (Keoke and Porterfield, 2002).

Something else that Native Americans did not introduce to the world was syphilis, according to Keoke and Porterfield. They pointed to archeological evidence that they say provides strong evidence that syphilis was present in Europe before Columbus (2002, xi). Excavations at a friary in Hull, England, have revealed at least a dozen skulls carbon dated to between 1300 and 1450 C.E. that display evidence of third-stage syphilis. Pre-Columbian skeletons with syphilis also have been found elsewhere in Europe, including Ireland, Naples, and Pompeii, as well as in Israel (Porterfield, 2002).

NATIVE MEDICINES IN THE PHARMACOPOEIA OF THE UNITED STATES

Several American Indian medicines have come into use among European Americans. By the late twentieth century, more than 200 drugs first used by American Indians were listed in the United States *Pharmacopoeia* (*The Pharmacopoeia of the United States of America*, 1863), an official listing of all effective medicines and their uses. These include quinine, laxatives, muscle relaxants, and nasal remedies, as well as several dozen drugs and herbal medicines. To this day, scientists are discovering more beneficial drugs in plants once known only to Native Americans. One reason that many people are concerned at the demise of the Amazon rain forests is that such destruction could keep us from learning more about the Native American uses of plants there.

Some Native Americans used foxglove (*Digitalis purpurea*) to treat heart problems. They administered it with extreme care because high doses are required, and the plant is extremely toxic. American Indian healers developed a sophisticated system of medical treatment compared to European healers of the time, who relied on bloodletting, blistering, religious penance, and concoctions of lead, arsenic, and cow dung to treat disease. In addition to performing surgery, American Indians from several areas understood the importance of keeping wounds sterile as they used botanical antiseptics. They made syringes from bird bones and animal bladders to administer plant medicines.

Native peoples in the Americas had developed so many botanical medications by the time of contact that the Spanish King Philip II sent physician Francisco Hernando to the Americas in 1570 to record Aztec medical knowledge and bring it back to Europe. As early as 1635, after less than a generation in America, English colonists were using herbal medicines introduced to them by the native peoples. "A Relation of Maryland," written to give prospective immigrants information on the new colony, included this passage:

> This Countrey affords naturally, many excellent things for Physicke and Surgery, the perfect use of which, the English cannot yet learne from the Natives: They have a roote which is an excellent preservative against Pyson, called by the English the Snake roote. Other herbes and rootes they have wherewith they cure all manners of wounds; also Saxafras, Gummes, and Balsum. An Indian seeing one of the English, much troubled with the tooth-ake, fetched of the roote of a tree, and gave the party some of it to hold in his mouth, and it eased the pain presently. (Birchfield, 1997, 5:705–706)

By the eighteenth century, European American observers, many of them missionaries, were compiling lists of Native herbal remedies; some of these lists were published in several European languages. One carried to Europe the knowledge that the bark of a particular tree that grows in North America could alleviate toothache. The Canada shrubby elder could be used to combat agues and inflammations. The jalap root could be used as a laxative and to relieve the pain of rheumatism; the ipecacaunha also functioned as an emetic as well as an antidote to snakebite. Peter Kalm, the Swedish botanist, visited the Middle Atlantic states between 1748 and 1750 to catalogue Native medicinal herbs.

Captain John Smith learned through Pocahontas that her people applied a root that she called *wighsacan* to wounds for its healing power. John Lawson, visiting the Carolinas about 1700, observed that Natives there chewed a root (which he did not name) to soothe stomach ailments. European observers also wrote of Indians who committed suicide by eating certain roots and mushrooms. William Penn wrote that a Delaware woman who had been betrayed by her husband "went out, plunk't a Root out of the Ground, and ate it, upon which she immediately died" (Birchfield, 1997, 5:706). Native peoples often warned Europeans which plants, if eaten, could make them ill, produce skin rashes, or kill them. In some cases, Native peoples also provided antidotes. The Delaware, for example, dealt with the rash produced by contact with poison sumac by preparing a tea from the inner bark of the sour gum tree, which gave off a distinctive odor that caused native peoples to compare it to raw fish.

Some Native plant remedies became popular among Europeans based on their biological record; others took Europe by storm on the basis of unsupported health claims. Use of sassafras root (the "saxafras" in the "Relation of Maryland" above) was noted as early as Shakespeare's time. The use of sassafras tea spread throughout Europe as a general health tonic, and a trading network grew up across the Atlantic specializing in its harvest, sale, and transport. At about the same time, all sorts of extravagant claims were being made for the tonic effects of tobacco that do not stand up to scientific scrutiny. Tobacco was said to aid digestion, cure toothaches, kill nits and lice, and even stop coughing. The advocates of tobacco seemed to draw their advice from Native peoples, who often used tobacco as a ceremonial herb and who only very rarely became addicted to nicotine.

Tobacco was one of many herbal weapons in the arsenal of Native medicine men, or shamans, across the continent. The role of the medicine man had no direct counterpart in Europe. The various Native names for the persons who performed these functions can be translated as shaman, juggler, conjurer, sorcerer, priest, and physician, as well as medicine man. Even the translation of Native words that correspond to medicine in English can be tricky because Western culture has no single term that incorporates all the aspects of the shaman's work. Whereas medicine in English connotes treatment of a disease with a drug or other specific remedy, a medicine man was a spiritualist as well as a person who had learned the basics of physical medicine and herbal cures. Native shamans combined the art of mental suggestion with physical cures as well; the mental attitude of the patient was often considered as important as any physical cure. The casting of spells (and other practice of sorcery) had as much to do with a person's state of mind as with physical and biological reactions.

Most Native American peoples used the by-products of animals, as well as plants, for medicinal and cosmetic purposes. English immigrants in Virginia and Massachusetts learned early that an emollient of bear grease allowed Native people to range in the woods wearing a minimum of clothing on hot summer days without being bitten by mosquitoes and other stinging insects. Goose grease and bear fat were widely used as hair dressings, and skunk oil was sometimes applied to the chest and throat to relieve the symptoms of colds, including chest congestion. The Delawares sometimes slowed the flow of blood from a cut by inserting spider webs, which probably helped with blood clotting.

Witch hazel is a commonly used Native botanical remedy that has been adopted generally by Euro-American society. Used as a first aid treatment for insect bites and cuts, witch hazel is the distilled extract of the witch hazel bush combined with alcohol. The shrub grows commonly in the eastern United States; its leaves were boiled and applied to bites and cuts by many Native peoples in that area. The root and leaves of the wintergreen contain methyl salicylate, which is used today in creams and other forms to treat rheumatic pain, muscular aches, and similar ailments. Salicylic acid is the main active ingredient of aspirin, probably the most widely used relief for minor pain in the late twentieth century. The inner bark of the white pine (the national symbol of the Iroquois Confederacy) today is used in cough syrups. Terpin hydrate, a prescription drug used to treat coughs and colds, is derived from the sap of pine trees (turpentine). The Indians also were the first people to utilize caffeine as a stimulant.

~

Native American Vegetal Remedies

Balm-of-gilead: Mixed with cream to form a balm for sores.

Blackberry: Root as tea; said to cure dysentery.

Black haw: Liquid boiled from bark; relieves stomach and menstrual cramps.

Black walnut: Tea boiled from bark relieves severe colds.

Catnip: Tea from the leaves may quiet a restless baby.

Corn silk: As tea, combats pain caused by kidney trouble.

Dogwood: Tea from the roots serves as a general tonic.

Elder: Tea made from flowers relieves colic in children.

Elm (American or white): Liquid from steeping the inner bark in water relieves symptoms of flu, such as coughs and chills. Elm is also a poultice for gunshot wounds. (General Washington's Army used it during the Revolutionary War.)

Fishweed (Jerusalem artichoke): A tea made from its leaves may rid children of worms.

Flannel mullein: Heated leaves in a compress provide relief from rheumatic pains.

Hog weed (ragweed): The root is a strong laxative.

Hops: Leaves serve (in a tea) to relieve symptoms of a cold or (as a compress) to relieve pain.

Jimson weed: Heated leaves relieve pain of burns; not to be taken internally.

Morning glory: A tea of the leaves relieves some types of stomach pain.

Peach: Crushed leaves used as a compress reduce swelling.

Peppermint: Boiled leaves sometimes relieve stomach pains.

Prickly ash: Tea made from the bark relieves symptoms of colds; the bark and root can be used to relieve toothache pain.

Sassafras: A tea may reduce high blood pressure.

Tobacco: A soft wad of chewed tobacco will reduce the pain of a bee sting.

Watermelon: Tea from boiled seeds may relieve pain of kidney trouble.

Wild grape: Juice conditions hair and scalp.

Wild strawberry: Crushed fruit applied to face may improve complexion.

Yarrow: Crushed roots boiled as tea reduce excessive menstrual flow.

White oak: Liquid steeped from bark helps heal cuts and scratches.

THE ORIGINS OF THANKSGIVING

Ceremonies of thanksgiving for the bounty of nature are a common element in many Native American cultures. Feasts of gratitude and giving thanks have been a part of these cultures for several thousand years. In Lakota culture, a feast of thanksgiving is called a *Wopila*; in Navajo, it is *Hozhoni*; in Cherokee, it is *Selu i-tse-i*; and in Ho Chunk (Winnebago), it is *Wicawas warocu sto waroc*.

Thanksgiving in many cases is a yearlong event, celebrated, for example, after the safe birth of a baby, a safe journey, or construction of a new home.

Native peoples introduced their thanksgiving celebrations to English colonists near Plymouth Rock in 1621. A fall thanksgiving holiday, usually accompanied by feasting on traditional Native American foods (turkey, corn, yams, squashes, cranberry sauce, etc.) has been widely practiced since about 1800 by most non-Native people in the United States and Canada. Thanksgiving was declared a national holiday in 1863 by President Abraham Lincoln in the midst of the Civil War. Canada declared an official Thanksgiving holiday in 1879; this day is celebrated six weeks before its counterpart in the United States.

Thanksgiving is part of an annual cycle. Many Native American peoples celebrate a number of seasonal thanksgivings each year, of which general American culture has adopted only one. At each season, thanks is given for nature's provision of an economic base, whether it be corn, buffalo, or salmon. According to José Barreiro, editor of *Native Americas*:

> The Thanksgiving tradition requires that human beings place themselves in a humble position relative to the natural, plant, and animal elements and to consider, in one mind, the contributions of these other species to our well-being and survival.... Among the Iroquois and other traditionalists, the "wish to be appreciated" is the fundamental shared perception—the first principle—of existence. (1992, 28)

Mohawk Nation Council subchief Tom Porter offered a traditional thanksgiving prayer, "words before all else," that is used for all of the Iroquois' nine thanksgiving celebrations:

> [Before] our great-great grandfathers were first born and given the breath of life, our Creator at that time said the Earth will be your mother. And the Creator said to the deer, and the animals and the birds, the Earth will be your mother, too. And I have instructed the earth to give food and nourishment and medicine and quenching of thirst to all life.... We, the people, humbly thank you today, mother earth.
>
> Our Creator spoke to the rivers and our creator made the rivers not just as water, but he made the rivers a living entity.... You must have a reverence and great respect for your mother the earth.... You must each day say "thank you" [for] every gift that contributes to your life. If you follow this pattern, it will be like a circle with no end. Your life will be as everlasting as your children will carry on your flesh, your blood, and your heartbeat. (Grinde and Johansen, 1995, 34–35)

A tribute to the creator and a reverence for the natural world is reflected in many Native greetings the span of the North American continent. More than 2,500 miles from the homeland of the Mohawks, the Lummis of the Pacific

A Hopi cornfield. (Courtesy of the Library of Congress.)

Northwest coast begin public meetings this way: "To the Creator, Great Spirit, Holy Father: may the words that we share here today give the people and [generations] to come the understanding of the sacredness of all life and creation" (Grinde and Johansen, 1995, 34–35).

The domesticated fowl that would come to be called turkey in English was first eaten by Native Americans in the Valley of Mexico, including the Aztecs, who introduced it to invading Spaniards. By the time the Pilgrims reached Plymouth Rock, Massachusetts, in 1620, turkey had been bred in Spain and exported to England for almost a century. The passengers of the Mayflower had some turkeys on board their ship, so when they prepared for the first Thanksgiving, the English immigrants were familiar with the wild turkeys that were hunted by Native American peoples in eastern North America. Wild American turkeys seemed larger and better tasting to many colonists than their European-bred brethren. They also were easy to hunt. Thomas Morton said that a hunter in early seventeenth century New England could shoot one turkey while others nearby looked on, "The one being killed, the other sit fast everthelesse" (Cronon, 1983, 23). By the late twentieth century, wild turkeys were scarce in much of New England.

Native Americans gathered the seeds of corn when it was a wild grass and selected for the most productive, hardiest varieties. By the time European immigrants made landfall in North America, corn was more productive per acre than any cereal crop in the Old World. Corn, along with squashes, beans, fish, venison (deer meat), and various "fowls" (probably turkeys, ducks, and geese) were consumed during the first Anglo-American thanksgiving. The abundance was welcomed by the Pilgrims, who had arrived in the New World with English seeds, most of which did not sprout in American soil. They nearly starved during their first winter. William Bradford, governor of the small colony, wrote in his diary that Squanto, who was able to teach the immigrants how to survive in their own language, was "a special instrument sent of God for [our] good" (Case, 2002).

AMERICAN GOLD AND EUROPEAN CAPITALISM

Jack Weatherford's *Indian Givers* (1988) takes the influence of Native American contributions to European capitalism beyond individual products. It begins with the birth of money capitalism, fueled by Indian gold and silver, which provided the necessary capital for the rise of industrial capitalism. Spain, England, and France did not set out to America as empires. Each acquired much of its riches in America and elsewhere around the world.

England's industrial revolution provoked urbanization, which also created a need for an agricultural revolution to feed the populations of burgeoning cities. Weatherford argues that without Native American corn, potatoes, and other crops, many increasingly urbanized Europeans could have starved to death. Some scholars may argue that Weatherford has something of an intellectual love affair with the potato. How greatly any one contribution shaped history as a whole is always a dandy point of departure for debate. Regardless of possible differences regarding emphasis, Weatherford makes his point for appreciation of native precedents.

In Weatherford's *Native Roots* (1991), ancient Native ingenuity is described in ways that bear on present-day problems. Read, for example, how the Anasazi fashioned their dwellings to take advantage of passive solar energy, as well as the shading of overhanging cliffs, blunting the seasonal extremes of the Southwest and reducing the amount of precious firewood they had to burn. Weatherford also describes how the Inuit created a kayak that fits its occupant like a wetsuit, a boat so watertight that its occupant can turn upside down, then right side up again, without getting wet.

The idea of personal equality in the societies of many Native peoples pervades both of Weatherford's books, especially as he contrasts Native concepts of liberty with European notions of hierarchy. Weatherford sometimes describes architecture to make his point: Nowhere did native peoples of the Americas create the cathedrals or palaces commissioned by European elites. Instead, the Anasazis (for example) built relatively comfortable housing for the average person that European peasants might have envied. In the world of ideas, liberty and equality have a long American lineage: Over time and space, the spacious homes of the Anasazi could be imagined as the precursor of Jefferson's freehold farmer in his snug log cabin and the tract housing suburbs of modern-day American urban areas. Could it be argued that the Anasazis helped create the type of housing that characterizes the American dream?

Europeans did not bring liberty and prosperity to America; they sought it here, meanwhile forcing on Native people its antithesis—slavery and indentured servitude. Weatherford, in *Native Roots*, reveals that Native Americans were forced into slavery in large numbers. The Spanish, French, and English all enslaved native peoples; the name of Labrador, for example, may have been handed down to us from a Portuguese term for slave coast, Weatherford wrote (1991, 138).

NATIVE LINGUISTIC TRACKS IN ENGLISH AND SPANISH

The communication of names between cultures goes both ways, of course, and often involves some semantic confusion. The names that we most often use to describe various Native tribes and nations are a linguistic mishmash. One could generally tell whose enemy was whose. *Iroquois* is French for people who called themselves "Haudenosaunee," meaning People of the Longhouse. The Algonquians called the Iroquois the Nation of Snakes. It has been said that *Mohawk* is an Algonquian derivation for "man-eater." *Sioux* is an archaic French derivation for "snake" or "enemy." *Huron* is French for "lout" or "ruffian," used to describe people who called themselves Wendat (also Wyandot), meaning "dwellers on a peninsula." Huron is a once-removed phrase from archaic French that describes the bristles on the snout of a wild boar, not the type of image that most peoples would cultivate for themselves.

Native American languages have left their linguistic tracks all over English and not just in thousands of geographical place names. Many of the following words come from the Algonquian languages spoken over much of what is now the eastern United States: hickory, hominy, moose, succotash, terrapin, tomahawk, totem, woodchuck. *Blizzard* is a Native American word, although we do not know which language it came from. The first published reference to a blizzard was handed down to us by Davy Crockett, who according to Weatherford, used it in 1834. Crockett himself was a walking cultural amalgamation, of course, from his coonskin hat to his leggings and moccasins. He was not, however, in the habit of giving credit to Native peoples for much of what he borrowed from them.

European Americans also adapted to their own needs many Indian articles of clothing and other artifacts, including hammocks, kayaks, canoes, moccasins, smoking pipes, dog sleds, and parkas, a type of hooded jacket they invented. Most European and American arctic explorers borrowed extensively from the clothing of the Inuit, whose sleds often were pulled by the husky, also an Inuit word. *Muckamuck* (applied in derision to someone in authority) comes from trading jargon Chinook, as does the slang term *hootch* for alcoholic beverages. Other Native words now used in English include cigar (Mayan), tobacco (Arawakan), potato (Taino), and tomato (Nahuatl).

~

State Names, Native American Derivations

Roughly half the states in the United States of America have names that derive, in some way, from Native American languages. Most are English or French adaptations of the original Native American words. Sometimes, more than one meaning has been attributed to a name, in which case both are listed.

Alabama: From *alipama*, or *alibamu*, a Muskogee tribal name meaning "those who clear the land."

Alaska: From the Aleut word for their homeland on the Alaska peninsula, *Alakhskhakh*; also Aleut for "great land."

Arizona: Pagago, airzonac, probably meaning "small springs."

Arkansas: From the Illinois name for the Quapaw, *akansea*. The same word has been said to mean "downstream people."

Connecticut: Mohegan or Pequot for "long tidal river" or "wind-driven river."

Dakota (North and South): A Dakota Sioux term for themselves (*dahkota*), meaning "friends" or "allies." It is interesting that the immigrants expropriated the Sioux's own name for themselves, with its friendly connotations, meanwhile assigning the Dakota a corruption of an old French word, *Sioux*," meaning "snake" or "enemy."

Idaho: The Native language from which this state name is derived is unknown; it is said to have meant "gem of the mountains"; some say it means "The sun is coming up."

Illinois: The name of an Algonquian confederation, meaning "original people" or "superior men," after a term that the Illinois Indians used for themselves. The name originated with the Algonquian *iliniwak*, modified by French traders as Illinois.

Iowa: For the Ioway Indians, modified through French, from the Fox language, as *aayahooweewa* (possibly from the Sioux *ayuhba*). Both words mean "sleepy ones."

Kansas: Kansa for "people of the south wind."

Kentucky: From *Kenta*, possibly an Iroquois word for "planted field." Some say the word is Cherokee for "meadowland."

Massachusetts: Meaning "people of the big hill," this name was used to describe an Algonquian people who lived near a steep hill near Boston.

Michigan: Meaning "great water" (*michigamea*) or "big lake," the name is probably derived from the Algonquian or Ottawa language.

Minnesota: From *minisota*, a Dakota word meaning "sky-tinted water."

Mississippi: A combination of two Algonquian or Ojibway words: *misi*, meaning "great" or "large," and *sipi*, meaning "water," usually taken to mean "big river."

Missouri: A French adaptation of an Illinois (*Iliniwak*) word meaning "people with dugout canoes." Missouri is also the name of a tribe that lived near the river; Missouri also may also be taken to mean "big muddy river," after the Missouri Indians' name for it, *Pokitanou*, which carries that meaning. To this day, inhabitants of cities along the river customarily call it "the Big Muddy."

Nebraska: From the Omaha name *Nibdhathka*, meaning "flat river" or "flat water"; named for the shallow but wide Platte River. Some sources say the word is from the Oto language; it may be from both.

New Mexico: As a province of New Spain, New Mexico's name was derived from *Mexica*, the Aztecs' name for themselves.

Ohio: Derived from a Seneca word meaning "beautiful river."

Oklahoma: "Red men" in Choctaw, a translation of "Indian Territory" into the Choctaw language.

Tennessee: From *Tanasi*, a Cherokee name for the Little Tennessee River, as well as a principal Cherokee town by the same name. It is said to mean "area of traveling waters."

Texas: First a Spanish (Tejas), then also an English derivation from *taysa*, a word used among members of the Caddo tribal confederacy meaning (like Dakota) "friends or allies."

Utah: From the tribal name Ute, anglicized from *yuuttaa*, the Utes' name for their homeland, "the land of the sun."

Wisconsin: The name of a tribal confederacy living near the Wisconsin River, "Wisconsin" is probably derived from the Ojibway *Wees-kon-san*, "gathering of the waters" and "grassy place."

Wyoming: This name, meaning "big meadows" or "big river flats," originated with the Delaware (Lenni Lenape) of present-day Pennsylvania and New Jersey and was carried by non-Indian migrants to the state that now bears the name. "Wyoming" is anglicized rather liberally from the Lenni Lenape *maughwauwame*, a name given first to the Wyoming Valley of Pennsylvania.

~

Examples of Foods Native to the Americas

Asparagus
Avocados
Blueberries
Cassava (tapioca)
Chewing gum (chicle)
Chocolate (cacao)
Corn

Corn products such as hominy, corn-
  starch, and cornmeal
Cranberries
Cucumbers
Currants
Green and yellow beans
Maple sugar and syrup

Mint and mint flavorings	Squashes, including pumpkins,
Peanuts and peanut products	watermelon, yams, and cantaloupe
Green and red peppers	Sunflower seeds
Pecans	Turkey
Popcorn	Vanilla
Potatoes and potato products	Venison
Sassafras tea	Wild rice

∽

CRISPUS ATTUCKS: FIRST CASUALTY OF THE BOSTON MASSACRE

Crispus Attucks, son of an African American father and a Massachuset Indian mother, was the first casualty of the Boston Massacre of March 5, 1770, the first death in the cause of the American Revolution. Attucks's father was a black slave in a Framington, Massachusetts, household until about 1750, when he escaped and became a sailor. Crispus's mother lived in an Indian mission at Natick.

Serious tension had begun to build in the late summer and fall of 1769 when Bostonians believed that the British Redcoats were becoming permanent residents. The soldiers were subjected to every form of legal harassment by local magistrates, to say nothing of mounting acts of violence against the men in uniform. The redcoats in the ranks, like all European soldiers of their day, were hardly of the highest character, often recruited from the slums and the gin mills, and stories of theft, assault, and rape by the regulars were not without considerable foundation.

On the night of March 5, 1770, a small crowd gathered around a soldier at the guard post in front of the Customs House at Boston, accusing him of striking a boy who had made disparaging remarks about a British officer. John Adams depicted the hecklers as "a motley rabble of saucy boys, Negroes and mulattoes, Irish teagues and outlandish Jack tars" ("Africans in America," 2003). The sentinel's call for aid brought a file of eight men from the 29th Regiment and Captain Thomas Preston, officer of the day. The crowd grew, especially after someone rang the bell in the old Brick Meeting House; men and boys hurled snowballs and pieces of ice at the crimson-coated regulars and taunted them to retaliate with cries of "lobster," "bloody-back," and "coward."

Attucks was known around Boston as one of the Sons of Liberty's most aggressive agitators. When the British claimed that he had provoked their soldiers, they may have been right. Attucks and Paul Revere were among the earliest Sons of Liberty, a clandestine society that agitated against the British by engaging in acts of agitation, propaganda, and creative political mischief. The Sons of Liberty tormented Tories and their supporters, often stripping,

The bloody massacre perpetrated in King Street, Boston, on March 5, 1770. (Courtesy of the Library of Congress.)

tarring, and feathering tax collectors, then walking free at the hands of sympathetic colonial juries. They later would form the nucleus of a revolutionary armed force, but in the early years their main business was guerilla theater.

The Boston Massacre was the first shedding of colonial blood during the American Revolution. "Massacre Day," as it was called, later was commemorated in Boston by the tolling of bells and speeches. In 1888, a monument to Attucks was erected at the Boston Common.

THE NATIVE AMERICAN IMPACT ON MODERN FEMINISM

The role of women in Native American life alternately intrigued, perplexed, and sometimes alarmed European and European American observers (nearly all of whom were male) during the seventeenth and eighteenth centuries. In many cases, women held pivotal positions in Native political systems. Iroquois women, for example, nominated men to positions of leadership and could "dehorn," or impeach, them for misconduct. Women usually approved men's plans for war. In a matrilineal society (nearly all the confederacies that bordered the colonies were matrilineal), women owned all household goods except the men's clothes, weapons, and hunting implements. They also were the primary conduits of culture from generation to generation.

Among the Cherokees (as with the Iroquois), women never held the office of *Uku* (civil chief) or Raven (war chief), but they often attended council meetings and acted as advisors behind the scenes. More than once, treaty council business stalled after English delegates objected to the fact that Cherokee women were doing what the English regarded as "men's business." After one such objection, the Cherokee chief Little Carpenter curtly informed the English that all men present had been born of women. He then diplomatically told the English delegates to sit down, shut up, and get on with business (Corkran, 1962, 110).

In the Cherokee home, the woman was supreme. An eighteenth century observer reported: "The women rule the rost [*sic*], and weres the britches and sometimes will beat thire husbands within an inch of thire life" (Corkran, 1962, 110). Father Joseph Frances Lafitau made a similar statement in a more elegant tone: "It is she who maintains the tribe, the nobility of the blood, the genealogical tree, the order of generations, and the conservation of the families. They are the souls of the council" (Exhibit, 1983). Women also were the souls of the Iroquois Grand Council; they were often so influential that the men have been characterized as political representatives of them (Carr, 1884, 217, 218). The Iroquois system has been styled a "gynocracy" (Axtell, 1981, 150–153).

The Iroquois have an elaborate description of the duties and rights of women in their confederacy. The Iroquois also recognized by law that the earth belonged to women. In Charles Abram's "Iroquois Law of the Woman Chief," an unpaginated manuscript held in the Smithsonian Institution, women's roles in governmental processes are described clearly:

> We shall make the rule that, in the place where the Federal titles are placed, among all our tribes, also among the clans—the several clans which exist—the several women who control the official titles, it shall then be that the Eldest woman, upon whom the eyes of her entire uterine family shall rest, shall be charged with all these duties. (1923, n.p.).

During the American Revolution, General Philip Schuyler of New York paid attention to the wishes of Iroquois women regarding diplomacy. On January 16, 1776, Schuyler met with a delegation of Mohawks near Schenectady, New York. Urging neutrality on the Mohawks and Abraham, their leader, Schuyler asserted that "Your women have sent us a belt. We beg you to assure them of our regard, and intreat [*sic*] them to prevent your warriors from doing anything that would have the least tendency to incur our resentment or interrupt that harmony which we wish to subsist to the end of time" (*Pennsylvania Magazine*, 1776, 96). After this admonition, a Mohawk chief replied that "You may depend on it that we will use our utmost influence with our warriors, to claim their minds. You may depend on it likewise that our sisters will use their utmost influence for the same purpose" (*American Monthly Museum*, 1776, 97).

At an early nineteenth century treaty conference, another Iroquois sachem said the following:

> Our ancestors considered it a great offence to reject the counsel of women, particularly the female governesses [clan mothers]. They were esteemed the mistresses of the soil. Who, said our forefathers, bring us into being? Who cultivates our lands, kindles our fires, and boils our pots, but the women? . . . They entreat that the veneration of our ancestors in favor of the women not be disregarded, and that they may not be despised. . . . The female governesses beg leave to speak with the freedom allowed to women and agreeable to the spirit of our ancestors. They entreat the Great Chief to . . . preserve them in peace, for they are the life of the nation. ("Substance," 1814, 2:115)

The character of women's influence in traditional Iroquois society has been maintained for centuries since Europeans first encountered it. John Kahionhes Fadden, a Mohawk teacher and artist, related the following story, which he said occurred during the mid-1960s, in the Akwesasne Mohawk Longhouse:

> There was a fellow who had been "de-horned." He was an eloquent speaker, and in a charismatic manner was able to hold people spellbound. During one summer there was a conference of traditional people that traveled from reserve to reserve, meeting with like-minded people. They finally came to Akwesasne and the event went on for the good part of a week. . . . There were Creeks and Cherokees from Oklahoma, Utes from Utah, Malecites from New Brunswick, Manawaki Algonquians from north of Ottawa, plus a good representation of the nations of the Haudenosaunee and others, such as Hopis. . . .
>
> At one point, when all of these people were gathered in the Longhouse many benches deep, with a lot of people standing in the doorways, and some outside craning their necks and cocking their ears to listen to what was going on, the "de-horned" former chief couldn't resist the temptation of that audience. He stood to talk to the gathered people, and, as you know, a "de-horned" chief isn't supposed to talk, and for sure no one is supposed to hear his words. He was able to get out about two or three brief sentences before he was abruptly interrupted by a slicing

voice from the women's end of the Longhouse. She was a clan mother, and standing less than five feet tall, she made it quickly and abundantly clear that this man could not speak anymore. He had lost that right by abusing his former position. The six-foot, two-hundred-plus pound "chief" snapped his mouth shut, sat down, waited about a minute or so, then quietly, with his head kind of low, left the Longhouse. Now, as I see it, that's feminism. (Grinde and Johansen, 1991, 224)

Marriage customs among American Indians elicited descriptions from eighteenth century European and Euro-American observers that strike a surprisingly modern tone. Robert Rogers noted that in many American Indian nations, vows of marriage were voluntary: "They take companions for a shorter or longer time, as they please" (1966, 232–233). Rogers wrote that children of such arrangements were fully accepted in Native societies at a time when such children would have been stigmatized as "born out of wedlock" in European cultures. Thomas Paine pointed to the hypocrisy of European customs in a supposed conversation with "an American savage." According to the savage:

> Either the Christian God was not as good and wise as he is represented, or he never meddled in the marriages of his people; since not one in a hundred of any of them had anything to do with either happiness or common sense. Hence, as soon as ever you meet, you long to part, and not having this relief in your power, by way of revenge, you double each others' misery. (Foner, 1945, 2:119–120)

Reverend Peters wrote that Indian women were better off as pagans than under Christian customs of his time, by which the woman was regarded as the husband's property. Before the arrival of Europeans in Connecticut during 1634, Indian women, according to Reverend Peters, had been "the most chaste set of people in the world. Concubinage and fornication are vices none of them are addicted to, except such as forsake the laws of Hobbomockow [the Great Spirit] and turn Christian" (Cameron, 1967, 158).

WOMEN'S RIGHTS AND NATIVE EXAMPLES

Pressure to broaden the ambit of natural and civil rights to women increased early in the nineteenth century at roughly the same time as the abolitionist movement against slavery. Although the landmark Seneca Falls conference, usually credited today with beginning the modern feminist movement in the United States, was not held until 1848, the ideological basis for the movement was set down by Lydia Maria Child in her *History of the Condition of Women, in Various Ages and Nations*, published in 1835. Child's book used the Iroquois and Wyandot cultures to counterpoise notions of European patriarchy, illustrating the importance of the woman's role in political decision making.

Matilda Joslyn Gage. (Courtesy of Sally Roesch Wagner.)

The Iroquois example also figured importantly in another important book in what feminist scholar Sally R. Wagner called "the first wave of feminism," Matilda Joslyn Gage's *Woman, Church and State* ([1893] 1980). In that book, Gage acknowledged, according to Wagner's research, that "the modern world [is] indebted for its first conception of inherent rights, natural equality of condition, and the establishment of a civilized government upon this basis," to the Iroquois (ibid., 10).

Gage was probably one of the three most influential feminist architects of the nineteenth century women's movement, with Elizabeth Cady Stanton and Susan B. Anthony, according to Wagner, whose research was among the first to provide a scholarly basis for a resurgent feminist movement in the late twentieth century. Gage was later "read out" of the movement and its history because of her radical views, especially regarding oppression of women

Elizabeth Cady Stanton, seated, and Susan B. Anthony. (Courtesy of
the Library of Congress.)

by organized religion. Knowledge of the Iroquois' matrilineal system of society and government was widespread among early feminists, many of whom
lived in upstate New York. The early feminists learned of the Iroquois not
only through reading the works of Morgan, Schoolcraft, and others, but also
through personal experience. Gage herself was admitted to the Iroquois
Council of Matrons and was adopted into the Wolf Clan, with the name
Karonienhawi, "she who holds the sky."

According to Gail Landsman, "Child's work was mined extensively by later
suffragists, including Gage, who furthered Child's concept of Indian culture as

a matriarchal alternative to American white patriarchy through her contact with the Iroquois" (1988, 8). With Stanton and Anthony, Gage coauthored the landmark *History of Woman Suffrage* ([1880] 1985). In her last book, *Women, Church, and State* ([1893] 1980), Gage opened with a chapter on "the matriarchate," a form of society she believed existed in a number of early societies, specifically the Iroquois. Gage discussed several Iroquois traditions that tended to create checks and balances between the sexes, including descent through the female line, the ability of women to nominate male leaders, the fact that women had a veto power over men's decisions to go to war, and the woman's supreme authority in the household. Gage also noted that Iroquois women had rights to their property and children after divorce (Landsman, 1988, 9).

The early suffragists developed their work about the same time as Lewis Henry Morgan, the pioneer anthropologist, whose descriptions of Iroquois society provided the groundwork for modern anthropology in the United States. According to Wagner, Stanton specifically referred to Morgan's work in her address (titled "The Matriarchate or Mother-Age") to the National Council of Women in 1891. Stanton referred to the influence of Iroquois women in national councils, to the fact that their society was descended through the female line, and to the irony that "our barbarian ancestors seem to have had a higher degree of justice to women than American men in the 19th century, professing to believe, as they do, in our republican principles of government" (1891, 2).

Wagner asserted that "Nineteenth century radical feminist theoreticians, such as Elizabeth Cady Stanton and Matilda Joslyn Gage, looked to the Iroquois for their vision of a transformed world" (1988, 32–33). Wagner also used the work of male students of the Iroquois who wrote at roughly the same time as Stanton, Gage, and other early feminists to illustrate just how appealing the Iroquois example must have been to women locked in a culture that considered them their husbands' property. She quoted Henry Schoolcraft, writing in 1846, two years before the Seneca Falls conference. "Marriage, among the Iroquois," wrote Schoolcraft, "appears to be a verbal contract between the parties, which does not affect the rights of property. Goods, personal effects, or valuables of any kind personal or real, which were the wife's before, remain so after marriage" (ibid., 32–33). Schoolcraft characterized marriage among the Iroquois as "a personal agreement, requiring neither civil nor ecclesiastical sanction, but not a union of the rights of property" (ibid., 32–33).

Stanton quoted the memoirs of the Reverend Asher Wright, who wrote that usually Seneca women "ruled the house." The stores were in common, "but woe to the luckless husband or lover who was too shiftless to do his share of the providing." No matter how many children, or whatever goods he might have in the house, he might at any time be ordered to pick up his blanket and move out; and after such an order, it would not be healthy for him to attempt to disobey. "The house would be too hot for him," wrote Wright, "and unless saved by the intercession of some aunt or grandmother he must retreat to his own clan, or go and start a new matrimonial alliance with some other" (1891, 4).

According to Stanton, Wright also noted that Iroquois women alone could "knock off the horns" of a sachem who had abused his office, as well as make the original nominations for sachemships. In early treaty negotiations, representatives of the United States, all male, often found themselves face-to-face with Iroquois women. Many of the treaties negotiated before 1800 are signed by both male sachems and their female advisors (1891, 4).

Paula Gunn Allen contrasted the woman's role in Native American societies with mass media portrayals of them: "I am intensely conscious of popular notions of Indian women as beasts of burden, squaws, traitors, or, at best, vanished denizens of a long-lost wilderness," she wrote. "How odd, then, must my contention seem that the gynocratic tribes of the American continent provided the basis for all the dreams of liberation that characterize the modern world. . . . Beliefs, attitudes and laws such as these became part of the vision of other human-liberation movements around the world." Allen continued: "Yet feminists too often believe that no one has ever experienced the kind of society that empowered women and made that empowerment the basis of its rules and civilization" (1986, 213–214). Even the history of feminism is too often overly Eurocentric. To Allen, lack of such knowledge robs feminists of their own history.

Realization of the Iroquois role in the history of feminism came to Wagner after seventeen years of studying feminism's European roots. Once she turned her attention to native inspirations, Wagner found them running throughout the primary sources of the period that she studied. Frances Wright, the first non-Quaker woman to speak publicly before audiences of both men and women in the United States, edited the pro-Indian *Free Enquirer* with Robert Dale Owen in the 1820s. Owen, like Child, inquired into the relative absence of rape by Indian men of Native women, wondering how their social structure influenced their behavior. To cite another example, Lucretia Mott, who called the Seneca Falls conference, met with the people of the Cattaraugus Seneca reservation just days before she met, during 1848, with Stanton and a group of Quaker friends to plan the Seneca Falls event, which became known as the world's first conference explicitly dedicated to women's rights.

FREDERICK ENGELS AND THE "MOTHER-RIGHT GENS"

Across the Atlantic, aging Karl Marx discovered the work of Lewis Henry Morgan during the late 1870s. After Marx's death, his copious notes on American indigenous societies were passed to Frederick Engels, who used them, with his own research, in preparing *The Origin of the Family, Private Property and the State* (1883). Engels picked up Morgan's refrain (which had also been a popular notion among many of the founders of the United States) that one could discern aspects of the political and economic future by using Native

American models as a window on the ancient past. Having discovered the "mother-right gens" (as he called the matriarchal society of the Iroquois) Engels could scarcely contain himself. "It has the same significance for the history of primitive society as Darwin's theory of evolution has for biology, and Marx's theory of surplus value for political economy," Engels enthused. "The mother-right gens," he wrote, "has become the pivot around which this entire science turns" (ibid., 3:201).

As contemporaries of Morgan, Engels, and Marx, the founding mothers of modern feminism in the United States shared their enthusiasm at finding functioning societies that incorporated notions of sexual equality. All seemed to believe that the Native model held promise for the future. Gage and Stanton looked to the Native model for a design of a "regenerated world" (Gage, [1893] 1980, 9). "Never was justice more perfect, never civilization higher than under the Matriarchate," Gage wrote (Wagner, 1989, 11; Gage, [1893] 1980, 246). She continued: "Under [Iroquois] women, the science of government reached the highest form known to the world" (Gage, [1893] 1980, 10.) Writing in the *New York Evening Post*, Gage contended that "division of power between the sexes in this Indian republic was nearly equal" (1875, 12).

In her 1891 speech before the National Council of Women, Stanton surveyed the research of Morgan and others indicating to her that, "Among the greater number of the American aborigines, the descent of property and children were in the female line. Women sat in the councils of war and peace and their opinions had equal weight on all questions" (Stanton, 1891, 1). In this regard, she mentioned the Iroquois' councils specifically. After surveying indigenous societies in other parts of the world as well, Stanton closed her speech with a case for sexual equality:

> In closing, I would say that every woman present must have a new sense of dignity and self respect, feeling that our mothers, during long periods in the long past, have been the ruling power and that they used that power for the best interests of humanity. As history is said to repeat itself, we have every reason to believe that our turn will come again. It may not be for woman's supremacy, but for, the as yet untried experiment of complete equality, when the united thought of man and woman will inaugurate a just government, a pure religion, a happy home, a civilization at last in which ignorance, poverty and crime will exist no more. Those who watch already behold the dawn of the new day. (Stanton, 1891, 7)

FURTHER READING

Abram, Charles. Law of the Woman Chief, May 21, 1923. Hewitt Collection, BAE Manuscript No. 1636, NAA, Smithsonian Institution. Cited in Grinde and Johansen, 1991, 259.

Africans in America: Revolution, Resource Bank, Part 2: 1750–1805: Crispus Attucks. Public Broadcasting Service. No date. Available at http://www.pbs.org/wgbh/aia/part2/2p24.html. Accessed February 20, 2003.

Allen, Paula Gunn. *The Sacred Hoop: Recovering the Feminine in American Indian Traditions*. Boston: Beacon Press, 1986.

American Monthly Museum [magazine], 2(February 1776), 96.

Anthony, Susan B., Elizabeth Cady Stanton, and Matilda Joslyn Gage, eds. *History of Woman Suffrage*. Salem, NH: Ayer, [1880] 1985.

Axtell, James. *The Indian Peoples of Eastern America: A Documentary History of the Sexes*. New York: Oxford University Press, 1981.

Barreiro, José. The Search for Lessons. In José Barreiro, ed., *Indigenous Economics: Toward A Natural World Order*. *Akwe:kon Journal* 9:2(Summer 1992):18–39.

Birchfield, D. L. *The Encyclopedia of North American Indians*. Vol. 5. New York: Marshall Cavendish, 1997.

Brown, Judith K. Economic Organization and the Position of Women Among the Iroquois. *Ethnohistory* 17:3–4(Summer-Fall 1970):151–167.

Cameron, Kenneth W., ed. *The Works of Samuel Peters*. Hartford, CT: Transcendental Books, 1967.

Carr, Lucien. *The Social and Political Position of Women Among the Huron-Iroquois Tribes*. Salem, MA: Salem Press, 1884.

Case, Nancy Humphrey. Gifts from the Indians: Native Americans Not Only Provided New Kinds of Food and Recreation; They May Have Given the Founding Fathers Ideas on How to Form a Government. *The Christian Science Monitor*, November 26, 2002. Available at http://www.csmonitor.com.

Child, Lydia Maria. *The History of the Condition of Women, in Various Ages and Nations*. 2 vols. Boston: J. Allen and Co., 1835.

Cohen, Felix. Americanizing the White Man. *American Scholar* 21:2(1952):177–191.

Cohen, Felix. *The Legal Conscience: Selected Papers of Felix S. Cohen*. Edited by Lucy Kramer Cohen. New Haven, CT: Yale University Press, 1960.

Corkran, David H. *The Cherokee Frontier: Conflict and Survival, 1740–62*. Norman: University of Oklahoma Press, 1962.

Cronon, William. *Changes in the Land: Indians, Colonists, and the Ecology of New England*. New York: Hill and Wang, 1983.

Crosby, Alfred W. *The Columbian Exchange: Biological and Cultural Consequences of 1492*. New York: Greenwood Press, 1972.

Edwards, Everett E. The Contributions of American Indians to Civilization. *Minnesota History* 15:3(1934):255–272.

Engels, Frederick. *The Origin of the Family, Private Property and the State*. 1883. Reprinted in *Karl Marx and Frederick Engles, Selected Works in One Volume*. New York: International Publishers, 1968.

"Exhibit on the Iroquois League," Yager Museum, Hartwick College, Oneonta, NY, June 1983.

Fenton, W. N. *Contacts Between Iroquois Herbalism and Colonial Medicine*. Washington, DC: Smithsonian Institution, 1941.

Foner, Philip S., ed. *Complete Writings of Thomas Paine*. New York: Citadel Press, 1945.

Forbes, Jack. *The Indian in America's Past*. New York: Prentice-Hall, 1964.

Frachtenberg, Leo J. Our Indebtedness to the American Indian. *Wisconsin Archeologist* 14:2(1915):64–69.

Gage, Matilda Joslyn. *Woman, Church and State*. Watertown, MA: Peresphone Press, [1893] 1980.

Gipson, Arrell Morgan. *The American Indian: Prehistory to Present.* Lexington, MA: D. C. Heath, 1980.

Grinde, Donald A., Jr., and Bruce E. Johansen. *Exemplar of Liberty: Native America and the Evolution of Democracy.* Los Angeles: UCLA American Indian Studies Center, 1991.

Grinde, Donald A., Jr., and Bruce E. Johansen. *Ecocide of Native America: Environmental Destruction of Indian Lands and Peoples.* Santa Fe, NM: Clear Light, 1995.

Keoke, Emory Dean, and Kay Marie Porterfield. *Encyclopedia of American Indian Contributions to the World.* New York: Facts on File, 2002.

Kraus, Michael. *The Atlantic Civilization: Eighteenth Century Origins.* New York: Russell and Russell, 1949.

Landsman, Gail. Portrayals of the Iroquois in the Woman Suffrage Movement. Paper presented at the Annual Conference on Iroquois Research, Rensselaerville, NY, October 8, 1988.

Myers, Albert Cook. *Narratives of Early Pennsylvania, West New Jersey and Delaware, 1630–1702.* New York: Charles Scribner's Sons, 1912.

New York Evening Post, September 24, 1875. Cited in Wagner, 1989, 12.

The Pharmacopoeia of the United States of America: by authority of the National Convention for Revising the Pharmacopoeia, held at Washington, A.D. 1860. 4th decennial rev. Philadelphia: Lippincott, 1863.

Porterfield, Kay Marie. Ten Lies about Indigenous Science—How to Talk Back. October 10, 2002. Available at http://www.kporterfield.com/aicttw/articles/lies.html.

Rogers, Robert. *Concise Account of North America.* New Haven, CT: Johnson Reprint, 1966.

Selsam, Millicent. *Plants that Heal.* New York: William Morrow, 1959.

Stanton, Elizabeth Cady. The Matriarchate or Mother-Age [address before the National Council of Women, February 1891]. *The National Bulletin* 1:5(February 1891):1–7.

Substance of the Speech of Good Peter to Governor Clinton and the Commissioners of Indian Affairs at Albany. Collections of the New York Historical Society, 1st Series (1814):2:115.

Wagner, Sally Roesch. The Iroquois Confederacy: A Native American Model for Non-Sexist Men. *Changing Men*, Spring-Summer 1988, 32–33.

Wagner, Sally Roesch. The Root of Oppression Is the Loss of Memory: The Iroquois and the Early Feminist Vision. *Akwesasne* Notes, Late Winter, 1989, 11.

Weatherford, Jack. *Indian Givers: How the Indians of the Americas Transformed the World.* New York: Fawcett Columbine, 1988.

Weatherford, Jack. *Native Roots: How the Indians Enriched America.* New York: Crown, 1991.

CHAPTER 11

Contemporary Issues in Native America

Native America today presents a varied mosaic of life, death, and pervasive struggle. Many issues are economic in nature, but others have to do with cultural respect, as well as for the earth we all share. This chapter is an attempt to sketch a sampling of contemporary issues—a few of many.

A survey of contemporary reservation economic conditions in South Dakota will be a corrective for anyone who thinks that modern-day gambling has made all Native Americans rich. Aside from some of the poorest counties in the United states (in and around reservations in South Dakota), Native peoples also occupy some of Canada's most desolate real estate, as characterized by the village of Pikangikum, Ontario, where major activities for young people are sniffling gasoline and suicide. Alcoholism is still a plague in the cities as well as on rural reservations. Readers will become acquainted with the hamlet of Whiteclay, Nebraska, where the major business is selling beer and other alcoholic beverages to Indians of the neighboring Pine Ridge Reservation, where such sales are illegal.

Is gambling the answer—the "new buffalo" as some Native Americans have called it? In some places, such as the Pequots' Foxwoods, in Connecticut, and some other locales, it has been, as small tribes' members have been enriched. In other places, such as the New York Oneidas' lands in upstate New York, gambling has provided an enriched upper class the means to hire police to force dissident antigambling traditionalists from their homes. Among the Mohawks at Akwesasne, people have died over the issue. Akwesasne's position on the border of the United States with Canada has made smuggling of cigarettes, liquor, other drugs, weapons, and human beings a major industry.

Environmental issues are very important in the contemporary Native American political equation. In this chapter, readers will come to know Navajos who mined some of the uranium that powered the nation's nuclear arsenal and have recently been dying of lung cancer. The U.S. fledgling Green Party is informed by Native American voices, including the naming of Winona LaDuke, an Anishinabe, as a candidate for vice president of the United States on its national ticket with Ralph Nader.

Today, Native activists campaign against the use of American Indian symbols as sports mascots, something that often has been handled with deft humor, as in the case of the "Fighting Whities," an intramural basketball team in Colorado, which stirred a national debate by adopting an upper middle class white mascot. Others struggle to remove the word *squaw* (often taken as a reference to Native women's vaginas) from place-names. Struggles are ongoing to return Native bones and burial artifacts to the earth and to revive Native languages that are on the verge of disappearing.

CONTEMPORARY RESERVATION ECONOMIC CONDITIONS

In some ways, life for Native people living on reservations was becoming more difficult as the twentieth century ended. By 1990, the Pine Ridge Oglala Lakota (Sioux) Reservation in southwest South Dakota, with people descended from Crazy Horse and Red Cloud and the site of the 1890 massacre at Wounded Knee and the 1973 confrontation there, had become the poorest area in the United States.

In the 2000 census, the rankings were little changed. In the 2000 census, Buffalo County, home of the Lower Brule Indian Reservation, had the lowest per capita income in the United States. Second-lowest ranking was Shannon County, home of the Pine Ridge Reservation. In Buffalo County, 61.8 percent of the children lived in poverty, the highest rate in the United States, followed by Zieback County (61.2 percent) and Shannon County (61 percent). These rates were much higher than those in any urban area.

The 2000 census indicated that South Dakota as a whole had the largest percentage increase in the United States for household median income between 1990 and 2000. At the same time, Buffalo County, home of the 3,500-member Crow Creek Sioux, exchanged places with Shannon County among the two poorest in the United States. In Buffalo County, the largest and most successful business during the 1990s was the Lode Star Casino. Shannon County has benefited somewhat from federal empowerment zone status that brought the county millions in federal dollars for economic development and a visit from President Bill Clinton.

In 1989, nearly seven of every ten people in Shannon County were unemployed, and virtually the only work, except for a few private businesses, came from government agencies and the underground economy. Pine Ridge village, the largest town on the reservation, had no railroad or bus connections and no bank, theater, clothing store, or barbershop. Big Bat's, the one major Native-owned business in Pine Ridge, was taken to court thirteen times by white land and business owners who tried to prevent its opening. Meanwhile, the pervasiveness of poverty shatters families and causes people to turn to alcohol and other drugs. Infant mortality at Pine Ridge was 29 per 1,000 children, three times the national average. The death rate from homicide was also three times the national average. People at Pine Ridge died from alcoholism at ten times the national rate (not taking into account damage caused by fetal alcohol syndrome). The death rate from adult diabetes was four times the national average. The tribal housing authority had a waiting list of 2,000 families for subsidized lodging, at least a quarter of the people on the reservation.

John Yellow Bird Steele, chair of the Oglala Sioux Tribal Council in 1992, advocated construction of three casinos to alleviate unemployment and provide private industry on the reservation. The Wounded Knee chapter of the American Indian Movement (AIM) believes that gambling will drive poor people on the reservation further into alcoholism and debt, a modern form of genocide. In the midst of deepening poverty and divisiveness, however, a tribal consensus to upgrade education produced improved schools and a number of well-kept school buildings. Since 1970, the tribe has gradually taken over administration of most reservation schools from the Bureau of Indian Affairs (BIA).

The indications of poverty in South Dakota were nearly duplicated in neighboring states. In Nebraska, unemployment on the Omaha reservation stood at 71 percent in the late 1980s; among the Santee Sioux, unemployment was 55 percent, compared to 65 percent among the Winnebago (Suzuki, 1991, 27–28). Nationwide, the civilian unemployment rate among Native Americans on reservations was about 30 percent in 1990. Unemployment on the Navajo reservation, with its workforce of 87,000 people (the largest in the United States) was 29.5 percent.

Nationwide, Native Americans' income level was falling in 1990 as measured against all other ethnic groups in the United States. According to the Census Bureau, the median household income for Native Americans (inflation adjusted) fell from $20,541 in 1980 to $20,025 in 1990; the same figure for citizens of European heritage rose from $29,632 to $31,435. The percentage of Native Americans defined as living below the "poverty line" increased from 27.5 percent in 1980 to 30.9 percent in 1990; the percentage for European Americans rose from 9.4 percent to 9.8 percent. In 1990, the Census Bureau found that 29.5 percent of blacks, 14.1 percent of Asians, and 25.3 percent of Hispanics lived in poverty. In 1989, the Children's Defense Fund found that 66 percent of Native American children in Minneapolis, Minnesota, were living in families with incomes below the poverty line.

Although many statistics indicate that Native Americans often were experiencing intensifying poverty at the end of the twentieth century, some indicators reveal improvement in some areas of health and welfare. For example, the Indian Health Service (IHS) reported that the homicide rate for Native

Americans (per 100,000 people) declined from 23.8 in 1955 to 14.1 in 1988, as the rate for all ethnic groups in the United States increased from 4.8 to 9.0 per 100,000. Although 57 percent of blacks and 47 percent of whites who died were killed with guns between 1966 and 1988, according to the Federal Bureau of Investigation (FBI), only 29 percent of Indians were murdered with firearms. Thirty-two percent were killed with knives. Deaths from alcoholism among Native Americans declined from 56.6 per 100,000 in 1969 to 33.9 in 1988; the rate for all races in the United States declined only slightly, from 7.7 to 6.3 per 100,000. Put another way, in 1969, the alcoholism death rate for Native Americans and Alaska Natives was 7.4 times that of the general population. In two decades, that figure fell to 5.4 times according to the IHS.

According to Jeffrey Wollock, writing in *Native Americas* (2003), from 1996 to 2001, crime rates on reservations rose while they fell elsewhere, Indians twelve to twenty years old are 58 percent more likely to be crime victims than whites and blacks. Indians under age fifteen years are murdered at twice the rate of whites.

The contemporary murder rate on Indian reservations is five times the average in the United States as a whole: 29,000 per 100,000 people compared to 5.6. The average in U.S. urban areas is 7 per 100,000 ("Crime Rate," 2003, 11). An Indian Country Crime Report, compiled from 1,072 cases prosecuted in U.S. District Courts, did not include felonies committed by non-Indians on reservations. Some small reservations have very high murder rates, according to this report. The Salt River Pima Maricopa Community in Arizona, for example, had 6 murders among 6,405 people, a murder rate 17 times the national average. The Gila River Reservation, with 11,257 enrollee members, suffered 11 murders, a similar rate (ibid., 11). According to Mac Rominger, an FBI agent on the Hopi and Navajo reservations, often-blamed problems such as alcoholism and poverty were being compounded by isolation. "Ninety-five per cent of the violent crime out there is directed towards family and friends," he said (ibid., 11).

Youth suicide among Native Americans is twice the rate of non-Indians. The American Medical Association reports that one in five Indian girls attempts suicide before leaving high school. The alcoholism death rate is four times the national average (Wollock, 2003, 30). In addition, more than 40 percent of Native Americans in the United States live in substandard housing compared with an average of 6 percent for the rest of the population. The crisis for Native American young people is closely tied to loss of culture, with youth "stuck between two worlds". Many more Native youths than in earlier times cannot speak their own languages and have little grasp of their traditional culture and history.

Similar statistics can assume a terrifying profile when they are described in personal context of a small village. Take, for example, the Ojibway-Cree village of Pikangikum, about 200 miles northeast of Winnipeg.

PIKANGIKUM'S CONTINUING DESOLATION ESCAPES CANADA'S MINISTRY OF INDIAN AFFAIRS

The Ojibway-Cree village of Pikangikum, about 200 miles northeast of Winnipeg, has the highest documented suicide rate in the world. It is a place where the main recreational pastime for young people is glue sniffing. The reserve's only school was closed for more than a year because of a fuel leak. Pikangikum's water treatment plant was closed nearly as long, also because of an accidental fuel leak.

Of the adults in Pikangikum, 80 to 90 percent are unemployed. The village is so overcrowded, with 400 homes for 2,100 people, that some people sleep in shifts to make beds available for others. All food is flown in, so prices are about five times the average for the rest of Canada.

What did Canada's Ministry of Indian Affairs do about all of this? It suspended the fiscal authority of the village band council, provoking anger at Pikangikum. On May 17, 2001, Indian Affairs Minister Robert Nault took control of the Pikangikum first nation's $9 million (Canadian) annual budget and then gave control to a private consulting firm, A. D. Morrison and Associates Limited, of London, Ontario, a situation known within the Canadian Indian bureaucracy as "third-party management."

Chief Louis Quill, a spokesman for the Pikangikum council, said the community was shocked to learn that A. D. Morrison and Associates was a first nations-operated company. "I don't think that's the way to treat other Natives," said Quill. "We shouldn't be going after our own people on behalf of Indian Affairs" ("Pikangikum Update," *Canadian Aboriginal*, n.d.). The local council called Indian Affairs' actions paternalistic. The band council was not running a deficit when its fiscal powers were removed; it had passed previous financial audits. Quill said the third-party managers "are not welcome in our community" ("Pikangikum Update," *Canadian Aboriginal*, n.d.).

When the residents of Pikangikum refused to cooperate with Nault and the third-party managers, Nault, whose jurisdiction in Canada's Parliament includes Pikangikum, suspended federal transfer payments to its council, meaning that most of the 10 percent of the town's adults who had jobs stopped receiving paychecks.

More than forty young people killed themselves in Pikangikum during the ten years ending in 2002. The same rate would have yielded 70,500 suicides in a city of 3 million people. During 2000, the community's rate of suicide was 380 per 100,000 population. The national average suicide rate in Canada is 13 per 100,000. "If [third-party management] is being forced on the community [Pikangikum] from the outside ... that just increases the sense of not having control, and that increases the distress," said David Masecar, president of the Canadian Association of Suicide Prevention (Elliott, June 7, 2001).

Most of the suicides were women who hung themselves (Elliott, June 7, 2001). During 2000 alone, nine Ojibway girls aged five to thirteen killed themselves in Pikangikum. Those suicides sent the year's suicide rate up to 470 deaths per 100,000, thirty-six times the Canadian national average. Three more young women killed themselves between mid-May and mid-June 2001. "When young women who are the bearers of life start to kill themselves, it's a real reflection on the health of the community," said Arnold Devlin, of Dilico Child and Family Services in Thunder Bay (Elliott, November 30, 2000).

Since 1995, the Pikangikum Youth Patrol, a team of young volunteers, has scoured Pikangikum almost every night looking for huddles of gas sniffers "whose spine-chilling howls permeate the community at night, but the young addicts often scatter into the darkness before patrollers can reach them. At peak suicide times like . . . summer and fall, there's an attempt or two every night" (Elliott, November 30, 2000).

Louise Elliott wrote for Canadian Press (November 30, 2000):

> The [suicide] problem, while worst in Pikangikum, is region-wide. On Monday, another 13-year-old girl took her life in Summer Beaver, a reserve 300 kilometers east of Pikangikum, bringing the total suicides on northern Ontario reserves this year [2000] to 25. "This is the worst year on record [for suicide]," said Arnold Devlin, of Dilico Child and Family Services in Thunder Bay."

"It's very, very difficult," said band councilor Sam Quill, 62, his eyes welling with tears. Quill, who recalled Pikangikum's first rash of youth hangings in 1993 and 1994 saw his daughter and granddaughter take their own lives (Elliott, November 30, 2000). "There are no resources here, whatsoever," said Bonnie-Jean Muir, of Pokangikum. "There's nothing for kids and because there's no place else to go when they're not sleeping, they're out roaming and sniffing. It's a community out of control" (Gamble, n.d.).

A Grand River Mohawk who is also a medical doctor, Michael Monture, 42, became lost in the bush while serving a rotation on the reserve (five doctors rotate; the reserve has no other medical services). Reports say the entire community joined in a search for Monture because he is so well loved. He was found after losing his way in the bush for two-and-a-half days.

The previous week, according to a report in the Brantford (Ontario) *Expositor*, during his second visit to Pikangikum, "Monture tallied up some of the dire social ills that plague the 2,100-member community and was angry," said Bonnie-Jean Muir, who had shared a dinner with Monture the evening before he went into the bush, beginning a two-day ordeal (Gamble, n.d.). "He joined us until 10 P.M. and about 12:30 A.M. he went out for a long walk, intending to spend the night in the bush," Muir told the *Expositor* from Pikangikum. "He found the state of the Pikangikum people absolutely deplorable" (Gamble, n.d.). Monture was known as a skilled hunter who is at home in the back country.

Each visiting physician is given a large box of food for his rotation in Pikangikum. Monture gave most of his food away. "The most common concern was the lack of food. What am I supposed to do? Write a prescription for food for these people?" Monture told Canadian Press (Gamble, n.d.). Recently, Monture had decided to dedicate a good part his medical practice to the people of Pikangikum. He moved to Sioux Lookout, near Pikangikum, so that he could fly in to offer medical treatment to the community once or twice a month.

With little food and dwindling gasoline supplies, town residents used their own all-terrain vehicles and boats to comb the area. They set out each morning of the search from a base camp north of Pikangikum. Spotted by an Ontario Provincial Police helicopter, Monture emerged from the bush seven miles from Pikangikum after two-and-a-half cold, wet days. According to one news account, Monture said that "The suffering and desperation . . . on the remote reserve of Pikangikum . . . prompted him to set out on a spiritual quest for help" (Elliott, June 18, 2001, A-14).

"I was concerned and frustrated at the lack of resources," Monture said after he was rescued (Elliott, June 18, 2001, A-14). "What galvanized me was how people were lacking in basic food and necessities," he said. "It's not a question of *what* you're going to eat, it's *whether* you're going to eat" (ibid., A-14). Monture described seeing young children huddled near a burning pile of refuse at Pikangikum. "They have a fire going in the garbage dump to keep warm while looking for things to eat," he says. "It's very upsetting to think that this is Canada" (ibid., A-14).

Chief Quill said that Monture's actions had raised the community's profile and its spirits, according to Canadian Press reports, which noted: "Residents, apparently overwhelmed by the doctor's actions, circled around him as he prepared to fly off the reserve Saturday night, reaching out to touch him as though he were a hero" (Elliott, June 18, 2001, A-14).

"It was a political stance he was taking," said Muir. "He could not believe what he saw" (Elliott, June 16, 2001, A-16). Stan Beardy, the grand chief of Nishnawbe-Aski Nation, the political organization that represents northern Ontario reserves, says he believed that fury over the government's appointment of an Indian agent to take control of Pikangikum's finances also played a role in Monture's sojourn into the bush.

About 200 students lost access to education when Pikangikum's only school closed for about a year after 24,000 liters of diesel oil were accidentally pumped into the crawl space under the school building. In addition, on October 2, 2000, the Pikangikum water treatment plant flooded, leaking more than 250 gallons of fuel oil into the town's reservoir. According to a report in a local newspaper, the *Anishinabek News*, "Health Canada closed down the water system and closed the hotel. The workers working on the school had to leave as well. . . . Chief Peter Quill has stated that unless the water situation is dealt with immediately, the impact on the community will be devastating—both in terms of water-related medical problems and youth suicide" (Goulais, 2000, n.p.). Many Pikangikum residents were forced to buy water at the local store for $5.99 (Canadian) per four-liter jug. Residents who could not buy drinking water used bottled water that is (occasionally, owing to weather conditions) flown in by Indian Affairs. Otherwise, they boiled lake water.

Canadian Indian Affairs provided $1.3 million in repairs to the water plant, which were completed January 22, 2001. "At no time," said an Indian Affairs press release, "was any resident of Pikangikum without clean water. In addition, the department also flew in a portable Zenon water plant at a cost of $4,500 per month. The community continues to use this portable plant."

A local news account said: "The water situation is no stranger to the communities of the Anishinabek Nation. In August, Gull Bay First Nation tested positive for *e-coli* contamination in their water supply. According to Chief Oliver Poile of Gull Bay, somebody may have died as a result of that contamination" (Goulais, 2000, n.p.).

In addition to the suicides, Pikangikum has been grappling with $10 million in failed infrastructure projects. In March 1999, workers were putting finishing touches on a business center in Pikangikum that community leaders had hoped would foster new ventures. *Northern Ontario Business* described "a 1,080-square-meter business center [which] will house a hotel, full-service restaurant, offices, rental space and classroom facilities. The project is expected to create 15 permanent jobs in Pikangikum" (Lynch, 1999). Two years later, Indian Affairs' embargo on funds closed the hotel.

The list of woes afflicting Pikangikum included construction delays and legal disputes with contractors over an all-weather road and a power line intended to connect the community to the provincial power grid—two necessary steps toward building the kind of infrastructure community members say is necessary.

Meanwhile, at Pikangikum, according to Louise Elliott of the Canadian Press:

> On the roads . . . young children play on makeshift sleds—sharp-edged fragments of wainscotting they've pulled from stalled construction projects. Band leaders say the community doesn't have enough electricity right now to fix its water treatment plant, or to keep up with the need for new houses. A grid line to pipe in electricity from Balmertown, 100 kilometers south, is only half-finished—it stalled when the contractor walked off the job last summer. (December 3, 2000)

Elliott continued:

> Outside the graffiti-scrawled homes with no indoor plumbing, crosses marking the graves of old and young are lined up seven or eight meters from the front doors, in a unique Pikangikum custom. No one seems to know where this tradition began—some say it happened when people left their traditional church for another, and could no longer use the church graveyard. (December 3, 2000)

As Indian Affairs and the Pikangikum Council remained in stalemate, the number of suicides continued to rise among First Nations youths across

Ontario's north country. As of the end of July, sixteen young people had killed themselves on forty-nine northern reserves during 2001, compared to twenty-six during all of 2001, with fall ("suicide season") still to come. Seven of those suicides had occurred in Pikangikum, compared to eight during all of 2000 (Elliott, July 31, 2001, A-6).

Nault had his own take on the rising suicide rate across Ontario's north country. In a letter, he said that Pikangikum band leaders had "perpetuated" the community's suicide crisis by talking to the media. "I'm very concerned that the decision to pursue a media approach may in fact perpetuate the suicide crisis," Nault wrote, adding that a 1996 report by the Royal Commission on Aboriginal Peoples "suggests the more publicity given to suicides, the more suicides that follow in their wake" (Elliott, June 22, 2001).

Joseph Magnet, a University of Ottawa law professor who undertook a constitutional challenge to Nault's decision to take over the band's finances, said the letter unfairly blames the community's interviews with media in recent weeks for the suicide epidemic. "It's a weird thing to say—'we shouldn't bring our lawyers in, we shouldn't call the press, we should let our kids die in private.'" Magnet said of the letter. "It's ridiculous" (Elliott, June 22, 2001).

ALCOHOLISM: THE CONTINUING TOLL

Second only to the ravages of smallpox and other diseases, alcoholism has been the major cause of early death and other forms of misery for Native Americans since the "discovery" of the Americas by Columbus. Scarrooyady, an Iroquois sachem, told Pennsylvania treaty commissioners in 1750: "Your traders now bring us scarce anything but rum and flour. The rum ruins us. . . . Those wicked whiskey sellers, when they have got the Indians in liquor, make them sell the very clothes from their backs!" (Johansen, 1982, 68). In 1832, the sale of alcoholic beverages to Indians was made illegal, an act that was not repealed until the early 1950s, when it became evident that prohibition produced a bootlegging industry little different from that which flourished nationwide during the 1920s and early 1930s.

Alcoholism continues to be a major problem today. The disease of alcoholism continues to be the leading single cause of death in many Native American communities. Today, the sharpest increases in alcoholism are being suffered in faraway places such as Alaska and the Canadian North, where Native peoples have only recently been deprived of their traditional ways of life. In Manitoba, for example, several hundred Native people whose lands were flooded have been moved to settlements where they are no longer allowed (or able) to wrest a living from the land. Alcoholism and other forms of social disorientation have followed suit. As many as 90 percent of adults have abused alcohol and other drugs, and juveniles frequently engage in fights. In a settlement of fewer than 1,000 people, suicide attempts averaged fifteen per month in the 1980s. At nearby Cross Lake, another small village, suicide attempts averaged twenty a month, ten times the provincial average.

In 1960, before widespread energy development on Alaska's North Slope, the suicide rate among Native people there was 13 per 100,000, comparable to averages in the United States as a whole. By 1970, the suicide rate had risen to 25 per 100,000; by 1986, it was 67.6 per 100,000. Homicide rates by the mid-1980s were three times the average in the United States as a whole, between 22.9 and 26.6 per 100,000 people, depending on which study was used. Death rates from homicide and suicide were related to rising alcoholism. In the mid-1980s, 79 percent of Native suicide victims had some alcohol in their blood at the time of death. Slightly more than half (54 percent) were legally intoxicated.

In 1969, the IHS appointed a Task Force on Alcoholism that a year later concluded that alcoholism was one of the most significant health problems facing American Indians and Alaska Natives. Seven years later, the American Indian Policy Review Commission, established by the U.S. Congress, found alcoholism and its medical consequences were the most serious and widespread health problem among American Indians. According to the IHS, alcoholism has an insidious multiplier effect. It contributes not only to elevated rates of traffic deaths, but also to the majority of Indian homicides, other assaults, suicides, and other mental health problems.

Even today, among Plains Indians, 80 to 90 percent of Native American men drink alcohol, as do 50 to 60 percent of Indian women. By age 17, a majority of Indian boys and a large minority of Indian girls are steady drinkers. Drinking among Indian young people has been related directly to the highest suicide rate in the United States for any age group. Alcohol abuse also relates to low educational achievement, poor health, high rates of unemployment, and crime among Indian youths.

Nationwide, Indians have for several years averaged twelve times the number of arrests per capita compared to the general population. Three-quarters of these arrests were alcohol related, almost twice the national average. In 1973, the General Accounting Office surveyed six IHS hospitals and found that 60 percent of the caseload could be directly or indirectly attributed to alcohol use. Cirrhosis of the liver was a frequent cause of hospitalization and eventual death. According to the IHS, cirrhosis of the liver occurs in American Indians at five times the rate of the general population. The IHS also reports that many child-battering cases are alcohol related.

A major cause of Indian alcoholism is deprivation and poverty, rejection by European Americans as inferiors, deterioration of traditional cultures, and a generally high level of anxiety that attends day-to-day reservation life. The Klamaths, who were dispersed by federal government termination policies during the early 1950s, had a high rate of arrests for alcohol-related crime, even when compared to the averages for Indians, which are a dozen times those for non-Indians. By contrast, the Pueblo Indians of New Mexico, who have maintained most of their traditional way of life through 150 years of U.S.

domination (and two centuries under Spain and Mexico before that) have relatively low rates of alcohol-related arrests.

Given the history of Indian alcoholism, treatment for it is a relatively recent development. As late as the mid-1960s, intoxicated Indians arrested in Gallup, New Mexico, were simply put in jail until it filled. On winter nights, those who were not arrested ran a risk of freezing to death. In a routine winter, many Indians froze to death on the streets of Gallup.

For a number of reasons, most of them cultural, traditional non-Indian treatments, from hospitalization to non-Indian chapters of Alcoholics Anonymous, had very little success dealing with Indian alcoholism. In the late 1960s, along with a general thrust of Indian self-determination, Native treatment programs began to open. The idea of Indians treating Indians was hailed as revolutionary in some quarters, but it is not really new. Since at least the days of the Iroquois spiritual leader Handsome Lake in the early 19th century, Indian religious figures have opposed the use of alcohol and achieved moderate success in sobering their followers.

THE POLITICS OF MALT LIQUOR

During the 1990s, protests from Native groups arose in several states regarding the sale of Crazy Horse malt liquor. The beverage was being sold by Hornell Brewing Company of New York in forty-ounce bottles bearing a likeness of Crazy Horse, the nineteenth century Lakota leader. The brew was being manufactured by G. Heileman Brewing Company.

In Congressional hearings, U.S. Surgeon General Antonia Novello and representatives of Native American groups contended that Crazy Horse malt liquor was specifically aimed at underage Native American drinkers. The surgeon general also was attacking other brands of alcohol, as well as cigarettes, which appeared to be aimed at minorities, women, and teenagers. The campaign already had resulted in the removal from shelves of PowerMaster, also a malt liquor, after complaints that it was targeted at young blacks.

Crazy Horse malt liquor was not the first marketing attempt aimed specifically at Indians, of course; traders have been getting them addicted to liquor since the earliest days of contact. It also is not the first alcoholic product to enter into contemporary Native politics. In the late 1980s, Native groups across the northern tier of states (roughly from Wisconsin to Washington) protested the marketing of "treaty beer" by sportsmen's rights groups raising funds to annul Native agreements with the federal government. At the time, the fund-raising brew was called "the Klan in a can" by Indians in Washington State (Johansen, 1988, 13).

WHITECLAY: THE BUSINESS IS BEER

On June 26, 1999, which was 123 years and one day after their ancestors had removed George Armstrong Custer's scalp, Lakotas gathered in

Whiteclay, Nebraska, to demand details describing how Wilson "Wally" Black Elk, 40, and Ronald Hard Heart, 39, had died. Their partially decomposed bodies had been found June 8. Many people at Pine Ridge believed that the way in which Black Elk and Hard Heart died was similar to how two other Lakota, Wesley Bad Heart Bull and Raymond Yellow Thunder, were killed in 1972—beaten to death by white toughs having what they regarded as a sporting time with inebriated Oglala Lakotas.

A month and more after the killings of Black Elk and Hard Heart, the men's reservation relatives knew little or nothing officially of how they died. Law enforcement officials in Nebraska and FBI agents talked vaguely of "foul play" and "following leads" while anger spread at Pine Ridge. Pine Ridge tribal police chief Stan Star Comes Out told the *Omaha World-Herald* that the remains of the two men had been wounded and bloody. He also said the two men had been bludgeoned to death. The bodies were found on the Pine Ridge (South Dakota) side of the line, but many Lakota believed the men were murdered in Nebraska, closer to Whiteclay, after which their bodies were dragged across the border.

Lakota community responses to the deaths of Yellow Thunder and Bad Heart Bull defined the AIM during 1972, becoming a provocation for the occupation of Wounded Knee the next year. Yellow Thunder was kidnapped and beaten to death during the middle of February, 1972, in Gorton, Nebraska (about twenty-five miles southeast of Whiteclay and thirteen miles south of Pine Ridge) by several white toughs. Four young men were charged with manslaughter (not murder), and two of them were convicted. By March, Gordon was the scene of rallies of more than 1,000 Lakota and allies demanding justice for Yellow Thunder. Two brothers who were convicted of manslaughter served ten months (of a two-year sentence) and two years (of a six-year sentence), respectively.

Shortly after the murder of Yellow Thunder in 1972, Lakota Wesley Bad Heart Bull was stabbed to death by a young white man near Custer, South Dakota (in the Black Hills southwest of Rapid City). The assailant was charged with second-degree manslaughter, provoking demonstrations organized by AIM, some of which turned violent, at the courthouse in Custer.

In 1999, some of the major organizers were the same as they had been in Gordon and Custer—AIMsters with many more lines on their faces. They listened to speeches by Russell Means, Clyde Bellecourt, and Dennis Banks, among others, protesting basic injustices, such as young white men's penchant for taking out their aggressions (sometimes with fatal results) on drunken Indians near the dusty streets of Whiteclay, population twenty-four, where the main business was selling $3 million a year worth of beer to the people of Pine Ridge (Johansen, 1998, 5).

In reaction to the murders of Hard Heart and Black Elk, a Rally for Justice— 250 people walking accompanied by about 150 automobiles—traversed the two-lane blacktop to "take Whiteclay back" on June 26. As the larger rally was breaking up in Whiteclay, about twenty-five to thirty people trashed a grocery store, V. J.'s Market, in Whiteclay. It was said that V. J.'s owner, Vic Clarke, had treated Lakota in a demeaning manner. The store's freezer cases were destroyed and its cash registers doused with lighter fluid. Groceries were strewn through the store.

Claims of Lakota control of the ground on which Whiteclay sits are based on surveys taken for the Fort Laramie Treaty of 1868, which place Whiteclay within reservation borders. Documents related to the Dawes (Allotment) Act, notably legislation passed by Congress in 1889 to break up what was then called "the Great Sioux Nation," also support this assertion. An executive order issued in 1882 by President Chester Arthur created a 50-square-mile "buffer zone" (which includes the site of Whiteclay) south of the Pine Ridge reservation expressly to curtail the liquor trade. This order was re-scinded on January 25, 1904, by President Theodore Roosevelt with the ratio-nale that non-Indians needed the land.

For years, Nebraska officials had been warned by activist Frank LaMere and others that the situation in Whiteclay could explode. One day during the summer of 1997, LaMere, a Winnebago who was executive director of the Nebraska Inter-Tribal Development Corporation, visited Whiteclay. He counted thirty-two intoxicated Indians on the town's streets at 5:15 in the morning and forty-seven drunks on the streets during the afternoon, some of whom were fighting with each other. Several other Indians were passed out at the intersection of Nebraska Highway 87 with the road that leads to the reservation. A few of them were urinating on the street (Johansen, 1998, 5).

Shortly after he visited Whiteclay, LaMere asked the Nebraska Liquor Con-trol Commission to shut Whiteclay down. "I don't know what constitutes in-fractions of liquor laws in Whiteclay, but my good sense tells me there is something terribly wrong," LaMere told Toni Heinzl of the *Omaha World-Herald*. "What I saw . . . in Whiteclay would not be acceptable in Omaha or Lincoln," LaMere continued (Johansen, 1998, 5).

The Pine Ridge Reservation in 1996 had an alcoholism-related death rate of 61.9 per 100,000 people, twice the average for Native American reservations and nine times the national average of 7.1. On the two-mile highway between Pine Ridge village and Whiteclay, tribal police issued at least 1,000 driving while intoxicated citations per year. Despite the police presence, residents who live along the road were constantly pestered by drunks. Several family dogs had been shot to death along the road as well.

On Saturday, July 3, 1999, about 100 sheriff's deputies and state patrol officers, many of them in riot gear, barricaded Whiteclay's business district. Ironically, the Nebraska State Patrol had met one of the protesters' demands: For Friday and Saturday at least, the beer stores of Whiteclay would be closed on one of their busiest weekends of the year. During Friday afternoon, car-avans of cars from Pine Ridge circled Whiteclay and its barricades in an air of ghostly quiet, using several back roads.

Aside from a few rocks thrown and nine brief arrests (one of them of Russell Means), the July 3 march came and went without notable physical contact between the Lakota Sioux and the hundred SWAT-suited police officers barricading Whiteclay. Many participants in the march stressed the spiritual nature of their actions. Marchers stopped four times to pray (and to give elderly marchers some rest) during the hour and a half it took the group of several hundred people to move from Pine Ridge to Whiteclay on a hot and unusually humid day.

As they approached Whiteclay, marchers debated whether to cross a line of yellow plastic tape that police had strung across the road into the village. Most urged restraint, but Russell Means urged the group on. One man on a pinto pony tried to run the line but was stopped by police. Means and the eight others who were arrested also stepped over the line briefly, as they were cited for failure to obey a lawful order, to establish a basis for a later court case (the activists contended that their arrests were illegal). They were released an hour later. Other marchers threw mud at the helmeted troopers. A few spit on them and cursed. One protester plastered a bumper sticker reading "You Are on Indian Land" across one officer's helmet.

As the dust settled in Whiteclay following the second rally, the beer stores opened briefly Monday morning, but closed once again after Clyde Bellecourt told Stuart Kozel, owner of the Jumping Eagle Inn, that opening his store would provoke another confrontation with AIM. Another beer outlet with a distinctly Indian-sounding name, the Arrowhead Inn, also remained closed for an extra day.

On Saturday, July 10, a smaller rally was held, followed by another march and motorcade from Pine Ridge to Whiteclay. Roughly 100 people on foot and in cars sang and drummed as they paraded up and down Whiteclay streets unimpeded by police this time. AIM members posted "eviction notices" on the four beer stores, then withdrew to tipis and tents erected on the site where the bodies of Black Elk and Hard Heart had been found June 8. The people in the camp pledged to maintain it (along with weekly demonstrations in Whiteclay) until the border town went "dry."

In the meantime, LaMere, one of nine people who had been arrested at the initial rally, appealed again to the Nebraska Liquor Control Commission to shut down Whiteclay's beer businesses permanently. Again, the board did not act; within days, the activists were gone, and most of the Indians on the streets of Whiteclay were falling-down drunk.

President Bill Clinton visited Pine Ridge later the same summer. The White House called the tour (which included communities in Appalachia, the Mississippi Delta, South Phoenix, and the Watts area of Los Angeles as well as Pine Ridge) the New Markets Initiative. The main purpose of the four-day tour was to lobby for business development of impoverished areas; some White House planners had suggested that the federal government match certain forms of private investment in such areas.

When President Clinton arrived at Pine Ridge July 7, he found a page out of the Meriam Report (Lewis, 1928), a state of reservation life in many cases little changed from the days of Franklin Roosevelt or Dwight Eisenhower. The Pine Ridge and its neighboring Rosebud Sioux reservations are among the poorest ten counties in the United States. Clinton arrived at Ellsworth Air Force Base, near Rapid City, early Wednesday morning and after a lengthy drive arrived at Pine Ridge village by midmorning. The president ceremonially signed documents creating an empowerment zone at Pine Ridge (the first such zone on an Indian reservation), toured a few housing areas, gave a speech at Pine Ridge High School, and was on his way back to Ellsworth after lunch.

Clinton thus completed a three-hour visit to Pine Ridge that made him the first sitting U.S. president to visit an Indian reservation since Franklin Delano Roosevelt, as well as the first to visit Pine Ridge since Calvin Coolidge (in 1927). During his 20-minute speech at Pine Ridge High School, Clinton greeted the 4,500 people in Lakota and promised such things as a doubling of the number of federal-backed mortgages at Pine Ridge, a move meant to add 1,000 homes to the reservation within a few years. As Clinton spoke, the waiting list for housing there stood at 4,000 units.

GAMBLING: THE NEW BUFFALO?

During the late twentieth century, commercial gambling became a major source of income on some Indian reservations across the United States. Although many Native American cultures traditionally practiced forms of gambling as a type of sport (such as the Iroquois peachstone game), no Native American historical precedent exists for large-scale experience with gambling as a commercial enterprise. The arrival of gaming has brought dividends to some Native American peoples and controversy culminating in firefights and death for others.

The history of reservation-based commercial gambling began during 1979, when the Seminoles became the first Native nation to enter the bingo industry. By early 1985, 75 to 80 of the 300 recognized Indian tribes in the United States were conducting some sort of game of chance. By the fall of 1988, the Congressional Research Service estimated that more than 100 Indian nations and tribes participated in some form of gambling, which grossed about $255 million a year. By 1991, 278 Native reservations recognized by non-Indian governmental bodies, 150 had some form of gambling. According to the Interior Department, gross revenue from such operations passed $1 billion that year.

Individual prizes in some reservation bingo games were reported to be as high as $100,000; bingo stakes in surrounding areas under state jurisdiction were sometimes limited to $100. The reasons for growth in gambling on Indian land were readily apparent. Native governments sensed an opportunity for income that could make a substantial improvement in their economic conditions. A lack of state or federal regulations provided them a competitive advantage over off-reservation gambling regulated by the states. These advantages included a lack of state-imposed limits on the size of pots or prizes, no restrictions by the states on days or hours of operations, no costs for licenses or compliance with state regulations, and (unless they were negotiated) no state taxes on gambling operations.

By the 1990s, gambling was providing a small galaxy of material benefits for some formerly impoverished Native peoples. A half-hour's drive from the Twin Cities, blackjack players crowded forty-one tables, while 450 other players stared into video slot machines inside the tipi-shaped Little Six Casino, operated by the 103 members of the Shakopee Mdewakanton Sioux tribe. By 1991, each member of the tribe was getting a monthly dividend check averaging $2,000 as a shareholder in the casino. In addition to monthly dividends, members became eligible for homes (if they lacked them), guaranteed jobs (if they were unemployed), and full college scholarships. The tribal government took out health insurance policies for everyone on the reservation and established day care for children of working parents.

The largest casino to open by mid-1991 was the $3 million Sycuan Gaming Center on the Sycuan Indian Reservation, near El Cajon, a suburb of San Diego, California. The casino's rakish neon sign flashed against a rocky patch of land onto which the government forced the tribe to move more than a century ago. The sign was visible miles away over scrub-covered hills.

Native American gaming revenue grew to $10.6 billion during 2000, representing 16 percent of the $64.9 billion generated by gaming in the United States as a whole (Wanamaker, May 13, 2002). By 2002, Indian gaming revenue had grown to $14.5 billion, but according to the National Indian Gaming Commission, 65 percent of the cash was flowing into only 7 percent of the gaming tribes (Fialka, 2004). By 2003, Native American casinos in the United States took in $16.2 billion annually, a 12 percent increase from the prior year according to a study by Alan Meister, an economist with the Analysis Group of Los Angeles. Indian casinos' revenue was about 35 percent of the U.S. total. Native American casinos paid $5.3 in taxes and $16.3 billion in wages, providing 460,000 jobs ("Fast Growing," 2004).

Also according to the National Indian Gaming Association, Indian gaming by 2002 contributed approximately $120 million in state and local tax receipts annually. Gaming patrons spent an estimated $237 million in local communities around Indian casinos (Marquez, 2002). Of the 562 federally recognized Native American governmental entities in the United States at that time, 201 participated in class II or III gaming by 2001. Class II includes such games as bingo, pull tabs, lotto, punchboards, and certain card games permissible under individual state laws. Class III includes everything else, such as casino-style table games like roulette and craps and card games such as poker and blackjack. Indian casinos operated in 29 states under a total of 249 separate gaming compacts (Wanamaker, April 5, 2002).

The Oneidas of New York: A Business Called a Nation

Thirty years ago, the New York Oneidas' landholdings were down to thirty-two acres east of Syracuse, with almost no economic infrastructure. Three decades later, the New York Oneidas owned a large casino, the Turning Stone, which had incubated a number of other business ventures. Many of the roughly 1,000 Oneidas who resided in the area were receiving substantial material benefits.

The Turning Stone earns an estimated net profit of $70 million a year on $230 million gross income. Roughly 4.2 million visitors passed through the casino's doors per year (many of these were repeat visits). The casino's influence on the tax base of nearby small towns was enormous. James Chapell, mayor of the town of Oneida, for example, said that the Oneidas had taken so much land off the tax rolls that the town's tax revenues fell from $700,000 to $139,000 in one year. The town of Oneida has resisted requesting financial help from the Oneida Nation, but nearby Verona, which faced similar declines in tax revenue, negotiated funding for a water project as well as $800,000 for local services (Randolph, 2003).

A substantial dissident movement has grown among Oneidas, who assert that Raymond Halbritter, "nation representative" of the New York Oneidas, was never voted into such an office. This group is centered in the Shenandoah family, which includes the notable singer Joanne Shenandoah and her husband, activist Doug George-Kanentiio. They believe that the New York Oneidas under Halbritter have established a business, called it a nation, and acquired the requisite approvals from New York State and the U.S. federal government to use this status to open the Turning Stone. The dissidents' benefits as Oneidas were eliminated after they took part, during 1995, in a "march for democracy" to make these points (Johansen, 2002).

The New York Oneidas under Halbritter's aegis appointed a men's council (a body unheard of in traditional matrilineal Iroquois law or tradition), which issued a zoning code to "beautify" the Oneida Nation. This code enabled his fifty-four-member police force (patrolling a thirty-two-acre reservation) to "legally" evict from their homes Oneidas who opposed his role as leader of the New York Oneidas. Halbritter's control also was supported by the acquisition of a number of other businesses, a phalanx of public relations spin doctors, several lawyers, and ownership of *Indian Country Today*, a national Native American newspaper.

The story of the New York Oneidas is a particularly raw example of conflicts that beset many Native American nations that have attempted to address problems of persistent poverty and economic marginalization by opening casinos. Supporters of the casinos see them as the new buffalo; opponents look at them as a form of internal colonization, an imposition of European-descended economic institutions and values on Native American peoples.

In few areas is the conflict as sharp as among the Haudenosaunee, or Iroquois Confederacy, where New York State governor George Pataki promoted plans to

Shenandoah

OPENS WOODSTOCK 1994

Joanne Shenandoah opened Woodstock '95 with an original song entitled "America". The award winning artist has achieved national acclaim for her conscientious and original compositions. From traditional chants to contemporary ballads, her music has been described as a "powerful, emotional experience" and a "Native American Trance". From love songs to melodies which reach deep into the soul, her stellar performances and music recordings have astounded and electrified audiences around the world. Her songs have been heard on many television productions such as PBS, Discovery and the popular CBS series "Northern Exposure". Her albums include: Joanne Shenandoah, Loving Ways (with A. Paul Ortega), Once in a Red Moon and Life Blood (with Peter Kater).

For further information and booking contact:
Joanne Shenandoah
Oneida Indian Territory, Box Ten, Oneida, NY 13421
Tel & Fax (315) 363-1655

Joanne Shenandoah at Woodstock II. (Photo credit: Henry Diorio. Courtesy of Joanne Shenandoah.)

open as many as six new Native-controlled casinos in an attempt to jump-start a state economy that was badly damaged by the attacks of September 11, 2001. On various Internet sites and chat rooms, supporters of Halbritter accused the Shenandoah family of supporting antitreaty groups, and opponents of the Oneidas' corporate structure routinely called Halbritter "the king" and "the despot."

The recent experience of the Oneidas of New York raised several significant questions for Indian Country as a whole. Is the Oneida model of an economic powerhouse key to defining the future of Native American sovereignty in the opening years of the twenty-first century, as many of its supporters believe? Materially, the New York Oneidas have gained a great deal in a quarter century, including repurchase of 14,000 acres of land. Have these gains been offset by an atmosphere of stifling totalitarianism and a devastating loss of traditional bearings, as many Oneida dissidents attest?

The Foxwoods Money Machine

Mashantucket means "the much-wooded land." The word *Foxwoods* is a combination of the notion of forest with the Pequots' reputation as "the fox people." Foxwoods started as a very small bingo parlor after roughly forty banks refused to loan money to the Pequots. The bingo parlor began operating in 1986 and became wildly successful, drawing its clientele mainly from the urban corridor that stretches from Boston to New York City. Having obtained backing from outside the United States, the Pequots opened their full-scale casino in 1992. At the time, Foxwoods was the only gaming establishment on the East Coast offering poker, which was banned at the time in Atlantic City.

The first day Foxwoods opened, February 14, 1992, its 1,700-car parking lot was full by 10:30 A.M. Roughly 75,000 people passed through the casino's doors there during that first day, and 2,000 of them were still present at the casino's 4 A.M. closing time. During the ensuing decade, Foxwoods expanded and became one of the most notable examples anywhere of Native American economic development.

By the year 2000, the Foxwoods complex was drawing about 50,000 people on an average day. By that time, the Foxwoods Resort Casino complex included five casinos housing more than 300,000 square feet of gaming space, 5,842 slot machines, 370 gaming tables, a 3,000-seat high-stakes bingo parlor with $1 million jackpots, a 200-seat Sportsbook, and a Keno lounge. Table games included baccarat, minibaccarat, big six wheels, blackjack, Caribbean stud poker, craps, pai gow, pai gow tiles, red dog, roulette, and a number of other games. The Foxwoods casino complex also included four hotels, ranging in size from 280 to 800 rooms each. In addition to gaming space and its four hotels, Foxwoods also offered twenty-three shopping areas, twenty-four food-and-beverage outlets, and a movie theater complex, as well as the

404   *The Native Peoples of North America*

Mashantucket Pequot museum and a Fox Grand Theater featuring Las Vegas-style entertainment.

Foxwoods quickly became a very large financial success for its sponsors, as well as the state government of Connecticut, to which the casino's management pledged a quarter of its profits. During the fiscal year beginning July 1, 1999, and ending June 30, 2000, Foxwoods' gross revenues on its slot and video machines alone totaled more than $9 billion. Foxwoods quickly became an integral pillar of Connecticut's economy and a multimillion-dollar contributor to the state's charities. The Pequots' casino even put up cash one year to help the state balance its budget.

By 2000, the Foxwoods casino complex was paying the state of Connecticut more than $189 million a year in taxes. The Foxwoods and a second, more recently constructed, casino, the Mohegan Sun, paid the state of Connecticut more than $318 million during the 1999–2000 fiscal year. The Mashantucket Pequots became the state of Connecticut's largest single taxpayer and, with 13,000 jobs, one of its larger employers. The casino complex employed a staff of lawyers and maintained its own permanent lobbying office in Washington, D.C.

At the same time, the Pequots also became a significant contributor to the Smithsonian's new National Museum of the American Indian at $10 million. That amount was soon matched by the New York Oneidas, drawing from its own casino profits. The Mashantucket Pequots also gave $2 million to the Special Olympics and $500,000 to the Hartford Ballet, as well as $5 million to the Mystic, Connecticut, aquarium. During June 2001, the Mohegans, owners of the neighboring Mohegan Sun casino, made an equal pledge.

To illustrate the volume of money changing hands in these casinos, consider that Mohegan Sun casino investors included Trading Cove Associates, headed by Sol Kerzner, creator of the Sun City casino and resort in South Africa. By 2000, this firm had received more than $800 million in fees, a sum the company argued was fair compensation for services rendered.

Death at Akwesasne

Although gambling has brought benefits to some Native American communities, it brought violence to the Akwesasne Mohawks of St. Regis in upstate New York. The violence erupted in part over the issue of gambling. As many as seven casinos had opened illegally along the reservation's main highway as the area became a crossroads for illicit smuggling of drugs, including cocaine and tax-free liquor and cigarettes.

Tension escalated after early protests of gambling in the late 1980s (including the trashing of one casino and the burning of another, to attempts by gambling supporters to brutally repress this resistance). Residents blockaded the reservation to keep the casinos' customers out, prompting the violent destruction of the same blockades by gambling supporters in late April 1990.

By that time, violence had spiraled into brutal beatings of antigambling activists, drive-by shootings, and firefights that culminated in two Mohawk deaths during the early morning of May 1. Intervention of several police agencies from the United States and Canada followed the two deaths; outside police presence continued for years afterward (Johansen, 1993).

Everyone who is familiar with Akwesasne Mohawk Territory knows it has been the scene of considerable smuggling between the United States and Canada, but no one knew the extent of the traffic until its volume drew the attention of prosecutors and police in both countries. By late 1999, with several convicted smugglers awaiting sentencing, the size of the smuggling "industry" outlined in court records was astounding even veteran observers. The evidence presented by prosecutors is outlining the largest smuggling operation since the border between the United States and Canada was established.

Akwesasne is the only Native American reservation that straddles the U.S.-Canadian border and as such has long provided a smuggling route for anything illegal that may be in demand across either border. This cargo varies from cigarettes and hard liquor (which are taxed much more heavily in Canada than in the United States), to several varieties of illegal narcotics, automatic weapons, and even human beings. Immigration authorities at one point broke a smuggling ring that was ferrying people (most of them illegal immigrants from Asia) across the border at a cost of $45,000 to $50,000 each.

The right of Mohawks to cross the border unimpeded is recognized by the Jay Treaty (1794), which Canadian authorities have occasionally contested. Various enterprising Akwesasne residents have become adept at selling their connections as border middlemen, the central link in the smuggling chain. A few years ago, a story floated around the reservation that a local "kingpin" was negotiating to buy a small island in the St. Lawrence River for about $225,000 for use as a smuggling base. After the two parties agreed on the price, the new owner walked to a closet in his home, which was stacked floor to ceiling with cash in large denominations. He peeled an inch or two off the top of the stack to pay for the island.

The Canadian federal government has asserted that taxing authorities in that country lost $750 million in potential revenue because of smuggling through Akwesasne between 1991 and 1997, when the biggest smuggling ring was busted. Nearly as much money was laundered through an armored car business in Massena, New York. Prosecutors requested that U.S. District Court Judge Thomas McAvoy sentence John "Chick" Fountain of Massena to seven years in prison and forfeiture of an unspecified amount worth of personal property for his role in laundering $557 million through his armored car and currency exchange business. Before he started this business, Fountain had lived much more modestly as a New York State trooper.

Fountain, convicted November 3, 1998, was one of twenty-seven people prosecutors alleged had important roles in a smuggling ring that at its height operated large warehouses and squads of motorboats which were used to ferry goods and people across the St. Lawrence River. When the river was frozen, smuggling often took place in automobiles. The smuggling ring drew some well-known names at Akwesasne into its ambit, including long-time gambling developer Tony Laughing and former St. Regis Tribal Chief Leo David Jacobs, who was convicted of taking $32,000 in kickbacks paid to link Miller with a number of Akwesasne businessmen. One of these businessmen was Loran Thompson, owner of a marina, a restaurant, and what New York radio reporter Neil Drew of Malone, New York, called "a very busy cigarette warehouse along the St. Lawrence River . . . where millions of cartons were purchased for smuggling into Canada" (2001).

The alleged kingpin of the smuggling cartel was Larry Miller of Massena, who traveled the world in a Lear Jet and owned five houses in Las Vegas as well as an estate not far from the source of his income: the porous international border through Akwesasne. According to court records, Miller made as much as $35 million a year at the height of the operation. Prosecutors suggested that Judge McAvoy fine Miller $160 million in cash and personal assets in addition to asking that he be sentenced to 17 to 22 years in prison.

INDIVIDUAL INDIAN TRUST ASSETS: WHERE HAS ALL THE MONEY GONE?

The Individual Indian Monies (IIM) mess has become the stuff of political and legal legend since the *Cobell v. Norton* (240 F.3rd 1081 [DC Cir. 2001]) class action was first filed in 1996. With 500,000 plaintiffs for whom the BIA played banker for a century or more, the case has grown to be the largest class action ever filed against the U.S. federal government. Employing more than 100 lawyers on the payrolls of the Interior and Treasury Departments, *Cobell v. Norton* (after Elouise Cobell, lead plaintiff, and Gale Norton, Secretary of the Interior) has become the largest single employer of federal legal talent in the history of the republic.

How much money is at stake? In 1997 (Johansen, 1997, 14–23), the commonly accepted figure was between $2 and $3 billion. By late 2002, lead prosecutor Dennis Gingold placed the figure at "far north of $10 billion" (Kennedy, 2002). A report prepared for the Interior Department suggested that the federal government's total liability might reach $40 billion. Tack on a few billion more, and you have Uncle Sam's annual bill for the Iraq war.

On December 21, 1999, Judge Royce C. Lamberth, who is overseeing the case in the Washington, D.C., federal district court, issued his first (Phase One) opinion (the case is divided into two phases). The 126-page opinion stated that the government had baldly violated its trust responsibilities to Native Americans. He called the IIM mess the "most egregious misconduct by the federal government." Although *Cobell v. Norton* is certainly a big-stakes case, such a superlative overstated its historical scope. Perhaps it is the most egregious example of *financial* misconduct in a trust relationship by the U.S.

government, which in its two-plus centuries has done worse to Native Americans than lose several billion dollars.

Judge Lamberth later ordered the government to file reports quarterly describing in detail its efforts to account for the monies. The judge also ordered the Interior and Treasury Departments to compile an audit of the IIM trust fund system reaching to its origins in 1887. At present, the Bush Administration's unwillingness to follow Lamberth's order comprises the legal line of scrimmage in what may turn out to be a decades-long battle.

Judge Lamberth is a Republican appointee, a Texan with a taste for fancy boots and large cars who seemed, on the surface, unlikely to take a serious interest in a Native American class action suit. However, he possessed a keen knowledge of bureaucratic politics and an ability to read and comprehend vast amounts of information. Like fishing rights judge George Hugo Boldt (also a Republican appointee), Lamberth has a sharp sense of justice, regardless of vested interests. He is, in other words (also like Boldt), hard working and ruthlessly honest.

During its eight-year run to 2004, the IIM case has produced evidence of what must have been the world's sloppiest banking record keeping. Even Elouise Cobell, who initiated the suit, has been amazed at the sorry state of the BIA's banking system, if it could be called that. Cobell, a member of the Blackfeet Tribe and a banker by profession, filed the suit in 1996. Cobell, of Browning, Montana, founded (and still has a hand in operating) the first Native American–owned bank in the United States. She also served as treasurer of the Blackfeet from 1970 through 1983.

Cobell's education in the BIA's ways of banking began with a detailed examination of the Blackfeet's trust accounts. After Cobell discovered a number of problematic transactions, she began asking questions. Her initial inquiries were rebuffed by the BIA. "They said, 'Oh! you don't know how to read the reports,'" Cobell recalled. "I think they were trying to embarrass me, but it did the opposite—it made me mad" (Awehali, 2003).

Cobell has spent much of her life in and near the reservation town of Browning, Montana. She was one of eight children in a house with no electricity or running water. The major form of entertainment was old fashioned: oral history, sometimes describing Baker's Massacre, during which U.S. soldiers killed about 200 Blackfeet, a majority of them women and children, following an ambush near the Marias River. She also sometimes heard stories from her parents and their neighbors about small government checks that bore no relationship to reality.

Today, Cobell spends much of her time tutoring Blackfeet and other Native peoples in ways to start their own businesses. She also helps with chores on a ranch that she co-owns with her husband, Alvin. During a sojourn off the reservation in her twenties (she is now nearly fifty), Elouise met Alvin, who is also Blackfoot, in Seattle. He was fishing off the Alaska coast, and she held a job as an accountant with a Seattle television station.

At the age of thirty, Cobell returned to Browning with Alvin to resume a life on the family ranch. She also was offered a job as the reservation government's accountant. At the time, Browning had practically no Native-owned businesses; unemployment rose to more than 70 percent in winter (which can last into May), when construction employment ceased. She found the Blackfeet accounting system "in total chaos." Some trust accounts were being charged negative interest. Checks were being posted against accounts without her knowledge, even though she was supposed to be the only valid signatory. In 1987, Cobell moved on to start the first Native-owned bank in the United States, mainly to help finance local business ventures. In a few years, she could point to several businesses that she had helped to finance: the Glacier Restaurant, Browning Video, the Dollar Store (Kennedy, 2002).

Years before the class action suit was filed, Cobell asked questions within the system. As she began to delve into the trust issue on a national basis, in Washington, D.C., Cobell was introduced to Dennis A. Gingold, who is now the lead prosecuting attorney for the case, who was quoted in the *Los Angeles Times* as saying of his first meeting with her: "From my experience, American Indians were not involved in banking. I was looking for a bunch of people with turbans" (Kennedy, 2003). Gingold admitted that he had a great deal to learn about how the government had separated Native Americans from their trust assets.

Cobell did not decide to file suit lightly, but only after several rebuffs by the government that displayed an unwillingness to take the trust accounts problem seriously. She realized that large legal actions were massively expensive. Her years of activism and her experience as the Blackfeet's accountant had suggested some sources of support, however. She contacted the Arthur Bremer Foundation of St. Paul, Minnesota, and won a $75,000 grant and a $600,000 loan. In 1997, a year after she filed the class action suit, Cobell also received, quite unexpectedly, a $300,000 "genius" grant from the John D. MacArthur Foundation, most of which went into the case. Shortly after that, J. Patrick Lannan of the Lannan Foundation read about Cobell's MacArthur grant and traveled to Browning to meet with her. Lannan eventually donated $4 million to the cause. By mid-2002, the cost of the legal action had reached $8 million, still barely a drop in the proverbial bucket next to the hundreds of millions of dollars in tax money that the federal government has spent to defend itself.

Some in the government saw the problem coming before Cobell filed suit. During 1992, the House of Representatives Committee on Government Operations issued a report, "Misplaced Trust: The Bureau of Indian Affairs' Mismanagement of the Indian Trust Fund." During 1994, Congress passed the Indian Trust Fund Management Reform Act, with the stated aim of cleaning up the mess. As part of this law's implementation, Paul Homan, an expert at cleaning up failing private financial institutions, was hired. Homan, having taken stock of the situation, later quit in disgust as he described a banker's nightmare.

The BIA, for example, did not establish an accounts receivable system, so it never knew how much money it was handling at any given time. Partial records indicated that more than $50 million was never paid because the BIA had lost track of account holders. About 21,000 accounts were listed in the names of people who were dead. Large numbers of records had been stored in cardboard boxes, left to soak (and smear) in leaky warehouses. About $695 million had been paid, but to the wrong people or Native governmental entities. One property record valued chain saws at $99 million each. Some of the records were contaminated with asbestos, and others had been paved over by a parking lot. As he resigned, Homan said he had never seen anything like this in his 30 years as a banker.

Before he quit, Homan reported that no one knew just how many people were owed money. Of the 238,000 individual trusts that Homan's staff located, 118,000 were missing crucial papers, 50,000 had no addresses, and 16,000 accounts had no documents at all. Homan further reported that one could assume money had been skimmed extensively from the trust: "It's akin to leaving the vault door open," he said (Awehali, 2003).

In the meantime, before a dime has been paid to any of the 500,000 Native people who are part of the class action, the Bush administration seems to have established some sort of perpetual motion lawyer employment fund. It requested $554 million in the 2004 budget to "reform" the trust fund, an increase of $183.3 million over $370.2 million budgeted in 2003. Reform in this case means, to a large degree, paying legal talent to protect Uncle Sam against the class action suit; as with John Ashcroft's Patriot Act, the terminology here is highly Orwellian. In a January 2001 interview with Harlan McKosato on the national radio show *Native America Calling*, Cobell noted that "just by not settling the case, it's costing the government and taxpayers $160,000 an hour, $7 million a day, $2.5 billion a year" (Awehali, 2003).

Pen-and-Ink Witchcraft

With the government's mismanagement now so widely known, a sensible person might conclude that the time has come to find a way to reimburse the many Native people who have been cheated. If you are one of the 500,000 Native Americans who unwillingly did your banking with the BIA, when might you expect a corrective check in the mail? Don't hold your breath. If the Bush administration has its way, you could turn very blue before the guarantor of your trust makes you, as they say in financial litigation circles, "whole."

The spin doctors in the White House probably do not realize that their designs resemble some treaty negotiations for their Alice-in-Wonderland quality (things are never what they seem). In 1791, the famed Ottawa speaker Egushawa, observing treaty negotiations, called such machinations pen-and-ink witchcraft.

What Egushawa witnessed had nothing on the trust money mess. After eight years of legal shuck and jive by the federal government, the central fact of the case is this: The BIA and Treasury Department never built a record-keeping system capable of tracking the money owed to Native Americans based on income from its supervision of their resources.

As time passed (the system, in its modern incantation, began with the advent of the Allotment Act in 1887), the lack of a functioning banking system made record keeping worse; the sloppiness of errant (or nonexistent) record keeping was compounded, for example, because of divisions of estate required by generations of fractional Native inheritances. By the time Cobell and a few other banking-minded Native Americans began asking seriously what had become of their IIM, the Interior Department by and large did not have a clue.

In an average year, $500 million or more was deposited into the Individual Indian Trust from companies leasing Native American land for grazing, oil drilling, timber, coal, and other natural resources. According to law and financial theory, the money is collected by the Interior and sent to the Treasury, which is supposed to place it into individual trust accounts. Problems began with the roughly 50,000 accounts that lacked names or correct addresses. One such account contained $1 million (Awehali, 2003). Along the way, it also was learned that some people simply neglected to pay as expected; they soon learned that, much of the time, no one seemed to be watching.

As early as 1999, the plaintiffs' legal team discovered that the Departments of Interior and Treasury had "inadvertently" destroyed 162 boxes of vital trust records during the course of the trial, then waited months to notify the court of the "accident." "You tell me if that's fair," Cobell told Mike Wallace in a *60 Minutes* interview shortly after the discovery. "When they have to manage other people's money according to standards, why aren't they managing our money to standards? Is it because you manage brown people's money differently?" (Awehali, 2003).

Judge Lamberth was shocked when he discovered, in the course of the lawsuit, that the Interior and Treasury Departments had, as a matter of course, destroyed accounting documents and filed false reports with the court. In the course of the litigation, thirty-seven past and present government officials, including Bush's Secretary of the Interior Gale Norton and Clinton's Interior Secretary Bruce Babbitt, have been held in contempt of court. On August 10, 1999, Lamberth ordered the Treasury Department to pay $600,000 in fines for misconduct.

As he delved into the trust account debacle, Lamberth found that some records were stored in rat-infested New Mexico warehouses. Others were dispersed haphazardly on several remote reservations. When the Interior Department kept computerized records at all, they were so inadequate and insecure that hackers could set up their own accounts (and presumably draw money from them).

During the first phase of the case, many experts testified that the Interior and Treasury Departments lack the records to render any semblance of true accounting for the monies that the government was supposed to be managing. Instead, the plaintiffs have suggested various methods of estimating what is owed. For example, the Geographic Information System (GIS) might use satellite mapping technology to estimate the amount of oil produced by wells on Native lands and thereby derive an idea of royalties owed.

Land of the Midnight Rider

During September 2003, Judge Lamberth ordered the Interior Department to conduct a thorough investigation into money that was supposed to be paid to Indians for oil, gas, timber, and grazing activities on their land dating back to 1887. He said that the accounting must be completed by 2007.

Responding to Lamberth's first-phase opinion and this directive, Cobell was enthusiastic at the time. "This is a landmark victory," she said. "It is now clear that trust law and trust standards fully govern the management of the Individual Indian Trust and that Secretary Norton can no longer ignore the trust duties that she owes to 500,000 individual Indian trust beneficiaries" (Awehali, 2003).

The idea of a complete accounting, which sounded so simple, suddenly became very problematic in the land of pen-and-ink witchcraft. Interior and Treasury Departments, with their allies on Capitol Hill and in the Bush White House, prepared a hastily inserted "midnight rider" to a federal spending bill that forbade spending that would have implemented Lamberth's directive. Funding, according to the rider, was to be frozen for a year or until an accounting methodology could be agreed on by the Interior and Treasury Departments and Congress.

In the meantime, the Interior Department was reported by several news organizations as complaining that the type of historical accounting required by Judge Lamberth's ruling would take ten years and cost $6 to $12 billion. Some feat of accounting that would be—the accounting equivalent, perhaps, of building the Panama Canal or putting many men on the moon, a rubber figure with an odor of obstructionist politics. (To illustrate just how rubbery this estimate is, let us crunch a few round numbers. At $100,000 each per year, very good pay for an accountant, $10 billion would hire 100,000 accountants. Even if they worked ten years each, $10 billion would still pay 10,000 number crunchers. Add a few zeroes here and there, and soon we are talking about some very serious money. Bear in mind that the folks who came up with these quick estimates work at the same agencies that lost track of all that Native American money in the beginning.)

With a federal budget deficit approaching $400 billion a year (including Iraq and Afghanistan wars and reconstruction liabilities running at least $87 billion a year), the Bush Administration and Republican-controlled Congress seemed unwilling to seriously consider paying a century-plus of Indian trust money bills that could cost as much as $40 billion—the bill that could come out of the second phase of the case, once Interior and Treasury Departments assessed the due bills as ordered by Judge Lamberth. The midnight rider was sponsored in large part by a Republican-controlled executive branch and Congress that added 721,000 federal jobs to the payroll since George W. Bush assumed office almost four years prior.

About fifty Republicans voted against the appropriations bill containing the rider, however, led by Representative Richard Pombo (R-Calif.), chair of the House Resources Committee, with Representative J. D. Hayworth (R-Ariz.), co-chair of the bipartisan House Native American Caucus. Pombo, who favored a legislative solution to the court case, called the rider a "poison pill that was added to the legislation in blatant violation of House rules and protocol" (Reynolds, 2003). The rider passed narrowly, 216–205, October 30.

The Senate passed the spending bill (with the midnight rider) 87–2 November 4 and sent it to Bush for his signature November 10. Cobell sharply criticized President Bush's administration, including Interior Secretary Norton, for sponsoring the rider. Said Cobell: "What this vote shows is the length that the Interior Secretary and the Bush administration will go to in their efforts to deny Indians the accounting for funds that belong to Indians—not the federal government. Now American Indians are being victimized once again by politicians in Washington" (Reynolds, 2002). Cobell said that she expected the courts to strike down the rider as an illegal interference with the judicial process, a violation of the Constitution's separation of powers.

"It's a clear act of bad faith to seek a stay based on an unconstitutional statute," said Gingold ("Appeals Court," 2003). The Senate's legal counsel and House members from both parties said the provision is probably unconstitutional because the administration cannot dictate to courts how to interpret the law.

Wither the Trust Fund Billions?

So, wither the trust fund case? When all is said and done, will the plaintiffs in *Cobell v. Norton* ever get anything close to what they are owed? Although optimism is always in season and justice sometimes does actually prevail, there is ample precedent in U.S. legal history vis-à-vis Native Americans to create doubts that right and reasonable outcomes follow the opinions of courts presided over by hard-working, honest judges, even after the government has copiously admitted its errors.

Some historical parallels present themselves: John Marshall, chief justice of the U.S. Supreme Court, found in favor of the Cherokees' sovereignty; President Andrew Jackson ignored him and his Court, leading to the Trail of Tears (Jackson's action was an impeachable offense, contempt of the Supreme Court, a violation of his oath of office. It was never prosecuted because

Georgia made a states' rights case that could have started the Civil War 30 years before it actually began.)

More recently, during the mid-1970s, the courts found in favor of a 250,000-acre land claim for the Oneidas. Thirty years later, they have yet to receive any land from this legal proceeding.

Might *Cobell v. Norton* end up being another perpetual motion employment engine for lawyers and another reminder that sometimes the legal system talks the talk as the executive branch fails to walk the walk of justice? Or might the contending parties, with Judge Lamberth's prodding, find a way at least to estimate what is owed the plaintiffs—and take the necessary steps to pay them? The next few years may provide an answer after the second phase of *Cobell v. Norton* is adjudicated and a final ruling is issued by Judge Lamberth.

Senator Ben Nighthorse Campbell, who is Cheyenne, has insisted that all parties to the Cobell litigation must work together to resolve the case; he believes, otherwise, that it may not be resolved. "We have one year to reach settlement on this issue," he said during a hearing of the Senate Committee on Indian Affairs as it considered his bill, S. 1770, to encourage individual beneficiary settlements in the lawsuit (Reynolds, 2003).

Native-owned companies could benefit from the requirement that the Interior Department compile an accounting for the 117-year record of Indian trust fund mismanagement. Earnings for such work may reach $50 million by some estimates. Tlingit and Haida Technology Industries has applied to do some of the court-ordered accounting work, according to Dan DuBray, an Interior Department spokesperson quoted in the *Fairbanks Daily News-Miner* and the *Juneau Empire*, both on November 5, 2003.

Blackfeet History at Ghost Ridge

"I've heard from friends that the government thinks I'm tired and that they'll wear me down, so that I'll just go away," says Cobell (Awehali, 2003). Near Cobell's hometown, a marker describes the winter of 1884, when 500 Blackfeet died of starvation and exposure while awaiting supplies promised them by the federal government. The dead were buried in a mass grave that is now called Ghost Ridge. During the more difficult stages of the lawsuit, Cobell said she has visited Ghost Ridge, thinking of her ancestors who perished in the cold 120 years ago while waiting for the government to fulfill its promises.

The Blackfeet starved as U.S. Indian Agent John Young hoarded food that would have allowed them to survive. From Ghost Ridge, it is not difficult to draw parallels to the entire course of Indian–European American relations, most notably to the case at hand. Again, Native land and fiscal resources were taken and hoarded in faraway places as the promises of the "trust" relationship between the United States and Native peoples were massively abused.

REPATRIATION: "WHOSE BONES ARE THEY, ANYWAY?"

Controversy regarding return and reburial of American Indian human remains and funerary objects has become a volatile issue in the United States. When the United States enacted legal measures requiring their return in 1990, the remains or burial offerings of 2 million American Indians were being stored in museums, state historical societies, universities, the National Park Service offices, private warehouses, and curio shops.

Many Native Americans resent retention of such human remains on religious, humanitarian, ethical, and legal grounds. American Indians have requested return of human skeletal remains and related funerary objects to the earth for several reasons. A large majority of American Indian religions believe that the souls of the deceased will not find rest unless the remains are properly interred. Decent and timely reburial of remains also has become a matter of religious freedom. These points of view were incorporated in U.S. national law, established in 1990, as the Native American Graves Protection and Repatriation Act (NAGPRA).

On the past practices of academic archeology, David Hurst Thomas, writing in *Skull Wars: Kennewick Man, Archaeology, and the Battle for Native American Identity* (2000), quotes Walter L. Echo-Hawk and Roger C. Echo-Hawk (Pawnee attorney and historian, respectively): "If you desecrate a white grave, you end up sitting in prison. But desecrate an Indian grave, [and] you get a Ph.D. The time has come for people to decide: Are we Indians part of this country's living culture, or are we just here to supply museums with dead bodies?" (p. 210).

It has been argued that the private market for human remains and funerary objects reflects a non-Indian belief that Native Americans are not fully human, that all aspects of American Indian culture were not accorded respect and equality under the law, and that traders in human remains and burial artifacts envisage Native peoples as brutal savages who lack essential qualities for civilization. As with non-Indians who support the use of Native sports mascots, traders in Native bones and burial artifacts often state openly that they are supporting and appreciating Native American peoples and their cultures.

Many American Indians have argued that civil rights laws and the U.S. Constitution (Thirteenth, Fourteenth, and Fifteenth amendments) render such points of view as legally as well as culturally obsolete. The same goes, by this line of reasoning, for the rationale that large numbers of Native American remains are being stored purportedly for future scientific use. The Native American Rights Fund contends that retention of American Indian human remains violates the Fourteenth Amendment (equal protection) and constitutional guarantees of religious freedom.

Native American historian Donald A. Grinde, Jr., made the following comparison (personal interview, October 22, 1991): When the remains of members of the armed forces who have died while missing in action and of pilots and other Vietnam veterans were returned to the United States, no one stated that these bones should be studied to give us some answers about the dangers and treatment of Agent Orange and other perils of war. Instead, the remains were respectfully reinterred with appropriate dignity and ceremony.

Many anthropologists, archeologists, state historical society personnel, and others oppose return and reburial of Native American remains for a number of reasons. Many of these arguments are based on the assumed need to hold Native American remains for the future use of scientists exercising their academic freedom. Opponents of reburial also believe that scholars or granting agencies that excavate Indian human remains "own" them and thus giving them back to Indians raises serious "property" questions.

The Case of Kennewick Man

The case of Kennewick Man became the first broad legal test of NAGPRA's provisions. A lawsuit was filed against the Corps of Engineers regarding Kennewick Man, a nearly complete, 9,200-year-old skeleton found in eastern Washington during 1996. The eight anthropologists who filed the suit represented the first major legal challenge to NAGPRA. The basic legal question became: How far into the past do Native American claims to remains extend? A federal judge in this case held during 2002 that, at 9,000-plus years, the age of Kennewick Man's remains exceeded the scope of the law.

Writing to the Corps of Engineers, physical anthropologists Douglas W. Owsley of the Smithsonian Institution and Richard L. Jantz of the University of Tennessee (Knoxville) warned: "If a pattern of returning [such] remains without study develops, the loss to science will be incalculable and we will never have the data required to understand the earliest populations in America" (Slayman, 1997, 19). In a letter to the editor in the *New York Times*, William D. Lipe, president of the Society for American Archaeology, asked that the "tribe that has claimed the ancient Washington skeleton . . . reconsider and permit additional studies to be conducted" (ibid., 19).

U.S. Representative Doc Hastings of Washington wrote to Lieutenant General Joe Ballard, commander of the Army Corps of Engineers, expressing alarm that the corps planned to give up the skeleton before it could be studied. He urged Ballard to "postpone action until the [skeleton's] origins are determined conclusively or until Congress has the opportunity to review this important issue" (Slayman, 1997, 19). In the meantime, Representative Hastings requested that the Corps allow scientists access to the bones.

The eight scientists filed their suit against the Corps of Engineers in Federal District Court, Portland, Oregon. They sought access to the skeleton and an indefinite delay of its repatriation. The scientists are Robson Bonnichsen, director of the Center for the Study of the First Americans at Oregon State University; C. Loring Brace, curator of biological anthropology at the University of Michigan's Museum of Anthropology; Dennis J. Stanford, chairman of the Smithsonian's anthropology department; Richard Jantz; Douglas Owsley; and anthropologists George W. Gill of the University of Wyoming, C. Vance Haynes, Jr., of the University of Arizona, and D. Gentry Steele of Texas A&M University.

During August 2002, after more than a year of deliberation (much of it spent reading several thousand pages of documentation) U.S. District court Judge John Jelderks found for the scientists, denying Native Americans possession of Kennewick man's remains under NAGPRA. "Allowing study is fully consistent with applicable statutes and regulations, which are clearly intended to make archaeological information available to the public through scientific research," Jelderks wrote ("Judge," 2002, 10). Jelderks' ruling was affirmed by the Ninth District Court of Appeals in San Francisco; Northwest Native groups that had been seeking repatriation then declined further appeal to the U.S. Supreme Court.

James C. Chatters, the first forensic specialist to handle the remains, supported the scientists. Chatters said that he could support the provisions of NAGPRA and oppose returning Kennewick Man to the tribes for reburial. "I have conducted repatriations for some of the same tribes who claimed this skeleton," Chatters wrote in the *Wall Street Journal*. "I support the purpose of the law" (2002, D-10). Chatters maintained that Kennewick Man's remains were outside the scope of NAGPRA. "The act," he wrote, "was not intended to turn over all ancient skeletons to some Indian tribe, regardless of relationship. . . . The past is not a possession" (ibid., D-10). To the Native nations seeking to rebury the remains, Chatters's statement was something of a simplification. They asserted that under NAGPRA, when it concerns human remains, the past is indeed a possession. The question was—and remains—how far back in time the legality of possession reaches.

Native American historian Donald A Grinde, Jr., believes the following (1993):

> While the reburial debate manifests itself in a freedom for scientific inquiry versus American Indian religious freedom, the real issue for the dominant society is control. For generations, American Indians have been decapitated and their skulls sent to the Smithsonian under the ruse of "science." In reality, the purpose was to demonstrate the utter subjugation of Native American people by the Euro-American community.

The subsidiary status of Native Americans was enshrined in U.S. law by court decisions, of which *Worcester v. Georgia* (31 U.S. [6 Pet.] 515 [1832]) is the best known. Legal doctrine established during the nineteenth century held Native Americans to be in state of wardship vis-à-vis the federal government and living in domestic dependent nations. The reclamation of remains and burial artifacts late in the twentieth century is in a way an extension of step-by-step liberation from these doctrines. Following passage of NAGPRA, the

Smithsonian Institution decided in 1991 that, because of the new federal law, it would offer to return almost 20,000 American Indian human remains from its collections.

The passage of NAGPRA at the federal level was pre-dated by similar laws in some states. In Nebraska, for example, Jim Hanson, then executive director of the Nebraska State Historical Society, responded to a state law mandating return of Native American skeletons and burial artifacts by calling it "censorship". "The work of a generation of scholars will be lost," Hanson, who often decked himself in nineteenth century cowboy gear, told an annual meeting of the historical society in Kearney, Nebraska. "For the first time in my professional career, a state government has decided to dictate" (Johansen, 1989, 15).

The "dictator," to Hanson, was Nebraska State Senator Ernie Chambers, who sponsored the act mandating return of remains and burial objects that had passed the state's Unicameral 30–16 in May 1989. Within three months, agreements along similar lines opened much larger collections to Indian tribes at Stanford University, the University of Minnesota, the Peabody Museum of Harvard, and the Smithsonian Institution.

Chambers, a Black Muslim who routinely wears a muscle shirt on the Unicameral floor, was no novice to initiating nationwide controversy. Chambers, who represents North Omaha, Nebraska's only sizable black community, sponsored legislation that made Nebraska the first state government to divest its financial interests in South Africa during the mid-1980s. Chambers's major ally in the effort to return remains and artifacts was the Pawnee Indian Nation, which had carried on a three-year campaign against the State Historical Society. The measure was drafted with the aid of the Native American Rights Fund of Boulder, Colorado.

Until passage of the Nebraska law and NAGPRA, most governmental bodies and academic institutions released skeletons and artifacts only to Native peoples who could prove familial relations to the deceased. Such relationships are usually nearly impossible to prove because very few of the remains have names or family lineages attached to them. The Nebraska measure (and others negotiated later) allowed claims of remains on a collective basis, a link that is much easier to document than familial association.

Like Hanson, the American Anthropological Association asserted that return of bones and artifacts to Indian tribes would infringe on the rights of scholars. The subject was a focus of intense controversy at an annual meeting of the association in Washington, D.C., during which Vine Deloria, Jr. (whose books, such as *Custer Died for Your Sins* (1969) and *God is Red* (1994) helped initiate Indian self-determination efforts), leveled a stinging address at the anthropologists. He said, in part, that even today many anthropologists regard Indians more as artifacts than as living human beings.

The repatriation debate ranged beyond bones and burial artifacts to such things as the wampum belts used to preserve memories of the Iroquois Great Law of Peace. Until late in the twentieth century, many of the Iroquois' wampum belts had been held by New York State. Three months after Nebraska passed its repatriation law, New York State agreed to return twelve of the belts to the Onondagas, who tend the central council fire of the Haudenosaunee Confederacy. "These belts are our archives. That's why we have been trying to get them back," said Raymond Gonyea, an Onondaga who specializes in Native American affairs at the New York State Museum (Johansen, 1989, 15).

During fall 1990, the Nebraska State Historical Society prepared, reluctantly, to return about 37,000 artifacts to the Pawnees. These included not only items manufactured by members of the tribe, but also spurs, bits, and buckles worn by Spanish conquistadors, a French medal, thousands of trade beads, and the bones of now-extinct animals such as the Great Plains grizzly bear and the ivory-billed woodpecker. The Nebraska Historical Society also returned the remains of 398 human beings to the Pawnees. More than 100 of the skeletons were taken from a village site near present-day Genoa, Nebraska, after a Pawnee village was devastated by disease about 1750. Some of the remains dated to about 1600, when the Pawnees moved into Nebraska from Kansas.

The changes in repatriation policy also benefited the Omaha Indian Tribe. About 280 artifacts were returned to the Omahas in late August 1990 from Harvard's Peabody Museum. The Peabody had held them for more than 100 years. The Smithsonian Institution returned an albino buffalo hide and a ceremonial pipe to the Omahas in 1991 after having held them since 1898. The two objects, believed to be at least 300 years old, were housed at the University of Nebraska's Lincoln campus until the Omahas completed a historical and cultural museum at Macy, the largest town on their present-day reservation. Near Macy, the Omahas also buried the remains of 92 tribal members whose skeletons were returned to them by the University of Nebraska. Although the skeletons were reburied, tribal members elected to keep artifacts above ground for exhibit and further study. The Omahas also planned to send their artifacts on tour around Nebraska on the theory that they belong to everyone.

The artifacts returned to the Omahas from the Peabody Museum included the tribe's cottonwood-and-ash sacred pole (Umon'hon'ti, the Venerable Man, the personification of the U'ma'ha Nation; Kehoe, 2002, 236), which was used for centuries to signify the life force that unified and renewed the Omahas.

"Basically, we want dead Indians out, and live Indians in," Susan Shown Harjo, executive director of the National Congress of American Indians, told the *Washington Post*. "It's a victory for America to solve a disgraceful situation where Indians are an archaeological resource, [and] our relatives are U.S. property—not quite human" (Johansen, 1989, 15).

THE INTERCOURSE ACTS: THE HISTORICAL BASIS OF MANY CONTEMPORARY LAND CLAIMS

In 1789, in one of his first acts as president, George Washington asked Secretary of War Henry Knox to prepare a report on the status of Indian affairs. Knox prepared a lengthy report on Native Americans' rights and mechanisms for dealing with them under the new U.S. Constitution. His conclusions closely resembled Spanish and English interpretations of the Doctrine of Discovery since the time of Francisco de Vitoria during the early sixteenth century. Knox found that the Indians had a right to their lands, and that land could not be taken except by mutual consent (as in agreement to a treaty) or in a "just" war as defined by the European powers of the day. Knox determined that that non-Indian squatters must be kept off Indian lands to keep the peace on the frontier.

From Knox's report emerged the first of several Trade and Intercourse Acts passed by Congress between 1790 and 1834. Congress, convening under the Constitution, passed the first such act in 1790 (25 U.S.C. paragraph 177), which said that no sale of Indian lands was valid without the authority of the United States. This initial act was extended and amended several times, in 1793, 1796, 1802, 1817, 1822, and 1834. In addition to extending federal authority to land sales, many of the Trade and Intercourse Acts forbade European American entry into Indian lands, regulated trade, and prohibited the sale of liquor.

Some of the Trade and Intercourse Acts made depredations by non-Indians against Native persons a federal crime in protected areas and promised monetary compensation to injured Natives who did not seek revenge by other means. The acts also set uniform standards for punishment of crimes by non-Indians against Indians (and vice versa) and enunciated a goal of "civilization and education" for U.S. Indian policy. Trade with Indians also came under federal regulation via the Trade and Intercourse Acts.

In a legal sense, the Trade and Intercourse Acts were a double-edged sword for Indian sovereignty. On one hand, they were passed to protect Indians from land fraud; on the other, they were an extension of federal law over Indian Country. The later intercourse acts were drafted under the theory that tribes should be considered foreign nations and that tribal lands protected by treaty, even though situated within the boundaries of a state, should be considered outside the limits of state jurisdictions (act of June 30, 1834, 4 Stat. 729, 733).

Federal jurisdiction over trade and land sales concerning Native nations had been an issue at least since the Albany Plan of Union (1754), when Iroquois delegates led by Tiyanoga (Hendrick) advised Benjamin Franklin and other colonial delegates to develop a single system for trade, land dealings, and diplomacy. The Albany Plan was rejected by the individual colonies, but the idea that the federal government retains authority over the states for dealing with Indians was written into the Constitution and has been central to American Indian law in the United States for more than two centuries.

The Trade and Intercourse Act of 1817 (3 Stat. 383) attempted the first systematic regulation of criminal jurisdiction in Indian Country. The act held that anyone, Indian or not, who committed an offense in Indian Country would be subject to the same punishment as if the offense had occurred in the United States, except for offenses defined as domestic. This exception became an important influence on subsequent court decisions delimiting juris-diction. This law became the source of opinions that defined the powers of Indian courts; generally, a non-Indian accused of a crime on Indian land has been held to be under the jurisdiction of the United States, while an Indian charged with an offense against another Indian is tried in a Native American court.

The Intercourse Acts are important today because violations of them form the legal basis for several large-scale land claims by Native Americans, es-pecially in the northeastern United States. The Penobscot and Passamaquoddy mounted a claim to two-thirds of the state of Maine during the 1970s based on violations of the Intercourse Acts. The long-standing claims by the Oneidas and other Iroquois Nation Indians also are based on similar grounds.

In *County of Oneida v. Oneida Indian Nation* (470 U.S. 226 [1985]) the Oneida people won rights to 100,000 acres of land transferred to New York State in 1795. The case was filed in 1970 and was originally dismissed in federal courts for lack of jurisdiction. The case was contested in the courts until the Supreme Court reversed the lower court decisions during its 1985 session. The court held that the Oneidas had a right to sue under common law, and that the right had not been diminished by the passage of time because it was not limited by a statute of limitations or any other form of abatement. The court also said that the Oneidas had an "unquestioned right" to their lands, and that the Indians' right of occupancy was "as sacred as the fee simple of the whites." The court's decision was split five to four, and the case was bitterly contested because it denied the property rights of some owners who had held title for as long as 175 years. As of 2003, the specifics of the settlement remained to be worked out between the Oneida Indian Nation and the state of New York. A key impediment to settlement had become the state and New York Oneidas' insistence on excluding Oneidas residing in Wisconsin and Ontario from any prospective settlement.

LEGAL STATUS OF NATIVE CLAIMS TO HAWAI'I

The 1893 overthrow of the Hawai'ian monarchy by the United States was invalid under international law. Native Hawai'ians have secured an apology from the U.S. House of Representatives for the overthrow and have been pressing a land claim that would return 1.8 million acres (of Hawai'i's 4.2-million-acre land area) to the jurisdiction of a government to be elected at a Native Hawai'ian constitutional convention. During the summer of 1996, about 30,000 Native Hawai'ians voted by a margin of three to one to establish such a government. Roughly 40 percent of Native Hawai'ians who were eli-gible to vote took part. The land claim includes all state and federal lands on the islands but leaves private owners untouched. The 200,000 acres presently occupied by U.S. military bases would be leased to the Department of Defense at market value for a fixed period of time.

This sovereignty movement had gained a large amount of support among the 200,000 members of Native Hawai'ian society by the 1990s, 100 years after the United States colonized the islands. During 1995 and 1996, Native Hawai'ians registered to vote in a referendum that will decide whether to initiate a Native legislature to press the land claim and other issues. On September 9, 1996, an overwhelming majority of Native Hawai'ians voted to elect delegates to a constitutional convention. This effort was being headed by the state government's Office of Hawaiian Affairs. In the 1990s, for the first time since 1893, the chief executive of Hawai'i was an ethnic Hawai'ian.

A modern "Hawai'ian renaissance" began in the 1970s. The Native language, which had nearly died, began to flourish again; Hawai'ians, who had once thought themselves homeless in their own land, began to recapture their heritage. Teams of seafarers built canoes capable of traveling to Tahiti to renew ties with indigenous people there. They sailed and practiced ancient navigational skills that tied together the people of widely dispersed islands centuries ago (Weinberg, 1996).

REQUEST AT WOUNDED KNEE: REVOKE THE ARMY'S MEDALS

During 1990, a century after the massacre at Wounded Knee, South Dakota's governor declared a "year of reconciliation" between Euro-Americans and Native peoples in that state. Even as South Dakota Governor George Mickelson smoked a ceremonial peace pipe with representatives of South Dakota's nine Indian tribes in the rotunda of the state capitol at Pierre as part of a year of reconciliation a century after the Wounded Knee massacre, he refused to advocate the revocation by the federal government of two dozen Medals of Honor awarded to members of the U.S. Army for their roles in the massacre.

About 9 percent of South Dakota's residents were of Indian descent in 1990, exactly one century after the territory became a state. "Should the American soldiers involved in My Lai in Vietnam have been awarded Medals of Honor for their actions?" asked Tim Giago, publisher and editor of the *Lakota Times* (Hill, 1999). The government should "stand tall, admit it was wrong, and atone for that massacre," said Mario Gonzalez, an attorney for the Wounded Knee Survivors' Association, which wants Congress to erect a national monument to the victims of Wounded Knee along with restitution (plus interest) for property taken from them. "We hurt and cry deep in our souls as we remember the stories told to us by our families," said Claudia Iron Hawk Sully, whose grandmother died at Wounded Knee in 1890. "Each of us here knows more about the truth of the blackest day than any historian or Indian expert, or classroom book will ever know" (ibid.). The Lakota say that more than 400 people died at Wounded Knee, while the Interior Department says that 153 Indians were killed and 44 wounded.

THE HIGH PRICE OF URANIUM MINING
AMONG THE NAVAJOS

About half the recoverable uranium on private land within the United States lies within New Mexico, and about half of that is beneath the Navajo Nation. Uranium has been mined on Navajo land since the late 1940s; the Indians dug the ore that started the U.S. stockpile of nuclear weapons mostly from 1,100 uranium mines on the Navajo Nation. The Grants Uranium Belt near the Four Corners, mainly on Navajo land, has been responsible for at least 80 percent of the U.S. production of uranium since it became a profitable commodity about 1950.

For thirty years after the first atomic explosions in New Mexico, uranium was mined much like any other mineral. More than 99 percent of the product of the mines was waste, cast aside near mine sites after the uranium had been extracted. One of the mesalike waste piles grew to a mile long and 70 feet high. On windy days, dust from the tailings blew into local communities, filling the air and settling on water supplies. The Atomic Energy Commission assured worried local residents that the dust was harmless.

The first uranium miners in the area, almost all of them Navajos, remember being sent into shallow tunnels within minutes after blasting. They loaded the radioactive ore into wheelbarrows and emerged from the mines spitting black mucus from the dust, coughing so hard they had headaches. Such mining practices exposed the Navajos to between 100 and 1,000 times the amount of radon gas later considered safe.

During the late 1940s and 1950s, Navajo uranium miners hauled radioactive ore out of the earth as if it were coal. Some of the miners ate their lunches in the mine and slaked their thirst with radioactive water. Some of their hogans were built of radioactive earth. Many sheep watered in small ponds that formed at the mouths of abandoned uranium mines that were called "dog holes" because of their small size. On dry, windy days, the gritty dust from uranium waste tailing piles covered everything in sight. The Navajo language has no word for radioactivity, and no one told the miners that within a few decades, many of them would die.

In their rush to profit from uranium mining, very few companies provided ventilation in the early years. Some miners worked as many as twenty hours a day, entering their dog holes just after blasting of local sandstone had filled the mines with silica dust. The dust produced silicosis in the miners' lungs in addition to lung cancer and other problems associated with exposure to radioactivity. As early as 1950, government workers were monitoring radiation levels in the mines, and the levels were as much as 750 times limits deemed acceptable at that time according to Peter Eichstaedt's account in *If You Poison Us: Uranium and American Indians* (1995). By 1970, nearly 200 of the miners already had died of uranium-related causes. Roughly one in four of the miners

INDIAN AWARENESS WEEK

CO-AUTHORS OF "WASI-CHU"

MAY 23   FRIDAY   7 P.M.

LOCATION

the New Life Baptist Church   Reverend Pitford
618 North Puget, Olympia, Washington

7–9 P.M.

Speakers: BRUCE JOHANSEN and ROBERTO MAESTAS
Co-Authors of "Wasi-Chu (Continuing Indian Wars)"

9 P.M.

Speaker: Dr. Naciyana followed by
MOVIE: "Six Days of Soweto"

FREE ADMISSION

THE NATIVE AMERICAN STUDENT ASSOCIATION

Indian Awareness Week, stressing opposition to nuclear power and uranium mining, Evergreen State College, Olympia, Washington.

had died, most of them from lung cancer, in an area where the disease had been nearly unknown before uranium mining began.

Some miners were put to work packing 1,000-pound barrels of "yellow-cake," ore rich in uranium. These workers carried radioactive dust home on their clothes. Some of the miners ingested so much of the dust that it was "making the workers radioactive from the inside out" (Eichstaedt, 1995, 62). Downwind of uranium processing mills, the dust from yellowcake sometimes was so thick that it stained the landscape a half-mile away.

With the end of the Cold War and the cloud of controversy cast over civilian uses of nuclear power, the uranium boom, and most of the mining, had ended by the 1980s. With the boom over, the mining town of Grants, New Mexico, tried to sell itself as a tourist destination with the slogan "Grants Enchants." In the meantime, many of the miners had been condemned to slow deaths by lung cancer. The U.S. government (particularly the Atomic Energy Commission) knew that uranium mining was poisoning the Navajos almost from the beginning. The government and the mining companies kept medical knowledge from the miners out of concern for national security and profits.

"We used to play in it," said Terry Yazzie of an enormous tailings pile behind his house. "We would dig holes and bury ourselves in it" (Eichstaedt, 1995, 140). The neighbors of this particular tailings pile were not told it was dangerous until 1990, twenty-two years after the mill that produced the tailings pile closed and twelve years after Congress authorized the cleanup of uranium mill tailings in Navajo country. Abandoned mines also were used as shelter by animals, who inhaled radon and drank contaminated water. Local people milked the animals and ate their contaminated meat.

Harris Charley, who worked in the mines for fifteen years, told a U.S. Senate hearing in 1979: "We were treated like dogs. There was no ventilation in the mines" (Grinde and Johansen, 1995, 214). Pearl Nakai, daughter of a deceased miner, told the same hearing that "No one ever told us about the dangers of uranium" (ibid., 214).

The Senate hearings were convened by Senator Pete Domenici, New Mexico Republican, who was seeking compensation for disabled uranium miners and for the families of the deceased. "The miners who extracted uranium from the Colorado Plateau are paying the price today for the inadequate health and safety standards that were then in force," Domenici told the hearing, held at a Holiday Inn near the uranium boomtown of Grants (Grinde and Johansen, 1995, 214).

Bills to compensate the miners were introduced, discussed, and died in Congress for a dozen years. By 1990, the death toll among former miners had risen to 450 and was still rising, even as (by 1997) more than 1,000 mines on the reservation had been closed. Compensation was finally approved by Congress and signed into law by President Clinton during the early 1990s. A small number of disabled miners and families collected $100,000, but many were screened out by stringent bureaucratic requirements of proof.

NAVAJO-KVINNE I KULLBRUDD (FOTO: BRUCE JOHANSEN)

Emma Yazzie at bottom of coal strip mine, Four Corners, 1976; inset of table of contents, exhibition program, University of Oslo Ethnology Museum, 1993. (Courtesy of Bruce Johansen.)

Part of uranium mining's legacy on the Navajo Nation was the biggest expulsion of radioactive material in the United States, which occurred July 16, 1978, at 5 A.M. On that morning, more than 1,100 tons of uranium mining wastes—tailings—gushed through a packed-mud dam near Church Rock, New Mexico. With the tailings, 100 million gallons of radioactive water gushed through the dam before the crack was repaired.

By 8 A.M., radioactivity was monitored in Gallup, New Mexico, nearly fifty miles away. According to the Nuclear Regulatory Commission, the contaminated river, the Rio Puerco, showed 6,000 times the allowable standard of radioactivity below the broken dam shortly after the breach was repaired.

A month after the spill occurred, United Nuclear Corporation, which owned the dam, had cleaned up only 50 of the 1,100 tons of spilled waste. Workers were using pails and shovels because heavy machinery could not negotiate the steep terrain near the Rio Puerco. Along the river, officials issued press releases telling people not to drink the water. They had a few problems; many of the Navajo residents could not read English and had no electricity to power television sets and radios. Another consumer of the water, cattle, also did not read the press releases.

Uranium was but one form of energy exploitation on the Navajo Nation; during the 1970s, coal strip mining (for electric power generation) was protested by Navajos in the Four Corners area. One of their leaders was an elderly sheep herder, Emma Yazzie, who took her protests into the mines, obstructing the draglines at risk of her life, because pollution from coal-fired electric plants was making her sheep sick.

GROWING NUMBERS OF NATIVE AMERICANS IN THE UNITED STATES

In 1900, anthropologists and government officials called Native Americans the vanishing race. By 1990, however, American Indians had become the fastest-growing ethnic group in the United States. The 1990 census reported that 1.8 million people classified themselves as Native American, more than three times as many as the 523,600 reported thirty years earlier. The 1890 U.S. Census reported 228,000 American Indians.

The same trend continued in the 2000 census, in which more than 4.1 million people said they were at least partially Native American, an increase of more than 100 percent in ten years and thirteen times the official figure of about 300,000 a century earlier. Part of the increase was caused by an excess of births over deaths among Native Americans. The census figures must be qualified for several reasons, however: First, they are based on self-identification. A century ago, asserting Native American roots could be harmful to one's physical health. Today, many people have become fond of claiming a Cherokee princess or two on the family tree, even if no blood links can be established. Second, in the 2000 census for the first time, people were allowed to claim more than one ethnic background. Of the 4.1 million people who selected "American Indian or Alaska Native," 40 percent checked more than one category. Of the 4.1 million counted, 2.5 million said they were solely American Indian or Alaska Native. This reflects a 26 percent increase between 1990 and 2000.

One in four of the 4.1 million American Indians and Alaska Natives counted in the 2000 census hailed from California or Oklahoma. California had the largest presence, 628,000 people. Aside from these two states, the other top ten states with Native population were Arizona, Texas, New Mexico, New York, Washington, North Carolina, Michigan, and Alaska.

Most American Indians and Alaska Natives live in the West, and a majority live in urban areas, most notably New York City (87,241 people) and Los Angeles (53,092). Other cities with large American Indian and Alaska Native communities were Chicago, Houston, Philadelphia, Phoenix, San Diego, Dallas, San Antonio, and Detroit.

Roughly 74 percent of those counted indicated a Native national identity. Aside from Cherokee and Navajo, the largest American Indian tribal groupings were Cherokee, Navajo, Latin American Indian (a census category comprising 181,000 people but not a single tribe), Choctaw, Sioux, Chippewa, Apache, Blackfoot, Iroquois, and Pueblo (Table 11.1).

TABLE 11.1
Largest American Indian Tribal Groupings, Year 2000

	American Indian Tribal Grouping Alone or in Combination with One or More Races	American Indian Tribal Grouping Alone
Cherokee	729,533	281,069
Navajo	298,197	281,069
Latin American Indian	180,940	104,354
Choctaw	158,774	87,349
Sioux	153,360	108,272
Chippewa	149,669	105,907
Apache	96,833	57,060
Blackfoot	85,750	27,104
Iroquois	80,822	45,212
Pueblo	74,085	59,533

Source: U.S. Census Bureau. Available at
http://www.census.gov/mso/www/pres_lib/c2k_aian/c2k_aian.ppt

THE DRIVE TO RETIRE INDIAN MASCOTS ACCELERATES

The mascot issue became active during the 1960s with the founding of AIM in Minneapolis. Because of AIM, some of the first Indian stereotypes were contested in the Midwest. At the University of Nebraska at Omaha, for example, a chapter of AIM spearheaded a change of mascot from Indians to Mavericks, a beef animal with an attitude, in 1971. The change was popular on campus in part because the visual depiction of Owumpie, the "Omaha Indian" was so tacky by comparison that he made the Cleveland Indians' Chief Wahoo look like a real gentleman. The student body of the university eventually voted to give Owumpie the boot. Stanford University (Stanford, CA) changed its Indian mascot to a cardinal at about the same time. During the late 1960s, the National Congress of American Indians launched a campaign to bring an end to the use of Indian sports mascots and other media stereotypes.

During the early 1980s, Choctaw filmmaker Phil Lucas addressed the mascot question on the pages of *Four Winds*, a short-lived glossy magazine devoted to Native American art, history, and culture, by asking how whites would react if a sports team was named the "Cleveland Caucasians." What would European Americans think, Lucas asked, if Indians adopted racial names (such as the Window Rock Negroes or the Tahlequah White Boys) for their sports teams (1980, 69)?

Since the early 1970s, about half of the 3,000 elementary schools, high schools, and colleges in the United States that once used American Indian nicknames and mascots have dropped them according to Susan Shown Harjo, president of the Morningstar Institute in Washington, D.C. Marquette University (Milwaukee, WI) has replaced Warriors in favor of Golden Eagles. Dartmouth (Hanover, NH) changed its Indians to Big Green, and Miami of Ohio (Oxford) changed Redskins to the RedHawks. At Seattle University in Washington, the Chieftains have become the Redhawks. In the meantime, producers of Crayola crayons have done away with the color Indian red (Babwin, 2000).

In 1994, Wisconsin's education department issued a directive urging school districts in that state to drop Indian mascots. Los Angeles schools have done the same (Gormley, 2000). Ten public schools in Dallas shed their Indian mascots during 1998, at a time when roughly fifty U.S. public high schools, thirteen U.S. colleges, and three colleges in Texas still used Indian mascots (Doclar, 1998).

Washington's Redskins

Susan Harjo, president of the Morningstar Institute, has sued the Washington Redskins over their use of Indian imagery. The Redskin lawsuit (*Harjo v. Pro-Football, Inc.*, 1999) was heard before a three-judge panel of trademark

Chief Owumpie, University of Omaha, ca. 1968, book cover.

judges of the Trademark Trial and Appeals Board (TTAB). In a case heard May 27, 1998, and decided April 2, 1999, the board found the following:

> Although the marks (Redskin logos) were not scandalous, they were disparaging to the relevant segment of the population (i.e., Native Americans) at the time of their registration. As a consequence, the marks had a tendency to bring Native Americans into contempt or disrepute. These findings were based primarily on a survey provided by the Petitioners, and the TTAB decided to cancel the registration of the word marks at issue, finding that the Petitioners' survey met their burden of proof by preponderance of the evidence. (*Harjo*, 1999)

The survey in question found that 46.2 percent of Native Americans questioned found the term *Redskin* offensive. The trademark board ruling against the Washington Redskins is under appeal, a legal process that could last for years. Washington Redskin imagery is, of course, still very visible. In 2003, a U.S. District Court judge, Colleen Kolar-Kotelly, denied the action on procedural grounds. That finding was appealed to circuit court, which agreed.

Cleveland's Indians

Cleveland entered professional baseball more than a century ago with a team named the Spiders; in the team's first year, the Spiders lost 134 games. Later, the team was called the Naps. The Cleveland Indian name was adopted by a vote of the fans during 1914. Chief Wahoo was created by a *Cleveland Plain Dealer* columnist during the 1940s and first sewn into Cleveland Indian uniforms in 1947.

Until the year 2000, the Cleveland Indians' official media guide maintained that the name was adopted in honor of Louis Sockalexis, a Penobscot who played for the Spiders between 1897 and 1899. Therefore, many Indians fans boasted that the name was an honor, not an insult. The media guide first mentioned the Sockalexis story in 1968 (just as early protests began to roll in from the new AIM).

Sockalexis was said to have been the first Native American to play in baseball's major leagues. It is unknown whether this is true or spin control meant to turn a slur into a belated act of affirmative action. In 1999, the media guide devoted an entire page to the Sockalexis "story," which was coyly declared bogus a year later. In January 2000, the wording of the guide was changed, with the reference to Sockalexis taken as "legend." The old version was proved factually inaccurate by Ellen Staurowsky, a professor at Ithaca College, New York, who maintained that the team should drop its Indian moniker. Any change could cost the baseball club a pretty penny because Chief Wahoo is among the best-selling sports images on clothing, caps, and other merchandise.

Sockalexis began playing baseball at Holy Cross College, Worcester, Massachusetts, less than five years after the massacre at Wounded Knee. He was raised on the Indian Island Reservation in Old Town, Maine. By 1897, he was playing baseball at Notre Dame in Ohio, a school from which he was expelled after only a month because of public drunkenness. The Cleveland Spiders then signed him to a professional contract for $1,500. At first, Sockalexis experienced something of a hitting streak. By the middle of his first season with the Spiders, he was hitting .335. It has been said that some fans "took to wearing Indian headdresses and screaming war whoops every time Sockalexis came to bat" (Nevard, n.d.). During July 1897, Sockalexis got drunk and injured himself. He spent most of the rest of his baseball career on the bench before being released in 1899. For a decade after that, Sockalexis performed manual labor in Cleveland as he continued to suffer from alcoholism. He died in 1913. A novel based on his life (*The Cleveland Indian: The Legend of King Saturday*) was written by Luke Salisbury (1992).

Atlanta's Braves

The Atlanta Braves moved to Georgia from Boston. Before the team adopted Braves in 1912, it was known as the Boston Beaneaters, the Boston Rustlers, and the Boston Doves. During October 1991, when the Atlanta Braves arrived in Minneapolis for the World Series, they found more than 200 protestors arrayed at the stadium's gates with placards reading (among other things), "500 Years of Oppression Is Enough." Minneapolis is AIM's hometown, and even the mayor had made a statement calling on the Braves to sack their Indian imagery. When the Twins management asked the police to move the demonstrators further from the Metrodome, they refused, citing the protestors' freedom of speech and assembly.

The Atlanta Braves' emphasis on Indian imagery has spawned a number of mascot wannabes, the best known of whom is Tomahawk Tom, also known as Tom Sullivan. According to the *Atlanta Journal-Constitution*, Tomahawk Tom arrives at the ballpark "in an Indian headdress, a catcher's mask, and a cape" (Pomerantz, 1995). Tomahawk Tom is not officially sanctioned by the Braves, but he leads fans in tomahawk chop cheers, signs autographs, and passes out free baseball cards to children. Sullivan also regards himself as an inventor. One of his inventions is an ice cream treat called the Tomahawk Chop Pop.

Tomahawk Tom has learned to walk gingerly during the last few years as protests against the Braves' logo and the tomahawk chop have intensified. During early October 1995, before a Braves playoff game, a Native protester named Aaron Two Elk took a swing at Tomahawk Tom, knocking his catcher's mask askew, as he told Tom that he was desecrating Native American cultures. Two Elk, a Cherokee, earlier had become well known at the Braves' ballpark for his handwritten placards in a free speech area near Hank Aaron's statue at the stadium's entrance. A week later, Sullivan called on Atlanta police for an escort into the ballpark. Sullivan later walked into the stadium in street clothes, changing into his buckskins in a restroom, to avoid several dozen protestors who gathered in the free speech area, carefully watched by a dozen Atlanta police.

Indian Mascot Controversies: A National Sampler

The struggle over sports mascots can evoke anger and even violence. In the otherwise peaceful town of West Hurley, New York, in the Catskills, a mascot struggle also sparked a contest for control of a local school board. A ban on use of racial images was enacted during April 2000 by the board governing the 2,300-student Onteora school board. The mascot then became a heated issue in a campaign for control of the school board. During May, supporters of the Indian image won a majority of board seats. In June, the school district's Indian imagery was reinstated.

During the fall of 2000, opponents of the Indian mascot found their cars vandalized, with nails and screws driven into tires and paint splattered, usually while the cars were parked at school board meetings. Tobe Carey, an opponent of the Indian mascot whose car was damaged, told *Indian Time* (a newspaper based at Akwesasne) that "A climate of intimidation makes it impossible to speak at public meetings. Citizens working to remove racial stereotypes in our public schools have endured criminal incidents for ten months" (Johansen, 2001, 59–60).

Supporters of Onteora's Indian imagery (which includes a tomahawk chop, totem poles in the school cafeteria, and various pseudo-Indian songs and dances) have been known to bristle at any suggestion that their images degrade Native Americans in any way. Joseph Doan, a member of the school board that voted to reinstate the Indian imagery, said that many white citizens see the Indian image as a symbol of honor and environmental protection. "Our Indian has nothing to do with degrading Indians. It's our symbol and we're proud of it," said Doan (Gormley, 2000). In West Hurley, the proms are called tomahawk dances. Onteora has used Indian images since the 1950s. Until 1997, no one had formally complained when a student in buckskins led cheers at football games or when songs and dances mimicked Native American religious rituals.

Regarding Chief Illiniwek, a mascot at the University of Illinois, a decades-old struggle continues. "The chief is a religious figure for Native American people and he doesn't belong as entertainment for drunk football fans at halftime," said Monica Garreton, a University of Illinois senior and anti-chief activist. "It's comparable to Little Black Sambo and *Amos 'n Andy*" (Babwin, 2000). Every Columbus Day since 1992, opponents of the Illiniwek imagery have held demonstrations on the University of Illinois campus.

In a paper titled, "Chief Illiniwek: Dignified or Damaging?" Joseph P. Gone, a Gros Ventre, wrote:

> One primary obstacle to political and economic renewal and self-determination
> in Indian communities around the country is the appalling ignorance of most

American citizens, including policymakers at local, state and federal levels of government, regarding Native American histories and cultures. As multi-dimensional peoples engaged in complex struggles for autonomy and equal-ity.... Indians are virtually invisible to the American consciousness, which gleans any awareness of Natives from caricatured Hollywood portrayals, tourist ex-cursions and, yes, popular symbols like Chief Illiniwek. Thus, the continued prevalence of Indian stereotypes fortifies a wall of misunderstanding between our peoples. ("Indian Mascots," 2000)

The faculty of Blacksburg High School in Roanoka, Virginia, voted late in 2000 to retire the school's Indian mascot. Other schools in the Roanoke area also have changed their mascots. The Shawsville High Shawnees became the Colts, for example. A citizens' coalition raised the issue in 1999, saying that the names "objectify Indians, teach negative stereotypes and abuse spiritual symbols such as eagle feathers" (Calnan, 2000). The University of California at San Diego retired its Aztec during the fall of 2000. At about the same time (in late September), Maine's Scarborough School Board voted to drop its Redskins nickname.

Most of the faculty in the University of North Dakota's Teaching and Learning Department in Grand Forks have petitioned the university's president to change its Fighting Sioux nickname because, they contend, "it dehumanizes Indian people" (Benedict, 2000). On October 6, 2000, three of the university's students were arrested for blocking traffic in protest of the Fighting Sioux nickname. The local newspaper, the *Grand Forks Herald*, reported that these were the first arrests of students engaging in protest at the university since the days of the Vietnam War.

Tim Giago, editor of the *Lakota Times*, commented: "Would you paint your face black, wear an Afro wig, and prance around a football field trying to imitate your perceptions of black people? Of course not! That would be insulting to Blacks. So why is it OK to do it to Indians" (Nevard, n.d.)? Still, after all this, Chief Wahoo endures. The tomahawk chop seems to have as-sumed the kind of historical inevitability that a quarter century ago was assigned to the Berlin Wall and the federal budget deficit—a rock-solid arti-fact of imperial popular culture. Ted Turner, who organized the Goodwill Games and gave $1 billion to the United Nations, has been unable, or un-willing, as owner of the Atlanta Braves, to touch the tomahawk chop.

Go Get 'em Fighting Whities!

During February 2002, an intramural basketball team composed of Native American, Latino, and European American students at Greeley's University of Northern Colorado decided to change its name from Native Pride to the Fighting Whites, a purposeful parody of North America's many Native mas-cots, most notably nearby Eaton High School's Fighting Reds.

The team printed a few T-shirts (their uniform of choice) with the team's new name; the computer clip art with a suited, clean-cut white man; and the slogan "Everythang's Gonna Be All White." There ensued a wave of nearly instant, continentwide publicity that stood the long-standing debate over the decency of Native sports team mascots on its head. The Fighting Whites set thousands of virtual tongues wagging. Everyone had an opinion, from AIM to affiliates of the Ku Klux Klan. The reactions provided a flash-frozen ideoscape of racial humor in an age of political correctness.

Within weeks, the Fighting Whites (or, as they soon became known in many circles, the Fighting Whities) had become nearly as well known as established professional monikers such as the Washington Redskins and the Cleveland Indians. A cursory Internet search under "Fighting Whities" (on Google.com) turned up 4,700 "hits"; "Fighting Whites" provided 2,930 Web page mentions, something of a media feeding frenzy for a mascot that had not existed three months earlier. The publicity helped to sell thousands of T-shirts and other items for a hastily endowed scholarship fund to aid Native American students. Within nine months, more than 15,000 articles of Whities team gear had been sold, raising roughly $100,000 for student scholarships (Cornelius, 2002).

As the official home page of the Fighting Whites explained, in a statement written by Ryan White (who is Mohawk), John Messner, and Charles Cuny:

> We came up with the "Fighting Whites" logo and slogan to have a little satirical fun and to deliver a simple, sincere, message about ethnic stereotyping. Since March 6, when our campus newspaper first reported on the Fighting Whites, we have been launched into the national spotlight, propelled by a national debate over stereotyping American Indians in sports symbolism. (Page, 2002)

The Fighting Whites' parody very quickly sprang from the sports pages to the front pages. From the student newspaper, the story spread to the *Greeley Tribune*, then over the state, regional, and national Associated Press wire services. Some of the stories popped up as far away as London's *Guardian*. The Whities also were contacted by Fox Sports Net and NBC News, among many other electronic media. Soon, the Fighting Whites had developed at least nine T-shirt designs for sale on an Internet Site, with receipts fueled by publicity in many major daily newspapers, electronic news outlets, and such other large-audience venues as the *Jay Leno Show*. The effect on sales was downright salubrious. Soon the merchandise was available not only on T-shirts, but also on sweatshirts, tank tops, baseball jerseys, several styles of caps, a coffee mug, boxer shorts, and mouse pads.

On the court, the Whities confessed that they were hardly championship caliber, but soon their prowess at basketball did not matter. Their reputation soon had very little to do with dribbling, jumping, or shooting and more to do with the incendiary nature of the ongoing debate regarding Native American names for sports teams. Brooks Wade, 23, a member of the Fighting Whites who is a Choctaw and an employee at the University of Northern Colorado Native American Student Services, told the *Rocky Mountain News* March 15, 2002: "It's a huge media rush. It kind of snowballed out of control, really. We started it as more of a protest so we could change things in our little world, and suddenly it's worldwide" (BeDan, 2002, 12-A).

The original protest had been aimed at Eaton (Colorado) High School's Indian mascot, the Fightin' Reds, after the wife of one of the Fighting Whites resigned a job there in anger over the issue. Solomon Little Owl, a Crow, whose wife resigned at Eaton, was director of the university's Native American Student Services when he joined the team. Little Owl's wife, Kacy Little Owl (who is European American), taught special education at the high school seven miles north of Greeley for two years before leaving at the end of the previous school year (Garner, 2002).

"The message is, let's do something that will let people see the other side of what it's like to be a mascot," said Little Owl ("Fighting Whities," March 12, 2002). The Whities had reason to agree with a comment on the *Wampum Chronicles* message board, a Native American Web site: "They'll swamp the country with publicity which has everyone laughing at their opponents, all the while our boys will be laughing all the way to the bank. Way to go, Fighting Whities. Give 'em hell" (*Wampum Chronicles*, n.d.).

WINONA LADUKE: VICE PRESIDENTIAL CANDIDATE FOR THE GREEN PARTY

Winona LaDuke (Anishinabe, born 1959) became one of the foremost environmental advocates in Native America during the last quarter of the twentieth century. She lectured, wrote, and pressed authorities for answers for issues ranging from the Navajo uranium mines, to Hydro-Quebec's construction sites at James Bay, to toxic waste sites on Native Alaskan and Canadian land along the Arctic Ocean. Twice during that period, she ran as Ralph Nader's vice presidential candidate on the Green Party ticket.

LaDuke was a daughter of Vincent LaDuke, who was an Indian activist in the 1950s, and Betty LaDuke, a painter. She was educated at Harvard University in the late 1970s, and in the early 1980s moved to the White Earth Ojibwa Reservation in Minnesota at Round Lake. LaDuke became involved in protests of environmental racism and in recovery of Native American land base. With the $20,000 Reebok Human Rights Award, she founded the White Earth Land Recovery Program, which took action to regain land base on her 36-square-mile home reservation, which by the early 1990s was 92 percent owned by non-Indians.

For much of the late twentieth century, LaDuke publicized her findings in numerous newspaper and magazine articles and as a founder of the Indigenous Women's Network, director of the White Earth Recovery Project, and board member of Greenpeace. In 1996 and 2000, LaDuke ran for vice president of the United States on the Green Party ticket with Ralph Nader, as she emphasized that the United States needs the following:

> [A] new model of electoral politics [regarding] . . . the distribution of power and wealth, the abuse of power, the rights of the natural world, the environment, and the need to consider an amendment to the U.S. Constitution in which all decisions made today would be considered in light of the impact on the seventh generation from now. (Johansen, 1996a, 3)

NATIVE AMERICAN LANGUAGE REVIVAL

At least 300 distinct Native American languages were spoken in North America at the time of Columbus's first landfall in 1492. Today, 190 languages remain, but a great many of them are in imminent danger of being lost. Michael Kraus, former president of the Society for the Study of Indigenous Languages, wrote, in his book *Stabilizing Indigenous Languages*, that only 20 of 175 surviving Native American languages in the United States are still being learned by children from their parents as a first language (Johansen, 2000, 57). The emphasis on language revival is arriving barely in time for some Native American languages, those that have reached stage eight of Joshua A. Fishman's eight stages of language loss (1996), when only a few elders speak the tongue which once served an entire people at home and in their working lives.

The people of the Cochiti Pueblo were moved to revitalize their language after they conducted a survey that disclosed that all of its fluent speakers were 35 years of age or older. The few speakers under age thirty-five were semiliterate, said Mary Eunice Romero. Romero then asked: "What is going to happen to our language in 20 years when those [who are] 35 years old become 55? In 20 more years, when they're 75?" (Johansen, 2000, 56). The Cochiti immersion program began in 1996 with a summer program for thirty children, under instruction from the Tribal Council that all instruction be carried out orally with no written texts. After that, according to Romero, the program grew quickly. "When the kids went home," she said, "They spread the news that, 'Wow, they're not using any English. They're not writing. It's just totally in Cochiti.' We started out with four teachers. The next day, we got 60 kids. By the third week, we had 90 kids. By the end of the summer, the kids were starting to speak" (ibid., 56).

Romero also watched the mode of instruction change the behavior of the children. "The behavior change was a major miracle," she continued. "These kids came in rowdy as can be. By the time they left, knew the appropriate protocol of how you enter a house, greet your elder, say good-bye. The fact that they could use verbal communication for the most important piece of culture, values, and love started a chain reaction in the community" (Johansen, 2000, 56).

Experiences at the Cochiti Pueblo illustrate a trend across North America. Native American languages, many of which are nearly extinct, have enjoyed a revival during the 1990s, largely because many Native nations adopted "immersion" programs, which teach a language as the major part of many tribal school curricula. Such programs are the historical opposite of the government's traditional emphasis on assimilation into English-speaking mainstream culture that was encapsulated in a slogan ("Kill the Indian, save the man") used by Richard Henry Pratt, who founded the Carlisle Indian Industrial School in 1879. The revival of Native languages has been a grassroots affair in many Native American communities, as immersion programs have spread across Turtle Island, from the Akwesasne Mohawk territory (which straddles the borders of New York State and Ontario and Quebec in Canada), to the Cochiti Pueblo of New Mexico and the Native peoples of Hawai'i.

Why teach language? Richard Little Bear said that, "Language is the basis of sovereignty" as well as the vessel of culture. During the nineteenth century, said Little Bear, the United States showed its respect for Native American languages' essential role in culture by trying to eliminate them.

> We have all those attributes that comprise sovereign nations: a governance structure, law and order, jurisprudence, a literature, a land base, spiritual and sacred practice, and that one attribute that holds all of these ... together: our languages. So once our languages disappear, each one of these attributes begins to fall apart until they are all gone. (Johansen, 2000, 56)

Little Bear said that, for the Cheyennes, the transition to a written language occurred about a century ago. As more and more communication took place in English, "Those in my generation who speak the Cheyenne language are quite possibly the last generation able to joke in our own language" (ibid., 56).

Many immersion programs were started after parents became concerned about (in the words of author Joshua Fishman) "what you lose when you lose your language." Fishman wrote the following:

> The most important relationship between language and culture ... is that most of the culture is expressed in the language. Take language away from the culture and you take away its greetings, its curses, its praises, its laws, its literature, its songs, riddles, proverbs, and prayers. The culture could not be expressed and handled in any other way. You are losing all those things that essentially are the way of life, the way of thought, the way of valuing the land upon which you live and the human reality that you're talking about. (Johansen, 2000, 57)

Darryl Kipp, codirector of the Piegen Institute, a language immersion program on Montana's Blackfoot Reservation, asserted that without programs to make young people fluent in Native languages, 70 percent of the Native languages spoken today in North America will die within the next few generations with the passing of the last elders speaking them. As on many other reservations, the Blackfoot Confederacy (totaling about 40,000 people) started language immersion as a response to the failure of education provided them by outside governments and agencies: "Out of the 17,000 that belong to my band, less than one per cent have a college education. Sixty-five per cent of the students in our schools never finish the tenth grade" (Johansen, 2000, 57).

A group of Blackfoot, including Kipp, spent five years developing ways to teach the language. They ran into some opposition from tribal members, who asserted that knowledge of the language was not of practical use. One woman asked him, "Can you make soup with your language?" Kipp replied, "I struggled and had a hard time with that one. While I can't necessarily make soup, we can make healthy children, and healthy children can make all kinds of soups" (Johansen, 2000, 57).

Julia Kushner, describing language-revival work among the Arikara) cited studies that indicate that 90 percent of the 175 Native languages that survived General Platt's educational gauntlet have no child speakers (Reyhner et al., 1999, 81). That figure dates from the mid-1990s. Elsewhere in the book, speakers mourn the continuing loss of several languages, more than a dozen of which lost their last living speakers during the first half of the 1990s alone. Revived Native languages become living tools of culture in daily life, not museum pieces of a presumably also-dead culture.

The reach of language revivals is worldwide; lessons and examples are freely borrowed from the Maori of New Zealand, who have conducted an active language-revival program for several decades. The New Zealand government has maintained a Maori Language Commission since 1987.

"Repatriated Bones, Unrepatriated Spirits," a poem by Little Bear that appears at the beginning of *Revitalizing Native Languages* (Reyhner et al., 1999), reveals a sense that revival of Native American languages close a historical and cultural circle:

> We were brought back here
> to a place we don't know.
>
> We were brought back here
> and yet we are lost.
>
> But now we are starting to sing our songs.
> We are singing our songs
> that will help us find our way.
>
> We came back to a people who
> look like us but whose language
> we do not understand anymore.
> Yet we know in our hearts
> they are feeling good too, to have
> us back here among them.
> —Reyhner et al., 1999, frontispiece

In *Revitalizing Indigenous Languages*, editor Jon Reyhner stresses the need to use a revitalized language as a living tool to teach academic subjects, not as a "second language." The language must be restored to its place in everyday life of a people, he believes.

One subject that provokes controversy in Native language revitalization studies is whether the revived language should be written or solely oral. Some language activists point out that many Native languages were first committed to writing by missionaries seeking, as Reyhner writes, "to translate their *Bible* and convert Natives from their traditional religions" (Reyhner, 1999, xiii). A wide range of programs have evolved locally, some in opposition to earlier efforts at written languages by church-affiliated programs, and others have grown from the same type of programs. Although some of the programs strive to maintain an emphasis on spoken language to the exclusion of written communication, others emphasize production of written bilingual sources in the Native language to be revived as well as in English. Some of the programs use computers extensively; others avoid them as a culturally inappropriate intrusion.

Fishman himself comes down squarely on the side of literacy: "Unless they are entirely withdrawn from the modern world, minority ethno-linguistic groups need to be literate in their mother tongue (as well as in some language of wider communication)" (Reyhner et al., 1999, 38).

The often-disputed distinction between oral and literate language may be culturally artificial because many Native American cultures possessed forms of written communication, even if many European immigrants did not re-cognize them as such. From the wampum belts of the Haudenosaunee, to the illustrated codices of the Aztecs and Maya, to the winter counts of the Plains, written communication was used in America long before Columbus. Reyhner et al. cited H. Russell Bernard, as he urged Native Americans to establish publishing houses (1999, xiii).

Language revival also is being used in some cases to encourage the expression of Native oral histories in both written and spoken forms as well as in musical composition. Some teachers of language are finding that music is an amazingly effective way to introduce young students to languages and cultural heritage. "Why music?" asks Amar Almasude, who writes about lan-guage revival in Northern Africa:

> It is perhaps the best vehicle for becoming acquainted with humans. It is the expression that is the most pervasive. In songs, human society is portrayed and every-day experiences are reflected. Their themes are usually social issues and historical events, including national and religious feasts and holidays.... Thus, music is a fundamental element in human life. (Reyhner et al., 1999, 121)

Two books edited by Jon Reyhner (1997; Reyhner et al., 1999) present precise descriptions and examples from teachers who have been involved in a wide variety of language-revival programs, from several Native bands in British Columbia, to the Cheyenne, Yaqui, Arapaho, and Navajo. While describing individual programs, these books also sketch the common pedagogical essentials basic to all language-revitalization efforts. Reyhner suggests use of the "3 M's" of language revitalization: methods, materials, and motivation.

> Methods deal with what teaching techniques will be used at what age levels and stages of language loss. Materials deal with what things will be available for teachers and learners to use, including audiotapes, videotapes, storybooks, dictionaries, grammars, textbooks, and computer software. Motivation deals with increasing the prestige (including giving recognition and awards to individuals and groups who make special efforts) and usefulness of the indigenous language in the community, and using teaching methods that learners enjoy, so they will come back for more indigenous language instruction. (Reyhner et al., 1999, xviii)

Language must become a familiar part of a student's life; immersion specialists believe that 600 to 700 hours of such contact is necessary to acquire the kind of fluency that allows for transmission of culture from generation to generation.

Language revitalization efforts across America now share a treasure trove of linguistic innovation describing how Native languages are being revived in some ways that are very old and in others use modern technology to extend the reach of oral cultures. In Mexico, traditional Aztec *Danza* (dance) is being used to teach classical Nahuatl. The dances are part of an eighteen-ceremony ecological calendar, so while learning the language, students also absorb some knowledge of Aztec history and culture. These ceremonies deal with rain, germination, ripening of corn, war victory, hunting, and [the] tribal dead, comment authors of a study on "revenacularizing" classical Nahuatl through Aztec dance. The authors listed the intertwined benefits of this approach, by which students acquire not only knowledge of language, but also "Nahua [Mexica, or Aztec] history from an indigenous perspective, a deeper understanding of Danza steps, creation myths, [and the] making and playing of indigenous [musical] instruments" (Reyhner, 1997, 71).

In Alaska, a number of Deg Hit'an (Ingalik Athabasken) people have been teaching each other their language, Deg Xinag, over the telephone, using conference calls. Telephone technology allows widely dispersed speakers of the language to create a space to practice their skills and to teach each other new phrases and words. Phone conferences are hardly immersive (because the calls last only an hour a week), but language still is being taught. Callers have joined the conversations from as far away as Seattle.

In a similar vein, KTNN AM 660, the Navajo Nation's official radio station, has been making plans to offer instruction in the Navajo language over the air in an attempt to follow Joshua Fishman's advice that revitalized languages, to be successful, must be shared by a people via the communications media of their communities. "The Voice of the Navajo Nation," as KTNN is called, has a signal that reaches from Albuquerque to Phoenix.

"SQUAWBLES"

The state of Minnesota has enacted a legal ban on the use of the word *squaw* in geographic place-names for lakes, streams, and points, agreeing with two Chippewa high school students on the Leech Lake Reservation that the word is degrading to Native American women. The state law was overwhelmingly approved by the state legislature and signed by Governor Arne Carlson. A debate has since developed that the Associated Press, with a straight journalistic face, called "a squawble" (Johansen, 1996b, 4). The law affected nineteen place-names in Minnesota. One Squaw Lake became Nature Lake, and another Squaw Lake became Wahbegon. Squaw Point became Oak Point, and Squaw Creek became Fond-du-Lac. Squaw Pond became Scout Camp Pond.

In Minnesota's Lake County, a swatch of forest, streams, and lakes with 10,000 residents that reaches the shores of western lake Superior near the Canadian border, non-Indian residents suggested that their Squaw Creek and Squaw Bay be changed to Politically Correct Creek and Politically Correct Bay, respectively. The state rejected Lake County's proposal, which arrived with a letter from Sharon Hahn, head of the Lake County Board of Commissioners: "The term 'squaw' is in common use throughout North America, far beyond its Algonquian origin," she wrote. "We find nothing derogatory in continued use of this term" (Johansen, 1996b, 4).

County officials in Lake County refused to change names as required by the state, citing standard dictionary definitions that define "squaw" as an Indian woman (generically). They also protested the expense of making the changes on signs and maps. Indeed, the 1983 edition of Webster's *New Universal Unabridged Dictionary* defined *squaw* as (1) an American Indian woman or wife; (2) any woman, chiefly humorous. Some dictionaries attribute the word to "squáas," in an Algonquian language (Massachuset, Natick, or Narraganset), and add that it is a derogatory word for women of any race or ethnic group. Unabridged dictionaries also sometimes list several derivations, such as "squaw winter," said to be a spell of unusually cold and stormy weather before Indian summer.

In *Literature of the American Indian* (1973), edited by Thomas E. Sanders and Walter W. Peek, however, squaw is said to be a French corruption of an "Iroquois" word, *otiska*, referring to female private parts. Which Iroquois language is involved here is not addressed. The phrase was probably carried into the north woods of Minnesota (and the rest of Anglo-American culture) by French fur trappers, with the word later anglicized by English-speaking colonists. According to the *Thesaurus of American Slang*, edited by Ester and Albert A. Lewis, the word *squaw* is used as a synonym for "prostitute" (Johansen, 1996b, 4).

The town of Squaw Lake, Minnesota, with 140 permanent residents and surrounded by the Leech Lake Indian Reservation, kept its name because non-Indian residents also grumbled about overindulgence in political correctness. Names of towns with the "S" word were omitted from the original law, but a movement is now afoot to include them as well. Muriel Charwood Litzau, a Native American who is a resident of Squaw Lake as well as the Leech Lake Reservation, loathes the "S" word so much that she does not want to tell people where she lives. She said that squaw is a French corruption of an Iroquois (possibly Mohawk) word for "vagina" (Johansen, 1996b, 4). Her daughter, Dawn Litzau and another student, Angelene Losh, began the campaign to eliminate squaw as a geographic place-name in Minnesota as part of a Native American studies class at Cass Lake-Bena High School, a public school within the Leech Lake Reservation. Students of the school's Name Change Committee also met with students at the Pequot Lakes High School in northern Minnesota and persuaded the student body to change its Indian mascot.

According to the U.S. Geological Survey's Board on Geographic Names, the word *squaw* has been affixed to 1,050 geographic names in the United States, most of them in the West and Midwest (Johansen, 1996b, 4). In California, for example, a request has been filed with the Survey Board to change the name Squaw Gulch, in Siskiyou County, to Taritsi Gulch. Also in California, questions are being raised about the name of the Squaw Valley ski resort. Activists in Arizona and Oregon (with 161 place-names that include "squaw") were taking up the refrain, advocating state laws similar to Minnesota's.

The Board on Geographic Names has exercised a role in "political correctness" debates before. In 1967, it directed that 143 places using the place-name *nigger* be changed to "Negro." The same year, the board ordered that *Jap* be changed to "Japanese" in 26 place-names across the United States.

FURTHER READING

Appeals Court Halts Indian Trust Accounting. *Billings Gazette*, November 14, 2003. Available at http://www.billingsgazette.com/index.php?id=1&display=rednews/2003/11/14/build/nation/42-indiantrust.inc.

Awehali, Brian. Fighting Long Odds: Government Continues to Shred, Evade, Obstruct, Lie, and Conspire in Indian Trust Case. *LiP Magazine*, December 15, 2003. Available at http://www.lipmagazine.org.

Babwin, Don. Opposition to Indian Mascots Mounts. Associated Press, November 6, 2000. Available at http://www.copleynewspapers.com/couriernews/top/e06mascots.htm.

BeDan, M. International Eye Drawn to "Fightin' Whities"; Protest of Mascot for Eaton High School "Has Kind of Snowballed." *Rocky Mountain News*, March 15, 2002, 12-A.

Benedict, Michael. UND: Another Voice; Faculty Group Gives Kupchella Petition Urging Nickname Change. *Grand Forks* [North Dakota] *Herald*, November 9, 2000. Available at http://web.northscape.com/content/gfherald/2000/11/09/local/MB1109UND.htm.

Brandon, William. *The Last Americans*. New York: McGraw-Hill, 1974.

Calnan, Christopher. Faculty Votes to Retire Mascot. *Roanoke Times*, November 8, 2000. Available at http://www.roanoke.com/roatimes/news/story102344.html.

Chatters, James C. Politics Aside, These Bones Belong to Everybody. *Wall Street Journal*, September 5, 2002, D-10.

Cobell v. Norton. 240 F3rd 1081 (DC Cir. 2001).

Committee on Government Operations, U.S. House of Representatives. "Misplaced Trust: The Bureau of Indian Affairs' Mismanagement of the Indian Trust Fund." April 1, 1992. Washington, D.C.: U.S. Government Printing Office, 1992.

Cornelius, Coleman. Fightin' Whites Fund Scholarships: T-Shirt Sales Reap $100,000 for Indians. *Denver Post*, December 1, 2002. Available at http://www.denverpost./com/Stories/0,1413,36%7E53%7E1021717%7E,00.html.

County of Oneida v. Oneida Indian Nation. 470 U.S. 226 (1985).

Crime Rate on Indian Reservations Much Higher than U.S. *Indian Time* [Akwesasne Mohawk Reservation, New York], October 9, 2003, 11.

Crisis at Akwesasne [transcript]. Hearings of the New York Assembly, July–August 1990. Albany and Fort Covington, NY: State of New York.

Deloria, Vine, Jr. *Custer Died for Your Sins: An Indian Manifesto*. New York: Avon Books, 1969.

Deloria, Vine, Jr. *God is Red*. Golden, CO: Fulcrum, 1994.

Department of Indian Affairs and Northern Development. Press release, June 20, 2001. Available at http://www1.newswire.ca/releases/June2001/20/c6060.html.

Diebel, Linda. $12 Billion Lawsuit Seeks Redress For Abuse In Residential Schools. *Toronto Star*, December 8, 2002. Available at http://www.thestar.ca/NASApp/cs/ContentServer?pagename=thestar/Layout/Article_Type1&c=Article&cid=1035775341135&call_page=TS_GTA&call_pageid=968350130169&call_pagepath=GTA/News&pubid=968163964505&StarSource=email.

Doclar, Mary. Protests Cause Reassessment of Dallas Schools' Indian Mascots. *Fort Worth Star-Telegram*, December 5, 1998. Available at http://www.startext.net/news/doc/1047/1:arl71/1:arl71120598.html.

Drew, Neil. Personal e-mail communication, July 1, 2001.

Eichstaedt, Peter. *If You Poison Us: Uranium and American Indians*. Santa Fe, NM: Red Crane Books, 1995.

Elliott, Louise. Ontario Native Suicide Rate One of Highest in World, Expert Says. *Vancouver Sun*, November 30, 2000. Available at http://www.vancouversun.com.

Elliott, Louise. Aboriginal Girls Taking Their Lives in Record Numbers Across Ontario's North. *Canadian Aboriginal*, December 3, 2000. Available at http://www.canadianaboriginal.com/health/health15b.htm.

Elliott, Louise. Hunger and Suicide Stalk Reserve after Feds Cut Funds. *Montreal Gazette*, June 7, 2001, A-15.

Elliott, Louise. Native Community Searches for Doctor. *Toronto Star*, June 16, 2001, A-16.3.

Elliott, Louise. Reserve's Doctor Safe After Two-Day Walk in Wilderness. *Montreal Gazette*, June 18, 2001, A-14.

Elliott, Louise. Band Talking to Media May Perpetuate Suicide Crisis, Says Nault. Canadian Press, June 22, 2001. Available at http://ca.news.yahoo.com/010622/6/6ei2.html.

Elliott, Louise. Native Groups Warn of Suicide Crisis. *Toronto Star*, July 31, 2001, A-6.

Fast Growing Indian Gambling Drew $16.2 Billion. *Omaha World-Herald*, July 8, 2004, A-5.

Federal Bureau of Investigation. *Crime in the United States: Annual Report, 1989.* Washington, DC: FBI, 1989.

Federal Paternalism Angers Pikangikum. *Canadian Aboriginal.* No date. Available at http://www.canadianaboriginal.com/news/news131a.htm.

Fialka, John J. Tribe Gets Private-Sector Jobs; Winnebagos Build Profitable Businesses with Casino Seed Money. *Wall Street Journal*, February 18, 2004, A-4.

"'Fighting Whities' Make a Statement; American Indian Students Try to Raise Awareness of Stereotypes." Associated Press, in *Philadelphia Daily News*, March 12, 2002. Available at www.philly.com/mld/dailynews/sports/2841746.htm.

Fishman, Joshua F. "Maintaining Languages: What Works, What Doesn't?" In G. Cantoni, ed. *Stabilizing Indigenous Languages.* Flagstaff, AZ: Northern Arizona University, 1996, 186-198.

Gamble, Susan. M.D. Shocked at Conditions on Reserve. *Brantford Expositor*, n.d., n.p. Available at http://www.southam.com/brantfordexpositor.

Garner, J. "Whities' Mascot about Education, Not Retaliation; Intramural Basketball Team Takes Shot at Indian Caricature Used by Eaton High School. *Rocky Mountain News*, March 12, 2002. Available at http://www.rockymountainnews.com/drmn/state/article/0,1299,DRMN_21_1026337,00.html.

Gormley, Michael [Associated Press]. State Commissioner to Take a Stand on Indian Mascots, Names. *Boston Globe On-line*, 11:42 A.M. October 28, 2000. Available at http://www.boston.com/dailynews/302/region/state_commissioner_to_take_a_s:.html.

Goulais, Bob. Water Crisis Latest Plague to Visit Pikangikum. *Anishinabek News*, November 2000. Available at http://www.anishinabek.ca/news/Past%20issues/2000/November%20issue/Nov00watercrisis.htm.

Grinde, Donald A., Jr. Personal interview, March 23. 1993.

Grinde, Donald A., Jr., and Bruce E. Johansen. *Ecocide of Native America: Environmental Destruction of Indian Lands and Peoples.* Santa Fe, NM: Clear Light, 1995.

Harjo v. Pro-Football, Inc. 1999 WL 329721 (P.T.O., April 2, 1999). The Trademark Trial and Appeals Board, Patent and Trademark Office. Available at http://www.kentlaw.edu/student_orgs/jip/trade/skins.htm.

Hill, Richard W., Sr. Wounded Knee, a Wound that Won't Heal. Did the Army Attempt to Cover Up the Massacre of Prisoners of War? October 7, 1999. Available at http://www.dickshovel.com/hill.html. Accessed February 13, 2003.

Hornung, Rick. *One Nation Under the Gun: Inside the Mohawk Civil War.* New York: Pantheon, 1991.

Indian Mascots: An Idea Whose Time Has Passed [editorial]. *Asheville, NC, Citizen-Times*, September 30, 2000. Available at http://www.main.nc.us/wncceib/PeweAC-T9300editorial.htm.

Johansen, Bruce E. *Forgotten Founders: Benjamin Franklin, the Iroquois, and the Rationale for the American Revolution.* Ipswich, MA: Gambit, 1982.

Johansen, Bruce E. The Klan in a Can. *The Progressive*, July 1988, 13.

Johansen, Bruce E. Dead Indians Out, Live Indians In. *The Progressive*, December 1989, 15–16.

Johansen, Bruce E. *Life and Death in Mohawk Country*. Golden, CO: North American Press/Fulcrum, 1993.

Johansen, Bruce E. Running for Office: LaDuke and the Green Party. *Native Americas* 13:4(Winter 1996a):3–4.

Johansen, Bruce E. "Squawbles" in Minnesota. *Native Americas* 13:4(Winter 1996b):4.

Johansen, Bruce E. The BIA as Banker: "Trust" Is Hard When Billions Disappear. *Native Americas* 14:1(Spring 1997):14–23.

Johansen, Bruce. Whiteclay, Nebraska: The Town that Booze Built. *Native Americas* 15:1(Spring 1998):5.

Johansen, Bruce E. Living and Breathing: Native Languages Come Alive. *Native Americas* 17:1(Spring 2000):56–59.

Johansen, Bruce E. Mascots: Honor Be Thy Name. *Native Americas* 18:1(Spring 2001): 58–61.

Johansen, Bruce E. The New York Oneidas: A Case Study in the Mismatch of Cultural Tradition and Economic Development. *American Indian Culture and Research Journal* 26:3(2002):25–46.

Johansen, Bruce E., and Donald A. Grinde, Jr. *The Encyclopedia of Native American Biography*. New York: Henry Holt, 1997.

Judge: Scientists Can Study Ancient Bones of Man Indian Tribes Claim as Ancestor. *Indian Time* 20:35(September 5, 2002):10.

Kehoe, Alice Beck. *America Before the European Invasions*. London: Longman, 2002.

Kennedy, J. Michael. Truth and Consequences on the Reservation. *Los Angeles Times Sunday Magazine*, July 7, 2002, cover story. Available at LATimes.com.

Kilborn, Peter. Pine Ridge: A Different Kind of Poverty. *New York Times*, in *Omaha World-Herald*, September 30, 1992, p. A-1.

King, C. Richard, and Charles Frueling Springwood. *Team Spirits: The Native American Mascots Controversy*. Lincoln: University of Nebraska Press, 2001.

Meriam, Lewis. *The Problem of Indian Administration*. Baltimore: Johns Hopkins University Press, 1928.

Lucas, Phil. Images of Indians. *Four Winds: The International Forum for Native American Art, Literature, and History*, Autumn 1980, 69–77.

Lynch, John. Pikangikum First Nation Looks Beyond "Opening a Store." It Wants to Create Private-Sector Partnerships. *Northern Ontario Business*, March 1999. Available at http://www.nob.on.ca/archives/mar99story/step.html.

Marquez, Deron. Indian Gaming Is Different from Other Forms of Gambling. *Indian Country Today*, February 12, 2002, n.p., in LEXIS.

Murphy, Maureen. Gambling on Indian Reservations. Congressional Research Service, Library of Congress, April 26, 1985.

Nevard, David. Wahooism in the USA. A Red Socks Journal. No date. Available at http://www.ultranet.com/~kuras/bhxi3d.htm.

Page, Charles. The "Fighting Whites" Offer Lesson in Cultural Diversity. *Newsday*, March 19, 2002, A-32.

Pomerantz, Gary. Atlanta Fan's Headdress Ruffles Indian Feathers. *Atlanta Journal-Constitution*, October 21, 1995. Available at http://www.fastball.com/braves/archives/stories/1995/66ws1021.html.

Randolph, Eleanor. New York's Native American Casino Contributes, But Not to Tax Rolls. *New York Times*, October 18, 2003, n.p.

Reyhner, Jon, ed. *Teaching Indigenous Languages*. Flagstaff: Center for Excellence in Education, Northern Arizona University, 1997.

Reyhner, Jon, Gina Cantoni, Robert N. St. Clair, and Evangeline Parsons Yazzie. *Revitalizing Native Languages*. Flagstaff: Center for Excellence in Education, Northern Arizona University, 1999.

Reynolds, Jerry. Bush Administration Likely Behind Cobell Appropriations Rider. *Indian Country Today*, November 1, 2003. Available at http://www.indiancountry.com/?1067709828.

Salisbury, L. *The Cleveland Indian: The Legend of King Saturday*. Brooklyn, NY: The Smith Publishers, 1992.

Sanders, Thomas E., and Walter W. Peek, eds. *Literature of the American Indian*. Beverly Hills, CA: Glencoe, 1976.

Seminole Tribe of Florida v. Butterworth. 658 F. 2d 310 (5th Cir., 1980).

Slayman, Andrew L. A Battle over Bones. *Archaeology* 50:1(January/February 1997): 16–23.

Smith, Dean Howard. *Modern Tribal Development: Paths to Self-Sufficiency and Cultural Integrity in Indian Country*. Walnut Creek, CA: AltaMira Press, 2000.

Spindel, Carol. *Dancing at Halftime: Sports and the Controversy over American Indian Mascots*. New York: New York University Press, 2001.

Suzuki, Peter T. Housing on the Nebraska Indian Reservations: Federal Policies and Practices. *Habitat International* 15:4(1991):27–32.

Thomas, David Hurst. *Skull Wars: Kennewick Man, Archaeology, and the Battle for Native American Identity*. New York: Basic Books/Peter N. Nevraumont, 2000.

U.S. Department of Health and Human Services. *Trends in Indian Health*. Washington, D.C.: Government Printing Office, 1991.

Walke, Roger. Gambling on Indian Reservations: Updated October 17, 1988. Congressional Research Service, Library of Congress, Washington, DC.

Wampum Chronicles message board. No date. Available at http://pub11.ezboard.com/fwampumchroniclescurrentevents.showMessage?topicID=265.topic.

Wanamaker, Tom. Indian Gaming Column. *Indian Country Today*, April 5, 2002, n.p., in LEXIS.

Wanamaker, Tom. Debunking the Myth of Unregulated Indian Gaming. *Indian Country Today*, May 13, 2002, n.p., in LEXIS.

Weinberg, Bill. Land and Sovereignty in Hawai'i: A Native Nation Re-emerges. *Native Americas* 13:2(Summer 1996):30–41.

Wollock, Jeffrey. On the Wings of History: American Indians in the 20th Century. *Native Americas* 20:1(Spring 2003):14–31.

Selected Bibliography

Abram, Charles. Law of the Woman Chief, May 21, 1923. Hewitt Collection, BAE Manuscript No. 1636, NAA, Smithsonian Institution. Cited in Grinde and Johansen, 1991, 259.

Adair, James. *History of the American Indians.* Edited by Samuel Cole Williams. Johnson City, TN: Wataugua Press, [1775] 1930.

Adams, Charles F. *Works of John Adams.* Boston: Little-Brown, 1851.

Adams, John. *Defence of the Constitutions . . . of the United States.* Philadelphia: Hall and Sellers, 1787.

Africans in America: Revolution, Resource Bank, Part 2: 1750–1805: Crispus Attucks. Public Broadcasting Service. No date. Available at http://www.pbs.org/wgbh/aia/part2/2p24.html. Accessed February 20, 2003.

Allen, Paula Gunn. *The Sacred Hoop: Recovering the Feminine in American Indian Traditions.* Boston: Beacon Press, 1986.

Ambrose, Stephen E. *Crazy Horse and Custer.* New York: New American Library, 1986.

American Monthly Museum [magazine], 2(February 1776):96.

American Friends Service Committee. *Uncommon Controversy: Fishing Rights of the Muckleshoot, Puyallup, and Nisqually Indians.* Seattle: University of Washington Press, 1970.

Anthony, Susan B., Elizabeth Cady Stanton, and Matilda Joslyn Gage, eds. *History of Woman Suffrage.* Salem, NH: Ayer Company, 1985.

Anderson, Eva Greenslit. *The Life Story of Chief Seattle.* Caldwell, OH: Caxton, 1950.

Anderson, Terry L. *Sovereign Nations or Reservations?: An Economic History of American Indians.* San Francisco: Pacific Research Institute for Public Policy, 1995.

Appeals Court Halts Indian Trust Accounting. *Billings Gazette*, November 14, 2003. Available at http://www.billingsgazette.com/index.php?id=1&display=rednews/2003/11/14/build/nation/42-indiantrust.inc.

Aquila, Richard. *The Iroquois Restoration: Iroquois Diplomacy on the Colonial Frontier, 1701–1754.* Detroit: Wayne State University Press, 1983.

Archuleta, Margaret L., Brenda J. Child, and K. Tsianina Lomawaima, eds. *Away from Home: American Indian Boarding School Experiences, 1879–2000.* Phoenix: Heard Museum, 2000.

Arden, Harvey. The Fire that Never Dies. *National Geographic,* September 1987, 374–403.

Armstrong, Virginia Irving. *I Have Spoken: American History through the Voices of the Indians.* Athens, OH: Swallow Press, 1984.

Associated Press. *Omaha World-Herald,* December 9, 1991, 16.

Associated Press. Canada's United Church Apologizes for Abuse at Indian Schools. *Associated Press Canada,* October 28, 1998.

Awehali, Brian. Fighting Long Odds: Government Continues to Shred, Evade, Obstruct, Lie, and Conspire in Indian Trust Case. *LiP Magazine.* December 15, 2003. Available at http://www.lipmagazine.org.

Axtell, James. *The Indian Peoples of Eastern America: A Documentary History of the Sexes.* New York: Oxford University Press, 1981.

Babwin, Don. Opposition to Indian Mascots Mounts. Associated Press, November 6, 2000. Available at http://www.copleynewspapers.com/couriernews/top/e06mascots.htm.

Baily, L. R. *Indian Slave Trade in the Southwest.* Los Angeles: Westernlore Press, 1973.

Baker, Leonard. *John Marshall: A Life in Law.* New York: Macmillan, 1974.

Ball, Milnar. Constitution, Court, Indian Tribes. *American Bar Foundation Research Journal* 1(1987):1–140.

Ballantine, Betty, and Ian Ballantine. *The Native Americans: An Illustrated History.* Atlanta: Turner, 1994.

Barbeau, C. M. *Huron and Wyandot Mythology with an Appendix Containing Earlier Published Records.* No. 11, Anthropological Series, Memoir 80. Ottawa: Government Printing Bureau, 1915:35–51.

Barreiro, José. The Search for Lessons. In José Barreiro, ed., *Indigenous Economics: Toward A Natural World Order. Akwe:kon Journal* 9:2(Summer 1992):18–39.

Barsh, Russel L. *The Washington Fishing Rights Controversy: An Economic Critique.* Seattle: University of Washington School of Business Administration, 1977.

Barsh, Russel, and James Henderson. *The Road: Indian Tribes and Political Liberty.* Berkeley: University of California Press, 1980.

Bates, Tom. The Government's Secret War on the Indian. *Oregon Times,* February–March 1976, 14.

Beal, Merrill D. *I Will Fight No More Forever.* Seattle: University of Washington Press, 1963.

Beals, Ralph L., and Harry Hoijer. *An Introduction to Anthropology.* New York, 1965.

Beckhard, Arthur J., *Black Hawk.* New York: Julian Messner, 1957.

BeDan, M. International Eye Drawn to "Fightin' Whities"; Protest of Mascot for Eaton High School "Has Kind of Snowballed." *Rocky Mountain News,* March 15, 2002, 12-A.

Benedict, Michael. UND: Another Voice; Faculty Group Gives Kupchella Petition Urging Nickname Change. *Grand Forks* [North Dakota] *Herald,* November 9, 2000. Available at http://web.northscape.com/content/gfherald/2000/11/09/local/MB1109UND.htm.

Bergh, Albert E., ed. *The Writings of Thomas Jefferson.* Washington: Jefferson Memorial Association, 1903–1904: vol. 11.

Bigelow, John, ed. *Autobiography of Benjamin Franklin.* Philadelphia: J. B. Lippincott, 1868.

Birchfield, D. L. *The Encyclopedia of North American Indians.* New York: Marshall Cavendish, 1997: vol. 5.

Blackbird, Andrew J. *Complete Both Early and Late History of the Ottawa and the Cheppewa Indians of Michigan: A Grammar of Their Language, Personal and Family History of the Author.* Harbor Springs, Michigan: Babcock and Darling, 1897.

Black Elk. *Black Elk Speaks, as Told to John G. Neihardt.* New York: William Morrow, [1932] 1972.

Black Elk. *The Sacred Pipe: Black Elk's Account of the Seven Rites of the Oglala Sioux.* Edited by Joseph Epes Brown. New York: Penguin Books, 1973.

Black Hawk. *Life of Ma-ka-tai-me-she-kia-kiak, or Black Hawk, Dictated by Himself.* Boston, 1834.

Bluecloud, Peter. *Alcatraz Is Not an Island.* Berkeley, CA: Wingbow Press, 1972.

Bolton, Herbet Eugene, ed. *Spanish Exploration in the Southwest, 1542–1706.* New York: Charles Scribner's Sons, 1916.

Bolton, Herbet Eugene. *Coronado on the Turquoise Trail.* Albuquerque: University of New Mexico Press, 1949.

Bone Shirt, Alfred. Via Internet to Marcel Guay. Canadian Aboriginal News/First Nations Skyvillage. Available at http://www.canadianaboriginal.com/.

Boorstin, Daniel J. *The Lost World of Thomas Jefferson.* New York: Henry Holt, 1948.

Borah, Woodrow. The Historical Demography of Aboriginal and Colonial America: An Attempt at Perspective. In William M. Denevan, ed., *The Native American Population of the Americas in 1492.* Madison: University of Wisconsin Press, 1976: 13–34.

Borah, Woodrow, and Sherburne Cook. *The Aboriginal Population of Mexico on the Eve of the Spanish Conquest.* Ibero-Americana No. 45. Berkeley: University of California Press, 1963.

Bourrie, Mark. Canada Apologizes for Abuse of Native Peoples. Interpress Service, January 8, 1998. Available at http://www.oneworld.org/ips2/jan98/canada2.html.

Boyd, Julian P., ed. *Indian Treaties Printed by Benjamin Franklin, 1736–1762.* Philadelphia: Historical Society of Pennsylvania, 1938.

Boyd, Julian P., ed. *The Papers of Thomas Jefferson.* Princeton, NJ: Princeton University Press, 1950 to date.

Boyd, Julian P. Dr. Franklin, Friend of the Indian. In Ray Lokken, Jr., ed., *Meet Dr. Franklin.* Philadelphia: Franklin Institute, 1981: 237–245.

Boyd, Robert. *The Coming of the Spirit of Pestilence: Introduced Infectious Diseases and Population Decline Among Northwest Coast Indians, 1774–1874.* Vancouver, BC: University of British Columbia Press, 1999.

Brack, Fred. Fishing Rights: Who Is Entitled to Northwest Salmon?" *Seattle Post-Intelligencer Northwest Magazine,* January 16, 1977, 8–10.

Bradford, William. *History of Plymouth Plantation.* Edited by Charles Deane. Boston: Private printing, 1856.

Bradford, William. *History of Plymouth Plantation.* Edited by Samuel Eliot Morison. New York: Modern Library, 1967.

Branch, Douglas E. *The Hunting of the Buffalo.* Lincoln: University of Nebraska Press, 1973.

Brand, Johanna. *The Life and Death of Anna Mae Aquash.* Toronto: Lorimer, 1978.

Brandon, William. *The American Heritage Book of Indians.* New York: Dell, 1961.

Brandon, William. *The Last Americans.* New York: McGraw-Hill, 1974.

Brandon, William. *The Rise and Fall of North American Indians from Prehistory through Geronimo.* Lanham, MD: Taylor Trade, 2003.

Bricker, Victoria R. *The Indian Christ, the Indian King.* Austin: University of Texas Press, 1981.

A Brief Notice of the Recent Outrages Committed by Isaac Stevens . . . May 17, 1856. In W. H. Wallace, *Martial Law in the Washington Territory, The Annals of America,* 1856, 384–389.

British Columbia Anglican Diocese Set to Close over Lawsuit. Canadian Broadcasting Corporation News On-line, December 30, 2001. Available at http://cbc.ca/cgi-bin/view?/news/2001/12/30/anglican_011230.

Brockunier, Samuel H. *The Irrepressible Democrat: Roger Williams.* New York: Ronald Press, 1940.

Brown, Bruce. *Mountain in the Clouds: The Search for the Wild Salmon.* New York: Simon and Schuster, 1982.

Brown, Dee. *Bury My Heart at Wounded Knee.* New York: Holt, Rinehart, Winston, 1970.

Brown, Jennifer S. H. *Strangers in Blood: Fur Trade Families in Indian Country.* Vancouver, BC: University of British Columbia Press, 1981.

Brown, Judith K. Economic Organization and the Position of Women among the Iroquois. *Ethnohistory* 17:3–4(Summer–Fall 1970):151–167.

Bryant, Martha F. *Sacajawea: A Native American Heroine.* New York: Council for Indian Education, 1989.

Burnham, Philip. Review *Seven Myths of the Spanish Conquest,* by Matthew Restall. *Indian Country Today,* August 5, 2004. Available at http://www.indiancountry.com/?1091714398.

Butterfield, Consul Wilshire. *History of the Girtys, Being a Concise Account of the Girty Brothers—Thomas, Simon, James and George, and of Their Half-Brother, John Turner— Also of the Part Taken by Them in Lord Dunmore's War, in the Western Border War of the Revolution, and in the Indian War of 1790–1795.* Cincinnati: Robert Clark, 1890.

Butterfield, Lyman H., ed. *The Diary and Autobiography of John Adams.* Cambridge, MA: Harvard University Press, 1961.

Byrd, Sydney. Wounded Knee: We Must Never Forget. *Lakota Journal,* January 3–10, 2003, 1. Available at http://www.lakotajournal.com/front.htm.

Caduto, Michael J., and Joseph Brudhac. *Keepers of the Earth: Native American Stories and Environmental Activities for Children.* Golden, CO: Fulcrum, 1988.

Calamai, Peter. Demise of Maya Tied to Droughts: Study Points to Climate Change Culture Depended on Growing Maize. *Toronto Star,* March 14, 2003. Available at http://www.thestar.ca/NASApp/cs/ContentServer?pagename=thestar/Layout/Article_Type1&c=Article&cid=1035779188042&call_page=TS_Canada&call_pageid=968332188774&call_pagepath=News/Canada&pubid=968163964505&StarSource=email.

Calloway, Colin. *The Western Abenakis of Vermont, 1600–1800: War, Migration, and the Survival of an Indian People.* Norman: University of Oklahoma Press, 1990.

Calloway, Colin. *New Worlds for All: Indians, Europeans, and the Remaking of Early America.* Baltimore: Johns Hopkins University Press, 1997.

Calnan, Christopher. Faculty Votes to Retire Mascot. *Roanoke Times,* November 8, 2000. Available at http://www.roanoke.com/roatimes/news/story102344.html.

Cameron, Kenneth W., ed. *The Works of Samuel Peters.* Hartford, CT: Transcendental Books, 1967.

Canby, Thomas Y. The Anasazi: Riddles in the Ruins. *National Geographic,* November 1982, 554–592.

Canby, William C., Jr. *American Indian Law.* St. Paul, MN: West, 1981.

Carr, Lucien. *The Social and Political Position of Women among the Huron-Iroquois Tribes.* Salem, MA: Salem Press, 1884.

Carter, Harvey Lewis. *The Life and Times of Little Turtle: First Sagamore of the Wabash.* Urbana: University of Illinois Press, 1987.

Carver, Jonathan. *Travels through the Interior Parts of North America.* London: C. Dilly, 1778.

Case, Nancy Humphrey. Gifts from the Indians: Native Americans Not Only Provided New Kinds of Food and Recreation; They May Have Given the Founding Fathers Ideas on How to Form a Government. *Christian Science Monitor*, November 26, 2002. Available at http://www.csmonitor.com.

Castillo, Bernal Diaz del. *Historia Verdadera de la Conquista de la Nueva Espana.* Edited by Joaquin Ramirez Cabanas. Mexico City: Editorial Purrua, 1968.

Castillo, Bernardino Diaz del. *Conquest of Mexico.* New York, 1958.

Chalmers, Harvey. *The Last Stand of the Nez Perce.* New York: Twayne, 1962.

Champagne, Duane. *American Indian Societies: Strategies and Conditions of Political and Cultural Survival.* Cambridge, MA: Cultural Survival, 1989.

Chapin, Howard H. *Sachems of the Narragansetts.* Providence: Rhode Island Historical Society, 1931.

Chatters, James C. Politics Aside, These Bones Belong to Everybody. *Wall Street Journal*, September 5, 2002, D-10.

Cherokee Nation v. Georgia (5 Peters 1, 1831).

Chittenden, Hiram M. *The American Fur Trade of the Far West.* New York: Press of the Pioneers, 1935.

Church, Thomas. *Diary of King Philip's War, 1676–77.* Edited by Alan and Mary Simpson. Chester, CT: Pequot Press, 1975.

Churchill, Ward. *Struggles for the Land.* Monroe, ME: Common Courage Press, 1993.

Churchill, Ward, and Jim Vander Wall. *Agents of Repression: The FBI's Secret War Against the Black Panther Party and the American Indian Movement.* Boston: South End Press, 1990a.

Churchill, Ward, and Jim Vander Wall. *The Cointelpro Papers.* Boston: South End Press, 1990b.

Chupack, Henry. *Roger Williams.* New York: Twayne, 1969.

Clark, Robert A. *The Killing of Crazy Horse.* Lincoln: University of Nebraska Press, 1976.

Coe, Michael D. *America's First Civilization.* New York: American Heritage, 1968.

Coe, William R. Resurrecting the Grandeur of Tikal. *National Geographic*, December 1975, 792–799.

Cohen, Felix. Americanizing the White Man. *American Scholar* 21:2(1952):177–191.

Cohen, Felix. *The Legal Conscience: The Selected Papers of Felix S. Cohen.* Edited by Lucy Kramer Cohen. New Haven, CT: Yale University Press, 1960.

Colden, Cadwallader. *The History of the Five Nations of Canada.* New York: Amsterdam, [1765] 1902.

Colden, Cadwallader. *The History of the Five Nations Depending on the Province of New York in America.* Ithaca, NY: Cornell University Press, [1727, 1747] 1958.

Cole, Donald B. *Presidency of Andrew Jackson.* Lawrence: University Press of Kansas, 1993.

Collier, John. *Indians of the Americas.* New York: New American Library, 1947.

Commager, Henry Steele. *Jefferson, Nationalism and the Enlightenment.* New York: George Braziller, 1975.

Cook, Sherburne F. Interracial Warfare and Population Decline among the New England Indians. *Ethnohistory* 20:1(Winter 1973):1–24.

Cook, Sherburne F., and Woodrow Borah, *The Indian Population of Central Mexico, 1521-1610.* Ibero-Americana No. 44. Berkeley: University of California Press, 1960.

Cook, Sherburne F., and Leslie B. Simpson. The Population of Central Mexico in the Sixteenth Century. *Ibero-Americana* 31. Berkeley and Los Angeles: University of California Press, 1948.

Converse, Harriet Maxwell [Ya-ie-wa-noh]. *Myths and Legends of the New York State Iroquois.* Edited by Arthur Caswell Parker. New York State Museum Bulletin 125. Education Department Bulletin No. 437. Albany: University of the State of New York, 1908: 31–36.

Copway, George [Kah-ge-ga-gah-bowh]. *The Life, Letters, and Speeches.* New York: S. W. Benedict, 1850.

Corkran, David H. *The Cherokee Frontier: Conflict and Survival, 1740–62.* Norman: University of Oklahoma Press, 1962.

Cornelius, Coleman. Fightin' Whites Fund Scholarships: T-shirt Sales Reap $100,000 for Indians. *Denver Post,* December 1, 2002. Available at http://www.denverpost. com/Stories/0,1413,36%7E53%7E1021717%7E,00.html.

Cornplanter, Jesse J. *Legends of the Longhouse.* Edited by William G. Spittal. Illustrated by J. J. Cornplanter. Ohsweken, Ontario, Canada: Iroqrafts, [1938] 1992.

Coulter, Robert T., and Steven M. Tullberg. Indian Land Rights. In Sandra L. Cadwallader and Vine Deloria, Jr., eds., *The Aggressions of Civilization.* Philadelphia: Temple University Press, 1984: 185–214.

Covey, Cyclone. *The Gentle Radical: A Biography of Roger Williams.* New York: Macmillan, 1966.

Cramblit, Andre. Survivor (Humor). October 25, 2002.

Cramblit, Andre. Item via IndigenousNewsNetwork@topica.com, March 31, 2003.

Cramblit, Andre. Item via IndigenousNewsNetwork@topica.com. May 17, 2003.

Cramblit, Andre. Item via IndigenousNewsNetwork@topica.com. June 1, 2003.

Cramblit, Andre. Reservations for Whites. E-mail newsletter item via Digest for IndigenousNewsNetwork@topica.com, issue 114, June 19, 2003.

Crevecouer, Hector Saint John de. *Journey into Northern Pennsylvania and the State of New York* [in French]. Ann Arbor: University of Michigan Press, [1801] 1964.

Crevecoeur, St. Jean de. *Letters from an American Farmer.* New York: Dutton, 1926.

Crime Rate on Indian Reservations Much Higher than U.S. *Indian Time* (Akwesasne Mohawk Reservation, New York), October 9, 2003, 11.

Crisis at Akwesasne [transcript]. Hearings of the New York Assembly, July–August, 1990. Albany and Fort Covington, NY: State of New York.

Cronon, William. *Changes in the Land: Indians, Colonists, and the Ecology of New England.* New York: Hill and Wang, 1983.

Crosby, Alfred W. *The Columbian Exchange: Biological and Cultural Consequences of 1492.* New York: Greenwood Press, 1972.

Crosby, Alfred W. *The Columbian Voyages, the Columbian Exchange, and Their Historians.* Washington, DC: American Historical Association, 1987.

Custer, Elizabeth. *Boots and Saddles.* New York, 1885.

Custer, George Armstrong. *My Life on the Plains.* Lincoln: University of Nebraska Press, 1966.

Darwin, Charles. *The Voyage of the Beagle.* Garden City, NY: Doubleday, 1962, 433–434.

Davis, Russell, and Brant Ashabranner. *Chief Joseph: War Chief of the Nez Perce.* New York: McGraw-Hill, 1962.

Deardorff, Merle H. *The Religion of Handsome Lake: Its Origins and Development.* American Bureau of Ethnology Bulletin No. 149. Washington, DC: BAE, 1951.

Deloria, Vine, Jr. *Behind the Trail of Broken Treaties.* New York: Delacorte, 1974a.

Deloria, Vine, Jr. *The Indian Affair.* New York: Friendship Press, 1974b.

Deloria, Vine, Jr. *The Nations Within.* New York: Pantheon, 1984.

Deloria, Vine, Jr. *American Indian Policy in the Twentieth Century.* Norman: University of Oklahoma Press, 1985.

Deloria, Vine, Jr. *Custer Died for Your Sins: An Indian Manifesto.* Norman: University of Oklahoma Press, 1988.

Deloria, Vine, Jr. *Behind the Trail of Broken Treaties.* Austin: University of Texas Press, 1990.

Deloria, Vine, Jr. *God Is Red.* Golden, CO: North American Press, 1992.

Deloria, Vine, Jr., and Clifford Lytle. *American Indians: American Justice.* Austin: University of Texas Press, 1984.

Demarest, Arthur A. The Violent Saga of a Mayan Kingdom. *National Geographic,* February 1993, 95–111.

Demarest, Arthur A., Prudence M. Rice, and Don S. Rice, eds. *The Terminal Classic in the Maya Lowlands: Collapse, Transition, and Transformation.* Boulder, CO: University Press of Colorado, 2003.

Denhardt, Robert M. *The Horse of the Americas.* Norman: University of Oklahoma Press, 1975.

Dennis, Matthew. *Cultivating a Landscape of Peace.* Ithaca, NY: Cornell University Press, 1993.

Department of Indian Affairs and Northern Development. Press release. June 20, 2001. Available at http://www1.newswire.ca/releases/June2001/20/c6060.html.

Deskaheh: Iroquois Statesman and Patriot. Onchiota, NY: Six Nations Indian Museum Series, n.d.

Deskaheh (Levi General) and Six Nations Council. *The Redman's Appeal for Justice.* Brantford, Ontario, Canada: Wilson Moore, 1924.

DeVoto, Bernard. *Across the Wide Missouri.* Cambridge, MA: Harvard University Press, 1947.

DeVoto, Bernard. *The Course of Empire.* Boston: Houghton-Mifflin, 1952.

Diamond, Jared. The Last Americans: Environmental Collapse and the End of Civilization. *Harper's,* June 2003, 43–51.

Diebel, Linda. $12 Billion Lawsuit Seeks Redress for Abuse in Residential Schools. *Toronto Star,* December 8, 2002. Available at http://www.thestar.ca/NASApp/cs/ContentServer?pagename=thestar/Layout/Article_Type1&c=Article&cid=1035775341135&call_page=TS_GTA&call_pageid=968350130169&call_pagepath=GTA/News&pubid=968163964505&StarSource=email.

Diehl, Richard A. *Tula: The Toltec Capital of Ancient Mexico.* London: Thames and Hudson, 1981.

Dillehay, Thomas D. *The Settlement of the Americas: A New Prehistory.* New York: Basic Books, 2000.

Dillehay, Tom D. Palaeoanthropology: Tracking the First Americans. *Nature* 425 (September 4, 2003):23–24.

Dittert, Alfred E., Jr. The Archaeology of Cebolleta Mesa and Acoma Pueblo: A Preliminary Report Based on Further Investigation. *El Palacio* 59(1952):191–217.

Dobyns, Henry F. Estimating Aboriginal American Population. *Current Anthropology* 7(October 1966):395–412.

Dobyns, Henry F. *Their Number Became Thinned.* Knoxville: University of Tennessee Press, 1983.

Dobyns, Henry F. More Methodological Perspectives on Historical Demography. *Ethnohistory* 36:3(Summer 1989):286–289.

Doclar, Mary. Protests Cause Reassessment of Dallas Schools' Indian Mascots. *Fort Worth Star-Telegram*, December 5, 1998. Available at http://www.startext.net/news/doc/1047/1:arl71/1:arl71120598.html.

Dozier, Edward P. *The Pueblo Indians of North America.* New York: Holt, Rinehart, and Winston, 1970.

Drew, Neil. Personal e-mail communication, July 1, 2001.

Drinnon, Richard. *Facing West: Indian Hating and Empire Building.* New York: Schoken Books, 1990.

Driver, Harold E. *Indians of North America.* 2nd ed., rev. Chicago: University of Chicago Press, 1969.

Drucker, Philip. *Indians of the Northwest Coast.* New York: McGraw-Hill, 1955.

Duby, Gertrude and Frans Blom. The Lacandon. In Robert Wauchope, ed. *Handbook of Middle-American Indians.* Vol. 7. Austin: University of Texas Press, 1969: 276–297.

Dugan, Bill. *Sitting Bull.* San Francisco: HarperCollins, 1994.

Eckert, Allan W. *A Sorrow in Our Heart: The Life of Tecumseh.* New York: Bantam, 1992.

Edmonds, Della and Margot. *Sacajawea of the Lewis and Clark Expedition.* Berkeley: University of California Press, 1979.

Edmunds, R. David., ed., *American Indian Leaders: Studies in Diversity.* Lincoln: University of Nebraska Press, 1980.

Edmunds, R. David. *The Shawnee Prophet.* Lincoln: University of Nebraska Press, 1983.

Edmunds, R. David. *Tecumseh and the Quest for Indian Leadership.* Boston: Little-Brown, 1984.

Edwards, Everett E. The Contributions of American Indians to Civilization. *Minnesota History* 15:3(1934):255–272.

Eggleston, Edward and Lillie Eggleston-Seelye. *Tecumseh and the Shawnee Prophet.* New York, 1878.

Eichstaedt, Peter. *If You Poison Us: Uranium and American Indians.* Santa Fe, NM: Red Crane Books, 1995.

Elliott, Louise. Ontario Native Suicide Rate One of Highest in World, Expert Says. *Vancouver Sun*, November 30, 2000. Available at http://www.vancouversun.com.

Elliott, Louise. Aboriginal Girls Taking Their Lives in Record Numbers Across Ontario's North. *Canadian Aboriginal*, December 3, 2000. Available at http://www.canadianaboriginal.com/health/health15b.htm.

Elliott, Louise. Hunger and Suicide Stalk Reserve after Feds Cut Funds. *Montreal Gazette*, June 7, 2001, A-15.

Elliott, Louise. Native Community Searches for Doctor. *Toronto Star*, June 16, 2001, A-16.

Elliott, Louise. Reserve's Doctor Safe After Two-Day Walk in Wilderness. *Montreal Gazette*, June 18, 2001, A-14

Elliott, Louise. Band Talking to Media May Perpetuate Suicide Crisis, Says Nault. Canadian Press, June 22, 2001. Available at http://ca.news.yahoo.com/010622/6/6ei2.html.

Elliott, Louise. Native Groups Warn of Suicide Crisis. *Toronto Star*, July 31, 2001, A-6.

Ellis, George W., and John E. Morris. *King Philip's War*. New York: The Grafton Press, 1906.

Emily of Kanesatake. Personal e-mail communication via John Kahionhes Fadden, March 21, 2003.

Engels, Frederick. *Origin of the Family, Private Property, and the State*. In *Karl Marx and Frederick Engels: Selected Works in One Volume*. New York: International Publishers, 1968.

Ernst, James. *Roger Williams: New England Firebrand*. New York: Macmillan, 1932.

Exhibit on the Iroquois Confereracy, Yager Museum, Hartwick College, Oneonta, NY, June 1983.

Fadden, John Kahionhes. Personal communication, June 14, 1989.

Fadden, John Kahionhes. Personal communication, March 20, 2001.

Fadden, John Kahionhes. Personal communication, February 22, 2003.

Fagan, Brian. *Before California: An Archaeologist Looks at Our Earliest Inhabitants*. Lanham, MD: Rowman and Littlefield, 2003.

Fahey, John. *The Flathead Indians*. Norman: University of Oklahoma Press, 1974.

Fahey, John. *The Kalispel Indians*. Norman: University of Oklahoma Press, 1986.

Fash, William L., Jr., and Barbara W. Fash. Scribes, Warriors and Kings: The Lives of the Copan Maya. *Archaeology*, May–June 1990, 28.

Fast Growing Indian Gambling Drew $16.2 Billion. *Omaha World-Herald*, July 8, 2004, A-5.

Federal Paternalism Angers Pikangikum. *Canadian Aboriginal*. No date. Available at http://www.canadianaboriginal.com/news/news131a.htm.

Fee, Chester. *Chief Joseph: The Biography of a Great Indian*. New York: Wilson Erickson, 1936.

Fenn, Elizabeth. *Pox Americana: The Great Smallpox Epidemic of 1775–82*. New York: Hill & Wang, 2001.

Fenton, W. N. *Contacts Between Iroquois Herbalism and Colonial Medicine*. Washington, DC: Smithsonian Institution, 1941.

Fenton, William N. *Roll Call of the Iroquois Chiefs*. Washington, DC: Smithsonian Institution, 1950.

Fenton, William N., ed. *Symposium on Cherokee and Iroquois Culture*. Smithsonian Institution Bureau of Ethnology Bulletin 180. Washington, DC: Government Printing Office, 1961.

Fenton, William N., ed. *Parker on the Iroquois*. Syracuse, NY: Syracuse University Press, 1968.

Fialka, John J. Tribe Gets Private-Sector Jobs; Winnebagos Build Profitable Businesses with Casino Seed Money. *Wall Street Journal*, February 18, 2004, A-4.

Fiscus, Carolyn. Personal communication, June 17, 2003.

Foner, Philip S., ed. *Complete Writings of Thomas Paine*. New York: Citadel Press, 1945.

Forbes, Jack. *The Indian in America's Past*. New York: Prentice-Hall, 1964.

Ford, Paul L., ed. *The Writings of Thomas Jefferson*. Vol. 3. New York: J. P. Putnam's Sons, 1892–1899.

Frachtenberg, Leo J. Our Indebtedness to the American Indian. *Wisconsin Archeologist* 14:2(1915):64–69.

Frazier, Joseph B. Humans in Oregon 10,000 Years Ago? Associated Press. November 25, 2002. Available at senior-staff@nativenewsonline.org.

Frazier, Neta L. *Sacajawea: The Girl Nobody Knows.* New York: McKay, 1967.

Furtwangler, Albert. *Answering Chief Seattle.* Seattle: University of Washington Press, 1997.

Gage, Matilda Joslyn. *Woman, Church and State.* Watertown, MA: Peresphone Press, [1893] 1980.

Gallay, Alan. Indian Slave Trade Thrived in Early America. *Daytona Beach News-Journal,* August 3, 2003, 3-B.

Gamble, Susan. M.D. Shocked at Conditions on Reserve. *Brantford (Ontario) Expositor,* n.d., n.p. Available at http://www.southam.com/brantfordexpositor.

Garner, J. Whities' Mascot about Education, Not Retaliation; Intramural Basketball Team Takes Shot at Indian Caricature Used by Eaton High School. *Rocky Mountain News,* March 12, 2002. Available at http://www.rockymountainnews.com/drmn/state/article/0,1299,DRMN_21_1026337,00.html.

Gates, Paul W., ed. *The Rape of Indian Lands.* New York: Arno Press, 1979.

Gerhard, Peter. *A Guide to the Historical Geography of New Spain.* Princeton, NJ: Princeton University Press, 1972.

Gerhard, Peter. *The North Frontier of New Spain.* Princeton, NJ: Princeton University Press, 1982.

Giago, Tim. Book Lacks Lakota View. *Indian Country Today,* August 4, 1993, n.p.

Gibson, Arrell M. *The American Indian: Prehistory to Present.* Lexington, KY: Heath, 1980.

Gibson, Charles. *The Aztecs Under Spanish Rule: A History of the Indians of the Valley of Mexico, 1519–1810.* Palo Alto, CA: Stanford University Press, 1964.

Giddings, James L. Roger Williams and the Indians [typescript]. Providence: Rhode Island Historical Society, 1957.

Gill, Richardson. *The Great Maya Droughts.* Albuquerque: University of New Mexico Press, 2000.

Gill, Sam. *Mother Earth: An American Story.* Chicago: University of Chicago Press, 1987.

Goebel, Ted, Michael R. Waters, and Margarita Dikova. The Archaeology of Ushki Lake, Kamchatka, and the Pleistocene Peopling of the Americas. *Science* 301(July 25, 2003):501–505.

Gonzalez-José, Rolando, Antonio Gonzalez-Martin, Miquel Hernandez, Hector M. Pucciarelli, Marina Sardi, Alfonso Rosales, and Silvina Van der Molen. Craniometric Evidence for Palaeoamerican Survival in Baja California. *Nature* 425(September 4, 2003):62–66.

Gormley, Michael [Associated Press]. State Commissioner to Take a Stand on Indian Mascots, Names. *Boston Globe On-line,* 11:42 A.M. October 28, 2000. Available at http://www.boston.com/dailynews/302/region/state_commissioner_to_take_a_s:.html.

Goss, Eldridge Henry. *The Life of Colonel Paul Revere.* Boston: G. K. Hall and Co./Gregg Press, 1972.

Goulais, Bob. Water Crisis Latest Plague to Visit Pikangikum. *Anishinabek News,* November 2000. Available at http://www.anishinabek.ca/news/Past%20issues/2000/November%20issue/Nov00watercrisis.htm.

Graham, W. A. *The Custer Myth.* Lincoln: University of Nebraska Press, 1953.

Green, Michael D. The Expansion of European Colonization to the Mississippi Valley, 1780–1880. In Bruce G. Trigger and Wilcomb E. Washburn, eds., *The Cambridge*

History of the Native Peoples of the Americas. Cambridge, England: Cambridge University Press, 1996: 461–538.

Green, Rayna. The Museum of the Plains White Person. In Arlene Hirschfelder, ed., *Native Heritage: Personal Accounts by American Indians, 1790 to the Present.* New York: Macmillan, 1995: 184–185.

Griffith, Benjamin W., Jr. *McIntosh and Weatherford: Creek Indian Leaders.* Tuscaloosa: University of Alabama Press, 1988.

Grinde, Donald A., Jr. The Reburial of American Indian Remains and Funerary Objects. *Northeast Indian Quarterly,* Summer 1991, 35–38.

Grinde, Donald A., Jr. Personal communication, March 23, 1993.

Grinde, Donald A., Jr., and Bruce E. Johansen. *Exemplar of Liberty: Native America and the Evolution of Democracy.* Los Angeles: UCLA American Indian Studies Center, 1991.

Grinde, Donald A., Jr., and Bruce E. Johansen. *Ecocide of Native America: Environmental Destruction of Indian Lands and Peoples.* Santa Fe, NM: Clear Light, 1995.

Guay, Marcel. Canadian Aboriginal. News. November 12, 2002. Available at http://www.canadianaboriginal.com.

Guild, Reuben Aldridge. *Footprints of Roger Williams.* Providence, RI: Tibbetts and Preston, 1886.

Gunther, Erna. *Indian Life on the Northwest Coast of North America.* Chicago: University of Chicago Press, 1972.

Hagan, William T. *The Sac and Fox Indians.* Norman: University of Oklahoma Press, 1958.

Hale, Horatio. *The Iroquois Book of Rites.* Philadelphia, 1883.

Hamilton, Charles. *Cry of the Thunderbird.* Norman: University of Oklahoma Press, 1972.

Harjo v. Pro-Football, Inc. 1999 WL 329721 (P.T.O., April 2, 1999). The Trademark Trial and Appeals Board, Patent and Trademark Office. Available at http://www.kentlaw.edu/student_orgs/jip/trade/skins.htm.

Harold, Howard. *Sacajawea.* Norman: University of Oklahoma Press, 1971.

Hassler, Peter. Cutting through the Myth of Human Sacrifice: The Lies of the Conquistadors. *World Press Review,* December 1992, 28–29. Reprinted from *Die Zeit,* Hamburg, Germany.

Haug, Gerald H., Detlef Gunter, Larry C. Peterson, Daniel M. Sigman, Konrad A. Hughen, and Beat Aeschlimann. Climate and the Collapse of Maya Civilization. *Science* 299(March 14, 2003):1731–1735.

Havighurst, Robert J., and Thea R. Hilkevitch. The Intelligence of Indian Children as Measured by a Performance Scale. *Journal of Abnormal and Social Psychology* 39(1944):419–433.

Haynes, Gary. *The Early Settlement of North America: The Clovis Era.* Cambridge, England: Cambridge University Press, 2002.

Hays, Wilma P. *Pontiac: Lion in the Forest.* Boston: Houghton-Mifflin, 1965.

Heckenberger, Michael J., Afukaka Kuikuro, Urissap Tabata Kuikuro, J. Christian Russell, Morgan Schmidt, Carlos Fausto, and Bruna Franchetto. Amazonia 1492: Pristine Forest or Cultural Parkland? *Science* 301(September 19, 2003):1710–1714.

Heckewelder, John. *History, Manners, and Customs of the Indian Nations Who Once Inhabited Pennsylvania and the Neighboring States.* The First American Frontier Series. New York: Arno Press and the *New York Times,* [1820, 1876] 1971.

Heckewelder, John. *Narrative of the Mission of the United Brethren among the Delaware and Mohegan Indians from Its Commencement, in the Year 1740, to the Close of the Year 1808.* New York: Arno Press, [1818] 1971.

Henderson, John F. *The World of the Ancient Maya.* Ithaca, NY: Cornell University Press, 1981.

Hendrix, Janey B. Redbird Smith and the Nighthawk Keetoowahs. *Journal of Cherokee Studies* 8:1(1983):17–33.

Henige, David. *Numbers from Nowhere: The American Indian Contact Population Debate.* Norman: University of Oklahoma Press, 1998.

Henige, David. Can a Myth be Astronomically Dated? *American Indian Culture and Research Journal* 23:4(1999):127–157.

Hertzberg, Hazel W. *The Search for an American Indian Identity: Modern Pan-Indian Movements.* Syracuse, NY: Syracuse University Press, 1971.

Hewitt, J. N. B. *Legend of the Founding of the Iroquois League.* Washington, DC: Smithsonian Institution, 1892.

Hewitt, J. N. B. Iroquoian Cosmology, First Part. In *Twenty-First Annual Report of the Bureau of American Ethnology to the Secretary of the Smithsonian Institution, 1899–1900.* Washington, DC: Government Printing Office, 1903: 127–339.

Hewitt, J. N. B. *A Constitutional League of Peace in the Stone Age of America.* Washington, DC: Smithsonian Institution, 1918.

Hewitt, J. N. B. Iroquoian Cosmology, Second Part. In *Forty-third Annual Report of the Bureau of American Ethnology to the Secretary of the Smithsonian Institution, 1925–1926.* Washington, DC: Government Printing Office, 1928: 453–819.

Hewitt, J. N. B. Notes on the Creek Indians. In J. R. Swanton, ed., *Bureau of American Ethnology Bulletin No. 123.* Washington, DC: U.S. Government Printing Office, 1939: 124–133.

Hill, Richard. Continuity of Haudenosaunee Government: Political Reality of the Grand Council. *Northeast Indian Quarterly* 4:3(Autumn 1987):10–14.

Hill, Richard W., Sr. Wounded Knee, A Wound that Won't Heal. Did the Army Attempt to Cover Up the Massacre of Prisoners of War? October 7, 1999. Available at http://www.dickshovel.com/hill.html. Accessed February 13, 2003.

Hipwell, Bill. Apology Should Have Been a Thank You. *Financial Post (Ottawa, Ontario),* February 3, 1998, 18.

Hobson, Charles F. *The Great Chief Justice: John Marshall and the Rule of Law.* Lawrence: University Press of Kansas, 1996.

Hodgson, Bryan. Buffalo: Back Home on the Range. *National Geographic* 186:5(November 1994):64–89.

Hoig, Stan. *The Sand Creek Massacre.* Norman: University of Oklahoma Press, 1961.

Holder, Preston. *The Hoe and the Horse on the Plains.* Lincoln: University of Nebraska Press, 1970.

Homaday, William T. *The Extermination of the American Bison.* Washington, DC: Annual Report of the U.S. National Museum, 1869.

Hornung, Rick. *One Nation Under the Gun: Inside the Mohawk Civil War.* New York: Pantheon, 1991.

Hoover, Dwight W. *The Red and the Black.* Chicago: Rand McNally, 1976.

Howard, Helen A. Hiawatha: Co-founder of an Indian United Nations. *Journal of the West* 10:3(1971):428–438.

Howard, Helen A., and Dan L. McGrath. *War Chief Joseph.* Caldwell, ID: Caxton, 1952.

Howard, Oliver O. *Nez Perce Joseph.* Boston: Lee & Shepherd, 1881.

Hughes, J. Donald. *American Indian Ecology.* El Paso: Texas Western Press, 1983.

Humor Can be Good Medicine. November 10, 2002. Available at nativeculture@ yahoo.com.

Hyde, George E. *A Sioux Chronicle.* Norman: University of Oklahoma Press, 1956.

Hyde, George E. *Red Cloud's Folk: A History of the Oglala Sioux Indians.* Norman: University of Oklahoma Press, 1967.

Indian Mascots: An Idea Whose Time Has Passed [editorial]. *Asheville, NC, Citizen-Times,* September 30, 2000. Available at http://www.main.nc.us/wncceib/PeweAC T9300editorial.htm.

Iverson, Peter. Taking Care of the Earth and Sky. In Alvin Josephy, ed., *America in 1492: The World of the Indian Peoples Before the Arrival of Columbus.* New York: Knopf, 1992: 85–118.

Jackson, Donald, ed. *Black Hawk: An Autobiography.* Urbana: University of Illinois Press, 1964.

Jackson, Helen Hunt. *A Century of Dishonor: A Sketch of the United States Government's Dealings with Some of the Indian Tribes.* New York: Harper and Brothers, 1881.

Jacobs, Wilbur. *Diplomacy and Indian Gifts: Anglo-French Rivalry among the Ohio and Northwest Frontiers, 1748–1763.* Stanford, CA: Stanford University Press, 1950.

Jacobs, Wilbur R. *Wilderness Politics and Indian Gifts.* Lincoln: University of Nebraska Press, 1966.

Jaimes, M. Annette, ed. *The State of Native America: Genocide, Colonization and Resistance.* Boston: South End Press, 1992.

Jefferson, Thomas. *Notes on the State of Virginia.* Edited by Willam Peden. Chapel Hill: University of North Carolina Press, [1784] 1955.

Jensen, Richard E., R. Eli Paul, and John E. Carter. *Eyewitness at Wounded Knee.* Lincoln: University of Nebraska Press, 1991.

Johansen, Bruce E. Peltier and the Posse. *The Nation,* October 1, 1977, 304–307.

Johansen, Bruce E. The Reservation Offensive. *The Nation,* February 25, 1978, 204–207.

Johansen, Bruce E. *The Forgotten Founders: Benjamin Franklin, the Iroquois, and the Rationale for the American Revolution.* Ipswich, MA: Gambit, 1982.

Johansen, Bruce E. The Klan in a Can. *The Progressive,* July 1988, 13.

Johansen, Bruce E. Dead Indians Out, Live Indians In. *The Progressive,* December 1989, 15–16.

Johansen, Bruce E. *Life and Death in Mohawk Country.* Golden, CO: Fulcrum/North American Press, 1993.

Johansen, Bruce E. Dating the Iroquois Confederacy. *Akwesasne Notes New Series* 1:3/ 4(Fall 1995):62–63.

Johansen, Bruce E. Running for Office: LaDuke and the Green Party. *Native Americas* 13:4(Winter 1996):3–4.

Johansen, Bruce E. "Squawbles" in Minnesota. *Native Americas* 13:4(Winter 1996):4.

Johansen, Bruce E. Wampum. In D. L. Birchfield, ed., *The Encyclopedia of North American Indians.* Vol. 10. New York: Marshall Cavendish, 1997: 1352–1353.

Johansen, Bruce E. The BIA as Banker: Trust Is Hard When Billions Disappear. *Native Americas* 14:1(Spring 1997):14–23.

Johansen, Bruce E. *The Encyclopedia of Native American Legal Tradition.* Westport, CT: Greenwood Press, 1998a.

Johansen, Bruce. Whiteclay, Nebraska: The Town that Booze Built. *Native Americas* 15:1(Spring 1998b):5.

Johansen, Bruce E. Living and Breathing: Native Languages Come Alive. *Native Americas* 17:1(Spring 2000a):56–59.

Johansen, Bruce E. Education—The Nightmare and the Dream: A Shared National Tragedy, a Shared National Disgrace. *Native Americas* 12:4(Winter 2000b):10–19.

Johansen, Bruce E. Native Languages: The New Phoenix. *Native Americas* 17:1(Spring 2000c):60–61.

Johansen, Bruce E. *Shapers of the Great Debate on Native Americans: Land, Spirit, and Power.* Westport, CT: Greenwood Press, 2000.

Johansen, Bruce E. Mascots: Honor Be Thy Name. *Native Americas* 18:1(Spring 2001):58–61.

Johansen, Bruce E., and Donald A. Grinde, Jr. *The Encyclopedia of Native American Biography.* New York: Henry Holt, 1997.

Johansen, Bruce E., and Roberto F. Maestas. *Wasi'chu: The Continuing Indian Wars.* New York: Monthly Review Press, 1979.

Johansen, Bruce E., and Barbara Alice Mann, eds. *Encyclopedia of the Haudenosaunee (Iroquois Confederacy).* Westport, CT: Greenwood Press, 2000.

Johnson, Lowell, ed. The Buffalo. In *The First Voices.* Lincoln, NE: Nebraska Game and Parks Commission, 1984: 60–61.

Johnson v. MacIntosh (8 Wheaton 543, 1823).

Jones, Louis Thomas. *Aboriginal American Oratory.* Los Angeles: Southwest Museum, 1965.

Joseph, Chief [In-mut-too-yah-lat-lat]. An Indian's View of Indian Affairs. *North American Review* 128(April 1879):415–433.

Josephy, Alvin, Jr. *The Patriot Chiefs.* New York: Viking, 1961.

Josephy, Alvin, Jr. *Red Power.* New York: McGraw-Hill, 1971.

Josephy, Alvin M. *The Nez Perce Indians and the Opening of the Northwest.* New Haven, CT: Yale University Press, 1965.

Josephy, Alvin M., Jr. Modern America and the Indian. In Frederick E. Hoxie, ed., *Indians in American History: An Introduction.* Arlington Heights, IL: Harlan Davidson, 1988: 251–272.

Journals of Captain John Montresor, 1757–1778. Vol. 14. April 4, 1766. Collections of the New York Historical Society. New York: Printed for the Society, 1868–1949, 2nd Set, 357, 367–368.

Judge: Scientists Can Study Ancient Bones of Man Indian Tribes Claim as Ancestor. *Indian Time* 20:35(September 5, 2002):10.

Kay, Jeanne. The Fur Trade and Native American Population Growth, *Ethnohistory* 31:4(1984):265–287.

Keefe, Tom, Jr. A Tribute to David Sohappy. *Native Nations,* June/July 1991, 4–6.

Kehoe, Alice Beck. *North American Indians: A Comprehensive Account.* Englewood Cliffs, NJ: Prentice-Hall, 1981.

Kehoe, Alice Beck. *America before the European Invasions.* London: Longman, 2002.

Kelley, David H. *Deciphering the Maya Script.* Austin: University of Texas Press, 1976.

Kelly, Lawrence C. The Indian Reorganization Act: The Dream and the Reality. *Pacific Historical Quarterly* 64(August 1975):291–312.

Kelly, Lawrence C. *The Assault on Assimilation: John Collier and the Origins of the Indian Reorganization Act.* Tucson: University of Arizona Press, 1983.

Kennedy, J. Michael. Truth and Consequences on the Reservation. *Los Angeles Times Sunday Magazine,* July 7, 2002, cover story. Available at LATimes.com.

Kennedy, John Hopkins. *Jesuit and Savage in New France.* New Haven, CT: Yale University Press, 1950.

Keoke, Emory Dean, and Kay Marie Porterfield. *Encyclopedia of American Indian Contributions to the World.* New York: Facts on File, 2002.

Kickingbird, Kirke. *Indian Sovereignty.* Washington, DC: Institute for the Development of Indian Law, 1983.

Kilborn, Peter. Pine Ridge, a Different Kind of Poverty. *New York Times* in *Omaha World-Herald,* September 30, 1992, 9.

King, C. Richard, and Charles Frueling Springwood. *Team Spirits: The Native American Mascots Controversy.* Lincoln: University of Nebraska Press, 2001.

Kraus, Michael. *The Atlantic Civilization: Eighteenth Century Origins.* New York: Russell and Russell, 1949.

Kroeber, A. L. *Cultural and Natural Areas of Native North America.* University of California Publications in American Archeology and Ethnology 38. Berkeley: University of California, 1939.

Labaree, Benjamin L. *America's Nation-Time: 1607–1789.* Boston: Allyn and Bacon, 1972.

Labaree, Leonard, ed. *The Papers of Benjamin Franklin.* Vol. 21. New Haven, CT: Yale University Press, 1950 to date.

La Fay, Howard. The Maya, the Children of Time. *National Geographic,* December 1975, 729–766.

LaMay, Konnie. Twenty Years of Anguish. *Indian Country Today,* February 25, 1993, n.p.

Landsman, Gail. Portrayals of the Iroquois in the Woman Suffrage Movement. Paper presented at the Annual Conference on Iroquois Research, Rensselaerville, NY, October 8, 1988.

Lara, Jesus. *La Poesia Quechua.* Cochabamba, Bolivia: Imprenta Universitaria, n.d., 193–194. Cited in Wright, 1992, 31.

La Republica, Lima, Peru. Reprinted in *World Press Review,* September, 1991, 50.

Las Casas, Bartolome de. *History of the Indies.* Translated and edited by Andree Collard. New York: Harper and Row, 1971.

Las Casas, Bartolome de. *The Devastation of the Indies.* New York: Seabury Press, [1542] 1974.

Lavender, David. *Let Me Be Free.* San Francisco: HarperCollins, 1992.

Leon-Portilla, M. *Los Antiguos Mexicanos a Traves de sus Cronicas y Cantares.* Mexico City: Fondo de Cultura Economica, 1972.

Leon-Portilla, Miguel. *The Broken Spears: The Aztec Account of the Conquest of Mexico.* Boston: Beacon Press, 1962.

Leon-Portilla, Miguel. *Pre-Columbian Literature of Mexico.* Norman: University of Oklahoma Press, 1969.

Leon-Portilla, Miguel. *The Aztec Image of Self and Society: An Introduction to Nahua Culture.* Salt Lake City: University of Utah Press, 1992.

Levitan, Sar A. *Big Brother's Indian Programs—With Reservations.* New York: McGraw-Hill, 1971.

Licon, Ernesto Gonzalez. *Vanished Mesoamerican Civilizations: The History and Cultures of the Zapotecs and Mixtecs.* Armonk, NY: Sharpe, 2001.

Linné, Sigvald. *Archaeological Researches at Teotihuacan, Mexico.* Tuscaloosa: University of Alabama Press, 2003

Lovell, W. George. *Conquest and Survival in Colonial Guatemala: A Historical Geography of the Cuchumatan Highlands, 1500–1821.* Montreal: McGill-Queen's University Press, 1985.

Lowey, Mark. Alberta Natives Sue over Residential Schools. *Calgary Herald,* January 3, 1999, A-1.

Lucas, Phil. Images of Indians. *Four Winds: The International Forum for Native American Art, Literature, and History,* Autumn 1980, 69–77.

Lynch, John. Pikangikum First Nation Looks Beyond "Opening a Store." It Wants to Create Private-Sector Partnerships. *Northern Ontario Business,* March 1999. Available at http://www.nob.on.ca/archives/mar99story/step.html.

Mails, Thomas E. *Fools Crow.* Lincoln: University of Nebraska Press, 1990.

Mann, Barbara A. The Fire at Onondaga: Wampum as Proto-writing. *Akwesasne Notes New Series* 1:1(Spring 1995):40–48.

Mann, Barbara A. *The Last of the Mohicans* and *The Indian-haters*; Forbidden Ground: Racial Politics and Hidden Identity in James Fenimore Cooper's Leather-Stocking Tales. Ph.D. dissertation, University of Toledo, 1997.

Mann, Barbara A., and Jerry L. Fields. A Sign in the Sky: Dating the League of the Haudenosaunee. *American Indian Culture and Research Journal* 21:2(1997):105–163.

Mann, Charles C. 1491: America before Columbus Was More Sophisticated and More Populous than We Have Ever Thought—And a More Livable Place than Europe. *The Atlantic Monthly,* March 2002, 41–53.

Marquez, Deron. Indian Gaming Is Different from Other Forms of Gambling. *Indian Country Today,* February 12, 2002, n.p., in LEXIS.

Marsh, Thelma R. *Lest We Forget: A Brief Sketch of Wyandot County's History.* Upper Sandusky, OH: Wyandot County Historical Society, 1967.

Martin, Calvin. *Keepers of the Game.* Berkeley: University of California Press, 1979.

Massey, Rosemary. *Footprints in Blood: Standing Bear's Struggle for Freedom and Human Dignity.* Omaha, NE: American Indian Center of Omaha, 1979, unpaginated.

Mather, Increase. *A Brief History of the War with the Indians in New England.* London: Richard Chiswell, 1676.

Mathes, Valerie Sherer. Helen Hunt Jackson and the Ponca Controversy. *Montana: The Magazine of Western History* 39:1(Winter 1989):42–53.

Matthiessen, Peter. *In the Spirit of Crazy Horse.* New York: Viking, 1991.

Maxwell, James A., ed. *America's Fascinating Indian Heritage.* Pleasantville, NY: Reader's Digest, 1978.

McDowell, Bart. The Aztecs. *National Geographic,* December 1980, 704–752.

McKee, Jesse O., and Jon A. Schlenker. *The Choctaws: Cultural Evolution of a Native American Tribe.* Jackson: University Press of Mississippi, 1980.

McIlroy, Anne. Canadians Apologize for Abuse. *Manchester Guardian Weekly,* November 8, 1998, 5.

McLaughlin, James. *My Friend, the Indian.* Boston: Houghton Mifflin, 1910.

McLaughlin, Michael R. The Dawes Act, or Indian General Allotment Act of 1887: The Continuing Burden of Allotment. *American Indian Culture and Research Journal* 20:2(1996):59–105.

McManus, John C. An Economic Analysis of Indian Behavior in the North American Fur Trade. *Journal of Economic History* 32(1972):36–53.

McNickle, D'Arcy. *They Came Here First: The Epic of the American Indian.* Philadelphia: Lippincott, 1949.

McNickle, D'Arcy. *Native American Tribalism.* New York: Oxford University Press, 1973.

McNickle, D'Arcy. *They Came Here First: The Epic of the American Indian.* New York: Harper and Row Perennial Library, 1975.

Meggers, Betty J., Eduardo S. Brondizio, Michael J. Heckenberger, Carlos Fausto, and Bruna Franchetto. Revisiting Amazonia Circa 1492 [letter to the editor]. *Science* 302(December 19, 2003):2067.

Meriam, Lewis. *The Problem of Indian Administration.* Baltimore: John Hopkins University Press, 1928.

Mexican Skull May Explain Indigenous Origins. Reuters, December 5, 2002. Available at http://story.news.yahoo.com/news?tmpl=story&u=/nm/20021205/sc_nm/science_mexico_skull_dc_1.

Miller, Bruce J. The Press, the Boldt Decision, and Indian-White Relations. *American Indian Culture and Research Journal* 17:2(1993):75–98.

Miller, Perry. *Roger Williams: His Contribution to the American Tradition.* Indianapolis, IN: Bobbs-Merrill, 1953.

Milner, Richard. Red Cloud. In Richard Milner, ed. *The Encyclopedia of Evolution.* New York: Henry Holt, 1990: 387–388.

Minge, Ward Alan. *Acoma: Pueblo in the Sky.* Albuquerque: University of New Mexico Press, 1991.

Mochtezuma, Eduardo Matos. Templo Mayor: History and Interpretation. In Johanna Broda, David Carrasco, and Mochtezuma, eds., *The Great Temple of Tenochtitlan: Center and Periphery in the Aztec World.* Berkeley: University of California Press, 1988: 15–60.

The Mohawk Creation Story. *Akwesasne Notes* 21.5(Spring 1989):32–29.

Molina Montes, Augusto F. The Building of Tenochtitlan. *National Geographic,* December 1980, 753–766.

Monoghan, Jay. *Custer.* Lincoln: University of Nebraska Press, 1959.

Mooney, James, Population. In F. W. Hodge, ed., *Handbook of American Indians North of Mexico. Bureau of American Ethnology Bulletin* 30(part 2):28–87. Washington, DC: Smithsonian Institution, 1910.

Mooney, James. *The Aboriginal Population of North America North of Mexico.* Smithsonian Miscellaneous Collections 80(7). Washington, DC: Smithsonian Institution, 1928.

Moore, John H. How Giveaways and Pow-wows Redistribute the Means of Subsistence. In John H. Moore, ed., *The Political Economy of North American Indians.* Norman: University of Oklahoma Press, 1993: 240–269.

Moore, John H. *The Cheyennes.* Oxford, England: Blackwell, 1997.

Moore, Oliver. Pre-Mayan Written Language Found in Mexico. *Toronto Globe and Mail,* December 5, 2002. Available at http://www.globeandmail.com/servlet/Article News/front/RTGAM/20021205/wlang1205/Front/homeBN/breakingnews.

Moquin, Wayne. *Great Documents in American Indian History.* New York: Praeger, 1973.

Morgan, Lewis Henry. *League of the Ho-de-no-sau-nee, or Iroquois.* New York: Corinth Books, [1851] 1962.

Morgan, Lewis Henry. *Houses and House-Life of the American Aborigines.* Edited by Paul Bohannon. Chicago: University of Chicago Press, 1965.

Morison, Patricia. Wisdom of the Aztecs. *London Financial Times.* Reprinted in Notes on the Arts, *World Press Review,* January 1993, 54.

Morris, Roy, Jr. *Sheridan: The Life and Wars of General Phil Sheridan.* New York: Crown, 1992.

Moulton, Gary. *John Ross: Cherokee Chief.* Athens: University of Georgia Press, 1978.

Moulton, Gary, ed. *The Journals of the Lewis and Clark Expedition.* Lincoln: University of Nebraska Press, 2001.

Mr. Penn's Plan for a Union of the Colonies in America, February 8, 1697. In E. B. O'Callaghan, ed., *Documents Relative to the Colonial History of New York.* Vol. 4. Albany, NY: Weed, Parsons, 1853–1887: 296–297.

Murphy, Maureen. Gambling on Indian Reservations. Washington DC: Congressional Research Service, Library of Congress, April 26, 1985.

Myers, Albert Cook. *Narratives of Early Pennsylvania, West New Jersey and Delaware, 1630–1702.* New York: Charles Scribner's Sons, 1912.

Nabokov, Peter, ed. *Native American Testimony.* New York: Viking, 1991.

National Resources Board, Land Planning Committee. *Indian Land Tenure, Economic Status, and Population Trends.* Washington, DC: U.S. Government Printing Office, 1935.

Nebard, Grace R. *Sacajawea.* Glendale, CA: Arthur H. Clark, 1932.

Neihardt, Hilda. *Black Elk and Flaming Rainbow: Personal Memories of the Lakota Holy Man.* Lincoln: University of Nebraska Press, 1995.

Nevard, David. Wahooism in the USA: A Red Socks Journal. No date. Available at http://www.ultranet.com/~kuras/bhxi3d.htm.

Notice. *Philadelphia Gazette.* 2705(April 17, 1782):2.

Oberg, Kalervo. *The Social Economy of the Tlinget Indians.* Seattle: University of Washington Press, 1973.

O'Brien, Sharon. *American Indian Tribal Governments.* Norman: University of Oklahoma Press, 1989.

O'Callaghan, E. B., ed. *Documentary History of the State of New York.* Vol. 1. Albany, NY: Weed, Parsons, 1849.

O'Callaghan, E. B., ed., *Documents Relative to the Colonial History of New York.* Vol. 6. Albany, NY: Weed, Parsons, 1853–1887.

Olexer, Barbara. *The Enslavement of the American Indian.* Monroe, NY: Library Research Associates, 1982.

Olson, James, and Raymond Wilson. *Native Americans in the Twentieth Century.* Urbana: University of Illinois Press, 1984.

Olson, James C. *Red Cloud and the Sioux Problem.* Lincoln: University of Nebraska Press, 1965.

Oskinson, John M. *Tecumseh and His Times.* New York: J. P. Putnam, 1938.

Oswalt, Wendell H. *This Land Was Theirs: A Study of North American Indians.* 7th ed. Boston: McGraw-Hill, 2002.

Page, Charles. The "Fighting Whites" Offer Lesson in Cultural Diversity. *Newsday,* March 19, 2002, A-32.

Page, Jake. *In the Hands of the Great Spirit: The 20,000 Year History of the American Indian.* New York: Free Press, 2003.

Paine, Thomas. *The Political Writings of Thomas Paine.* New York: Peter Eckler, 1892.

Parker, Arthur. *Parker on the Iroquois.* Edited by William Fenton. Syracuse, NY: Syracuse University Press, 1968.

Parker, Arthur C. *The Code of Handsome Lake, the Seneca Prophet.* New York State Museum Bulletin 163, November 1, 1912. Albany: University of the State of New York, 1913.

Parkman, Francis. *History of the Conspiracy of Pontiac.* Boston: Little, Brown, 1868.

Parman, Donald L. *The Navajos and the New Deal.* New Haven, CT: Yale University Press, 1976.

Parrington, Vernon Louis. *Main Currents in American Thought.* New York: Harcourt, Brace, 1927.

Pascua, Maria Parker. Ozette: A Makah Village in 1491. *National Geographic*, October 1991, 38–53.

Peckham, Howard H. *Pontiac and the Indian Uprising.* Chicago: University of Chicago Press, 1947.

Peopling the Americas: A New Site to Debate. *National Geographic (Geographica)*, September 1992, n.p.

Perdue, Theda. Indians in Southern History. In Frederick E. Hoxie, ed., *Indians in American History: An Introduction.* Arlington Heights, IL: Harlan Davidson, 1988.

Phillips, Kate. *Helen Hunt Jackson: A Literary Life.* Berkeley: University of California Press, 2003.

Phillips, Paul C. *The Fur Trade.* 2 vols. Norman: University of Oklahoma Press, 1961.

Philp, Kenneth R. *John Collier's Crusade for Indian Reform, 1920–1954.* Tucson: University of Arizona Press, 1977.

Pitulko, V. V., P. A. Nikolsky, E. Yu. Girya, A. E. Basilyan, V. E. Tumskoy, S. A. Koulakov, S. N. Astakhov, E. Yu. Pavlova, and M. A. Anisimov. The Yana RHS Site: Humans in the Arctic Before the Last Glacial Maximum. *Science* 303(January 2, 2004):52–56.

Pohl, Frederick Julius. *The Viking Settlements of North America.* New York: Potter, 1972.

Pohl, Mary E. D., Kevin O. Pope, and Christopher von Nagy. Olmec Origins of Mesoamerican Writing. *Science* 298(December 6, 2002):1984–1987.

Pomerantz, Gary. Atlanta Fan's Headdress Ruffles Indian Feathers. *Atlanta Journal-Constitution*, October 21, 1995. Available at http://www.fastball.com/braves/archives/stories/1995/66ws1021.html.

Porter, C. Fayne. *Our Indian Heritage: Profiles of Twelve Great Leaders.* Philadelphia: Chilton, 1964.

Porter, Joy. *To Be Indian: The Life of Iroquois-Seneca Arthur Caswell Parker.* Norman: University of Oklahoma Press, 2001.

Porterfield, Kay Marie. Ten Lies about Indigenous Science—How to Talk Back. October 10, 2002. Available at http://www.kporterfield.com/aicttw/articles/lies.html.

Powers, William K. *Indians of the Northern Plains.* New York: Capricorn Books, 1973.

Pratt, William Henry. *Battlefield and Classroom: Four Decades with the American Indian, 1867–1904.* Edited by Robert M. Utley. Lincoln: University of Nebraska Press, 1987.

Proceedings of the Commissioners Appointed by the Continental Congress to Negotiate a Treaty with the Six Nations, 1775. Papers of the Continental Congress, 1774–89, National Archives (M247, Roll 144, Item No. 134). See Treaty Council at German Flats, New York, August 15, 1775, unpaginated.

Prucha, Francis P. *Documents of United States Indian Policy.* Lincoln: University of Nebraska Press, 1975.

Radell, Davis R. The Indian Slave Trade and Population of Nicaragua During the Sixteenth Century. In William E. Denevan, ed., *The Native Population of the Americas.* Madison: University of Wisconsin Press, 1976: 67–76.

Ramenofsky, Ann F. *Vectors of Death: The Archeology of European Contact.* Albuquerque: University of New Mexico Press, 1987.

Randolph, Eleanor. New York's Native American Casino Contributes, But Not to Tax Rolls. *New York Times,* October 18, 2003, n.p.

Reaman, G. Elmore. *The Trail of the Iroquois Indians: How the Iroquois Nation Saved Canada for the British Empire.* London: Frederick Muller, 1967.

Recer, Paul. Researchers Find Evidence of Sophisticated, Pre-Columbian Civilization in the Amazon Basin. Associated Press, September 19, 2003, in LEXIS.

Recer, Paul. Evidence Found of Arctic Hunters Living in Siberia Near New World 30,000 Years Ago. Associated Press, January 2, 2004, in LEXIS.

Recinos, Adrian, and Delia Goetz, trans. *The Annals of the Cakchiquels.* Norman: University of Oklahoma Press, 1953.

Reilly, Bob, Hugh Reilly, and Pegeen Reilly. *Historic Omaha: An Illustrated History of Omaha and Douglas County.* San Antonio, TX: Historical Publishing Network, 2003.

Reilly, Hugh. Treatment of Native Americans by the Frontier Press: An Omaha, Nebraska Study, 1868–1891. Masters thesis, University of Nebraska at Omaha, 1997.

Resek, Carl. *Lewis Henry Morgan: American Scholar.* Chicago: University of Chicago Press, 1960.

Restall, Matthew. *Seven Myths of the Spanish Conquest.* New York: Oxford University Press, 2004.

Reyhner, Jon, ed. *Teaching Indigenous Languages.* Flagstaff: Center for Excellence in Education, Northern Arizona University, 1997.

Reyhner, Jon, Gina Cantoni, Robert N. St. Clair, and Evangeline Parsons Yazzie. *Revitalizing Native Languages.* Flagstaff: Center for Excellence in Education, Northern Arizona University, 1999.

Reynolds, Jerry. Bush Administration Likely Behind Cobell Appropriations Rider. *Indian Country Today,* November 1, 2003. Available at http://www.indiancountry.com/?1067709828.

Rice, Julian. *Black Elk's Story.* Albuquerque: New Mexico University Press, 1991.

Richter, Daniel K. *The Ordeal of the Longhouse: The Peoples of the Iroquois League in the Era of European Colonization.* Chapel Hill: University of North Carolina Press, 1992.

Rider, Sidney S. *The Lands of Rhode Island as They Were Known to Caunonicus and Miantunnomu When Roger Williams Came in 1636.* Providence, RI: Sidney S. Rider, 1904.

Roberts, David. Geronimo. *National Geographic,* October 1992, 46–71.

Roe, Frank Gilbert. *The Indian and the Horse.* Norman: University of Oklahoma Press, 1955.

Rogers, Robert. *Concise Account of North America.* New Haven, CT: Johnson Reprint, [1765] 1966.

Rogin, Michael Paul. *Fathers and Children: Andrew Jackson and the Subjugation of the American Indian.* New York: Alfred A. Knopf, 1975.

Rosenberg, Bruce A. *Custer and the Epic of Defeat.* University Park: Pennsylvania State University Press, 1974.

Rosenstiel, Annette. *Red and White: Indian Views of the White Man, 1492–1982*. New York: Universe Books, 1983.

Rostkowski, Joelle. The Redman's Appeal for Justice: Deskaheh and the League of Nations. In Christian F. Feest, ed., *Indians and Europe*. Aachen, Germany: Edition Herodot, 1987.

Royal Commission on Aboriginal Peoples. Vol. 1, chapter 10. No date. Available at http://www.prsp.bc.ca/vol1ch10_files/Vol1%20Ch10.rtf. Accessed February 25, 2003.

Roys, Ralph L. *The Book of Chilam Balam of Chumayel*. Norman: University of Oklahoma Press, 1967.

Rozema, Vicki, ed. *Voices from the Trail of Tears*. Winston-Salem, NC: John F. Blair, 2003.

Ruby, Robert H., and John A Brown. *Indian Slavery in the Pacific Northwest*. Spokane, WA: Arthur H. Clark, 1993.

Russell, Don. *The Lives and Legends of Buffalo Bill*. Norman: University of Oklahoma Press, 1960.

Sahagún, Bernardino de. *General History of the Things of New Spain: Florentine Codex*. Translated by A. J. O. Anderson and C. E. Dibble. Salt Lake City: University of Utah Press, and Santa Fe, NM: School of American Research, 1950.

Sahagún, Bernardino de. *Historia General de las Cosas de Nueva Espana*. 4 vols. Edited and translated by Angel Maria Garibay. Mexico, D.F.: Porrua, [ca. 1555] 1956.

Sahagún, Bernardino de. *Historia de las Cosas de la Nueva Espana*. 1905–1907. Cited in Portilla, 1992.

Sahagún, Fray Bernardino de. In Arthur J. O. Anderson and Charles E. Dibble, eds. *Florentine Codex: General History of the Things of New Spain*. 12 vols. Salt Lake City: University of Utah Press: 1950–1982.

Sando, Joe S. *The Pueblo Indians*. San Francisco: Indian Historian Press, 1976.

Sandoz, Mari. *Crazy Horse: Strange Man of the Oglalas*. New York: Alfred A. Knopf, 1942.

Satz, Ronald N. *American Indian Policy in the Jacksonian Era*. Lincoln: University of Nebraska Press, 1975.

Saum, Lewis. *The Fur Trader and the Indian*. Seattle: University of Washington Press, 1965.

Schele, Linda. The Owl, Shield, and Flint Blade. *Natural History*, November, 1991, 7–11.

Schmitt, Martin F., and Dee Brown. *Fighting Indians of the West*. New York: Ballantine Books, 1948.

Scholars Rewrite Mayan History after Hieroglyphics Found. *Omaha World-Herald*, September 20, 2002, 12-A.

Segal, Charles M., and Stineback, David C. *Puritans, Indians, and Manifest Destiny*. New York: Putnam, 1977.

Sell, Henry B., and Victor Weybright. *Buffalo Bill and the Wild West*. New York: Oxford University Press, 1955.

Selsam, Millicent. *Plants that Heal*. New York: William Morrow, 1959.

Seminole Tribe of Florida v. Butterworth. 658 F. 2d 310 (5th Cir., 1980).

Seymour, Flora W. *Sacajawea: American Pathfinder*. New York: Macmillan, 1991.

Sherzer, Joel. A Richness of Voices. In Alvin Josephy, ed., *America in 1492: The World of the Indian Peoples Before the Arrival of Columbus*. New York: Knopf, 1992.

Siegel, Beatrice. *Fur Trappers and Traders*. New York: Walker, 1981.

Slayman, Andrew L. A Battle Over Bones. *Archaeology* 50:1 (January/February 1997):16–23.

Slotkin, Richard, and James K. Folsom, eds. *So Dreadful a Judgement: Puritan Responses to King Philip's War 1676–1677*. Middleton, CT: Wesleyan University Press, 1978.

Smith, Dean Howard. *Modern Tribal Development: Paths to Self-Sufficiency and Cultural Integrity in Indian Country.* Walnut Creek, CA: AltaMira Press, 2000.

Smith, Henry A. Early Reminiscences. Number Ten. Scraps from a Diary. Chief Seattle—A Gentleman by Instinct—His Native Eloquence, etc., etc. *Seattle Star,* October 29, 1887, n.p.

Smith, Jean Edward. *John Marshall: Definer of a Nation.* New York: Henry Holt, 1996.

Smith, Michael E. The Aztec Migrations of the Nahuatl Chronicles: Myth or History? *Ethnohistory* 31:3(1984):153–186.

Smyth, Albert H., ed. *The Writings of Benjamin Franklin.* Vol. 3. New York: Macmillan, 1905–1907.

Snake, Reuben. Personal communication to Bruce E. Johansen, in Seattle, October 12, 1991.

Snell, William Robert. Indian Slavery in Colonial South Carolina, 1671–1795. Ph.D. dissertation, University of Alabama, Tuscaloosa, 1972.

Snow, Dean. *The Iroquois.* London: Blackwell, 1994.

Snow, Dean. The First Americans and the Differentiation of Hunter-Gatherer Cultures. In Bruce G. Trigger and Wilcomb E. Washburn, eds. *The Cambridge History of the Native Peoples of the Americas.* Cambridge, England: Cambridge University Press, 1996: 125–199.

Snow, Dean R., and Kim M. Lanphear. European Contact and Indian Depopulation in the Northeast: The Timing of the First Epidemics. *Ethnohistory* 35:1(Winter 1988):16–24.

Snow, Dean R., and Kim M. Lanphear. "More Methodological Perspectives:" A Rejoinder to Dobyns. *Ethnohistory* 36:3(Summer 1989):299–300.

Soustelle, Jacques. *Daily Life of the Aztecs on the Eve of the Spanish Conquest.* Translated by Patrick O'Brian. Palo Alto, CA: Stanford University Press, 1961.

Spicer, Edward H. *Cycles of Conquest.* Tucson: University of Arizona Press, 1962.

Spindel, Carol. *Dancing at Halftime: Sports and the Controversy over American Indian Mascots.* New York: New York University Press, 2001.

Stannard, David E. *American Holocaust: The Conquest of the New World.* New York: Oxford University Press, 1992.

Stanton, Elizabeth Cady. The Matriarchate or Mother-Age [address before the National Council of Women, February, 1891]. *The National Bulletin* 1:5(February 1891):1–7.

Stevens, William K. Andean Culture Found to be as Old as the Great Pyramids. *New York Times,* October 3, 1989, C-1.

Stokstad, Erik. Oldest New World Writing Suggests Olmec Innovation. *Science* 298 (December 6, 2002):1872–1874.

Stokstad, Erik. Amazon Archaeology: "Pristine" Forest Teemed With People. *Science* 301(September 19, 2003):1645–1646.

Stone, Richard. Late Date for Siberian Site Challenges Bering Pathway. *Science* 301 (July 25, 2003):450–451.

Stone, Richard. A Surprising Survival Story in the Siberian Arctic. *Science* 303(January 2, 2004):33.

Straus, Oscar S. *Roger Williams: Pioneer of Religious Liberty.* New York: Century, 1894.

Stuart, George E. Riddle of the Glyphs. *National Geographic,* December 1975, 768–791.

Stuart, George E. Etowah: A Southeast Village in 1491. *National Geographic,* October 1991, 54–67.

Stuart, George E. Mural Masterpieces of Ancient Cacaxtla. *National Geographic*, September 1992, 120–136.

Stubben, Jerry. Iowa State University. Personal communication, October 30, 2002.

Substance of the Speech of Good Peter to Governor Clinton and the Commissioners of Indian Affairs at Albany. *Collections of the New York Historical Society, 1st Series* 2:(1814):115.

Suzuki, Peter T. Housing on the Nebraska Indian Reservations: Federal Policies and Practices. *Habitat International* 15:4(1991):27–32.

Swan, Bradford F. New Light on Roger Williams and the Indians. *Providence Sunday Journal Magazine*, November 23, 1969, 14.

Swanton, J. R. The Social Significance of the Creek Confederacy. *Proceedings of the International Congress of Americanists* 19:(1915):327–334.

Talbot, Steve. *Contemporary Indian Nations of North America: An Indigenist Perspective.* New York: Prentice-Hall, 2004.

Tebbel, John, and Keith Jennison. *The American Indian Wars.* New York: Bonanza Books, 1960.

Tehanetorens [Ray Fadden]. *Tales of the Iroquois.* Rooseveltown, NY: *Akwesasne Notes*, 1976.

Tehanetorens [Ray Fadden]. *Basic Call to Consciousness.* Rooseveltown, NY: *Akwesasne Notes*, 1986.

Tehanetorens [Ray Fadden]. *Wampum Belts.* Onchiota, NY: Six Nations Museum, n.d.

Thomas, David Hurst. *Skull Wars: Kennewick Man, Archaeology, and the Battle for Native American Identity.* New York: Basic Books/Peter N. Nevraumont, 2000.

Thornton, Russell. Cherokee Population Losses during the Trail of Tears: A New Perspective and a New Estimate. *Ethnohistory* 31(1984):4.

Thorpe, James, and Thomas F. Collinson. *Jim Thorpe's History of the Olympics.* Los Angeles: Wetzel Publishing Co., 1932.

Thwaites, Reuben Gold. *The Original Journals of Lewis and Clark.* New York: Dodd, Mead & Co., 1904–1905.

Tibbles, Thomas Henry. *The Ponca Chiefs: An Account of the Trial of Standing Bear* (1880) Edited by Kay Graber. Lincoln: University of Nebraska Press, 1972.

Tocqueville, Alexis de. *Democracy in America.* Translated by Henry Reeve. New York: Century, 1898.

Todd, Douglas. Natives' Abuse Suits Creating a Dilemma. *Vancouver Sun*, December 15, 1998, A-1.

Townsend, Camilla. Burying the White Gods: New Perspectives on the Conquest of Mexico. *American Historical Review* 108(June 2003):659–687.

Trelease, Allen W. *Indian Affairs in Colonial New York: The Seventeenth Century.* Ithaca, NY: Cornell University Press, 1960.

Trigger, Bruce G. *Children of the Aataentsic: A History of the Huron People.* Montreal: McGill-Queen's University Press, 1976.

Tucker, Glenn. *Tecumseh: Vision of Glory.* Indianapolis: Bobbs-Merrill, 1956.

Turtle Island Native Network. British Columbia Residential School Project. No date. Available at http://www.turtleisland.org/healing/infopack1a.htm.

Young, Calvin M. *Little Turtle.* Fort Wayne, IN: Public Library of Fort Wayne and Allen County, 1956.

U.S. Commission on Civil Rights, Report of Investigation: Oglala Sioux Tribe, General Election, 1974. Mimeograph. Washington, DC: Civil Rights Commission, October 1974.

U.S. Department of Health and Human Services. *Trends in Indian Health*. Washington, DC: U.S. Government Printing Office, 1991.

United States v. Washington 384 F. Supp. 312 (1974).

Utley, Robert. *The Lance and the Shield: The Life and Times of Sitting Bull*. New York: Henry Holt, 1993.

Vanderwerth, W. C., ed. *Indian Oratory: Famous Speeches by Noted Indian Chieftains*. Norman: University of Oklahoma Press, 1971.

Van Doren, Carl, and Julian P. Boyd, eds. *Indian Treaties Printed by Benjamin Franklin 1736–1762*. Philadelphia: Historical Society of Pennsylvania, 1938.

Van Every, Dale. *Disinherited: The Lost Birthright of the American Indian*. New York: William Morrow, 1966.

Van Kirk, Sylvia. *Many Tender Ties: Women in Fur Trade Society, 1670–1870*. Norman: University of Oklahoma Press, 1983.

Vaughan, Alden T. *New England Frontier: Puritans and Indians, 1620–1675*. Boston: Little, Brown, 1965.

Vestal, Stanley. *Sitting Bull: Champion of the Sioux*. Norman: University of Oklahoma Press, [1932] 1957.

Virtual Truth Commission. Telling the Truth for a Better America; Reports by Name: Col. John M. Chivington. June 22, 1998. Available at www.geocities.com/~virtualtruth/chiving.htm. Accessed February 24, 2003.

Wagner, Sally Roesch. The Iroquois Confederacy: A Native American Model for Non-sexist Men. *Changing Men* (Spring–Summer 1988):32–33.

Wagner, Sally Roesch. The Root of Oppression Is the Loss of Memory: The Iroquois and the Early Feminist Vision, *Akwesasne Notes*, Late Winter, 1989, 11.

Waldman, Carl. *Who Was Who in Native American History*. New York: Facts on File, 1990.

Walke, Roger. Gambling on Indian Reservations: Updated October 17, 1988. Washington, DC: Congressional Research Service, Library of Congress.

Walker, Carson. Man Is Arrested in Activist's Death. Associated Press item in IndigenousNewsNetwork@topica.com, e-mail newsletter, April 2, 2003.

Walker, James R. *Lakota Society*. Edited by Raymond J. DeMallie. Lincoln: University of Nebraska Press, 1982.

Wallace, Anthony F. C. *The Death and Rebirth of the Seneca*. New York: Random House, 1969.

Wallace, Paul A. W. Captivity and Murder. In Paul A. W. Wallace, ed. *Thirty Thousand Miles with John Heckewelder*. Pittsburgh: University of Pittsburgh Press, 1958: 170–207.

Wallace, Paul A. W. *The White Roots of Peace*. Santa Fe, N.M.: Clear Light Publishers, 1994. (Originally published in 1946 by University of Pennsylvania Press)

Walton, Marsha, and Michael Coren. Archaeologists Put Humans in North America 50,000 Years Ago. Cable News Network, November 17, 2004. Available at http://www.cnn.com/2004/TECH/science/11/17/carolina.dig/index.html.

Wampum Chronicles message board. No date. Available at http://pub11.ezboard.com/fwampumchroniclescurrentevents.showMessage?topicID=265.topic.

Wanamaker, Tom. Indian Gaming Column. *Indian Country Today*, April 5, 2002, n.p., in LEXIS.

Wanamaker, Tom. Debunking the Myth of Unregulated Indian Gaming. *Indian Country Today*, May 13, 2002, n.p., in LEXIS.

Washburn, Wilcomb E., ed. *The American Indian and the United States: A Documentary History.* New York: Random House, 1973.

Washburn, Wilcomb E. *The Assault on Indian Tribalism: The General Allotment Law (Dawes Act) of 1887.* Philadelphia: Lippincott, 1975.

Waters, Frank. *Brave Are My People: Indian Heroes Not Forgotten.* Santa Fe, NM: Clear Light, 1993.

Weatherford, Jack. *Indian Givers: How the Indians of the Americas Transformed the World.* New York: Fawcett Columbine, 1988.

Weatherford, Jack. *Native Roots: How the Indians Enriched America.* New York: Crown, 1991.

Webster, David. *The Fall of the Ancient Maya.* London: Thames and Hudson, 2002.

Weeks, Philip. *Farewell, My Nation: The American Indian and the United States, 1820–1890.* Arlington Heights, IL: Harlan Davidson, 1990.

Weinberg, Bill. Land and Sovereignty in Hawai'i: A Native Nation Re-emerges. *Native Americas* 13:2(Summer 1996):30–41.

Weir, David, and Lowell Bergman. The Killing of Anna Mae Aquash. *Rolling Stone,* April 7, 1977, 51–55.

Weisman, Joel. About That "Ambush" at Wounded Knee. *Columbia Journalism Review,* September/October 1975, 28–51.

Wheaton, Henry. *Elements of International Law.* Boston: Dana, 1866.

Wilson, James. *The Earth Shall Weep: A History of Native America.* Boston: Atlantic Monthly Press, 1998.

Wissler, Clark. The Influence of the Horse in the Development of Plains Culture. *American Anthropologist* 16(1914):1–25.

White, Richard. The Winning of the West: The Expansion of the Western Sioux in the Eighteenth and Nineteenth Centuries, *Journal of American History* 65:2(1978):319–343.

White Roots of Peace. *The Great Law of Peace of the Longhouse People.* Rooseveltown, NY: White Roots of Peace, 1971.

Wilford, John Noble. Did Warfare Doom the Mayas' Ecology? *New York Times* in *Miami Herald,* December 22, 1991, 7-L.

Wilkerson, Jeffery K. Following the Route of Cortes. *National Geographic,* October 1984, 420–459.

Wilkinson, Charles F. *American Indians, Time, and the Law: Native Societies in a Modern Constitutional Democracy.* New Haven, CT: Yale University Press, 1987.

William Penn to the Society of Free Traders, August 16, 1683. In Richard S. and Mary M. Dunn, eds., *The Papers of William Penn.* Vol. 2. Philadelphia: University of Pennsylvania Press, 1982.

Williams, Richard B. The True Story of Thanksgiving. November 19, 2002. Available at IndigenousNewsNetwork@topica.com.

Williams, Roger. *A Key into the Languages of America.* Providence, RI: Tercentenary Committee, [1643] 1936.

Williams, Roger. *The Complete Writings of Roger Williams.* Vol. 1. New York: Russell and Russell, 1963.

Williams, Stephen. *Fantastic Archaeology: The Wild Side of North American Prehistory.* Philadelphia: University of Pennsylvania Press, 1991.

Wilson, Edmund. *Apologies to the Iroquois.* New York: Farrar, Strauss, and Cudahy, 1960.

Wilson, Terry P. *The Underground Reservation: Osage Oil.* Lincoln: University of Nebraska Press, 1985.

Winslow, Elizabeth Ola. *Master Roger Williams*. New York: Macmillan, 1957.

Wishart, David J. *The Fur Trade and the American West, 1807–1840*. Lincoln: University of Nebraska Press, 1979.

Wishart, David J. *An Unspeakable Sadness: The Dispossession of the Nebraska Indians*. Lincoln: University of Nebraska Press, 1994.

Wollock, Jeffrey. On the Wings of History: American Indians in the 20th Century. *Native Americas* 20:1(Spring 2003):14–31.

Wood, Gordon S. *The Creation of the American Republic*. Chapel Hill: University of North Carolina, 1969.

Wood, H. Clay. *The Status of Young Joseph and His Band of Nez Perce Indians*. Portland, OR: Assistant Adjutant General's Office, Department of the Columbia, 1876.

Wood, William. *New England's Prospect*. Amherst: University of Massachusetts Press, 1977.

Woodbury, Hanni, Reg Henry, and Harry Webster, comps. *Concerning the League: The Iroquois League Tradition as Dictated in Onondaga by John Arthur Gibson*. Algonquian and Iroquoian Linguistics Memoir No. 9. Winnipeg, Manitoba, Canada: University of Manitoba Press, 1992.

Worcester, Donald, ed. *Forked Tongues and Broken Treaties*. Caldwell, ID: Caxton, 1975.

Worcester v. Georgia 31 U.S. (6 Pet.) 515(1832).

Wright, Ronald. *Stolen Continents: The Americas through Indian Eyes since 1492*. Boston: Houghton-Mifflin, 1992.

Zorita, Alonso de. *Life and Labor in Ancient Mexico*. Translated by Benjamin Keen. New Brunswick, NJ: Rutgers University Press, 1963.

Cumulative Index

Army Signal Corps, borrowings from Native signals, 359

Articles of Confederation, 176

Aspirin (*methyl salicylate*), Native American origins, 364

Assimilation, 297–305, 307, 308, 309–15, 326–28; education and, 308–15; reservations as "legalized reformatories," 298; Sun Dance banned, 298, 315; wardship, 307–8

Astronomy, Mayan, 361

Atlatl (hunting tool), 22

Attucks, Crispus, 372

Aztecs (Mexicas): arrival in Valley of Mexico, 78–79; blood sacrifice, 65, 79–80, 82–84, 85–86; Calendar Stone, described, 85; *calpulli* (local government), 84, 85; clans and government, 85; class structure, 84; growth of empire, 79–80; meaning of term, 78; military training, 81; music and war, 81; origins of, 78–79; religious cosmology and beliefs, 65, 81, 83, 85–86; Spanish conquest of, 88–93; warfare and rituals, 80–82

Bad Heart Bull, Wesley, murder of, 396–97

Ball games, origins, 361

Banks, Dennis, 342, 344, 348; federal charges, 345

Barreiro, José, 366

Battle of Black Ax, 197

Baum, L. Frank, on Indian extermination, 282

Beaver Wars, 147–48

Benedict, Ruth, 107

Benson, Paul, 345, 346

Bering Strait theory, challenges to, 11, 14, 18, 22

Bering, Vitus, 225

Bigfoot, at Wounded Knee (1890), 285

Big Hawk Chief (Kootahwecoosoolele-hoolashar), 313–14

Big Snake (Standing Bear's brother), killed, 279

Black Elk (Hchaka Sapa), at Battle of Little Bighorn (1876), 271; describes Wounded Knee massacre, 288–89

Blackface, Jackie, 316

Black Hawk (Makataimeshekiakiak), 196–98; sense of honor, 196; sketch of life, 196; defiant in surrender, 197; meets Andrew Jackson, 197–98; described, late in life, 198; death, 198

Black Hawk's War, 197–98

Black Kettle (Moketavato), 265–66; death, 266

Black Shawl (Crazy Horse's wife), 273

Blood sacrifice: Aztec, 65, 79–80, 82–83; Maya, 66–67

Blue Jacket (Weyapiersenwah), 189, 190

Boarding schools, Canada, 316–24; beatings, 316, 318, 319; church apologies, 321, 322; church sponsorship, 316; government apology, 320–21; lawsuits, 321–22; number of students, 316; sexual abuse, 317–18, 321

Boarding schools, U.S., 308–15; curriculum, 310, 314; described by Luther Standing Bear, 310; methods of operation, 309; number of, 315; racism, 314–15; suicides at, 314

Boldt, George, 353

Boston Massacre (1770), 372

Boston Tea Party, Mohawk images, 169–71

Bounties, for scalps, 135

Boyd, Julian P., 169

Bradford, William: credits God with spreading smallpox, 121; on Mystic massacre (1637), 126–27

Brando, Marlon, refuses Oscar during Wounded Knee occupation, 344; at fishing-rights protests, 352

Brant, Joseph, 149

Brodhead, Col. Daniel, 185

Brown, Dee, 344

Brown, W. O., 349, 350

Buffalo, 246, 250–52; as basis of Plains Indian economy, 250; cultural sanctions on hunting, 251; economic

influence of on housing sizes and styles, 248; as measure of wealth, 245, 248; as "mystery dogs," 246; Pawnee, as horse traders, 246; prosperity stems from, 247; raiding enabled by, 248

Houston, Sam, peace policies, 199, 261, 262

Howard, Oliver O., in Apache wars, 257

Hudson's Bay Company, 225–26

Hurons. *See* Wyandots

If You Poison Us (Eichstaedt, 1995), 422

Incas, writing system of, 29–31

Indian Citizenship Act (1924), 328–29

Indian Claims Commission, 333–34, 335; expiration of (1978), 334; number of cases, 334

Indian Reorganization Act (1934), 331–33; Native opposition t, 332–33

Individual Indian Monies (IIM), 302, 406–13; amount at stake, 406, 410, 412; *Cobell v. Norton*, 406, 413; Elouise Cobell, 406, 407, 408, 410, 412, 413; number of plaintiffs, 406, 410

Intercourse Acts: and land claims, 418–20; Maine land claims, 420; Oneida land claim, 420

In the Spirit of Crazy Horse (Matthiessen, 1991), 347–48

Inuit, defined, 227; "summer drunk," 227

Iroquois (Haudenosaunee) Confederacy, 37–38, 136–44, 159–62; Aionwantha (Hiawatha), 137, 140; Beaver Wars, 147–48; childrearing practices of, 38; clans, 37, 161; date of founding debated, 138–40; Deganawida (the Peacemaker), 137, 139, 141; gender roles, 141; government described, 136–37, 160–61; Grand Council, 136; Great Law of Peace, 136; influence of on treaty diplomacy, 141–44; as kinship state, 37; matrilineal nature of, 37; passports issued to, 144;

persuasive abilities of leaders, 160; pivotal diplomatic role, 136–38, 160; Tadadaho, role of, 137, 139; translation of, 141

Jackson, Andrew, 198–213; as U.S. Army officer, 198; defeat of William Weatherford and Creeks, 198–201; Horseshoe Bend "treaty" (1814), 199; Seminole war, 201–3; allied with land-industry business, 203–4; attitudes toward Indians, 203–4; view of treaties, 206–7; support of Removal Act, 199, 207–8; election of as U.S. president (1828), 203; ignores Marshall rulings on Cherokees, 212–13

Jackson, Helen Hunt, 299, 330; *Century of Dishonor* (1881), 299

Jackson, William Henry, discovers Anasazi ruins, 105

Jacobs, Leo David, 406

Jamestown, Virginia, 118–20; Indian uprisings against (1622, 1641), 119; tobacco culture, 119, 120

Janklow, William, 347

Jefferson, Thomas, 22, 135; as student of Native American languages, 13; and Native American origins, 13; and Native American "census," 44; and Native American political ideas, 173–76

Jelderks, John, 416

Jesup, Thomas S., 202

Jingosaseh, 140–41

Johnson, Sir William, 168

Joseph, Elder, 237

Joseph, Younger (Hinmaton Yalatik), 237–41; Long March, 239–40; surrender of, 239; appeal to Congress, 240; imprisoned, 240; return to homeland, 241; death, 241

Kalm, Peter, 363

Karlsefni, Thorfinn, 40

Keefe, Tom, Jr., 355

Kennedy, John F., 341

Pine Ridge reservation, economic
conditions, 386
Pitt, Lord William, 170
Pizzaro, Francisco, 43
Plano (Plainview) points, 22
Plenty Horses, 289–90
Pocahontes (Matowake), 119
Pohl, M. E. D., 23
Poncas, 276–79; land given to Sioux,
276; newspaper campaign, 277–78;
"persons" under the law, 278–79;
removed to Indian Territory, 276;
sheltered by Omahas, 278; tribal
status restored (1990), 279
Pontiac (Ponteach), 183–84
Poor Bear, Myrtle, 345–46
Pope (Pueblo leader), 111
Pope Paul III, 110
Population, Native American, U.S.
(1880–1920), 301–3; U.S. Census
(2000), 426–27
Population density, indigenous, at
contact, 42–48; debates regarding,
42–48; interpretation of evidence, 42,
43, 44; losses, by nation, 46
Porter, Joy, 324
Porter, Tom, 366
Porterfield, Kay, 360
Potlatch, 222–25; cannibal dance, 225;
ceremony and political economy,
222–25; described, 223; display of
wealth, 223; gift-giving, 223; "grease
feast," 223; rehearsed insults, 224
Poverty Point, Louisiana (archeological
site), 111–12
Powhatan (Wahunsonacock), 117–18
Powhatan Confederacy, 117–20; extent
of, 118; location, 118; Pocahontes
(Matowake), 119; relationship with
English at Jamestown, 118–20;
uprisings, 119–20
Pratt, G. Michael, 190–91
Pratt, Richard Henry, 300, 308–10
Pueblo Bonito, 105–6
Pueblo Revolt, 110–11
Pueblos, 35–36, 106–9; agriculture
and irrigation, 35–36; government,

107–8; revolt (1680), 110–11; Spanish
exploration, 106–9
Puget, Peter, 225

Quakerism, and Code of Handsome
Lake, 150
Quatie (Henley Elizabeth Brown), wife
of John Ross, death on Trail of Tears,
214–15
Quetzalcoatl, 84, 86
Quiche (Maya), 94
Quill, Louis, 391
Quill, Peter, 391

Railroad, as aid to migration, 245
Raynal, Abbe, 173
Red Cloud (Makhpiya-luta), 266–68;
sketch of life, 266–67; forces conces-
sions from U.S. Army, 268
Red Sleeves, death, 256
Reilly, Hugh, 285, 286
Relocation program, 334, 336; numbers
moved, 336
Removal Act (1830), 203–8, 214–15;
Cherokees, 203–5, 213–15; Choctaws,
205; Creeks, 207; hunger, 204;
number affected, 214–15; origins of,
206–8; spread of cholera, 205; spread
of cotton culture related to, 203;
support from Andrew Jackson, 207–8;
Tocqueville on, 205. *See also* Trails
of Tears
Repatriation, 414–18; early Nebraska
law, 417; Omahas' remains returned,
418; Pawnees' remain returned, 418
Reservation economic conditions,
386–88, 395; alcoholism, death rates
from, 388; arrest rates, 394; homicide
rates, 387–88; infant morality, 387;
Omahas' unemployment, poverty,
386, 387–88; youth suicide, 388
Restall, Matthew, 90
Revere, Paul, engravings, 170–71
Revolutionary War, in Ohio, 185
Reyhner, Jon, 439, 440
Rio Usumacinta, battle at, 63
Rogers, Rix, 319, 320

Rogers, Robert, 184; on Native marriage, 376
Romero, Mary Eunice, 436
Roosevelt, Franklin D., 295–96
Roosevelt, Theodore, 296, 302; on Allotment, 302
Ross, John (Coowescoowe), 209–10, 214; opposes Removal, 209; serves with Andrew Jackson, 209; sketch of early life, 209; principal chief of Cherokees, 210; evicted from home, 214
Royal Commission on Aboriginal Peoples (Canada), report on boarding schools' abuses, 317, 318, 319, 322
Russians, and Northwest Coast peoples, 226–27; slaughter of wildlife, 226

Sacajawea, 182–83
Sahagun, Bernadino de, 77, 87, 230; on Aztec slavery, 230
Sand Creek Massacre (1864), 264–66; Black Kettle, 265; described, 266; incited by J. M. Chivington, 264–65; Southern Cheyennes killed, 265; White Antelope, 265
Sandia, New Mexico, archaeological site, 21, 22
Sandoz, Mari, _Cheyenne Autumn_, 240
San Lorenzo, 55
Sapling (Haudenosaunee creation story), 7–8, 10
Sassafras, 363
Satanta, suicide, 262
Saukenuk, 196, 197
Scalping: amounts paid (1703), 172; origins, 361–62
Scarrooyady: on alcoholism, 393; at Carlisle Treaty (1753), 165
Schele, Linda, 28
Schoolcraft, Henry, 379
Schurr, Theodore, 17, 18
Scott, Gen. Winfield, 197
Scout, Warner, 316
Sea'th'l, 222; sketch of life, 234; farewell speech, environmental themes, 235–36

Seminole War, 201–3
Seneca Falls Women's Conference (1848), 376, 380
Sequoyah, 208, 210–11; invents written Cherokee, 210–11; sketch of early life, 210–11; accused of witchcraft, 211; death, 211
Settlement frontier: population figures (1800 and 1830), 182; speed of movement (1800–1900), 182
Shenandoah, Joanne, 401, 402
Sheridan, Philip, 251–52, 297
Sherman, William Tecumseh, on Chief Joseph, Younger, 239
Sitting Bull (Tatanka Yotanka), 239, 273–76, 280, 282; harbors Nez Perce (1877), 239; exile in Canada, 273–76; life described, 273–76; friend of William Cody, 280–82; death, 282
Six Nations Indian Museum (Onchiota, New York), 23
Skywoman (Haudenosaunee creation story), 4, 5, 6, 7, 8
Slavery and Native Americans, 228–31, 232; Apaches, 228; Aztecs, 229; California, enslavement of children, 232; combined with horse trading, 228; The Dalles slave market, 228–29; de Soto expedition, 228; Florida, as source of slaves, 228; Los Angeles slave market, 229; Mission system as, 230–31; Pequots, 228; prices, in blankets, 229; South Carolina slave market, 228; Spanish, 230
"Sleep on it," Iroquois origin of term, 161, 361
Smallpox, 43, 46, 47, 48, 120, 125, 135–36, 225, 248–50; intentional spread advocated, 135–36; Maya, 95; Mexico, 46, 88; Native deaths from, 249–50; New England, 47, 120, 125; Pacific Northwest, 48, 225. _See also_ Amherst, Jeffrey
Smith, Henry, 235, 236
Smith, John (Jamestown, Virginia), 119
Snake, Reuben, on assimilation, 298
Snow, Dean, 45, 46, 246

ABOUT THE AUTHOR

BRUCE E. JOHANSEN is Professor of Communications and Native American Studies at the University of Nebraska, Omaha. He is the author or editor of twenty books, the most recent being *Enduring Legacies: Native American Treaties and Contemporary Controversies* (Praeger, 2004), *Indigenous Peoples and Environmental Issues: An Encyclopedia* (Greenwood, 2003), *The Dirty Dozen: Toxic Chemicals and the Earth's Future* (Praeger, 2003), and *The Global Warming Desk Reference* (Greenwood, 2001).